PRAIS̶_ _ER AND

California Dish

"I'm glad to have [Tower's] riveting, frontline perspective, which is at once fascinating, illuminating, and poignant. Those of us who have built American hospitality careers over the past couple of decades owe a major debt to this bushwhacking pioneer of product, pleasure, and promotion."

—Danny Meyer, coauthor, *Union Square Cafe Cookbook*

"Jeremiah Tower dishes better than almost anybody."

—Robert Mondavi

"This book is a celebrity-studded literary 'tasting menu,' combining the raw, tell-all energy of Anthony Bourdain with the worldliness of Jeffrey Steingarten."

—Rick Smilow, President, The Institute of Culinary Education

"Tower's place in culinary history is assured, and his message still needs to be heard by striving young chefs today."

—*San Antonio Express-News*

"Jeremiah Tower is a beloved legend of America's food business. He was at the forefront of the new era when America got serious about its own cuisine. He ranks up there with Wolfgang Puck and Emeril Lagasse and all the other pioneers of today's great food styles in putting the new American cuisine really on the world map. This book is an absolute must-have for both the serious cookbook collector and the casual reader."

—Robin Leach

"Serves up a longtime insider's juicy perspective on the key players of the American culinary revolution and recounts, course by course, a career's worth of exceptional meals. It's a great read. I couldn't put it down."

—Sara Moulton, host, Food Network's *Sara's Secrets*

"A gifted writer, when he tells his own story, will project himself as a character in scenes as craftily shaped as any fiction writer's. A gifted writer senses that the restaurant world and the harried chef are ripe materials for comedy, so he goes at it full blast to get the laughing reader on his side. And that's just what Jeremiah Tower has done in his hilarious account."

—Betty Fussell, *Food Arts*

"What a pleasure. . . . Tower captures the real spirit of California cuisine—simple, fresh, and crisp. Thank you, Jeremiah."

—André Soltner, chef and owner, Lutèce

"Twenty years ago I met Jeremiah Tower and I fell in love with his food. I think [he] is one of our great chefs. For anyone interested in the food revolution and the innovative cuisine of California . . . [this] book is a must."

—Colette Rossant, author of *Apricots on the Nile* and *Return to Paris*

"His memoir is fascinating, offering tantalizing glimpses of restaurant operations and insights into many culinary personalities."

—*Library Journal*

ALSO BY JEREMIAH TOWER

Jeremiah Tower's New American Classics
Jeremiah Tower Cooks

California Dish

WHAT I SAW (AND COOKED) AT THE
AMERICAN CULINARY REVOLUTION

JEREMIAH TOWER

FREE PRESS
New York   London   Toronto   Sydney

fP

FREE PRESS
A Division of Simon & Schuster, Inc.
1230 Avenue of the Americas
New York, NY 10020

FREE PRESS and colophon are trademarks
of Simon & Schuster, Inc.

First Free Press trade paperback edition 2004

For information about special discounts for bulk purchases,
please contact Simon & Schuster Special Sales:
1-800-456-6798 or business@simonandschuster.com.

Designed by Paul Dippolito

Manufactured in the United States of America

1   3   5   7   9   10   8   6   4   2

Library of Congress Cataloging-in-Publication Data
Tower, Jeremiah.
California dish : what I saw (and cooked) at the American culinary revolution / Jeremiah Tower.
p.   c.m.
Includes biobliographical references and index.
1. Tower, Jeremiah—Biography. 2. Cookery, American—California style.   I. Title.
TX 649.T.68T68 2003
641. 5'092—dc21   2003049124
[B]

ISBN 0-7432-2844-8
0-7432-2845-6 (pbk)

For Orlando

In the 1970's, some California chefs found inspiration in their own backyards, and the cuisine they invented radically changed the way America dines . . . and so succeeded that its principles completely dominate the way we eat today.

—*The Wine Spectator*, March 31, 2001

You have to be psychotic to be a restaurant owner, let alone its chef as well. It has something to do with mother, I'm sure. Nurturing and taking care of people and all that. All chefs have this in common.

—Jeremiah Tower

Contents

California Dish

Prologue: Taming the Fire

CALIFORNIA CUISINE, as it came to be heralded in the national media, might never have been discovered if it weren't for a bunch of pushy French chefs.

In the spring of 1983, the ad agency for Ocean Spray was charged with placing cranberries at the forefront of American gastronomy. Their idea was a weekend headlined "Innovations in Food" at Beechwood, the Astor mansion in Newport, Rhode Island, for one hundred syndicated food journalists. The main event would be a dinner showcasing the "innovative sauceless cuisine" of Paris's Guy Savoy, with my crew from the Santa Fe Bar & Grill in Berkeley, California, preparing a little lunch to keep up the strength of the writers for the all-day workshops on culinary trends.

I didn't mind the supporting role. In the three years since Savoy had opened his own Paris restaurant, the New York food press had fallen in love with his originality and dash. I had profound respect for the French and especially for the Young Turks of nouvelle cuisine, as well as for Guy himself.

If it was obvious why Savoy had been invited, it wasn't clear why I had been. Although the two celebrated Jameses of the food world, Beard and Villas, had lavished praise on my cooking at both Chez Panisse and the Santa Fe Bar & Grill, only one restaurant (Panisse) had as yet become a national sensation. But I didn't press the agency for a reason. I was grateful for the opportunity to put the Santa Fe in front of the national food press and, since I had no formal training as a chef, eager to see a master at work.

Beyond that, I could never resist a challenge. I was sure we could do it—I just wasn't sure what "it" would turn out to be. We'd fake it as we went along.

My assignment was to provide a simple California lunch using cranberries. It was an odd request for April, but I could see one of the agency's points: Demonstrate that you can cook with cranberries all year. Top it off with a famous French chef including them in three-star Michelin food, and the press would go wild. Or perhaps it was just an agency budget waiting to happen. Whatever the reason for the cranberries, I decided to use them to marinate racks of lamb, despite the obvious fact that, if you factored in the travel expenses we incurred getting to Newport, it would be the most expensive marinade in history.

The first challenge was to get the cooks and food to our first stop, New York, from California. What kept me up at night was how to get past the airport check-in with fifteen hundred pounds of food and luggage. At that time anyone at airport check-ins was familiar with the demands of first-class traveling socialites with mounded Louis Vuitton hatboxes and toy poodles, but when my crew and I arrived, the five of us pushing a long line of carts, we looked like anything but first-class passengers. Airports in 1983 were as yet innocent of chefs and their entourages. Up to that point road shows were the purview of only rock bands and circuses, both of which chefs soon came to resemble, as only a year later one could see toques on famous chefs in every major airport in the United States, blue and white ice coolers dominating the luggage carousels, and fans lining up for autographs in the passenger lounges.

The list of our "bags" was staggering: 125 individual California goat cheeses, two hundred grape leaves (in April that was like asking a winery to give up a whole vineyard), five gallons of sauce essences, and twenty-five California lamb loins. Everything was packed in four enormous coolers, one of them full of noisily scratching Bay Area Delta crayfish, another full of fresh coconut ice cream. It was for this trip that I developed an elaborate traveling system: vacuum-packed foods stacked with the blue ice in coolers and, in two huge suitcases on wheels, a massive on-site support system that held everything from cheesecloth to extension cords, food mills to pepper mills, first-aid kits to baling wire and clip-on lights.

The greatest of my nightmares was getting eight fifty-pound bags of mesquite charcoal, whose purpose in life was to spew fine black dust onto everything in its path, on a plane to New York. All that charcoal seemed a bit obsessive even to us, and we knew that the chances of finding a foodie in all those grim faces behind the ticket counters were less than slim. But mesquite was one of our "innovations," and no mere gate agent was going to stand in the way of our publicizing it. Halfway to the check-in window I saw the agents whispering. Closer I saw the face behind the window in front of us: as a bulldog at the Westminster, she would have taken best in show. Our eyes locked. "Nothing doing" was her unmistakable look. I could see she was focused on the coolers, no doubt convinced they were full of dry ice that could have blown up the plane.

As we both braced for combat, I searched for another window. The staff had seen the bulldog look and were cowering behind their carts. A whispered "Oh shit, no" was all I heard from them. I raised an arm in a full-speed-ahead gesture and then, feeling like Patton in the lead tank, swerved with the team toward the check-in with the long red carpet, crowd-control ropes, and an agent wide-eyed with shock. I remembered that my PR folder had a very complimentary James Villas *Town & Country* article on the Santa Fe Bar & Grill with a full-page color photograph of me. So before the customer relations agent could say a word, I whipped out the photograph and launched into a spiel about "local kids" on a mission to show those Easterners how to cook. Impressed, she unhooked the first-class rope and took us to the window. Nothing could describe the look on her face as she tried to understand the scratching of hundreds of tiny claws against the cooler walls, but minutes after my explanation, the five of us had first-class tickets and increased luggage allowances.

"Kids," I said, as the plane left the runway, "this is just the beginning."

The plane ride is a blank. I must have gone through the shopping list over and over again, wondering where in New York we would find California-quality vegetables and fruit at their peak of perfect ripeness and flavor, let alone restaurant-quality fish and shellfish.

It was not going to be easy, so to reward my staff for their work so far, and to get them in the mood for going that extra mile in the days ahead, I decided that a lunch at the great Four Seasons, my home away from home, was just the ticket. It was my idea of America's finest restaurant, created by people I adored and admired—James Beard, Joe Baum, and Barbara Kafka—and now the realm of two great restaurateurs, Tom Margittai and Paul Kovi, and one of the nicest chefs in America, Seppi Renggli. It didn't hurt that the restaurant was in a Mies van der Rohe building with a perfect interior by my other favorite architect, Philip Johnson.

I wanted my team to experience perfect service in a perfect room, taste one of my favorite white wines (Condrieu), and ogle the enormous silver chariot of desserts crowned with the pastry chef Albert Kumin's famous cake—shaped like a half cantaloupe turned upside-down, covered in chocolate, and topped by a foot-high chocolate version of a scarf Loretta Young would have tied around her head. None of us could figure out how Albert had spun chocolate into this couture shape of silk settling in a light wind. Now, ten years after I first encountered this creation, I told Albert I had waited all that time to ask him the secret of his gossamer construction.

"I would have told you anytime," he said with a huge grin. "It's simple: I use a hand pasta machine. (Of course, the chocolate has to be the right temperature and it's only that way for a minute or two.)"

Yes, I thought, time enough for a master who knows all chocolate's intimate secrets (and for the rest of us to screw it up completely).

The next morning, full of fine memories of our magnificent lunch and the spectacle of New York seen from the bar on the 107th floor of the World Trade Center, it was time to return to earth. We picked up an enormous van from our uptown hotel and headed downtown to Balducci's, the only place where I thought we could get the quality of produce we were used to in California and wanted to show off in Newport. As it turned out we could—at five times the price. We shopped for boxes of red and gold bell peppers, leeks, zucchini, red torpedo onions, ripe mangoes and passion fruit. At the meat counter I saw beautiful coils of fresh fennel sausage; they turned out to be a last-minute inspiration for a snack with drinks. The veteran Balducci's staff was as impressed by the mountain of crates on the Sixth Avenue sidewalk as I was by the proportionately small mound of cash left in my hand. Later, the ad agency told me I was crazy to buy food for one hundred at what was then New York's most expensive boutique grocery. But the quality was worth it, even if I did end up having to split the tab.

My sous-chef, Steven Vranian, was thin, wiry, and pale-skinned to the point you could see the blue veins pumping an intense energy. He had dropped us off in front of the store with the intention of circling the block. After an hour standing behind the pile of crates and boxes on the sidewalk looking anxiously for the van, we realized it really was gone. We still had to buy fish and shellfish before finding our way through the nightmare of parkways and bridges out of New York to make it to Newport on time. But with no van, no food-filled coolers, no clothes, and no money or directions, we had no way of getting to Newport. Our California boy had disappeared in the maze of alien West Village one-way streets, and since this was before cell phones, he was truly lost. He finally showed up, red-faced, sheepish, his shoulders in a shrug, giving us the both-hands-palms-up gesture. If I hadn't needed him so much I would have killed him.

I had planned to buy the fish at its source in Newport, but now the team overruled me with "Let's have it in hand." Perilously off schedule, we raced to the Fulton Fish Market for an aquarium's worth of live clams, mussels, crab, and shrimp—leaving only lobsters and oysters to purchase live the next day—then barreled up the New England Thruway.

We drove around Newport searching for our lodgings, expecting something grand (given the mansions we saw), but the address on the slip of paper I was clutching turned out to be a motel. Not a bad motel, but a motel nonetheless, and that meant no room service. Since chefs never eat at normal times (defined as when we're cooking for everyone else), we survive on room service. My staff knew I could put up with just about anything provided I could get a chicken club sandwich and champagne twenty-four hours a day, so two of them peeled out of the motel driveway for the makings of club sandwiches and a case of bubbly—because, in the words of my all-time heroine, Madame Lilly Bollinger, who when asked "Why champagne?" replied, "I drink it when I'm happy and when I'm sad. Sometimes I drink it when I am alone. When I have company I consider it obligatory. I trifle with it if I'm not hungry and drink it when I am. Otherwise I never touch it—unless I'm thirsty." I would add the wonderful words from the Pink Panther: "Champagne is a minimum of alcohol and a maximum of companionship. It takes care of all extremes." And this was going to be an extreme weekend.

I wanted my staff in tip-top shape in the early morning, so I grabbed a bed by the door to ensure that no one would slip out during the night, but the boys were too quick. Newport had been the stomping ground of Brad Barker, one of the cooks, and he decided to give Steven a tour of his old watering holes. Oxsana Czuczman, another cook from the Santa Fe, stayed behind to watch over my nerves. Staff legend has it that she sacrificed her entire stash of pot to calm her nerves while I paced our little room and fumed, waiting for the errant boys. They staggered back in the middle of the night drowned in Coors, but at least without the companions they reeked of.

The next morning was quiet, tense, and hot for April, even in those early hours. The heat made the shaky staff even shakier, and I felt worse than they did—grimly low on adrenaline and nourishment. The sunlight was already far too bright, so I stopped off in town and bought a pair of large fire engine red plastic-framed Ray-Bans, very Doris Duke or Barbara Hutton, to be worn for photographers.

We pulled up in front of the Beechwood gates, then drove up an endless, impeccably tailored gravel driveway to the mansion—a two-story Palladian house with Doric columns set a few feet above a lawn that stretched for a mile or so down to the water. I saw an open porch around two sides and the back of the house covered with the as yet unset tables for the lunch. It was all very impressive, and I expected a kitchen of comparable grandeur with space for two teams of cooks, mine and Guy Savoy's. It was not.

It was the size of a large closet.

Then just as we had figured out how to make it work and started to cook, the French arrived. I had heard Savoy was a decent bloke, but that day I never had a chance to find out. His crew preceded him, and they were armed with attitude. At first they ignored us, but packed into that small kitchen that wasn't easy, so they asked us to leave. Their needs took precedence, they said, because the serious meal—dinner—was theirs.

All was quiet for a moment. I don't know what made me keep silent, possibly my English-schooled manners, possibly my status as a guest in someone else's kitchen, but all I could think of was keeping our focus. Every moment of energy had already been spoken for, and realizing that a pissing match at that moment would get us nowhere, I stepped aside.

"All right, girls and boys," I said. "Grab everything and follow me."

I had read Sun-tzu for years, but stepping aside was my first *Art of War* move. By not making a scene, I let the force of the French arrogance fire up my cooks and give them a powerful sense of purpose and determination to show these guys what they could do. In an instant, they forgot their throbbing heads, and we searched for a new place to cook.

"This," I told my team, sweeping an arm over the landscape in front of all the tables, " is the place for us, right in front of the bloody press."

I dropped the red sunglasses down on my nose and got to work. We lined up four five-food grills with white, cloth-covered tables behind them—just far enough from the press to keep the smoke from their eyes but close enough so they could see the color of ours. The grills were meant to have been kept out of sight; now they would be the focus of everything—a great stage and the center of our entertainment. I insisted that only the most beautiful things should show, that all the mechanics be stowed away under the tables, so the food would "appear" with seeming effortlessness.

Two hours later, the press materialized. Their schedule gave them thirty minutes to wander around with glasses of wine before sitting down, so we served them a snack that I could cook and talk about simultaneously: the fresh fennel sausage from Balducci's, coiled into large rings, skewered, and grilled whole, then cut into bite-size pieces on large wooden planks. They were served still sizzling from the grill with the juice from our newest exotic ingredient, Rangpur limes, and sprinkled with a salt we flavored with ground, oven-dried peel of lime and cumin seeds. On the side were bowls of grilled tomatillo salsa.

A hundred food journalists took one look at us and one bite of sausage, raised their eyebrows with expectation, and away we went: salsa, grilling, and California were suddenly *it*.

We played up grilling as essential to the California style and mesquite charcoal as the only one we used because it burned very hot and added a slightly acid taste to the food. We didn't mention that it was the only kind of real charcoal we could get. It was perfect for fish, but in the cooking business every perfection has its flaw, and mesquite's was the occasional unspent .22 bullets put there by Mexican baggers as revenge against the gringos. A bullet blasting off and whizzing by inches from a cook's head was not something I needed journalists to see, so the press watched us sort through a huge black mountain of the charcoal before setting it in the grills. "Just the choice pieces," I lied, while keeping an eye out for bullets.

Luncheon on the Terrace

April 28, 1983

Grilled Fennel Sausage with Rangpur Lime & Orange-Cumin Salt

Grilled Mixed Shellfish with Grilled Garlic & Ancho Chili & Herb-Shellfish Butter Sauces

Cranberry Puree Marinated Grilled Lamb Loin
Mixed California Vegetable Salad
Cranberry Chili Relish

Grilled California Goat Cheese
With Garden Greens

Tropical Fruit Compote
With Coconut Ice Cream

The first course was shellfish, marinated and grilled, the lobsters cooked initially on a bed of fresh seaweed (to give them maximum ocean flavor), then finished off on the charcoal fire, which also pushed all the flavor of the shells into the lobster meat. Each guest was served a big white plate with two ramekins, one for the warm lobster butter sauce, made from the crushed shells and mussel stock, the other with a sauce made from my secret dried ancho chili puree and sour cream laced with mayonnaise. Warm towels scented with fresh tarragon and Meyer lemon gave them all the confidence to eat with their fingers.

We decorated the guest tables with vegetables instead of flowers—huge platters of leeks, red and gold bell peppers, yellow zucchini, and red torpedo onions. The vegetables were oiled, to glisten and reflect the sunlight as well as to marinate them for the grill. As soon as the shellfish was served, the waiters removed the table decor in unison, then marched over and emptied the platters onto the grills to create the illusion of vegetables cooked to order when, of course, we had the ones we were to serve already done.

Next came the lamb loins marinated in the juice of crushed cranberries with thyme, bay leaf, and olive oil. To our astonishment, the berry juice worked beautifully, making a sweet-sour caramelized glaze that was a perfect counterpart to the richness of the lamb fat and the slightly musky flavor of the meat.

So far, so good. But we had planned, while the lamb was on the grills, to use the kitchen ovens for the Sadie Kendall California goat cheeses, which were sandwiched between two thin pounded-out slices of oven-dried tomatoes (a new product in those days), a sprig of fresh flowering wild thyme on each side, and wrapped in fresh grape leaves. Only in that way could we achieve a seamless transition between the courses and hold the lunch to ninety minutes. But one last pleading at the kitchen door was like Oliver Twist in the orphanage asking for more gruel—the answer was a firm *Non*. The little cheeses came back to me on the rebound, so we stoked up the fires, furiously brushed off the grills, and laid out the cheeses. If we didn't have the journalists in the palms of our grillers' hands by then, the sight of all of us coolly turning (and turning) 125 individual goat cheese packages certainly did the job.

But they weren't totally floored until we grilled the dessert.

By now high on fatigue and adrenaline poisoning, I pushed the red sunglasses up on my head and commanded each cook to down a glass of champagne and pick up two huge sauté pans. On a signal from me, they filled them with mixed tropical fruits, raspberries, and passion fruit sugar syrup; then all of us in unison tossed the fruit compote up in the air like master omelet makers. That got a standing ovation. We plated the tropical fruit ragouts, scooped fresh coconut ice cream into the center of each plate, added shortbread cookies—and we were done.

At the end of the lunch the cooks collapsed on the lawn, while I went from table to table. I remember a flood of journalists blaming me for nearly killing them with food, but all were smiling. I kissed the cooks—mine, not the ones standing around on the sidelines stage-whispering furiously in French (which they assumed we didn't speak) about our use of a "nonculinary" herb like lemon thyme and our lack of chefs' hats and embroidered names on our jackets. I heard a hint of admiration in their voices, but the tone reversed when I helped my cooks clean up and wash the pans.

I took a bottle of champagne and went down to the water. I was numb. I knew that we had to pack and that I had to attend the dinner in four hours' time, coherent, with a smile, and acting as if everything the press had seen had been carefully rehearsed. In truth, I could never have planned that level of success. In those days we would have been declared insane if we had announced a meal cooked entirely out-of-doors on an East Coast early spring day. And to have grilled dessert? Certifiable.

The press had no preconceptions of what we would cook, but Guy Savoy was not so lucky. The journalists had been told to expect no sauces, no flour, no cream, and no butter. But this is what they saw:

Dinner at Beechwood

Potage de Homard aux Airelles

Saumon au Persil

Rillons de Ris de Veau aux Truffes

Bavarois aux Airelles

Savoy didn't use flour, but sauces, cream, and butter were everywhere. There was cream in the lobster soup with cranberries, cream in the salmon with parsley sauce, and the Bavarois with cranberries was packed with cream. The sweetbreads had a flourless veal stock and truffle sauce. To say the least, we were confused. The advance press from the agency had lauded Guy's innovative cooking in the same breath as that of the famous restaurant L'Ami Louis, over which I got a good laugh. A normal dinner there was an eighteen-ounce slab of goose liver, a whole chicken or entire leg of baby lamb served with a potato pancake cooked in butter and duck fat, and pastry crust and butter-sugar caramelized apple tarte Tatin for dessert, all of it weighing in at around seven thousand calories.

Actually none of my team cared whether the food was sauced or not—it was delicious. But the press still didn't get it. *The California Union* explained that what was meant by sauceless cuisine was actually "sauces that are done at the last minute." Having told everyone it meant no sauces was not an especially good PR hook for Savoy unless you understood the sauce tradition against which he and the other Young Turks had rebelled.

People who rail against traditional French sauces often mean the espagnole or advanced version of the flour-thickened "brown" sauce that has been screwed up for decades by hotels, luxury resorts, and the majority of French restaurants, all of which render it a muddy, opaque brown, the color of the water a child is left with after painting for hours with watercolors. A true espagnole takes three days to make, including the initial stock, and demands a monogamous relationship: full devotion from a sauce maker who never abandons his charge. Each day there has to be a rest period so that the fat on the top and the detritus on the bottom of the jellied mass can be easily removed. Then it sits on the edge of a burner for several hours finishing, cooking at such a slow rate that it barely shimmers—it merely "smiles" at the cook skimming off its last traces of fat, scum, and skin.

This accomplished, and poured over a few bones and carcasses of whatever creature it is meant to enhance, then strained and made to "smile" again, it becomes a sauce so easy on the body that four hours later you're ready for the next meal. And the flour? Transformed like the silk cocoons that become an Hermès scarf. The fat? Not a drop. The stock-becoming-sauce has never vigorously boiled, and so the fat, unincorporated and removed, can neither ruin the diners' plumbing nor mask the true flavors of what is being sauced.

Even the revolutionary Turks Paul Bocuse, the Troisgros, and the great unsung Jacques Manière knew that this great basic brown sauce could be magnificent, and a test of a truly great kitchen. But when you're starting a culinary revolution, it's easier to blame the sauce than the saucier, to guillotine the aristocrats instead of overturning the regime. It was the restaurant critics and guidebook writers Gault and Millau and then their following in the American press that lined up all the figures of classicism and beheaded them indiscriminately. Gone were the creamed crayfish-sauced quenelles of the master Fernand Point at La Pyramide in Vienne, drawn and quartered were the butter-based sauces of Henri Soulé at New York's Le Pavillon, rack-and-pinioned any flour-thickened meat essences. Fat was now labeled treason and its eaters, traitors.

All these crazy thoughts pounded through my exhausted brain as I sat at Savoy's dinner in the ballroom at Beechwood. Everything seemed to move in slow motion, the sounds coming out of the writers' mouths like a tape at half speed. I was so tired that I could not remember anyone's name, barely even what I was doing there. I knew this was Guy's night, and these journalists were professional. They wanted to give him equal time, even if they could be in no possible way as physically interested as they were before lunch. But with nine powerful journalists to my right and left, I sat just waiting to hear about my party and which way the thumbs were pointing, up or down. I knew right after lunch that we had pulled off a success, but now, at the evening table, doubts crept in. It was my first big public performance, and I wanted praise strong and constant enough to overwhelm my fears, of both failure and, oddly enough, success.

As it turned out, the French handed the event to us on a platter. Not that their event wasn't wonderful; one just couldn't *feel* it. *The Christian Science Monitor* gave France forty words and California two thousand. "Berkeley Chef's Magic Grill Dazzles Eastern Experts at Al Fresco Lunch" one headline trumpeted. Phyllis Richman in *The Washington Post* made our lunch one of the first full-page color cover sections, writing of a "far from down-home barbecue, with white tablecloths . . . and a hushed silence." Nina Simmonds quoted Ruth Reichl, then at *California* magazine, in *The Boston Globe* on July 6, 1983: "Tower's cooking is a brand of California cooking that is instantly recognizable. It is understated and depends on local ingredients, unusual flavor combinations and impeccable timing." Simmonds then quoted me, making a first stab at a characterization. I said that nothing had changed as far as the fundamentals. What was new was the marriage between "the aesthetic chasteness of nouvelle cuisine and the hearty, robust hominess of bistro food: New American Cuisine." Within weeks of the Newport event, that term was repeated widely.

The press had France on their minds when they arrived, but they left with their hearts in San Francisco—or just across the bay. The love affair between the American food press and California had begun.

Another affair began, too—with me. "Tower is a photographer's fantasy. He stands tall and regal, cool enough to tame the fire," wrote one reporter. I ate this up, of course. It would have taken a stronger person than I was not to see this as a way to get our message across and make money doing it.

Great success is supposed to be followed by great elation, but with me a great performance has always brought on that "little death" feeling. The greater the success, the more devastating its successor. I didn't have it as bad as my pal Rudolf Nureyev, who would vacuum down a bottle of Stoli in the wings right after the last curtain call. But almost. As W. S. Gilbert (of Sullivan) puts it in the wonderful film *Topsy-Turvy*, "There is something inherently disappointing in success."

My California kids felt they had "kicked French butt." The next morning, as we loaded up the van, I felt as if I had been kicked in the head. As soon as the road was a clear shot to JFK, I crawled into the rear of the van to find a sleep that never arrived. While my cooking team raved with delight and was filled with pride in the front of the van, I ended up in a fetal position in the back. I felt sorry for myself that I was going to get everything I ever wanted because I knew at that moment that some part of me didn't want it. I felt an awakening pain of the old adage of being careful what you wish for, and I was fairly certain that my life would never be the same again.

Something had been born, and I did not want to know what. And something was surely about to die—the unselfconscious "anything goes" exuberance of my little band of outlaws that had made our triumph possible.

Steven Vranian wrote a note afterward describing his feelings about the event. He said that the staff felt that the sight of my moving from table to table, face still flushed from the grill, revealed something new and vaguely disturbing: "The half of him that he pretends to be, and the half that others expect him to be, merged together and created the new Jeremiah." I had chosen, Steven said, "a path that would consume and redefine" me.

Did I want to be redefined by success? In my youth I'd been defined by the lack of it—first as a "Yank" in Australia, then as an "Aussie" in England, and then in the United States, where everyone assumed I was English. The truth is that I was a bit of an alien wherever I was. But at Newport I learned that my vision—of a new, serious simplicity that could change the way people thought of fine dining—had power.

I was learning that people who are best at keeping their huge success are somehow detached from it, able to regard it as something outside themselves. Only then can one stay focused, both when being lionized and then, inevitably, when being torn down. If the press loves first to proclaim "Long live the king," they love just as much to cry, "The king is dead."

As I slumped, fallen in my seat in the plane headed westward, Steven noticed me and leapt over the back of his seat—somehow not spilling a drop of his gin and tonic. "Are you all right?" he said, a note of panic in his voice.

"All right," I said. "Quite all right."

At that moment I knew I would go for it, whatever the ultimate cost. I knew that what was coming wasn't an occasional ride on the tiger's back but a life living on it. I decided to go for the crown, in full view of the guillotine.

Grilled Garlic & Ancho Chili Sauce

Serves 4–6

2 dried ancho chili pods
1 head fresh spring first-crop
    garlic
2 sprigs fresh thyme
½ cup mild extra-virgin olive oil

1 ripe lime, zested and juiced
½ tablespoon fresh oregano leaves,
    chopped
4 ounces unsalted butter
Salt

Grill the chilies over a charcoal, wood, or low gas flame until they puff up, or about 3 minutes. Put them in a bowl with enough warm water to cover them.

Weight them down with a small saucer, and soak for 2 hours. Drain, saving the water, and remove and discard the stems and seeds.

Meanwhile wrap the head of garlic loosely in foil with the thyme and a tablespoon of the olive oil. Cook over low fire or under a broiler until the garlic is tender, or about 20 minutes. Remove the stem and rough outer layers of the skin and discard. Put all the cloves in a food processor and puree the garlic with the remaining olive oil. Pass through a sieve and discard the residue.

Puree the chilies with just enough of their soaking water to make a smooth puree. Sieve. Clean out the food processor.

Put the garlic and chili purees in the processor with the lime zest and juice, oregano, butter, and a teaspoon of salt. Puree until soft and smooth. Add more salt if necessary.

Serve on top of grilled fish and shellfish.

Tropical Fruit Compote

Serve the warm compote with either custard, vanilla or coconut ice cream, mascarpone, English clotted or heavy cream, and cookies of your choice, like shortbread or warm gingersnaps 5 minutes out of the oven.

Serves 4–6

2 ripe mangoes, peeled, cut in $\frac{1}{4}$-inch slices	$\frac{1}{2}$ cup medium sugar syrup
1 ripe papaya, peeled, seeded, cut in $\frac{1}{4}$-inch slices	1 basket raspberries
2 ripe passion fruit, cut in half, pulp and juice saved	1 teaspoon fresh lime juice
	1 tablespoon unsalted butter
	Salt

Put the mango and papaya slices in a medium-size nonreactive frying pan. Whisk the passion fruit pulp with the sugar syrup for 1 minute to break up the pulp, and add to the fruit.

Warm the fruit over medium heat until just heated through—about 3 minutes. Add the raspberries, lime juice, butter, and pinch of salt. Turn up the heat, and swirl the pan around until the butter is just melted.

Serve immediately in soup plates with the cream or ice cream in the center.

Early Imprints

Grills, Galaas, and Budgerigars

IT IS FITTING that my national fame as a chef should have come while standing over an outdoor grill in Newport, since a grill was the setting for my first momentous cooking lesson. I was six years old, and my teacher was an old aborigine named Nick, whom I had seen out back behind the kitchen of an island resort in Australia's Great Barrier Reef peeling potatoes.

After my first lunch, I went back to meet Nick, and he took me on as a cause. First he taught me how to spike coconuts on a log, whack them with a machete to clean the husks away, open them up, drink the water, eat the flesh, and then semidry the rest of the meat to carry in my pocket. Sucking down the young coconuts, the meat still jellylike and mixed with fresh molasses from sugarcane, seemed to me so sinful, indulgent, and antiparental that it is to this day one of my favorite things on a hot, steamy day. Nick also tried to teach me about the birds and the bees, without the benefit of bees, making do with lizards instead. I preferred coconuts, and the cooking lessons.

From Nick's dugout canoe I had caught a barracuda, which he showed me how to roast over a coconut-shell fire on the beach. It tasted awful—musty and off, like a meat loaf with fish in it—but I put on a good face. Most of it, however, went to the ravenous cats lurking in the banana trees outside the restaurant. As did my portion of the wild parrots, or galaas, which he cooked on spits on the beach. Eating those was to me like cooking the Australian family budgie—all I could see were the bright raspberry pink plumage of the birds in the palms above the beach, and even though there were thousands of them, I couldn't imagine killing one. Let alone eating one. Seeing my disappointment in both these treats, my mentor took me off to the tide pools on the reef, some Olympic-size, some small enough to reach into for oysters, mussels, little crabs for frying, big black shiny sea urchins, and the short-spined purple urchins, which we ate on the spot.

I was then allowed to watch a fishing expedition, which was carried out by the adults at dusk. It was in the failing light that the big and best eating fish like barramundi came in to shore to get away from the tiger and hammerhead sharks, who themselves would prowl closer to the beach for their evening meal. My father, fueled with several pink gins, went chin-deep into the water to provide a strategic "anchor" for one end of the net while the other end was towed around in deeper waters by a little rowboat. The rest of us watched, breathless, from the shore, knowing that a scream meant no dinner, at least not for us.

The ever-darkening waters were screamless, and the catch was brought in, gutted, cleaned, and slathered in coconut oil, salt, and chili pepper. The coals of a big bonfire, started to provide light for the cocktail hour, were raked down into a three-inch bed, over which the grill grates were laid and, when Nick declared them sizzling hot enough by spitting on them, oiled. The fish were set on the grill, big ones first, and then in stages all the rest. And with the fire engine red and Macedonian gold parrots, pink and gray galaas, and thousands of multicolored budgerigars swirling overhead, their deafening shrieks descending into murmurs in the inky equatorial darkness, we ate our fish, crayfish, and grilled oysters—just with fresh limes squeezed over, or chili powder mixed with salt, or a sauce made from coconut milk, oil, fresh chilies, and lime juice. This, I realized, was how life must be.

Cooking these exotic animals from the sea in this tropical setting fixed a love for grilling in my mind forever. I didn't yet know the word *paradise,* but I knew the concept; I sensed that tropical islands mean abundance, color, the perfumed life I would always crave. My instincts told me to savor every moment of it and, in the future, never to let the feelings get very far away.

The Family

Deprived at an early age of being an orphan, I was forced to live with my parents: a childhood hardly suitable for children. I was a stranger to my father until he came back from World War II when I was three, and our status had not changed much, having deteriorated after I bit him in his groin at our first meeting.

My father, Sheldon "Pete" Tower, was an international managing director of Western Electric (or Westrex, the company that invented stereo motion picture sound systems), living off an inheritance from his family's and America's first oil company and internationally strong dollar. He was adored by the people who worked with him because of his ability to project an interest in what others (if not his family) were saying and doing. It did not hurt that as a young man he was beautiful enough to charm everyone and later, even with his girth expanding from so many perfect lunches, continued to do so. He was tall, with a typically Ivy League neat haircut parted at one side and kept in place with brilliantine from a small St. James's (London) shop. His black hair would eventually turn an elegant pepper and salt, but with never a hair out of place unless he was sailing, and then kept in place with an L.L. Bean sword fisherman's hat. His clothes were Brooks Brothers, the shirts always white and buttoned down. When my mother died he was over seventy, and still a flurry of women from all around the world called and wrote to rekindle the flames.

My mother, Margaret, was a beautiful, passionate, intelligent, and multitalented woman. Photos of her at thirty show a woman not of a usual kind of great beauty but of an intensity in her eyes and a powerful presence that was highly attractive: tall, with china blue eyes, platinum white hair, and a lovely mouth painted the same color as her nails (scarlet). She was an artist who had played the saxophone and guitar, could paint cabinets with birds-of-paradise, sew us pajamas out of Viyella or vicuña, decorate a house or a garden with a frenzy, drive by herself with two children (my two older siblings) in a Model T Ford in the thirties from Connecticut to Mexico, and cook in several cuisines, her favorites being American, Mexican, and Indonesian. My memory of her two looks shows the two forces holding sway in her—elegant in Jean Patou suits, pearls, and Cartier diamond brooches pinned to her lapels, her shortish hair swept back in a Coco Chanel, or plunked down in the garden in old mannish clothes gardening in the dirt all day with no gloves, the rings taken off and put on the back stoop.

Having volunteered during World War II in a Rosie the Riveter role, my mother emerged from the war as an independent woman. That spirit was immediately and systematically neutralized by my father. Deeply compromised by this emotional abuse, and by the fact that her Catholic upbringing had not taught her what to do with your abusive husband when you adore him, my mother increased her dependence on alcohol for companionship, which had begun during the war. As her drinking increased, so did my father's subsequent abuse, which turned physical. Some evenings turned bloody.

The eldest of the three children was my sister, Mary, who after four years in Australia was sent to America to boarding school to get her out of the atmosphere at home. So I never really saw much of her until years later. My older brother, Jonathan, wanted little to do with me in Australia since I was a drag on his lifestyle and he considered me my mother's favorite.

On these rocky foundations of my life at six years old, I fixed my attentions on our world of food, wine, and gardening. They were at once a balm (an escape into a private universe of glorious sensation) and my only potential realms of mastery. As I came to know food at its earthiest, plucked from trees or pulled from the sea and thrown on hot coals, and at its most glamorous, in the grand dining rooms of the poshest restaurants and in the kitchens of luxury ocean liners or hotels, these passions—a love of things cooked with bravura in their elemental state, an where they came from and how they were grown, and a fascination with "fine dining"—became the foundation and structure of my life.

The Great Barrier Reef visit had been one of the few blessed respites from an otherwise horrible five years that had begun when I was four, in early 1947, when my parents moved us from Connecticut to Australia. My father was sent by Westrex to Australia to make sure their movie houses or cinemas had the right equipment to take the soon to be developed stereo sound.

I had never been on a plane until the trip from San Francisco to Honolulu, where we stopped over in Waikiki at the very grand Royal Hawaiian Hotel. But the trip was horrendous enough for me (travel sick) to never want to get on a plane again, and to stay in Hawaii forever. That beach out in front of our balcony and the balmy tropical climate bonded me with Hawaii forever, but especially then with increasing misery as I watched the hours go by before we had to once again get in that little plane to head out for Sydney.

The three-day plane trip across the Pacific was so traumatizing that my memory of anything leading up to the coral landing strip in Fiji is almost entirely erased. I do recall a few things from those eighty hours in the twin-engine prop DC-3 plane: the smell of the DDT bomb set off in the cabin before we left Honolulu, the dry air, the turbulent plunges, and the French convicts seated behind us on their way to Devil's Island (only the French would send their convicts first-class), who kept propositioning my thirteen-year-old sister. I screamed, threw up repeatedly, and pleaded ceaselessly for the plane to be stopped. By the time we skidded to a halt on Fiji's bleached coral atoll, I was frantic to get out. As we arrived at the little corrugated-iron terminal building, I slung my arms around the nearest pole and shrieked at the top of what was left of my lungs that I would never leave.

And I stayed (and was left by my exhausted mother) there until approached by a huge man in a tapa cloth skirt, black hair teased straight up about a foot and tied with a red ribbon, his torso filling firmly a white military jacket with brass buttons that looked impressively like the ones on my toy soldiers. The fact that he had no shoes on his size fourteen feet fascinated me so much I forgot that I was going to live and die on that pole. I loosened my grip, a failing of spirit encouraged by the fact that he was holding in his hands an enormous, condensation-covered glass of golden yellow liquid, and by his voice, which was like a singing cello as it told me to come and sit in his tapa-cloth lap and have some pineapple juice. I am pretty sure that I had never heard of a pineapple, but as he waved the glass under my nose I knew I wanted to.

The smell and sight of that juice is my first and still one of my most vivid culinary memories. The pineapple had undoubtedly been picked only a few hours before in the cool morning and not refrigerated but chilled near chunks of ice to a temperature kind to your teeth as the juice goes down. Cool, sweet, refreshing juice shut me up for the first time in two days, so when I asked for a whole pineapple that I saw in the terminal, my mother nodded wearily. The pineapple itself is my second culinary memory: a whole fruit seemingly half the size of me, its top cut off, and so ripe that I could dig into it with my whole hand and eat the entire inside with my fingers. The irritation that greeted me when I returned covered in pineapple did not matter. I had found paradise.

Promises of juice lured me back onto the plane, and I drove the stewards mad with demands for more and more, until I was yet again violently ill, this time from all the acid of the canned variety. But I was hooked on tropical fruit, and within hours of arrival in Sydney, now on firm ground at the Hotel Australia, I lunged for the ripe fruit that was sent up by the manager in a huge basket covered in colored cellophane and tied with an enormous ribbon: passion fruit, ripe finger bananas and, of course, more ripe pineapples.

From a culinary standpoint, we were lucky that when we arrived in Sydney there were still wartime shortages. The refrigerator was powered only some of the time, so we had to rely on an old stand-up ice chest on the banana-tree-covered porch. That meant we ate all the tropical fruit—which now included papayas, mangoes, rambutans, mangosteens, and custard apples—only mildly chilled. By the time the thirties power stations were updated with American machinery, even with our refrigerator working, we knew that refrigerated fruit loses the scent of its ripening in the sun, of the heady vapors of papaya and pineapple tropical jungle plantations. The ice chest remained.

I loved all the tropical fruit, with its different seasons for the various varieties of mangoes and the excitement when the garnet red, pepperysmelling papaw arrived. But my favorites were the passion fruits, still warm from the summer sun, that grew along our backyard fence. Listening to the kookaburras overhead in the gum trees, I would bite the top of a hot, ripe fruit and suck out the juices while inhaling the perfume, a taste memory that came to play a constant part in my menus and recipes thirty years later, because perfectly ripe tropical fruit—the only thing I had in abundance in my early childhood—was a measure of happiness and success.

Although we lived in the wealthy Vaucluse suburb of Sydney, the grandeur of our house was a distinct disadvantage during routine power outages and their resulting lack of heating and hot water. In cold weather we ended up living in one room with an illegal heater monopolized by the dog; the smell of singeing hair reminds me to this day of deprivation. Home was far preferable to school, however, with its bare stone chapels, rank confessionals, enforced silence, and promises of life perfect only after death. As a Yank, I was mercilessly brutalized by my peers when I wasn't subjected to the wandering hands of priests.

My oasis was our vegetable garden, which my mother opted for after enduring six months of Australian vegetables: cabbage and its entire family, huge potatoes and carrots, the potatoes revoltingly full of deep-set black rotting spots, the carrots more wood core than sweet flesh. The garden was laid out in an old tennis court at the back of the property. Since it was set ten feet down below the level of the garden above, the top of the retaining wall was planted with nasturtiums, and the whole face of the hundred-foot wall was covered in a blanket of multicolored flowers— which I adore to this day. The nasturtiums attracted snails, and since I was paid for my small bucket full of snails, I took on the job of planting and carefully tending these flowers—my first gardening project. As a five-year-old I made sandwiches of nasturtium flowers (an Australian treat) and later, in 1974, put the blossoms in salads in California. (When I did so on *Good Morning America*, Joan Lunden announced, "I hate flowers [in food]," and went to a commercial.)

It was decided that we'd all pitch in to make the garden a special place. After my success with the nasturtiums, I chose what I wanted from a seed catalog airmailed from Burpee in the United States and took responsibility for five rows, including "runner" beans (green beans), broad (fava) beans, and lima beans, all of which required almost daily harvesting. With great love and prodigious labor—Australia is the land of extreme climate, droughts alternating with month-long deluges—we produced sweet corn that made the conservative Australians, unaccustomed to eating with their fingers, uncomfortable, but delighted our guests from home.

The rest of the Australian diet was lamb chops for breakfast, lamb sandwiches for lunch, and roast lamb for dinner, interspersed with a bit of flathead, a fish that was all we could come by when the fishermen were too nervous to venture out through the harbor (to the ocean), where the Communists had taken to blowing up the Pan American flying boats. From our house we had the best view in Sydney of those explosions, but the thrill was significantly lessened by the thought of having to go back to eating lamb or flathead.

After a couple of years, things like fresh shrimp showed up in abundance, and my mother added a jambalaya to her party repertoire. Some of my fondest memories of that huge house are the sideboard groaning with the little there was to cook with, the jambalaya in the center of the display, and the arrival in Sydney of meat other than lamb, even if it was only silverside (top round), corned and as tough as nails. My treat on my way out of the butcher shop was to pinch some of the wet corning salt surrounding the beef as it sat in a ten-inch marble table by the door, and suck on it until it dissolved.

The city's hotels and restaurants, meanwhile, featured twee interpretations of English food in the sort of atmosphere Dame Edna Everage would have coveted as source material. So whenever it was time for the annual visit to the one renowned French restaurant, Prunier, for my mother's birthday, I would be beside myself with excitement. Since arrival was an hour before my usual bedtime, the deep gloom then fashionable in deluxe dining rooms made me sleepy. But when the smiling maître d' handed me a huge menu with a silk tassel longer than I was and all the words in French, my mind began to race. From my many visits over the next three years, I memorized the menu and would insist on ordering for myself—a source of pride to my parents and eye rolling from nearby diners appalled by my French pronunciation. But I loved Chez Prunier so much that I was an angel of restraint and good manners, the deal being that I could put my head down on the table and sleep between the main course and dessert.

As obnoxious as my mangled French must have seemed, the owner-chef was charming to me and always brought me special things to taste. I was enchanted by his glamour, this man in starched white who had such authority in his domain. And he was a long way from my grizzled, half-naked, aborigine cooking teacher.

Forty years later, after a lunch promoting California Cuisine at the Regent Hotel in Sydney, an old man summoned me to his table. "I'd have recognized you instantly, you're your father's son," he said. Then the owner of Prunier told his guests, "This is the little boy who used to order by himself in horrible French and after the main course put his head on the table to sleep it all off." Prunier was still open, and this wonderful old man was still cooking.

The World Is a Dining Room

One night in 1950 my father announced we were going around the world on a ship. "The world" was still a vague concept in my mind, but missing two months of school was splendidly unambiguous. With a delicious sense of "living well is the best revenge," I announced to the school's head priest that I was seriously out of there, bound for Ceylon, India, the Red Sea, Egypt, Italy, New York, and San Francisco, before returning to Sydney.

The ship to India was Italian and brand-new. It would have made a fine steamer on Lake Como, but our first major storm in the Great Australian Bight nearly upended it. Many people were badly injured, the captain was seasick, and I begged for someone to kill me after smelling the banana oil used to clean up someone's smashed bottle of nail polish in the corridor outside my cabin. (To this day I cannot go near banana flavoring or the smell of heating bananas, Mr. Foster's delicious dessert notwithstanding.) Taking pity on me for the pounds I'd lost after three days of not eating, our stewardess, Maria, wheeled in a dish of eggs shirred in garlic and green Neapolitan olive oil. Green is what I turned, and she took it personally when I threw up on the spot.

After these upheavals of every kind, all I could think of was cereal and cold milk. The only milk onboard was canned unsweetened condensed milk, and after one taste of that on cornflakes (the only choice for twenty-eight days), I gave up in disgust. It was a disappointment all the more felt because I loved sweetened canned milk, which at that point was the only thing I could cook by myself. Australian food lore, born out of deprivation, had designated sweetened condensed milk, cooked in boiling water while still in the can, a national delicacy. And it was, though one could hardly call the fabulous ensuing goo delicate. Its name now is dulce de leche; then it was just what every kid begged for. Probably because it is as sweet as anything can be.

Pudding

14-ounce can sweetened condensed milk

Do not open the can, but take off the label and put the can in a saucepan 4 inches deeper than the can is high.

Pour water in the saucepan to cover the can by 1 inch. Bring the water to a boil, and continue simmering for 2 hours, adding water when necessary to keep the can covered with boiling water.

Take the can out and let cool completely before opening it.

Eat with a spoon right out of the can if you are a kid, and if an adult, think of something else to do with it, like make ice cream, or pour it over vanilla ice cream or, if you are a real adult genius, like George Lang, use it to dip pretzels into.

On board the ship, if my mother and sister thought I had been a pest about fresh pineapple juice on our first plane to Australia, they could have killed me over an every-day twelve-hour nag for fresh milk. In those days I didn't know there is no point complaining about what you cannot change, so I begged and plotted. My mother and sister became alarmed when I insisted I'd find some in Bombay, our first port after two weeks out of Australia.

"Eat *nothing* from the vendors," I was told.

When we docked and I peered over the rail at the forty or so vendor boats pressed against the ship's hull, I saw a little canoe far beneath us selling fresh milk. Down went my money in a can on a string, up came the milk, and down my throat it went. It was tropically warm but, to me, ambrosial. Then it came up and kept on coming up, until the doctor, seeing that he could have put a pencil between my ribs and it wouldn't have rolled away, gave me up for dead. My mother courageously washed me with cool, jasmine-scented towels and tried to fill me up with chilled Schweppes India tonic water, the only thing that had a prayer of staying down. Within a day or so I rallied, and to this day I am not sure which acts more as a tonic in difficult times, Schweppes and gin, or jasmine anything. And although my first brush with the "East" had nearly killed me, having been for the first time the center of so much attention, I was now forever hooked on its flavors, smells, and unending exotica.

After Egypt and Port Said, we were soon headed up the Mediterranean and into Rome, where I encountered my first truly grand city hotel. While my mother went off to save a life (someone else's for a change, this time that of a fellow passenger now in the hands of the Sisters of Charity, whose medical attentions consisted mostly of prayers), I was left in the care of the hotel staff. They had been warned to make sure I touched no dairy. If I stole anything to drink, they were instructed, it had better be wine.

It was at this wonderful old hotel that I discovered room service, the kind that only great luxury hotels can give. The Quirinale was like the nearby presidential palace of the same name. And it had milk—which, despite my sister's best efforts, I managed to order from room service and scarf down. Only minutes later was it on its way up again, and this time my family said, "Why not just let the little bugger die?"—and quite rightly. But my second near-death experience left me surprisingly sanguine, as I could now luxuriate in heavy linen sheets and silk bedcovers and listen to the soothing clatter of horse carriages and the presidential guard outside the huge windows.

From that week on, hotels like the Quirinale became an obsession and room service my favorite hobby.

The pampering would continue on the ship that left Genoa for New York, the vast American SS *Independence*. She was so modern, with identical stainless-steel and pale enamel walls in all the public areas, that I'd get hopelessly lost. So I decided to spend all my time in the dining room. In those days the menus of luxury liners were enormous, with sixty or more items for breakfast alone. It was my first real encounter with American food, and the only impression I took away was of quantity. My brother ate pancakes, waffles, and French toast with maple syrup until he could no longer stand; I ate rafts of smoked salmon.

We landed in New York, settled into the Waldorf-Astoria, and hit the restaurants: Cavanaugh's, Lindy's, Lüchow's, and Schrafft's, all of which had the same huge menus I'd seen on the ships. Certainly Lüchow's dining room, "The Gourmets' Rendezvous," was the size of an ocean liner. Here I found fried Long Island scallops with tartar sauce (a princely $2.35) and lobster Newburg, a favorite because it was served tableside by a maître d', and everyone in the restaurant would turn and look. At Lindy's I discovered Welch's Concord Grape Wine, Maryland lump crabmeat, and jumbo shrimp "cocktails," a very grown-up moment since I couldn't get the real thing. I loved Lindy's menu because it was a voyage in itself, like the painting on the wall of American travel spots. There was Boston sole, Maine lobster, Nova Scotia salmon (my new favorite), Great Lakes sturgeon, Canadian bacon, Jersey pork chops, and California strawberries. I ate as much of it as I could. The only dud was the Cold California Fruit Salad, with Cottage Cheese and Raisin Bread, which put me off "California" food for years. As did the Halekulani Salad I had at the St. Francis Hotel in San Francisco on the way back to Sydney. It was Fresh Half Pineapple, Papaya, Prunes, Banana, and Cottage Cheese. Suddenly full of nostalgia for Fiji and the Queensland pineapple fields, I ordered it, despite some misgivings now about bananas, let alone with prunes. At its arrival I knew my experience at Lindy's was true, and for the next several years whenever anyone in Australia or England asked me about food in California (the land of Hollywood to them), I told them it was all about fruit and cottage cheese, and to be avoided at all costs. Their opinions that American food was silly and not very good were confirmed.

America's Food

In 1951 the news came that we were moving again, this time to England by way of the United States. My father felt we knew nothing of the heartland of our native country, so he decided to show it to us. His plan was to fly to California, purchase a car, drive leisurely across the country with stops at major landmarks, sell the car in New York, and board the HMS *Queen Elizabeth* for Southampton. My memories are of the restaurants on each coast, with something of a blank in between.

The highlight of our West Coast leg was a pair of trips with my grandfather in and around Carmel, where he had retired. The first was to a California Spanish hacienda restaurant on the Holman Ranch, an oasis at the center of hundreds of acres of sunburnt, golden brown hills. We sat on a raised terrace beside a courtyard where white-robed and red-sashed Mexican staff gathered around huge grills and spits. It was a series of firsts: Caesar salad tossed at the table, garlic bread in huge rustic slabs, wild boar sausages grilled over mesquite charcoal, avocado "pears," and two-inch-thick T-bone steaks. The memory of a perfect evening lingered: the brown summer hills of California suffused in pink early evening light, an ambush of bougainvillea, the dense dark green of live oaks, the perfume of the fully flowering jasmine hedge mingling with the smells of charcoal-cooked wild boar, and my first taste of California wine. Later, when I was a professional chef, the place remained a benchmark of pleasure for me: simply grand food and perfect service in an unpretentious but beautiful setting.

The second excursion was to the Garrapata Trout Farm, located in one of those magical canyons off Big Sur. Catching fish in the pond was guaranteed, and we soon had enough to grill on open fires under huge overhanging California bay trees. Again the smells and aromas invaded and captured my brain: the summer-baked grass, the spice of the bay leaves, the charcoal smoke, the fish wrapped in sizzling bacon. The family was happy as a group, something rare enough in itself to incise this day in my memory. When I started working at Chez Panisse, the Garrapata trout were among the first resources to which I turned.

Heading east in our Ford station wagon, we stopped in Needles, home of motels, pickup trucks, lots of dust, and an enormous sign with thousands of lightbulbs flashing in sequence that read THE COCKY CACTUS. Bedazzled, I begged my parents to stop there for dinner. The decor was an original of the "family restaurant," a prototype for copies that line the U.S. interstates today. The menu was Pacific seafood, steaks, salads, and flaming desserts like hot plums ladled over a gigantic pile of coconut ice cream. I adored it. But what kept it in my mind was the birthday card the restaurant sent every year for at least the next decade. Years later, when I opened my restaurant Stars in San Francisco, I put two lessons from The Cocky Cactus at the top of my list: a restaurant can be fairly humble and still feel world-class, and nothing will build loyalty like "loving" relationships with customers.

The dinner in that dusty town was the last thing I remember of the trip, except for an endless succession of stainless-steel diners serving fresh pies and wonderful regional American food, until our stop in Washington, D.C., to visit my aunt and Russian uncle. Both would come to play an enormous role in my upbringing. She was my mother's sister, the eldest in a wealthy Irish Catholic family of thirteen kids. But she had been raised apart. Bedridden from a childhood illness, she was passed to my grandfather's even wealthier brother and his wife, who brought her up as a debutante in opulent Philadelphia Main Line settings. Her first marriage, to a prince of Philadelphia society, had ended after her husband's alcoholism became more pronounced than his homosexuality.

The uncle I knew was her second husband, a celebrated rocket scientist who, as an eighteen-year-old Russian naval cadet, had captured an imperial frigate in Communist hands, and then as captain of the ship had sailed it to India to escape the revolution. He was my hero. That was fine with my mother, but there is no doubt she was jealous of the loving relationship that grew between me and my veritable Mame of an aunt. I could hardly help revering this woman, with her meticulous sense of order in all the areas in which my mother's life was in chaos, her flamboyant wardrobe, her passion for galleries, Russian emeralds, a perfectly made-up face before lunch, old textiles, restaurants, and cooking.

When I had told her that in New York we'd be dining at Lüchow's and Lindy's, she gave a shudder and handed me a small pad of English blue notepaper. "Write these down," she commanded. "Delmonico's, The Colony, and Le Pavillon."

"Are those your favorites?" I asked.

"No," she replied. "Those would be Le Voisin, L'Escargot, and Maud Chez Elle, but don't write them down."

I did. And when I showed the entire list to my mother, she swore to keep me away from my aunt forever. My father was impressed but told me to forget all those places.

I didn't: They've been anchored in my mind ever since. The Delmonico's cookbook, *The Epicurean*, by its chef, Charles Ranhofer, inspired me to do the first Chez Panisse California Regional Dinner in 1976. In 1985, after opening Stars, I tried to buy L'Escargot to have a restaurant in New York. At Stars I posted the menu of Le Pavillon in a place of honor above the kitchen entrance and incorporated quotations from its imperious owner, Henri Soulé, into our training manuals.

Michael and Ariane Batterberry's *On the Town in New York* says Soulé was "to French cuisine what de Gaulle was to the Third Republic," but that his personality was closer to Napoleon's. He was a martinet and a snob, but above all a perfectionist who lived for his art. And he was nothing compared with his mentor in France, Fernand Point who, as George Lang, the first great promoter and manager of The Four Seasons in New York and later owner of Café des Artistes, told me, once threw out a party of four at his restaurant La Pyramide because one of the men was holding his glass of champagne by the bowl instead of the stem, ruining the otherwise perfectly achieved temperature of the wine.

What would I have eaten if my parents had taken me to Le Pavillon? What would I eat now? There were eleven ways to start the meal, from smoked salmon to cherrystones to crabmeat (all in French of course). Following those were eggs (ten dishes), fish (eleven), plats du jour (fourteen), grillades (seven), cold plates (six), vegetables (nine), and desserts (eight). Traveling on ships and trains had made me fall in love with cold plates like York Ham and Tongue, but I would have mercy on my guests and not confuse the order of the meal by ordering them (since no one knew any longer where to put them in the order of dishes served).

I'd begin with the Bayonne ham with a glass of champagne for sure, most likely followed by the Goujonettes de Sole, Sauce Tartare. Then, though tempted by the kidneys from the Grillades section, or the Rognons Maître d'Hôtel (with a simple unmelted butter and parsley, salt, freshly ground pepper, and lemon juice), and wondering about the daring of featuring "Irish Stew," I would have the poached chicken Bordelaise with fresh little peas steamed in lettuce. For dessert my eye would light upon the Désir du Roi as I looked on the Duke of Windsor or the Aga Khan across the dining room. Knowing that one of my companions would have a wild strawberry soufflé, I would order the Coupe aux Marrons, as I always did as a child. The cost for my meal would have been ten dollars.

Would anyone not want to join me?

My World Is a First-Class Dining Room

On boarding the Cunard liner *Queen Elizabeth* in New York, we found that the enormous cabin reserved for my brother and me was filled with huge trays of canapés—more than the two of us could eat—and our first caviar and goose liver. We were in heaven. But this very grand ship was to teach me more than how to fill my belly with wonderful food. The first morning I found the promenade deck and a deck chair with a card that read "Master J. Tower" in its holder. After tucking me into my blanket, the white-coated steward served me hot beef bouillon in a bone china cup. Too small to see over the rail, I stared at the sky and listened to the hum and vibrations of the ship, allowing myself to be voluptuously enveloped in the perfection of the moment. I remember thinking that whatever my future held, the freedom of this morning—without adults, the only supervision from a perfect waiter folding blankets around my feet and providing delicious food—would be what I'd live for. Whatever happened (and it usually did, I thought), I would always have this.

The next area to conquer was the dining room. My brother and I were scheduled for the first dinner seating, my parents the second; and since my brother was embarrassed to sit with me (he wanted the beautiful daughter of the Firestone family), I was left alone with the waiter and the immense menu in French. I found the things I knew I liked, and the words I could understand: Saumon Fumé écossais, Caviare, Jambon de Paris, l'Homard Newburg, Pommes Chips. The Mock Turtle Soup and Baked Alaska in English were easy, so I had those too. Then I had the Assiette de Petits Fours all to myself. Within days I was bedridden, sick as a dog from greedy and enthusiastic overeating.

Most any calm-sea afternoon before my downfall, I could be found in the dining room waiting for dinner, or waiting to be asked into the kitchens, where I had become something of a mascot. So one evening when I did not appear, my parents were compelled to explain that I was in bed, incapable of looking at more food. That night, there was a knock at my cabin door. In came a dining room waiter—not a cabin steward but my real dining room waiter. I was honored—but then my stomach tightened at the sight of the trolley piled high with domed dishes, among them an enormous silver cloche that obviously held a huge roast of beef or a goose. My heart sank. I knew if I said, "Please go away and let me die," I'd insult the kitchen and lose my standing. If I ate any of it, I doubted I'd survive the night.

I should have noticed the sympathetic smile on the waiter's face and the grin on the steward behind him. I recoiled in horror as the waiter, with a dramatic flourish, removed the dome. My queasy stomach perversely expected fatty meat, but I saw only a small green earthenware pot. My pal from the dining room laughed as he removed the lid to reveal a dish of simply water, lamb, potatoes, a hint of sage, and nothing more. The clean aromas of a Lancashire hot pot wafted across to my bed, and my appetite was immediately restored. The next morning I felt good enough to consume a quantity of smoked salmon, but I never dove blindly into a menu again. The chef had taught me balance, if not moderation.

We left the ship in Southampton in November 1951 and headed up to London by the Golden Arrow Boat Train, with a wonderfully magical dining car, and its afternoon tea of Toasted Teacake, Buttered Toast, Crumpets & Scones, Hovis Bread & Butter, Teatime Biscuits & Quality Cake. I was in heaven, although how much I was later to learn when we got to London and found ourselves in the desert of nationally rationed and very scarce food.

In London it was cold and damp, and through a thick fog we made our way to the Hyde Park Hotel, our rooms looking out on trees, horse guards in red and blue, and nannies whose big black prams could be discerned through the gloom. Our house in Sydney had been vast, but these hotel rooms were the biggest I had ever seen—so large that I don't remember my brother after this. Maybe he was in school. Alone and bored, the city too fog-swathed to venture into by myself, I turned to the only entertainment I knew: room service and the dining room.

During the day I'd run the carts around the corridors with my favorite waiters, Bill and Ben, who would let me accompany them into the rooms of the less uptight guests. They showed me how to carve game birds, open wine bottles, and hold the tops of huge tureens as they ladled out turtle soup or consommé Célestine.

Meanwhile, my first lesson in shopping for perfect ingredients was just a few blocks away in Knightsbridge, at Harrods' magnificent Food Hall. I went every day to see the twenty-foot-high, ten-foot-wide display of fish and shellfish, the fish laid out on a sloping, light gray marble slab, so fresh they needed to be cooled only by a mist of water. As food became more readily available in the next two years, sometimes the white belly of a forty-pound turbot would be decorated in a Prince of Wales fleur-de-lis of tiny shrimp, their pink in contrast to the orange coral of sea scallops still in their shells; and sometimes it would be covered in an arabesque of fresh herring and lobsters. If the fishing weather had been bad, the display would be all smoked fish, with miles of kippers and mounds of smoked salmon, four-foot-long smoked eels biting down on the tails of whole smoked sturgeon.

Even with rationing, the poultry section had the usual ducks, wild and white domesticated Aylesbury, if only one or two of each, but there were all kinds of wild pheasants and other game birds hanging in rows along the marble hall. I was astonished not so much by the numbers of hares and rabbits as by the fact they were there at all: In Australia, rabbit was known as "bush chicken" and so common a pest that no one ate it. In those days in England, chickens were more expensive than beef. The meat section boasted twenty or so whole lambs, half beef carcasses, and every kind of offal, including calves' heads scrubbed and white and ready for Tête de Veau, Sauce Gribiche—my favorite lunch at the hotel. The routine was to order something new on the hotel menu and then run to Harrods to see what it looked like raw.

My career as a food tourist was cut short one night when my parents unexpectedly stayed in the hotel for dinner and I, seizing my chance to have some wine, sat down at their table. Bill, Ben, the headwaiter, and the maître d' all came to greet me. This caught my father's attention, and he looked at me with new focus. "What are you doing here?" he asked. "I thought you were in school."

"I am," I said, "they're teaching me to slice smoked salmon."

Admiration and disgust were in a close race on my father's face, but he knew I had him for the moment.

It says something about the size of our adjoining suites that I had been in residence for two months without my father noticing. It says something about my father, too. He turned to my mother, and I could read the looks on their faces. Each wanted to say to the other: "I thought you put him in school!" The waiters and I were devastated: my reign as Eloise of the Hyde Park Hotel was over.

That evening was about the extent of my parents' attention span with me, because we remained at the Hyde Park for another month before eventually landing in a very *Separate Tables* hotel in the Surrey countryside nearer schools. It was another month before they found one; in the meantime, I attempted to reproduce my old routine by befriending the chef and the room service waiters. I failed: The entire staff thought I was a pest. So I turned my attention to the guests, particularly to an ancient (to me) English lesbian dressed in impeccable tweed suits. Mrs. Charlesworth let me take her two Russell terriers around the grounds while she played canasta with the beautifully mannered unmarried colonels, majors, reverends, gym teachers, and dressmakers who lived in the hotel. Then she'd let me finish off her gin and have a puff on her ivory cigarette holder.

Finally, I was sent off to school, where I was miserable, and where for the first time in my life I ate bad food. The food at the hotel had been very English, with very good ingredients, and I learned to love most of them. But unlike the Hyde Park Hotel, we were now on English food rationing coupons. I had two eggs a week, no sugar or desserts, just lots of kippers, bread fried in bacon fat, and steamed puddings. It was a long way from shipboard lobster Newburg and grand hotel roasted teal duck.

The school food was cooked for hours and covered with sauces reconstituted from powders labeled "brown," "fish," or "custard." It was a diet made for scurvy; in my six years at English "public" (i.e., private) schools, I never saw a piece of fresh fruit.

For that I'd have to wait for the weekends, when I'd be home in my mother's kitchen at our country house near Guildford, Surrey, to which we had moved after the country hotel.

My Mother's English Kitchen

Food and entertaining were the way my mother communicated. She had never cooked before her marriage, but she was a natural and quickly learned her way around the kitchen. My father's making light of all her talents save cooking and gardening meant they became her only artistic outlets. Hopeless in most maternal respects, she took food and hospitality very seriously. Parties meant mountains of food, rivers of drinks, and the carpet rolled up at midnight for dancing until dawn.

We would often shop together, visiting the greengrocer, the butcher, the poulterer (who had fresh game as well), the fishmonger, and, twice a week, the farmers' market, where one could find fresh herbs and salad greens, honeys, more game, and potatoes dug that morning. Everything was local or regional because it had to be. There were no large industrial farms and no refrigerated transportation, and rural England in the throes of rationing meant that the only meats and poultry in plentiful supply were locally caught wild things. I would walk down the streets of Guildford ogling all the wild hare and rabbits hanging outside the shops, with little buckets under their noses to catch the blood for "jugged hare" or lièvre à la royale.

At the fishmonger's they would try to frighten me with tasting a raw oyster, a game I kept up for as long as I could, and in the greengrocer my mother taught me to pick out the best Channel Islands new potatoes and green beans, which had to be small and of the same size so they would cook evenly. The watercress had to shine, the Brussels sprouts had to be tiny and firm, and the lettuces were to have no brown spots. The vegetables and fruits we bought were to supplement our orchard of pears, apples, and quinces, and our one-acre vegetable garden of herbs, edible flowers, green "runner" beans, and American crops like squashes, corn, and lima beans that the gardeners thought were devil's work. Most of the time the weather agreed. There were also strawberries and raspberries (both of which were my project and responsibility), and blackberries, mulberries, and hazelnuts from the wild "common" land where I'd go horseback riding.

When I managed to get myself suspended or expelled from school on several occasions, being sentenced to the garden was a haven, not an exile. Even if Mullins, one of the gardeners, did insist on pinching my bottom, I got used to it after a while, since this was England, after all.

I cannot think of a more important education from my mother than gardening, and certainly no education I enjoyed as much. There were no big concepts like "organic" or "pesticide free"—I'm not even sure there were chemicals. It was all manure and plowing under, and double digging, and the dung from the horse stables and my pet twin goats kept the strawberries and asparagus very happy. "They need to be fed a lot," my mother would explain, firing my imagination about plants that had to eat before we ate them.

I often ended up cooking these wonderful ingredients because I had to, when my mother had become distracted or couldn't manage. Her ambition sometimes did not outlast the martini consumption, and there were memorable disasters. There was the time we received a shipment from the U.S. embassy of what appeared to be vegetable shortening, which she promptly used to cook eggs and lamb chops. It was only after she rendered the house uninhabitable that she realized she had just fried with pure lanolin meant to keep naval leather in good condition at sea. And then there was the time I came home from school, sniffed the air, and said, with dripping contempt, "What are we having, fried cheese?" Her face fell. She had gone to great lengths to obtain wild pheasant that, according to true English tastes, had been hung to their desired level of putrefaction. But rationing was off by then, money talked, and there was always a "larder" full of food to choose from. On any given day there would be a whole poached wild Scottish salmon, a fresh ham (meaning leg of pork brined and poached), leftover game birds and beef, as well as cakes and puddings made by the housekeeper. So that night my mother gave us all up to what was in the larder and, in disappointment at not having made a hit with her family, got drunk.

My mother was not an alcoholic in the usual sense. She didn't drink during the day. What she had, I realize in retrospect, was a problem metabolizing alcohol. She'd consume two martinis and it was as if you'd hit her with a sledgehammer. So I was used to taking over the kitchen from her every weekend. But the large summer garden parties were the most dramatic and heart pounding for me. At age fourteen I would find myself doing the second half of a meal for a hundred people, carefully removing huge wild Scottish salmon from their poaching liquid, peeling them and decorating them and giving them to waiters to take out to the backyard tent, where my mother would inevitably be reeling. The boiled leg of mutton served cold with sauce gribiche or the grilled steak would have been done in advance, and I had been taught how to carve and slice a few years before, so they were no problem to finish. Nor were the green bean salad vinaigrette, the twenty-odd pounds of strawberries served in a bowl my mother had had made in Venice for that purpose, or the ice cream, usually wild blackberry, which we had taken turns all day churning. The quantities were heart stopping for me, but our waiters Bill and Ben from the Hyde Park Hotel knew how much to put out.

If alcohol drove a wedge between my mother and the family, it was my one point of connection with my father. I lived for the wine ritual that anchored the weekend, when I'd return from school, determine what was being served at Saturday's dinner, and discuss with him the appropriate bottles. I would push for my favorite wines, of course, even when they were too expensive for the occasion—maneuvers he didn't always appreciate—but on the whole he was pleased by my performance as his private sommelier, and proud that I would accompany my mother to Berry Brothers in St. James's (London) to taste and pick out the English bottlings of "Claret" or "Pomerol" house wines for the year.

The routine of retrieving the bottles was nonetheless fraught. The cellar was cavernous, with five or six rooms, and we had to descend a long, gray stone staircase into the darkness. I had seen all the Hammer horror films, so I had nightmares about those rooms throughout my teens. Yet I made the descent, white-knuckled, because the happiest moments of my week revolved around choosing the wines, decanting them, tasting them, and drinking them with dinner. When there was no company, we served only red wine, since my father considered white "effeminate" and champagne "frivolous." Perhaps that's why I adore both.

Home Alone

By the time I was sixteen, my parents felt I could hold down a kitchen of my own, so one summer, when my mother left for the United States to put my brother in university, my father and I were alone in our Knightsbridge mews flat. It was my job to cook. I had Harrods to shop in, food was plentiful, and my stint a success, even though I blew the week's budget the first day and melted the plastic colander over boiling water while keeping the pasta warm to go with my Veal Marengo for my father and his Australian mistress.

My aunt wrote constantly with cooking advice: "I have an easy recipe: Take a cut-up bird—chicken, grouse, or what have you (even rabbit)—wipe it dry and clean, and brown it in butter (salt and pepper) in a pan on top of stove. When brown pour heavy cream over it, put a tight lid on pan and turn heat low, and let cook half an hour. Serve with wide noodles in butter and a green salad." She told me about whole Mediterranean sea bass baked in the oven. My father was proud, if aghast at the expenses, which only mounted as more recipes arrived: "The first and second ribs of beef," wild mushrooms with potatoes, "an honest to goodness Indian curry," "coquilles" in their shells, and "last but not least, rump pot roast."

My aunt and uncle decided to send me to Paris to eat, learn, and buy them truffles. My thank-you note to them says I had "six escargots, a croustade de crabe, salade verte, gâteau des pêches (de la maison), and café. The crab was in a white wine sauce (very light) and served on a vol-au-vent. I don't usually like them, but this one was exceptional. The food was good and down to earth! So many restaurants have very fancy food that tastes of nothing but money."

Money was a problem if you were a young glutton, even a subsidized one. I wrote of passing Fauchon's, "which makes Fortnum & Mason look ill. Fresh truffles, mangoes, mountains of chocolate truffles, cakes enough to make you smash the windows to get at them. The only trouble was it reeked of money, so I was forced to stay out—just as well, I suppose." But my father was just as indulgent when it involved teaching by traveling. In 1956 he sent my brother and me alone to California and back, traveling on the French ship *Liberté*, the 20th Century Limited crack train to Chicago, and the California Zephyr to San Francisco, which would stop in the Rockies to pick up wild trout for the dining car.

Such indulgences could not last, and I was soon back in boarding school, where I finally complained to the headmaster about the food. For breakfast there was white bread, margarine, and cheap marmalade; for lunch, typically shepherd's pie and bread pudding with powdered custard sauce; and for the evening meal a repetition of breakfast. I was surprised when he offered a challenge instead of the usual caning for speaking out: Cook a meal that could be reproduced, on a given budget, for the students. I enlisted a friend and cooked meat loaf with fresh vegetables, green salad, and an upside-down apple tart served with cheddar. I was applauded—and the food stayed the same.

But nothing of English food and ingredients had prepared me for the weird swill dished out at the New England prep school to which I moved for my junior year in 1959: chipped beef in flour sauce on a rusk that would choke a giant, and lime Jell-O with marshmallow and bacon. I thought of a hunger strike but decided instead on illegal trips to town for the newly discovered luxury of hamburgers and malted milk shakes. Threats to expel me didn't work (been there, done that), even after I tried to run away to Cuba anyway and join the revolution. I was made head of the student committee on food, a position that meant nothing in the face of a phalanx of dietitians drumming up lime Jell-O and bacon. For the headmaster, it was an admirable act of revenge.

Two years later, at Harvard College, the Freshman Union eating hall was worse—worse even than the food I had at army camp in England with the Royal Fusiliers when I was fifteen and a cadet. Once again I spoke up, this time to the deaf ears of a home economist and the huge women cooks who had been serving that slop for thirty years with firmly muttered Boston Irish oaths. So I backed off, and plotted to get out of Harvard's "houses" and into a house of my own. Or anyone's, for that matter.

"Anyone" appeared in the form of a teaching fellow from Paris, and soon I was ensconced in a Directoire-decorated apartment on Beacon Hill. We called it the Champagne Palace.

The Champagne Palace

The teaching fellow turned out to have lived in Paris, so we loved the same things. The champagne flowed, the candles stayed lighted, and the Piaf songs played on. There wasn't much of a kitchen, but I did manage a mean steak au poivre, and since my aunt continued to send recipes, we enjoyed a chicken in cream, spaghetti in clam sauce, lobsters, and all sorts of risottos and omelets. The apartment was above the English consul general's house, the site of constant cast parties, so many a bored actor found his way up the stairs at the advice of the consul's (and our) risqué maid. So there was a lot of impromptu cooking for actors, hustlers, pill pushers, and even Etonian sons and nephews at the small hours of the morning. Here I could practice my own full-blown candlelight Alexandria Quartet hospitality for the first time.

A diary entry in 1963 is marked "Freddy and the Champagne Palace":

Steak au poivre
Jack Daniel's
Chambolle-Musigny
Courvoisier
Pills

Substitute Chicken Club, Omelet

After two years of this masked ball, my Champagne Palace friend became unhinged, the creditors showed up and commandeered my Directoire gilt-bronze swan-neck and dolphin chandelier. So after a few more parties, the palace was disbanded and bare, and I went back to my allotted rooms at Adams House, where, deprived of a kitchen, my time was now filled more with Baudelaire, Mallarmé, William Burroughs, studies of Egyptian funerary temples, and wishing I didn't understand why Oscar Wilde would take a cab to cross the street than it was with food. My friend and roommate, Michael Palmer, already on his way to becoming a first-rate poet, developed friendships with Louis Zukofsky, Allen Ginsberg, Gary Snyder, and the Creeleys, who were among those who visited our room. After smoking marijuana for the first time, I said I preferred a good champagne any day, Lafite-Rothschild or Otard, and offered some to that evening's guests. But we still needed to cook for whoever had the munchies.

I set up a kitchen in the closet with the hot plate and blue Le Creuset frying pan sent by my aunt, who was worried that years of bad school food would stunt my mind. Recipes and advice on how to entertain my friends kept coming: one for romaine lettuce dressed with sour cream, mayonnaise, and imported Parmesan cheese; others for her incredible coleslaw; iced coffee with ice cream and vanilla bean; and the names of importers on the East Coast that sold Ratsherrn Bockbeer and a particular 1957 Rosé d'Anjou (with advice never to spend money on any older ones).

At the end of that letter in 1962 she wrote, "Your uncle's prediction for the past five years came to pass yesterday—two Soviets in space and he expects them to try for a rendezvous and to train for a rescue in space." Back on earth, she knew it was time to check out my mental health, so she invited me with several of my friends, including Michael, still uninitiated in the lessons of aristocratic Russia, to come to Washington.

CHAPTER 2

First Lessons

The Old World First

MY FRIENDS HAD indulged in my aunt's chicken liver with hundred-year-old Madeira recipe, which I'd cooked in our little college rooms' closet, but before we disbanded from Harvard I wanted them to experience the source and a lifestyle of the only perfect harmony I had ever known. I wanted them to hear the conversations at the table with my uncle's circle of aristocratic Russians, their talk ranging from underwater missiles and galactic travel to space stations and the real story of Rasputin's death, by Count Cheremetev, childhood friend of his assassin (Prince Yusupov). I wanted my friends to see the last vestiges of a grand world whose real players were about to disappear. I certainly wanted them to meet my favorite, a discreet crown prince of Poland who when my aunt had offered an aspirin to a guest complaining of a headache said: "Take the *France* instead, it sails at eleven."

So in our junior year we made the trip. My friends paled when they saw the silk and malachite apartment, but it was nothing compared with the pallor they'd acquired after three de rigueur frozen vodka toasts: "To our meeting!" "To the promise of your young minds!" and "May you leave the world a better place than you found it!" Only a Russian could greet you and speak to your death within five minutes—and it all seemed so normal to me.

With the vodka were the famous chicken livers and blini with caviar. The first Russian culinary lesson was that blini should be drenched in enough melted butter for it to run down into one's lace cuffs, if one had them. The second was in the social nerve and dexterity to pick up a vodka in one hand, a beluga-laden, butter-soaked, sour-cream-covered blini in the other, and pop the whole blini in one's mouth seconds after the burn of the vodka hit one's throat.

After several more courses and lots of wines, dessert was a quart of ice cream per person. Then my uncle repeated the before-the-war/after-the-war tutorial, giving each of us a taste of his favorite liqueur partnered with its far more magnificent prewar incarnation. The pousse-café—"to settle our stomachs"—was what legends are made of: a sixteen-ounce Scotch and soda. Our lessons had begun, and we returned to Cambridge.

Beef and d'Yquem

Stories of this Russian meal survived better than we did, and it became a challenge to repeat as much of it as possible back in Cambridge. This was easier with a kitchen of my own. When we couldn't stand Adams House any longer (or they us), Michael and I took a little two-story house with a garden on Green Street in Cambridge. I pulled out my Elizabeth David *Gourmet* articles on the London restaurateur of the thirties X. Marcel Boulestin and put aside Radiguet and Ho Chi Minh's *Le Dragon de Bambon* for Montagné's *Larousse Gastronomique*.

We never did get around to planting the planned little lettuces and mesclun in the garden, but the kitchen was well enough equipped for serious cooking. Michael loved food as much as I did: he came from a Scarsdale Italian family with several maiden aunts who specialized in organizing Old World feasts. His Wellesley girlfriend, Cathy Simon, loved cooking as well. Her Danish mother in Manhattan was a friend of the legendary cooking teacher Michael Field, and Cathy had learned from the best. Not that she needed much education, she was one of the best natural cooks I had ever seen. And our Texan friend John Sanger, another passionate cook and Michael Field fan, had the allowance to cook all the things we couldn't afford.

For my junior-year birthday, Michael had given me a can of truffles and a book of H.D.'s poems, setting the tone for the coming year—my year spent in the college library listening to Noël (Coward) and Gertie (Gertrude Lawrence) reading *Private Lives*, and cooking. Nothing else seemed to make much sense.

Once we had our kitchen, I couldn't wait to use the truffles and an 1884 Madeira Michael had also given me:

First Dinner in Our Own Kitchen

Cambridge, 1965

Pâté

Frozen Vodka

Consommé Madrilène

Saumon en gelée aux truffes
Pouilly-Fumé 1962

Filet de Boeuf périgourdine
Château-Neuf-du-Pape 1957

Strawberries and French Cream
Asti Spumante

Coffee
"Napolean" Armagnac
Sercial Madeira 1884

Guests at that dinner included Cathy, John Sanger, and Colin Streeter, the most beautiful young man at Harvard, only recently, it was said, out of the arms of Leonard Bernstein.

Fired up by this success, I filled my notebook with recipes for salt beef, how to make hams, turbot with Meyer lemon salad, sturgeon with cream and caviar, green bean and nasturtium flower salad, and Soufrières lime punch. I wrote that my goal was to cook the way Balenciaga cut clothes—simple in form, without ornamentation, always in harmony with the lines of the body.

Everyone who had been on the Washington trip wanted to test what Cheremetev had told us was Prince Yusupov's definition of decadence: drinking Château d'Yquem with roast beef. The Russians considered the point of it to be the richness of the fat (it had to be prime and aged beef) and the age of the wine, which could not be too young or too old. Too young, the wine would lack the complexity to match the richness of the meat, and too old it would pale under that same richness. A twenty- to thirty-year-old d'Yquem was thought to be just about right.

We served the beef with a 1955 d'Yquem because that was all we could find and afford. But the ten-year-old wine did its job: I remember the moment of silence that fell around the hot, early summer kitchen as I cut salty fat off the roast ribs and everyone (as instructed) sucked on a hunk while washing it down with the cool wine. One felt a stagger in the knees, the body sending a silent but eloquent message to the brain to *stop!* We had reached the benchmark. Or so we thought.

Our final dinner, a year later, just before we graduated in June 1965, was in a kitchen that had reached one hundred degrees by the time I had roasted the goose. I served it room temperature with more d'Yquem. That fatty goose and its Peking duck–like skin paired with the old sweet wine pushed us momentarily out into a world where eating and tasting were as powerful forces as any we knew.

But enough of all that, I thought. We were leaving the college nest, and so time to find a job. An offer from *The New Yorker* seemed from the other side of the moon, so I thought of architecture. And Italy and Greece. Would they move me enough to go back to school for more?

I sailed for Europe.

The Horse & Groom

My mother's treat for surviving Harvard and for never having successfully made it all the way to Cuba to meet Che, or Venezuela for the Peace Corps, was to take me to her ancestral Ireland before going on to England. I chose the liner *Maasdam* because of my parents' stories of Trimalchian feasts on Dutch freighters before the war. I had great expectations of eel and rijsttafel, of two-hour midmorning breakfasts of cold fish and fowl followed by more of the same throughout the day. But the food was so bad that I spent my time writing an outline for a cookbook called *Quick & Cheap*. It included a fifteen-minute tomato soup, green bean salad, citrus chicken, and a lamb-potato casserole modeled on the hot pot that had saved my life aboard the *Queen Elizabeth*. Then I wrote a regimen for a carbohydrate-free diet (fish, eggs, smoked salmon, melon, prawns, clear soups, watercress salads, trout, vegetable ragouts) before drawing up a list of all the famous restaurants in the world and a travel plan to visit them.

Ireland in those days had no famous restaurants, so we were a bit adrift after we left Galway's (where we had landed) Ashford Castle, with its ease and splendor and fine old Amontillado. On the way to Dublin we ended up at the Welcome Home guesthouse, where it was a shock to learn that if you didn't eat a high tea of eggs, fried bread, and grilled tomatoes at 6 P.M., you didn't eat at night at all. Gone were the famous teas of Lady Portarlington, who replaced tea with Sidecars, and gone as well the fashion of cold grouse washed down with ancient Malmsey. Now it was sausage rolls.

All this my mother forgave when she discovered that every tiny village grocery store had a bar, and that a little tot of enlightenment was always just around the corner. Never one for whiskey during the day, I distracted myself by keeping records of every meal, in macabre fascination at the contrast between the richness of the countryside (lily-covered peat bogs and endless undulating hills covered in rhododendrons and fuchsia hedgerows) and the ubiquitous watery tomatoes, powdered oxtail soup, and canned peas.

In England I retraced my childhood culinary past. At Brown's Hotel, beloved of my aunt and Russian uncle and a mecca for country eccentrics, gone also were its breakfasts of cold meats and ptarmigan, haddock, eggs and kidneys, ham and nectarines, and small mountains of scones and buttered toast. Gone were Brown's vodka iced to perfection, and the hundreds of different kinds of pies that Leonard Woolf said had limbs peeking through the crusts, gone the grand dinners with ten courses and the suppers that followed (deviled chicken and potted shrimp and a huge brandy or Scotch and soda). Gone also was this last attempt at something timeless in everyday life, like the party in Sir Alfred Manning's painting *Picnic on a River*. These thoughts cascaded through my mind in the bar at Brown's while I listened to the Texas, not Gloucestershire, accents. I shed a tear into my champagne for everything wonderful that had passed, and headed for the village of our old house, an hour southwest of London in the county of Surrey.

We stayed in Surrey with my English guardians, who had always looked after me when my parents were away and during the year I was left at school in England (1958) when my parents returned to the States. They shared my mother's passion for gardens and gardening, and their grounds were an ocean of color, of enormous careless poppies, ceanothus scented like honey, columbines in various shades of night, fritillaries and delphinium, and a whole garden of roses, both tea and Peace. Filled with nostalgia, we rushed to see our old house, with its acre kitchen garden lined with box hedges and framed with rose-covered arbors and trellises, its lawn tennis courts, vast orchard, goat paddock, and croquet lawn that held the huge tents of my mother's garden parties. Eight houses now sat in its place.

Back amongst my guardians' flowers, two Pimm's before lunch assuaged the growing sadness that you can never go back; I learned that even this huge garden of my wealthy guardians was probably doomed by the vast cost of keeping it up. I realized that gardening, which so far was the only thing life had prepared me for, was not a way out. My mother went back to New York, a piece of her heart forever left in the eighteenth-century property we had seen in the Wicklow Mountains outside of Dublin, my father having decided they would live in Connecticut. I would have stayed in Ireland happily, but not Connecticut, so looked around in England for a job.

I had no leads for any jobs, so perhaps the wine business could be the answer? My first visit to a wine company led only to the director's bed and the advice that I was too ambitious to settle for never being able to own this, his boss's family's company.

Cooking was my last hope. But for whom? Back in Surrey I ran into my old girlfriend, the daughter of the publican at the Horse & Groom, next to our old house. It turned out she was fed up with cooking the simple pub menu and offered me the job. The prospect of requisitioning ingredients and facing a row of orders at the rush while using such strange equipment as infrared steak griddlers and deep-fat fryers was terrifying, but not as much as being penniless. The food, I figured, would be easy. All I had to do was cook everything a little less than this English kitchen had, put some butter and cream in the mashed potatoes, banish packaged sauces, and salt the previously tasteless soup. After a few disasters—among them not shutting the valve in the fryer when filling it back up with oil—I got the hang of it. Or so I thought. The public hated my Frenchified food, thinking it too rich and strangely flavored. Their thumbs-down gesture meant I was soon out pounding the pavement again.

I had just finished James Baldwin's *Another Country*, with its line about security as a vast, gray sleep, so I fell on my grandfather's offer to pay for graduate school in architecture, as long as it was back at Harvard, and left England for good. I docked in New York in hundred-degree heat with my great-uncle's fur coat over my arm and a handkerchief wet with the tears of an admiring chief steward in my breast pocket. My family took the wetness in my own eyes as a sign of my happiness to be back in America.

Lafite in the Streets

I set out for Cambridge, where Cathy and Michael were back in the same Green Street house, but this time they had planted the backyard garden with rows of baby lettuces from seeds brought from Italy and France. That street held too many memories for me, so I found a place in Boston's Italian North End to be near the food markets, in the romantic notion that it would be like living in Europe. But the only European thing about the neighborhood was that it was more violent than Naples. The Italian mama across the hall turned out to be the mother of the local boss, so I was declared off-limits to stranger bashing. But my friends were not, so brushing aside the pasta hanging in the corridor, I made my peace with Mama and crossed the Charles River again. This time it was for a blue-collar Irish block near Inman Square in Somerville, where the rents for houses with big kitchens and dining rooms were cheap. There was also a decent fish market called Legal Sea Foods, where after a few months I convinced the owner to use the space next door as an experimental restaurant. Use up all the left-over fish in fish and chips so that what's in the case each day is fresh, was what I told him, and later I was his first customer.

Protests against the Vietnam War were breaking out across the nation, and Harvard Square was no exception. My disdain for a revolution without the proper Jacobite fashions had brought down polite but dedicated calumny on my head, so I invited two street-kid dancers, poets, my Green Beret brother just in from Vietnam for R & R, radical architecture students, and the son of a senior official at the FBI to dinner to discuss my artistic and revolutionary stance.

After my radical guests had a few Polish frozen vodkas, the veins of their currently politically correct thinking ran not as deep as when they had first walked in the door and seen the enemy, my brother, who at my request was in full uniform. By the time we were deep into the red wine, they all saw him as having the same dignity as the rare and expensive Château Beychevelle 1962. Then I asked my brother's advice for making Molotov cocktails.

"Use strong bottles," he said.

We drank Dom Pérignon and I filled the empty bottles with gasoline siphoned from my car, ripped up an old Hermès scarf to use for fuses, and hauled them in a Tiffany shopping bag to the campus. My champagne Molotovs bounced off the architecture school building, where I threw them, rolled down the street into a storm drain, and exploded.

So much for my militant radical phase.

I had about the same success at the School of Design. Neither my underwater habitat project nor my bridge-tunnel design for linking England and France went over well. They insisted instead that I involve myself with the real world of public housing. So I decided on a multimedia effort: cooking, film, music, and drugs. My presentation was called "Champagne While the World Crumbles," and consisted of a film loop of the atom bomb going off amid footage of the worst public housing projects and urban sprawl I could find. The music was Lou Reed, the food a huge platter of marijuana cookies—the recipe adapted from *The Alice B. Toklas Cookbook*.

All the cookies were consumed, most by people who didn't know what they were—despite a sign that said eating more than two was at the eater's risk. At least five were gobbled up by a juror, who was found three days later in some louche sink in Boston. He later told me that I was lucky not to be kicked out of school, and that I would have been had there not been a student revolution going on. In my senior year, he said, I would have to work on socially responsible projects—and over the summer think long and hard about myself.

I did.

And I realized that food was a more powerful weapon than architecture.

Mary Jane Butter

The quality of the grass you use to make this butter is up to you and your budget. We used to use whatever leftover sticks and seeds there were after harvesting the leaves. Obviously fresh is better. As for quantity, anything from two to six handfuls.

The butter is very good under the skin of a turkey to be roasted for Thanksgiving.

Handfuls cannabis   2 pounds butter

Put the cannabis in a 4-quart saucepan and fill 2/3 with water. Add the butter and bring to a boil. Simmer over very low heat for 1 hour, adding more water if necessary.

Drain through a fine sieve, discarding the plant material. Put the water with the butter floating on top in the refrigerator until the butter is hard. Discard the water, unless you have a penchant for it, and use the butter for cooking.

Grass Cookies

Makes about 20

2 cups all-purpose flour, sifted	1 cup Mary Jane butter
1/2 cup powdered sugar, sifted	(see above), cut in
1/4 teaspoon salt	1-inch cubes

Preheat the oven to 325 degrees.

Mix the flour, sugar, and salt in a bowl, and then mix in the butter. Form the mixture into a ball, and then roll out on a very lightly floured surface until 1/2 inch thick.

Cut out into your favorite shape with a cutter, place the pieces on a cookie-baking sheet, and bake for 30 minutes.

Cool on a rack and eat while still just warm.

My only plans that summer were to give political revolution one more chance—at the Black Panther conference in Northern California—and to sweet-talk my grandmother in Carmel. My grandfather had just died, and the question of my very generous allowance was very much up in the air. So a week after the academic year ended, I packed my copy of Carlos Castaneda, started a new journal with a quote from John Cage about circumstances being in charge, and began a cross-country trip in my brother's little green MG. I had no set itinerary since I dreamed of a Norman Douglas *South Wind* kind of life (of giving in to one's "fool") and followed my stomach. What was to have been a tour of American architecture turned into a tour of its food, especially Louisiana and Southwest culinary festivals, New Mexico chili cookouts, and Texas barbecues. After a stop at my aunt Mary and Russian uncle Kot's and a dinner of eighteenth-century Madeira and my requested chicken Kiev, I set off on the Blue Ridge Highway out of Washington bound for Louisiana.

In Lafayette, I headed straight and ravenously for the crayfish festivals and a gumbo and crayfish dinner ($3.65) at the famous Normandie. Then to Morgan City and Don's with its dozen freshwater oysters for $1.50, and on to New Orleans's Hotel Pontchartrain, where I thought to myself if there was better Creole food in the United States it must be in heaven itself. After a breakfast at Brennan's and "buster" crabs at Joe Casamento's, I headed west for Texas.

It was too late for any restaurants to be open, so I ate peyote instead, driving along the interstate listening to B. B. King and watching the oil burn-off lighting up the wide open Texas night sky. In the ninety-eight-degree heat my iced ripe white peaches dipped in freezing Coca-Cola from my backseat cooler were heaven. Then after a wrong turn, I ended up in Houston's ghetto and found an all-night and all-black soul food café where I had perfectly delicious barbecued meat loaf, if in a silence as thick as the glutinous mashed potatoes.

I stopped in San Antonio to visit some friends of my mother's whom she adored for their huge warehouses of chilies and every conceivable Tex-Mex seasoning as much as their love of dancing tangos till dawn. After a five-hour lesson in southwestern spices, I headed to the Four Corners and the chili at Kelly's Bar in Chama. After the superb green chili, which I noted was hotter even than the rocks of the Sangre de Cristo Mountains at high noon, I tore myself away, drove my four cylinders up into the Rockies, and drank from the cool upland glacier springs in Yosemite. Then down into Carmel to negotiate my allowance and stock up for the Black Panther conference with a 1959 Lafite and 1963 Romanée-Conti from a local market.

Annoyed by the crude fascism of the SDS, I headed back to Big Sur to see the trout farm again, and to meet a forbidden couple.

Now that my grandfather was gone, I was finally emboldened to look up the Big Sur legends Emile Norman and Brooks Clement. My step-grandmother couldn't have dealt with two male artists living together with scandalous frankness and enormous success, so her ancient Chrysler and I were off alone down the coast to the top of a mountain and their house set in the center of four hundred acres. After I knocked on the door, it slid open to reveal Emile Norman clad only in a towel. I was dressed as I would have been for lunch at my grandmother's, in a jacket and tie.

"You can stay just the way you are, or get naked for lunch. It's up to you."

Until this trip, I had never been seen in public without a jacket unless it was at a pool or on the rugby field. So this was a turning point in my life, and why I had come to California.

With pounding heart I took off my clothes and joined the two of them at a table set by an indoor pool surrounded by a vegetable garden in planters. The sun shone through an overhead vine of New Zealand climbing spinach, from which Emile was cutting leaves for a salad, while Brooks played Bach on an organ that was a replica of the composer's own. Standing with my glass of champagne, looking out over the brown hills to the Pacific Ocean, I realized then that one could love and cook in a world entirely of one's own choosing.

After a couple of magnums of red wine and a screening of films they had taken of the young Masai holding hands and elephants and giraffes doing things no nature program had ever shown, it was time for the next course.

"May I help with dessert?" I offered.

"You are dessert," they replied.

A few hours later, I told Emile I would be moving to California as soon as possible.

Back in Cambridge there was more revolution in the streets, Moratorium Day, and the March on Washington. Two dancers I'd met the previous spring took up residence with me in Somerville, and when Rudolf Nureyev came to town, my new friend the Harvard undergraduate and painter Philip Core called him up, and we went to see him at the Ritz. Philip had his script for a ballet on Nijinsky with Rudi in mind. While one of the dancers spent an athletic night with Rudi, he with a bottle of Stoli in one hand, a boy in the other, Philip and I drank champagne and smoked Sobranie cigarettes nonstop. In the morning Rudolf told us that Margot

Fonteyn was coming to town, and that we should look after her. Most often it's lonely being famous, he told me, and she's both.

A few weeks later we summoned the nerve to call her and invite her to dinner at my house—an invitation which, to our huge surprise, she accepted.

We had three hours to shop and cook. One of the streetwise dancers called me from the store. "I have some wine called L-A-F-I-T-E. Is it OK?"

It's fine, I said. But who had the money?

"Don't worry about that," he said, and then: "Is a ten-pound rib roast big enough?"

Half an hour later he returned, triumphantly. With no time for questions, I started to cook. Two hours later, when we answered a knock at the door, there was a breathtakingly beautiful Margot in floor-length white mink covering a basic black Yves St. Laurent dress, ropes of pearls, and a huge, disarming smile. And a slightly Cockney accent: "May we come in?"

Her partner in dance—Richard Cragun from the Stuttgart, also in black, but full leather, his crotch delicately festooned with chains—stood behind her.

Dinner for Margot Fonteyn, Richard Cragun, Philip Core, and the Street Dancers

February 16, 1970

Salmon canapé

Roast beef ribs
Château Lafite, 1962

Creamed spinach
Château Lafite 1964

Green salad vinaigrette

Raspberry and lemon sherbet

Pirouettes

Café

Cointreau

After Margot's second slab of beef and heavily into the Lafite, she commented on my generosity. I said she'd have to thank the two dancers as well. With great pride at having ripped off the Establishment, the dancers related how, to support the revolution, they'd stolen the Lafite, beef, and Cointreau. I blushed, the boys beamed, Richard helped himself to more Lafite, and Margot let out peals of laughter. "Well," she said, "if it has to be Lafite in the streets, so be it."

A blizzard had set in, so I drove them back to the Ritz in John Sanger's old silver Porsche, the boys squashed into the tiny back, Richard in the passenger seat with Margot on his lap. As we skidded around the deserted streets, all I could think of was how many millions of dollars of legs I had in that car—and how to drive so as not to spill the champagne being passed around over her white mink.

The next morning we awoke to riots in the streets again, and headed to Cambridge for a look. As we sat on top of the news kiosk in the center of Harvard Square, we were suddenly surrounded by police. One of the dancers pushed me off the roof into the arms of the other, did a grand jeté onto the roof of a squad car, and rebounded down into the subway with the two of us in hot pursuit. I went home to work on underwater space stations again, and after that close call the boys were in the mood for revolution eighteenth-century French style: more for dining while America burned than for burning it.

Pride's Crossing

Soon after, while I was having an all-aquavit dinner with my new girlfriend, Annie Meyer, a granddaughter of the *Washington Post* and *Newsweek* founder Agnes Meyer, the windows of her apartment were blown out by some firebombing "students" in the street. We decided it was time to get out of town. I thought that it was time to grow up, or at least that that time was fast approaching. So I decided to leave the dancers behind and to move in with Annie. We rented a farm in Pride's Crossing outside Boston, where we started a vegetable garden and raised birds. But first we packed up the cats into her Aston Martin DB5 and headed north to her family's island in Maine.

The first day I read Euell Gibbons's *Stalking the Wild Asparagus,* and as I contemplated the difference between stealing great ingredients and walking outside and gathering them, cooking took on a whole new life for me. I switched from reading Escoffier's *Ma Cuisine* to a culinary mix of Rachel Carson, nineteenth-century American housewives' companions, and James Beard.

Dinner in Maine (Hog Island), Having Read Euell Gibbons

May 22, 1970

Four nests of Eider ducks, each with four eggs.

In one, the eggs still wet. Took one.

Found samphire, sour sorrel, and lovage—or seacoast angelica.

As well as young dandelion.

Mussels, a bushel or so, some for salad.

Steamed mussels with samphire
Niersteiner Meisterkroner 1967

Spinach-sorrel noodles

Asparagus vinaigrette

For lunch the next day we had a mussel salad with a mayonnaise made with more wild sorrel, shallots, wild horseradish, and mustard, thinned with a reduced white wine mussel broth. To eat with a 1961 Bollinger, I dressed cooked lobster meat with a "lobster cream"—a paste of the coral, the fat lining the shell, and the liver mixed with mayonnaise and garnished with sea sorrel.

Back in Pride's Crossing I noted that my life now was books and food, and Philip Core sent me a note: "Food and Wine are the sex of art, and pasta is the bridge between the two." I wrote back with Tristan Tzara's "Thought is made in the mouth." Cooking for friends was now more powerful a revolution than politics. The directness of the menus at Pride's Crossing said it all:

Cold salmon, fresh herb mayonnaise
Château d'Yquem 1947

Strawberries
Château d'Yquem 1966

The next night, after a pound of caviar and '62 Dom Pérignon, Annie made the accusation that the only way I could communicate was by writing menus and then cooking them. We decided to take some time off from each other. While she was in Washington visiting her aunt Kay Graham, I read Robert de Montesquiou, wrote the outline for a book from one of his best phrases, "A Carnage of Geraniums," planted fifty, and cooked.

Youth on the Prow and Pleasure at the Helm

I finished my "politically acceptable" public housing project—but my notebooks were now filled with the glories of old American picnics, systems of farming and aquaculture (using dolphins as the staff), designs for the World's Fair in Hawaii that I heard was to be on the water, and California wines I should try. The allure of California and Hawaii became real, but not before one last-gasp attempt to create the European world that was as comfortable to me as old clothes—if increasingly tattered.

After graduation, I tried to make a living in Pride's Crossing designing gardens for the rich. But they were not as rich as the people who had built the gardens, and thus knew and cared little about them. So I ended up just a gardener. It was a year in which our band of aesthetes graduated and dispersed—a year, as Philip Core said, that was "crowded with the wreckage of exhumed conversations."

Meanwhile I followed the advice of Carl Van Vechten to "write as you feel and you will discover that your feeling is greater than your knowledge of it"—because I wanted to know what I did feel. I wrote "An Outline of Pleasures" after Colette, subtitled "The Sauce for Being Served Up." I loved her "Pride in giving pleasure relieved them of the need for any other pleasure," and "To receive from someone happiness—is it not to choose the sauce in which we want to be served up?"

I found myself truly beginning to travel into the silent and self-absorptive world of cooking.

So when Richard Olney's *French Menu Cookbook* came out in 1970, it bowled me over. I adored his claim that cooking the first time for his mentor, Georges Garin, he dared only "simple preparations." I had a sneaking suspicion that I must be one of the few readers who felt calm at his calling Artichoke Bottoms with Two Mousses followed by ortolans, then cheeses and a "Tepid Apple Charlotte," simple.

When I read, "The rock on which my church was built was the provincial kitchen of my home in Iowa," I wondered what he would think of my rock: eccentric lives and the life of travel around the world with its great hotels, ships, and trains. I had been, like Olney, "cooking with a passion that could be gleaned from books—Escoffier, in particular." Olney's rock was Iowa. I looked around for mine.

I wrote Richard, opened a bottle of 1888 Boal Madeira, and jotted down a rash of titles for proposed cookbooks: *Casting Pearls Before Wine, Culinary Suicides, Mental Cuisine, Octopus Bouquet,* and *Fraises Musclées.*

Something had to give.

Just as I was rethinking that old offer to work at *The New Yorker*, a call came from Clay Shaw (the New Orleans architect who was accused of masterminding the Kennedy assassination) to work on the revival of New Orleans's French Market. It was tempting, but I knew if I lived there I would fall even further back into my longing for the past: I would never leave lunch at Galatoire's. So I left Annie and the farm, and headed on down to my sister's beachfront apartment on the Jersey shore to put aside my "Carnage of Geraniums" and rewrite it as my memoirs, *Camphor Ice.* Perhaps then I could put the past behind me.

California: Simple Pleasures

In June 1972 I finished *Camphor Ice.* Writing it did not cure me of the past, so I decided I could find the cure in Big Sur—the land of the naked lunch. I cooked a last dinner on the East Coast for my sister's fortieth birthday, finding parts of the menu from the book by Lucien Tendret (that Richard Olney had told me about in a letter), *La Table au Pays de Brillat-Savarin.* I served Tendret's famous "Le gâteau de foies blonds de poulardes de Bresse, baigné de la sauce aux queues d'écrevisses." I poured my last two bottles of wine, a 1962 La Tâche and an unlabeled 1927 vintage port. So now, with no wine and no money, I set out for California.

Heading west in a huge old Lincoln delivery car, I landed in San Francisco with seventy-five dollars, not enough to fund the final leg of my journey to Honolulu with my designs for the World's Fair half under and half above the water. I showed the project around architectural offices, with no success. So once again I worked as a gardener.

The rest of the year was one of agony and attacks of nerves that left my nights full of demons, my days full of looking for a job, my skin scrofulous, and writing a letter at 4:00 A.M. to the only pal who would understand, Philip Core: "As I lie here recovering from yet another evening of unsuccessful job-seeking charm and brilliance, wondering how could I again, in a room full of Indians from ancient Mexican jungles, Chinese, Japanese Burroughs, Swiss and Argentinian *L'Uomo Vogue* bathing-suit extravaganzas, end up tangoing 'til dawn in the arms of a García Lorca lesbian from Cuba? Feeling like a venomous orchid, and am teetering on an edge beyond bankruptcy which has led better men than me to prison and to say 'the only vice is shallowness.' These last weeks have been a tornado of vortices, leading nowhere."

On my thirtieth birthday I was down to twenty-five dollars.

On November 6, 1972, I wrote in my journal: "Good thing to do at 1:15 am: sit on toilet, drink beer, and read Dumas' *Grand Dictionnaire de Cuisine*." The bookmark that fell out of that book was a menu from the RMS *Mauretania* dated forty-three years before to the day. An omen, if the food was not. My father at Herbert Hoover's table ate grapefruit Maraschino before a petite marmite, fillet of sole, roast pheasant, "pomme chips," salad of the season, and "pouding glace Nesselrode." After reading the menu, I fell into a troubled sleep.

5 am: in a dream—in a restaurant:

Steak with marrow bone filled with marrow soufflé

Baba (au rhum)

Puree of celery root

Sauce Périgord on steak

All on plate together.

My last hope, I felt, was the cure of Big Sur and Emile, who had given me the courage to embrace the freedoms of California in the first place. At a lunch he gave for Elizabeth Gordon (later editor of *House Beautiful*), the menu was cannelloni stuffed with wild boar, then persimmons with a mayonnaise flavored with fenugreek (to this day I love this dish) and a superb, velvety Chapelle-Chambertin 1961. Elizabeth talked for hours of Alice B. Toklas, with whom she had traveled. Even on a trip to Venice when Alice was very old, Elizabeth said, she showed great courage and knowledge of where to find the best food in the markets along the canals. At the end of the lunch Elizabeth said, "Alice would have loved cooking with you." I took that as an omen as well.

The next day at 1:00 A.M. I was werewolf awake at the sound of coyotes outside my door, my sleep plagued with Mozartian black-sheeted figures trying to strangle me. After writing a suicide note—"The last of my silk shirts just died"—I read Wilde's *De Profundis* again and, back in San Francisco, cooked a last meal: goose soup and a Chambertin 1934, Cuvée Héritiers Latour. I recovered and decided to live.

In San Francisco for a New Year's apartment sitting for Michael and Cathy, I made a feast for one, and recorded the menu.

Dinner for One, San Francisco, 1972

The virtues of boiled garlic. Spread on new bread and French butter.
I put it with marrow, a paste for toast.

Château d'Yquem 1967

"Simple pleasures are the last refuge of the complex." Oscar.

When Michael returned, he told me that the little French café in Berkeley
we had visited once was looking for a chef.

"So what?" I said.

All I remembered was the most perfect slice of fresh raspberry tart I had
ever tasted. But by now any job was looking good. It seemed he could be
right when he replied: "There's more to it than a simple raspberry tart."

Or could be.

First Interlude

TO ME, MENUS are a language unto themselves.

I have been collecting and reading them since I was ten, composing and acting them out since I was a teenager. They spoke to me as clearly as any childhood fantasy novel. Reading an old menu slowly forms in my mind's eye its era, the sensibility of the restaurateur or the chef, even the physical details of the dining room. I can picture the guests even when I don't know who they were. Sometimes I can conjure up an entire evening, a three-act play orchestrated around the food. And from my own past, it is the menus and the food that are the fixatives for the memories. When I think again about one of my mother's summer garden party menus, the whole day is conjured up—my mouth waters as I see, taste, and smell the lovage-mayonnaise-covered poached whole salmons laid out in the tents. I can see everyone who was there.

I have used the language of menus as the basis for dialogues with mentors, colleagues, and friends. And I had always assumed that this language was universal. When I began to write this book, I outlined it with menus—some that had aroused my appetites, others that I'd designed and cooked myself—and eagerly passed them on to a few editors and publishers as a way of revealing my mission.

The silence was deafening—broken later by only a single comment poised in a question: What do they mean? After a long pause, that question was followed by two more: What were the stories behind the menus, and were any famous people present at the meals? I couldn't have been more stunned. I thought the menus told their own stories. And eloquently.

Menus are liberally sprinkled through this book, and so that you do not find them silent, let me tell you how they speak to me.

The first menu I wrote in my culinary notebooks in the late sixties, knowing at that time only that the dinner was given by Cecil Beaton in a private dining room in Paris's Lapérouse restaurant, for two dozen male friends, was probably in the early 1930s.

Fat of a turtle
Château d'Yquem 1860

Cold foie gras

Truffles poached in champagne

Canard rôti Lucullus
Burgundy, a priceless one

Doyenne de Comice pear, juste à point

Coffee

Crusted port

Cognac Napoleon

Romeo and Juliettas

At first glance it seems way over the top. But it has a discipline. The kind created by Beaton in the horse-racing scene in *My Fair Lady*, with its miles and miles of extravagant ruffles and hats, but all in black and white, and the singing in a controlled chant about the perfection of the Ascot afternoon . . . until, of course, Liza screams, "Move your bleedin' arse," to her horse, lagging in third place. In this menu, that scream is the duck.

The mixed language suggests an Englishman wrote it, since a Frenchman would never use English with food, and with the same taste and delight in the language as in the food. *Gras* has a onomatopoeic ring to it, but only when pronounced by a lower gratin butcher from Marseilles. Using the English word for it, *fat*, tells you that in relishing the word, probably pronounced with the very upper gratin Oxford accent so that it sounded like *fiat*, the dinner guests were undoubtedly rail-thin young things in perfect Boldini-portrait tailored frock coats and Charvet floppy bow ties, giggling at the irony of slipping so much of that fat between their tightly compressed lips, otherwise opened only for the latest quip, gossip, or fingernails-on-metal analysis of the most recent *Brideshead Revisited*–type scandal. And I would automatically, without thinking, have used *rôti* once *canard* had been used, and slipped into French once the word *doyenne* had been put on paper. It would just be natural, without affectation, in bilingual company.

Following the turtle fat with foie gras tells me also that whoever ordered the menu was very securely a gourmand of deep appreciation for the art of dining: knowing how to push one's guests' sensibilities to the limit without embarrassing them with a troubling surfeit later in the meal. Obviously they all were aesthetes, and saw themselves that way. They were not unfamiliar with this kind of expensive living, and whoever was paying was wealthy. Maybe a younger Tennant or Devonshire son, if his millionaire father had him on a liberal leash.

I have never been in a private dining room at Lapérouse, but one can count on it having a rectangular table seating two at each end, leaving no room for dropped conversation. And just as the meal was far more than a token, so the table decor would not have been one shrimp pink geranium in a vase—a degree of sophistication with which Beaton would have been out of sympathy. Rather there would have been an impression of enthusiastic spontaneity. Probably there was just a tulipiere filled with enough camellias so that after each guest was served one for the buttonhole, enough were left to make an impression on the room of expense but not extravagance.

Very likely there was a small sofa in the corner. Somewhere off the room fur coats, top hats, and silver-tipped Malacca canes were stored, since it was obviously winter. It was the kind of scene Ken Russell portrayed in *The Music Lovers*, but with more restraint, at least until the port showed up, at which point the sofa was the scene of more intimate conversations, the waiters long since having ceased entering before knocking—after the "my dears" amongst the young men had become a bit thick.

And the food?

Our minds now might reel at a slab of turtle fat apiece. Even at this dinner the cold-blooded English, who would easily rip out the throat of a partridge with their teeth, might have thought twice to plunder further an endangered species so baldly. So the slab of fat in the Limoges soup plate in front of each of the two dozen guests must have given them a slight frisson. I had fat of a turtle in my youth, but only small cubes in turtle soup. Here it is obviously served hot, perhaps moistened with a little sherry-perfumed consommé (but only a little), since it is followed by a cold foie gras. Well, not exactly cold, more like the temperature of the pantry off the dining room, which in those days clocked in at a bone-chilling (were it not for the embroidered silk waistcoats) sixty degrees. Obviously Beaton knew that to stimulate the senses and keep them going is to sample something hot, then something cold, then something hot again.

To follow turtle fat with foie gras—100 percent more fat—is a heady statement in an already heady room. I remember the turtle fat texture as more foie gras than hot foie gras, and I love the knowledge here that, as the turtle should be hot, the foie gras should not. Heated until the fats are released, foie gras seems to me too slippery; the flavor is deeper and more satisfying when the fat melts slowly in one's mouth: a reluctant companion in excess, rather than a dancer in your lap.

Next, a whole truffle per person poached in champagne, served in a starched napkin, says again, "This is a person who knows the best of the best," and needs no ostentatious show of it. The roasted duck Lucullus, however, gives one pause: What duck dish could be worthy of the name of ancient Rome's most sumptuous banqueter? I don't know what the preparation consists of, but need to believe it had no truffles, and ideally no coxcombs, testicles, or sweetbreads either. "Doyenne de Comice pear"— housewife's pear, a frivolous and funny label that could easily rev up the fragile conversation. The simplicity is pleasantly startling. And then the "crusted" port: nonvintage, but to those in the know, a much more satisfying value for your money, all the while accompanied by Havana's best and most expensive cigars. The waiter appears again for the last time, to crack open the windows onto the Quai des Grands Augustins.

In college I devoured all the Lord Peter Wimsey books. In my diaries at the time I noted a menu that to me is still perfection in language, balance, and progression of food.

Oysters
Chablis Moutonne 1915
Chevalier Montrachet 1911

Consommé marmite

Sole
"Echter" Schloss Johannisberger

Poulet
Lafite 1875

Pré-salé
Clos Vougeot 1911

Dessert
Genuine Imperial Tokay
True "Napoleon" with seal

"Short and lovely" was my noted comment when I first read it.

Auguste Escoffier, the father of modern French cooking (and chef to

Ritz), considered oysters such a natural way to raise one's juices and expectations for the food following that he hardly deemed them part of the "opus" and often left them off the written menu. Or merely listed them as "natives," deliciously the same word in French and English. Here they are part of the menu, and probably Colchesters or flat oysters like Bélons. A great Colchester is rich enough to need a palate cleanser, but as important, a dozen of them would need a mental one so that they did not dominate the beginning of the rest of the food. That is up to the sole.

So the consommé of the broth "marmite" is beef rather than the lighter chicken, since white poultry broth wouldn't send the oysters into memory quite completely enough.

It is obvious that Bunter is not cooking this himself, and a bachelor like Peter is used to simple food. So I guess the sole is simply meunière or grillée, since his mouth will be hungering for a bit of richness after the consommé broth, though not enough so Peter would not recoil at the fish being covered with lobster sauce. The chicken, however, is obviously à la crème after the austere fullness of the sole, as simply served by Henri Soulé years later in Manhattan's Le Pavillon.

Obviously the pré-salé is that perfect lamb from the salt marshes of Brittany around St. Michel, or from the coastlands of Suffolk or Cornwall. Simply roasted.

And the dessert? Well, no need to call that out, since it's chosen from a trolley of them. Peter would have either a little baba au rhum or just a big plate of raspberries covered with Devon or Jersey/Guernsey cream—if the chicken was not.

After reading this I wrote myself a note: "Taste an old Lafite and Tokay."

Years later in Berkeley I would taste the Tokay, and then in my San Francisco restaurant Stars I would hold the West Coast tasting of the old Lafites, and finally taste the 1875.

Cecil Beaton was definitely in the air my spring of 1969, when I wrote a self-consciously "decadent" menu. This was in Cambridge, Massachusetts, at the height of the counterculture, when revolution was in the air as well. The guests included two close friends and a Boston poet.

Pirozhki
Vodka Wyborova

Prosciutto & Figs
Niersteiner Spiegleberg Spätlese Kabinet 1966

Consommé Marijuana

Roast Beef, sauce nature/madère
Château Beychevelle 1962

Spinach cream puree

Pommes de terre château

Watercress salad vinaigrette

Fraises, crème Carême
Korbel, brut California

Coffee

Meringues
Madeira (Cossart)

Cigars Royal Jamaica, Churchill

It was hot outside and inside, and since nothing gets a party going or the juices flowing faster than a slug of vodka right out of the freezer followed by anything warm and rich, that's what we did. The vodka was buffalo grass flavored—Zubrovka—and then we immediately popped a little pastry—pirozhki, little bites—into our mouths, the perfumed buffalo grass (made from hay from the steppes of the Ukraine) playing off against coriander-flavored buttered cabbage-filled pastry, with the burn of the alcohol just in time smoothed by the butter. Heaven.

Then prosciutto and figs, salty and sweet, dry against moist fig flesh (not dry against wet, like melon), the complex flavors brought together even further by the fruity young Spätlese.

The consommé cleansed the palate, and this one—from marijuana plants, the stems soaked in a rich chicken stock—provided another level of stimulation. But not stoned: The brew takes forty-five minutes to reach the brain, by which time (as the menu planned) we were on to dessert, tasting strawberries and cream as we'd never tasted them before. Meanwhile, against the fat of the roast beef (the juices bolstered with sweet Madeira), the bitterness of the creamed spinach was a perfect foil accompanied by a second-growth Bordeaux in an especially hard year that I adored and defended for its non-easy virtue. The wine did not yield easily, but when its personality finally, stubbornly, emerged, it proved a glorious match with the meat.

Why roast beef in ninety-five-degree weather? In love with memories of my own and in the spirit of Beaton at Lapérouse, it was the way I knew best to push culinary senses to the limit. The fat of beef dry-aged for twenty-four days had all the complexity of the long-cellared wine with which it was paired, with a kind of power that met the intensity of the ninety-five-degree weather. The beef, the heat, the wine all said what the evening was all about, what it meant to be at table that night: our manners meeting the challenge of the menu, ingesting forbidden drugs, and talking of my heroes Ho Chi Minh, Che, and Nureyev, whose pictures were on the kitchen wall.

Watercress with vinaigrette was a different kind of bow to the heat, and cleared the palate. The commercial strawberries were tossed in fresh red currant syrup, a trick that always intensifies their strawberryness. Served with a custard containing white Maraschino, this simple cream has so many layers of flavor that you can't put your finger on what makes it so mysteriously and magically delicious. And of course the drugs would have just been kicking in . . .

Consommé Marijuana

6 cups rich chicken stock	1 loose cup freshly picked
1 packed cup marijuana stems	nasturtium flowers (mixed
and seeds	bright colors)
½ cup fresh basil leaves	sea salt

pepper mill

Preheat the oven to 275 degrees.

Bring the chicken stock to a boil in a 4-quart saucepan.

Meanwhile, spread the marijuana out on a metal cookie sheet or tray and put in the oven for 10 minutes. After the stems and seeds are "toasted," put all of them in the chicken stock and turn off the heat. Steep for 1 hour.

Put the stock through a very fine strainer, and return to the cleaned-out saucepan.

Chop the basil leaves coarsely (1/8 inch), and shred the nasturtium flowers. Heat the consommé to boiling. Put the basil and nasturtium in warmed soup plates, and pour the consommé over. Pass the sea salt and pepper mill separately.

❧

My outlaw early efforts notwithstanding, it was reading Richard Olney's *French Menu Cookbook* in 1970 that firmed up my ideas of what a seriously enjoyable but also controlled menu should be. In the progression of his dishes you sense the workings of his mind and heart, his discipline and his sense of play. In his first chapter, he lays out principles of menu creation that I live by to this day, even while tweaking them:

"Each course must provide a happy contrast to the one preceding it [see the Beaton menu]; at the same time the movement through the various courses should be an ascending one from light, delicate, and more complex flavors through progressively richer, more full-bodied, and simple flavors.... [See Cambridge, Massachusetts, menu.]

Essentially the only thing to remember is that the palate should be kept fresh, teased, surprised, excited throughout a meal. The moment there is danger of fatigue, it must be astonished or soothed into greater anticipation until the moment of release and post-prandial pleasures. [See both.]

Inspired by his philosophy, I created the following menu in 1971 for a late-winter dinner with Annie Meyer and friends at our farm. We ate to the sounds of dogs, and geese, guinea fowl screaming, and quail chattering.

Pâté de foie (perdrix) moelle
Frozen vodka Wyborova

Garlic soup

Perdrix à la Souvaroff
Château Léoville 1959
Château Ausone 1937

Soufflé of hominy
Château Cheval-Blanc 1959

Salade Doria

Stilton (aged)
Martinez Port 1927

I made a pâté of beef marrow and the livers of the farm partridge/perdrix, spread it on wonderful country bread, and served it with frozen buffalo grass vodka. I wanted that satisfying jolt at the beginning of the menu: the rich game flavors, the scent of juniper berries, the perfumed bite of black pepper—and the bite of the cold vodka. The garlic soup brought us back to earth: Long-simmered and very mild, it was like a consommé with a vegetable puree—rich and austere at the same time. The partridge was stuffed with a truffled foie gras, while the hominy (white cornmeal) soufflé that accompanied it was simple and clean, the perfect foil for the luxuriant meat and liver. The Léoville had a slightly truffled aroma and was particularly good with the foie-gras-stuffed partridge. Of course, in those days there was no fresh foie gras; it was canned.

No dessert—the rest of the menu was so rich—but a flashy salad instead: potatoes in white truffle mayonnaise, asparagus tips, and red and gold chopped baked beets sprinkled on top. Aged Stilton and 1927 port stopped time. The best part, actually, was the breakfast the next morning, when I made a mousse of all the leftover foie gras stuffing and partridge meat, spread it in a gratin dish, buried coddled eggs in it, and covered it with fresh cream before baking it just until it started to bubble. Served with Black Velvets (half champagne, half Guinness), it blew what was left of our minds.

⁂

A menu doesn't always need to be a grand wallow.

In summer in particular, it is best to be calculatingly offhand as well as to indulge in the occasional roast beef gesture. Begin, for example, with bruschetta because it's colorful (especially made with yellow and red tomatoes), light, immediate, and delicious. The acid and sweetness of the fruit and the olive oil, the spice from pepper, the aromas of garlic and fresh herbs make for a perfect palate teaser.

A great summer menu can be as simple as this one, cooked by Cathy Simon to cheer me up following the harrowing experience in June 1969 of my year-end presentation at Harvard's Graduate School of Design:

Asparagus, sauce alsacienne
Niersteiner Domtal

Tuna, fresh, over charcoal

Salad, lettuce of the garden

Mushrooms

Pie, strawberry & rhubarb

Scotch & soda

The asparagus was poached and served at room temperature with a thin demi-glace and olive oil; the fresh grilled tuna was showered in basil from the garden, which also supplied the lettuce salad served alongside mushrooms mixed with cream, mustard, and olive oil. Strawberry and rhubarb pie and Scotch and soda were accompanied by the sound of chanting students bent on overthrowing the established social order, but I, for one, was happy to keep the best of the old one (its food and cellars) while investigating, by cooking, a new one.

❧

These four menus show what kind of new food I started cooking. I had no thought in my mind other than the power of simplicity (and the ease of cooking it) for creating the most effect with my guests. Foraging on the beaches of islands in Maine, and tasting lobsters and mussels right out of the water had reminded me of the power also of perfect, and perfectly fresh, ingredients.

Dinner for Two Street-Kid Dancers— My House, Somerville (Massachusetts)

1970

Avocado-Lobster Mayonnaise
Château d'Yquem 1959

Chicken (cold) in tarragon butter

Asparagus

Cheesecake

Lunch in the Heat, Using Up the Somerville Cellar

June 11, 1970

Poached red snapper, cold
Dom Pérignon 1959, 2 bottles

Lunch by Myself at the Farm, Eating the Produce Before Moving to California

May 3, 1971

Cold roast pheasant
Iced lemon vodka
Vosne-Romanée 1961 (superb!)

Lunch with Annie, for Michael Palmer, in from California. Pride's Crossing

July 1971

Cold poached salmon, garden mayonnaise
Château d'Yquem 1947

Caesar salad

Wild strawberries
Château d'Yquem 1966

The Caesar was a flop since it was impossible to find good lettuce. I wrote in my notes that we *must* grow our own lettuces again, including mesclun and eight-inch-long romaine. Michael raved about the wines he was trying out there in California, and we drove down to the local store to look for some. All we found was bulk California "Burgundy."

CHAPTER 3

Three Women Called Alice

MY FIRST MEETING with Alice Waters was scheduled for 6:00 P.M., an unusual time to interview a prospective chef on a day when a restaurant is open for business. But Chez Panisse was less than a year and a half old. Did anyone know any better?

I walked around outside until a minute to six and had plenty of time to survey the building in which I hoped to work for the next few months, when I would have enough money to continue my journey to Hawaii. The remodeled old Victorian house looked like a cross between Frank Lloyd Wright and Charles Rennie Mackintosh, with a little bow to Berkeley's Julia Morgan. There were a couple of brick steps dodging under an enormous monkey puzzle tree, then a few more leading up to the front door, which said, "Pull."

I did, the ice in my stomach doing nothing to stop the fear from bubbling into my throat. When I'd applied for jobs in the past, it had always been through an introduction by family or friends; but no one influential called to set up this appointment. My terror of entering was overcome only by the knowledge of how much I needed the money.

The ad in the newspaper had read: "Immediate opening in a small innovative french [sic] provincial restaurant for inspired energetic chef who will plan and cook menus weekly for a single entrée five course dinner à la Elizabeth David and Fernand Point. Send resume and sample menus to Chez Panisse." The restaurant had opened in the summer of 1971 with the first chef, Victoria Kroyer. She lasted a year; since then the kitchen had been run by anyone who was a friend and could cook. In desperation, this ad appeared.

I had no résumé, but I knew how to compose menus, and I'd read David's book *French Provincial Cooking* a few times. I was, however, a bit confused by the Fernand Point reference. Point, with a powerfully direct simplicity, had simplified the grand cuisine of the nineteenth century and started the modern cooking movement in France. His unadorned versions of the great classics were not "provincial" food, and there was no clue that Point had breathed life into any of the old Panisse menus I was given to guide me. Perhaps in the turkey sandwiches and Cristal dinner that one of the partners, Gene Opton, had wooed me with, but nothing else.

Point had famously commanded the équipe (including the young Paul Bocuse, later and for a while the world's most famous chef) to make a gratin de queues d'écrivisses every day for two years before he thought it fit for the public—and this for a dish with only five ingredients! And where in the San Francisco Bay Area would I find the makings of my favorite dishes from his great book *Ma Gastronomie*—omble chevalier, bécasses, foie gras d'oie, salade de truffes, perdreaux, marcassin, and palombes en beatitude?

My eighteen sample menus were without desserts, which were the bailiwick of the raspberry tart maker and Chez Panisse pastry chef, Lindsey Shere:

Tuesday

Gougère à la bourguignonne

Haricots verts natures

Matelote à la normande

Wednesday

Oeufs rémoulade

Madrilène of beet and onion

"Haricot" of oxtail, Alice B. Toklas

I could make the cheese puff gougères in my sleep since I had used them a lot at my dinner parties in Cambridge; the green beans had been drilled into me by my growing them as a child and by my aunt's fierce teaching; I had already made a lot of fish stews; the eggs rémoulade were a personal favorite from all those hungover days with Philip Core in New Orleans at Mardi Gras; the consommé was another dish made in advance and just heated to order; and the oxtail, once made, was easy to serve out to a hundred people without compromising any of the quality, as if it had been made for six.

Menus in hand, I walked into an unheated dining room with fresh flowers in marmalade jars, unmatched old silver, and checkered oilcloths. The room was small, the floors bare. Anything but formidable. Through a door to the tiny kitchen I glimpsed a confusion of bodies under the direction of a diminutive, bandannaed young woman who seemed oddly in and out of charge.

"That's Alice," said a tall, blond, and whiskered waiter. "Just go in."

At the door I was stopped by a man with a black beard, severe eyebrows, and wire-rim glasses. "Alice can't see you now," he said, frowning. "She says come back tomorrow."

And so I left, down the first set of steps, through the bare courtyard, dodging the lethal leaves of the huge tree, to Shattuck Avenue. Then I did the math: My round-trip fare had used up a third of all my money in the world. I'd have barely enough to return.

Biting my lip, rubbing sweat from my palms onto the backs of my thighs (where it wouldn't be visible when I reentered the restaurant), I strode back along the irregular brick sidewalk. I turned into the unruly honeysuckle-covered gate and went up the steps, sliding my right hand along the railing to wipe off the last of the perspiration. Hard to remember that this panic had nothing to do with fame or famous people. There was and were none in Panisse in those days. The cold sweat dripping down my back in that foggy Berkeley winter air came from fear of this new position of supplication. I was not used to being on my knees. For a moment I envisioned a safer route out of poverty: perhaps I should ask for the job of gardener. By the looks of the garden, they needed one as much as they did a chef.

At the kitchen entrance once more, I declared that an interview had been scheduled and an interview there would be. To my amazement, Alice received me with a beaming smile, then swiftly returned to finishing the dinner that was already overdue in the dining room. "Do something to that soup," she said.

I turned to the biggest aluminum pot I had ever seen, twenty gallons, full of a liquid puree of some kind. I stuck a finger in and tasted it. All it needed was salt, but I added a bit of white wine and cream, to show off.

Alice took a spoonful and smiled. "You're hired," she yelled across the counter.

I stood there awkwardly, the taste of uncooked white wine in my mouth, imagining her next words would be "On the other hand . . ." But there was no other hand.

The man with the beard and the severe eyebrows shot a furious glance at Alice, then turned to me. "Call Gene. And come back tomorrow," he said curtly. It wasn't a promising start for our relationship, but this man—my soon to be sous-chef, Willy Bishop—would turn out to be my greatest ally.

The menus had gotten me in the door; salting the soup got me the job.

The next day, Gene Opton, who had kept Panisse financially afloat in those haphazard first years, gave me a cash advance to pay for the next two weeks' buses. Two days later a letter appeared:

> Dear Jerry,
> We would like to offer you the position of chef, with the responsibility for developing and executing the cuisine of the restaurant— assuming a common interest in integrity and high quality without pretentiousness.

I knew I was imprinted with cooking integrity and high quality; lack of pretentiousness I was not so sure about. It was sobering to read the rest of the letter, which said that in addition to menu planning and food preparation my responsibilities would include "directing kitchen operation and personnel, ordering of supplies, budgeting food costs, ordering and storing food, maintaining inventory control, routine cleaning, and all other considerations that are relevant to making the restaurant a smoothly operating, profitable enterprise." Thirty years later I received another letter from a friend from that time: "All I can think of is that rainy night when I went with you on the bus to Berkeley and you interviewed at Panisse. I remember that on the bus back home you said you weren't sure if you could do this, and I said, if you don't try, you'll never find out."

I accepted the job. The salary was to be four hundred dollars a month.

My official entrance a week later coincided with the arrival of the produce, which was stacked at the dining room entrance to the kitchen. As I was fresh from my farm in Massachusetts and our hunter-gatherer menus from summers in Maine, the stack of commercial-grade crated fruits and vegetables did not look terribly impressive to my eyes. I separated out the more pathetic specimens and told the delivery boy to take them back. "But," he protested, "they usually just sign the invoice." I told him that a chef has to approve all the ingredients (how would I know?) and that the green beans were especially a joke, so large and tough that an elephant would pass them up. I told him I'd come across the road to look for replacements.

Seconds more than the time it took for the goods to make their way from the restaurant back to Ron's Produce Center, the kitchen phone rang. It was Alice. "You can't send produce back to Ron," she said. "He's a friend."

"That very well may be," I told her, "but this is junk. The green beans are ridiculous. I'm going over to find whatever looks good."

Precious time was being wasted—I still had no idea how to cook for a hundred people. But I knew mediocre ingredients when I saw them and was prepared to hold my ground.

A few minutes later, Alice appeared with two members of the restaurant's board, one of them now a famous rock-star attorney. Her eyes told the story, and her mouth agreed. It was a little spoiled, the lines around it defiant, just in case. At a nudge from Alice, the lawyer explained that I was out of order and would not be allowed to refuse product from suppliers who were part of our community. I was confused by the quick intervention of a stranger but would soon become accustomed to Alice's technique of using front men to implement unpleasant tasks.

I took off my apron and laid it carefully on the table—watching, in a kind of slow motion, my hand throw away a paycheck more sorely needed than anything in my life. My money was gone. I was living with a friend and a dog in a ghetto dump across the hall from pornography stars. I felt especially bad for the dog, who deserved to go hungry even less than we did.

"If that's the way it's going to be," I heard myself say, "you cook."

That was probably the moment my reputation for being "difficult" was born, a tag that has now been glued to me for thirty years. Certainly my East Coast manners were oil in the Berkeley waters, and not extra-virgin.

Alice backed down. As Willy Bishop arrived, she was all squirming and cooing to get that apron back around my then thirty-two-inch waist. He laughed, if a bit grimly, having seen her act before.

The altercation had used up a couple of hours on my first day of work, and panic was beginning to set in. As the apron strings tightened, so did the feeling of a noose around my neck. It would all be up to me now. Me, that is, and the bearded Beatnik menthol-cigarette-chain-smoking, English-atomic-mint-sucking painter, drummer, and sous-chef, Willy Bishop. And the dishwasher, who came out from hiding, after the altercation, to peel potatoes.

On that first day in the first week of February 1973, Alice gave me the menus for the week her team would have cooked if I had not taken the job. The first menu was:

Quiche d'aubergine

Velouté volaille [*sic*]

Gigot d'agneau, sauce soubise

Salad or cheese

Fruit & coffee

for six dollars per person.

An eggplant quiche seemed no problem, especially since I had a pastry chef to make the shells. I had no idea what Alice intended for the velouté de volaille, since by itself and unadorned it's the French version of chicken soup and mother's love. The leg of lamb was easy, but for eighty people a daunting task. The soubise of onions cooked lovingly down and mixed with some white sauce or sauce Béchamel was definitely easy, although I wondered if anyone wanted it after the rich soup, or if anyone in Berkeley knew that Count Soubise had been executed for politically incorrect sexual crimes. My other menu challenges that week, beyond the variable produce, included game hens that arrived frozen solid and a menu with "haricot" of oxtail and a "saupiquet de jambon," both of which I'd cooked before but for only five people and with a whole weekend to work on them. So I started immediately to write my own menus.

To get a better angle on the Panisse style, I read what had come out of the kitchen in the previous year and a half and how it had been received. Gene gave me press clippings, all local, and the gist was reassuring. Reviewers felt warmly toward the restaurant: "What faults there are seem somehow more tolerable than they might be elsewhere," wrote one. "Funny how much easier it is to appreciate a slightly flawed culinary work of art than a mass-produced, perfect appearing but tasteless meal."

The reviewer's biggest complaint was a "Chicken Demi-Deuil" with no truffles. As there were no fresh truffles to be had in those days in California, I wasn't surprised. But she loved the "remarkable raspberry tart," viewed as doubly remarkable in December, with raspberries out of season. There were more out-of-season amazements, among them "hors d'oeuvres varies [*sic*]: marinated broiled green pepper and fennel(!)," and disappointment in "a tasty substance on a buttered crouton that seemed like lamb marrow but no one could identify for sure since that particular cook had gone."

The most important Bay Area restaurant reviewer was Jack Shelton, and in May 1972 he introduced his review by saying that the food in the "unassuming circa 1900 wood-frame house" had shaken him with "imbalances" in some menus and "slipups" in presentation. But, he added, "I have never, ever been bored."

He said also that the soup "called for a soupçon more salt"—which brought a smile to my face.

I jotted down his final warning: "Watch your marketing."

Gene had also given me a sheaf of menus, the first from 1971. The format was (and still is) to serve a single set of dishes each night with no choices. The menus were printed a week in advance for regulars to pick up and decide which meal they wanted to eat. Sunday through Thursday menus started with "hors d'oeuvres varies [sic]" and included one dessert, with more available à la carte. For Monday the first of November 1971, the menu was:

Hors d'oeuvres variés

Calamari farci

Salade

Zabaglione

and the cost $4.50 per person.

For Friday the twelfth of November the menu cost $6.00 and was:

Celery mimosa

Fresh tomato soup

Lamb en croûte

Salade

Cheeses

Mousse aux poires

Other menus of the period featured "consommé bellevue," "crab quiche," "manicotti and meat balls," "orange and carrot soup," "gigot de Provence," and lots of "poulet basquaise." I was confused.

Seasonal it wasn't, with tomato soup in November years before the Holland ones were available year-round. Nor was it Elizabeth David, who stood for "excellence of ingredients, simplicity of preparation, seasonality, and respect for tradition (as long as that tradition embraced the first three principles) and for region." She would have hated the lamb en croute: This I knew from her book, in which the lamb is braised or grilled and in which nothing is served in pastry unless a tart or pie. It wasn't the Grande Bourgeoise cooking of Fernand Point either. But it was all food that I wouldn't mind eating.

By late 1972, Alice was in the kitchen with anyone who would help, and the menu on Saturday, October 21, was again "celery mimosa," followed by:

Onion soup

Châteaubriand

Salade or cheese

Apple tart

The cost was now up to $7.50 per person, and the dishes did not as a whole thrill me. I took heart when I saw the 1972 New Year's menu, just months before I'd been hired. The $12.00 menu was:

Pâté de poisson à la guillaume tirei [*sic*]

Consommé royal à l'oseille

Pigeoneaux farcis

Choux rouges braisés

Fromages variés

Gâteau moka, paris brest ou tartes aux oranges

followed by "bonbons assortis Chez Panisse."

This was more along the lines of where I wanted to go, and where I had gone in the menus I submitted to get the job: from my Russian cooking, "pellmenes de blancs de volaille au beurre," sauced with a little raw onion juice and parsley; oeufs durs au gratin X. Marcel Boulestin; Queches de Nancy, Alice B. Toklas; Potage Untel froid; cervelles de veau froides à la crème," and the "poulet farci à l'ariégoise."

Shelton had said that Panisse was a "rule-breaker" if not a "revolutionary." As my Dom Pérignon–bottle Molotov cocktails would suggest, I had revolutionary aspirations—if somewhat elitist ones. But I knew that I had to learn the rules of running a restaurant before I could break them.

With a lot of support from Alice and Gene, and devoted teamwork from Willy, it took six months for me to hit my stride. They patiently guided me through the mysteries of quantity. Willy and I would look at the numbers from the previous week for each day and make a guess about how many would turn up that night. Then he would draw a chalk mark on the soup pot and say, "Make soup to here."

You could tell that Willy had been a drummer by the way he'd turn twenty pounds of mushrooms into a mound of finely chopped duxelles in about ten minutes. He'd lay the button mushrooms out in a long row, then attack them with two Chinese cleavers while moving around and around the six-foot table. Unlike those of the young male cooking-school graduates I'd see over the years, convinced that the louder their chopping the more virile they'd look, Willy's blades barely touched the wooden top. It was a light and soothing staccato, the sound of an unassuming master at work.

Willy's real love was painting. His works were in the style of very early Francis Bacon, complete with toilets, sexual emissions, and text (Mallarmé, Genet, *Fear and Loathing in Las Vegas*). Cooking gave him money for cigarettes, rent, and a weekly blowout of oysters and drinks at one of the local fish restaurants. Later it would keep him in cocaine. Barely.

Willy was the only one who consistently saw through Alice's wiles. He called her Tiny, in part because of her stature and in part because whenever she'd be caught in some brazen act of manipulation, she'd try to become small; she'd raise one hand to her mouth to hide the lower part of her face and emit little squeaks of contrition. Later, at the end of service, with a glass of wine, she would sit in his lap and coo sweet nothings to calm him down, and it generally worked. Alice was good.

I am often asked about Alice's role in the kitchen in those early days, and the truth is that we worked together, but in different realms, she in the dining room and I in the kitchen. She was out front every night, and I was in the back. Our relationship was like an alternating current—little shocks backward and forward between us, a current of creativity. I was Apollinaire to her Breton. But most of the time it was Willy and me against the world.

Alice believed strongly in the no-choice five-course single menu, and so did I: It focused all my attention on three courses, some burden lifted by the waiters, who made the green salads and cut the cheese, and by Lindsey Shere, whose stunning desserts were by far the consistently best food in the restaurant when I got there. It was like a dinner party, albeit for an average of eighty people, and I loved the novelty of cooking something different every night: It was like a repertory theater with a new play a day.

Less clear to us was how to make this particular theater great. I knew the grand things I had grown up with and had cooked for my friends, but "grand" was not a part of the Chez Panisse persona. And it was all too clear that we were a long way from Harrods' Food Hall, my favorite street markets in Paris, my farm in Massachusetts, and the wild beaches of Maine. I was determined to bring a bit of *Stalking the Wild Asparagus* to the challenge of provisioning the kitchen.

I didn't yet know Alice well, but I could tell she was a kindred spirit: She loved the way I encouraged the fishing boat boys to come to the back door with stuff that no one else would accept—wolf eels and other unappreciated "trash" fish. It didn't take long to find Sacramento River Delta crayfish; wild boar from the Stuyvesant Fish ranch in Carmel; trout from my teenage stomping grounds in Big Sur's Garrapata; and fresh spot prawns from Monterey Bay's Fisherman's Wharf, where my grandfather had indulged my childhood insistence that we survey the fish stores before hitting the restaurants on the wharf.

By the summer of 1973, my menu format was new, with an English version on the back page. Panisse the "experiment in dining" was becoming a real restaurant. A menu in July shows the food was now heading more into the Fernand Point *Ma Gastronomie* style, but the price was still six dollars per person:

Salade de champignons
Salad of Fresh Mushrooms

Potage à la Florentine
Cream of Spinach Soup

Truite jurascienne
Trout Cooked in Rosé Wine, served with a Hollandaise Sauce and Buttered Croutons

In another few months the price had gone up fifty cents, the food another notch (more luxurious):

Escargots en cocotte languedocienne
Snails with garlic, fennel, ham, and wine

Crème de champignons
Cream of mushroom soup

Thon poché, sauce beurre blanc
Fresh poached tuna with shallots, butter, and white wine

I had always loved my parents' books of the compiled *Gourmet* articles of Samuel Chamberlain and his wife on their tours of the gastronomic regions of France, so I came up with the idea of doing special dinners of the regions of France to increase the awareness of the restaurant staff and the range of customers beyond Berkeley. I was after the national press as well. Among the inspirations were my books by Curnonsky, Jean de Gouy (1896), Gaston Derys, Robert Courtine, and my handy 1931 *Larousse Gastronomique*.

In September 1973 I wrote the menu for "Brittany" and decided to charge $8.50 per person, pushing the prices for a Wednesday night. Attendance had been forty-five to seventy on weeknights and seventy to ninety on weekends; weekly gross sales were averaging $3,600. If I was ever going to earn enough to move out of my Oakland flophouse—not to mention make it to Hawaii—I needed to raise the revenue, then my salary.

Local Oysters on the Half Shell

Mussel Crêpes

Roast Duckling with Baby Peas

Watercress Salad

Pont-l'Evêque Cheese

Almond Cake with Almond Paste and Chantilly

The attendance was 104 and the sales $1,200 for one night. I knew then what we had to do.

In October I wrote a menu for a Provence Region dinner. Everyone had a Kir before starting with an aioli de province which included fish, vegetables, and snails. This was followed by sea scallops, spit-roasted pork loin with wild sage (from Sonoma), artichauts à la barigoule, and goat cheese. The finale was fresh figs we'd picked in the Sierra foothills and poached in red wine, served with crème fraîche we made ourselves (since there was no other way of getting it). That was another weekday night, and another 104 people came, boosting the weekly revenue to five thousand dollars.

We were on a roll, I was convinced, so I decided to tempt the gods on November 29 by serving a Champagne dinner featuring a real truite au bleu, or live trout cooked in vegetable broth.

Boudin de lapin à la Sainte Ménehould
White sausage of rabbit breaded and grilled

Truites au bleu au champagne
Fresh trout poached in champagne

La brioche de ris de veau au champagne
Sweetbreads in a brioche pastry with a champagne sauce

Salade verte
Field greens salad

Plat du fromages de Champagne
Special cheeses of Champagne

Sorbets de poire et de cassis

We charged an astonishing ten dollars per person on a Thursday night. We offered various champagnes from the middle sixties: Roederer Cristal was sixteen dollars and Dom Pérignon a dollar more. Best of all, we introduced the new and superb California Schramsberg Blancs de Noir for eleven dollars.

The first time I ever saw truite au bleu was at Stonehenge, the Ridgefield, Connecticut, restaurant of Albert Stockli, the first chef of The Four Seasons. In the sixties I would make special pilgrimages there to eat the trout, and not just for the spectacle of watching the live fish caught from the pond outside the dining room window just after it was ordered. Albert served it perfectly "blue," meaning none of its color-giving protective slime had been rubbed off as he gilled, gutted, and immersed it in a bath of simmering vegetable broth. Very soon after it was caught, the trout would appear on a huge silver platter, this time swimming in an inch of melted butter. Then, in one magnificent gesture, Albert would slide the skin off and serve the fish with whipped cream–lightened hollandaise sauce spooned over. I couldn't wait to serve these blue trout in his honor when I started cooking professionally.

The day of our Champagne dinner, the trout arrived from Big Sur in a huge tank on a flatbed truck. We filled every available sink with the Big Sur mountain-stream water in which they'd been raised, and kept the water bubbling and aerated with a compressor from the garage across the street.

The printed menu notwithstanding, the trout weren't poached in champagne: They were dribbled with a little before leaving the kitchen. The champagne was more to fit the theme of the dinner. Actually, it was to give me an ample supply so that I could face killing and cooking over a hundred trout myself.

Then it was killing time.

The first trout slipped out of my hands and went flapping into the dining room, spraying slime over some dowager's ankles. The entire neighborhood heard her ensuing shrieks. My last trout, the one hundred and tenth, was even worse: It looked up at me as I prepared to bash it over the head with my little rubber mallet, and croaked a complaint as I stuck my fingers in its gills. I couldn't go on—the dishwasher had to finish off the rest. We never did them again in such large numbers at one time.

Blue Trout in Pink Champagne

4 8-ounce live trout
$\frac{1}{2}$ gallon vegetable broth
1 cup clarified butter

$\frac{1}{2}$ bottle pink champagne, at room temperature
1 cup savory (shellfish) sabayon

Prepare the trout: Being very careful to handle the trout as little as possible so that the protective slime is not rubbed off, hit it over the head, put your fingers into the gill opening, wrap a finger around the esophagus, and pull out the entire intestinal tract along with the gills. You will get really good at this after the fiftieth trout, so just do your best with the first four.

Bring the broth to a gentle simmer. The moment you have cleaned the trout, put them in the hot broth and cook for 8 minutes.

Have ready a heated rimmed 2-inch-deep platter that will just hold the trout and melted butter. Stand the fish up on their bellies on the platter in a swimming position and pour the butter over each trout. Take the platters to the table, open the champagne, and pour the pink wine over the trout.

Serve the trout with the champagne butter scooped over them. Each person draws back the skin, then spoons some sabayon on each bite of trout.

That year of experiments culminated in the New Year's Eve dinner, a menu that I hoped would set the stage for the new Chez Panisse. We charged fifteen dollars per person.

Crabe au Macôn, Sauce Moutarde
Fresh crab poached in Macôn wine, mustard sauce

Tarte de Bresse, Nantua
Tart of chicken livers and fish quenelles with a crayfish butter sauce

Civet de Lapin lyonnais
Civet of rabbit cooked in red wine

Fromage Saint-Marcellin
Saint-Marcellin cheese marinated in olive oil, juniper berries, and garlic

Sorbet de cassis aux poires
Pears poached in red wine served with a black currant sorbet

Success we could bask in seemed just around the corner. A letter from the head of KQED, one of the country's flagship National Public Radio stations, waxed lyrical about the Champagne dinner, saying it was "extraordinary for the originality of the courses and concept . . . the best of Panisse." Our work, he added, was as important to the Bay Area as that of San Francisco Symphony conductors Kurt Herbert Adler and Seiji Ozawa. We'd become a cultural institution.

"The few flaws we found [earlier have] virtually disappeared, and there is a feeling of life and creativity," read one June 1974 local review, in *A La Votre*, which used terms like "poetic" and "a wonder." The reviewer also applauded our effort to promote California wines, among them the Santa Cruz and Ridge Geyserville Zinfandels. She gave us three and a half stars out of four, saying she needed to keep a half star back to give us something to strive for.

And strive we did. As one of the equal general partners in Chez Panisse (we were five), I was still hoping one day to collect my winnings and finally head off to Hawaii: I was still ambivalent about being in business, especially in a place like Berkeley. But if we were starting to become famous, we were a long way from rich. The restaurant's finances were in a shambles, and the lone partner with financial smarts, Gene Opton, had also been alone in regularly standing up to Alice—with the upshot that Alice had successfully lobbied the rest of us to buy her out.

Alice pretended she didn't care about profits, until she needed them to travel or buy a new car, or to subsidize the business of one of her close friends—a crazed but wonderful woman who looked like Marlene Dietrich in *Touch of Evil*, lived with ocelots, and ran a vintage clothing shop. Alice was disarmingly casual about expenses. She would take a bunch of checks and never bring back the dupes, so operating as we did on a day-to-day (sometimes, it seemed, a half-day) cash flow, it was common for the principal food and wine buyer—me—to be in constant terror of bouncing checks. This, I felt, was a waste of energy. And energy, in the days before cocaine fueled a chef's eighty- to ninety-hour week, was what it was all about.

So I commandeered the checkbook and took over the books, keeping track of the food costs and attendance each day. After twenty-eight years of the world's most expensive schooling, I still had no experience handling money: in my youth when I had problems balancing my checkbook, I would just give in to my grandfather's constant offers to send me more money. But I was determined, some said ruthlessly, to make money and get out, and I quickly learned my way around accounting. I must have inherited something of my grandfather's Yankee Puritan instincts. If my Irish side promptly spent whatever I made for myself, I fiercely guarded the restaurant's takings.

Our first financial statements were an exciting "grown-up" moment— even if no one knew how to read them. For the first six months of 1975, we had assets of $24,000 and a long-term debt of $60,000. Sales averaged $25,000 a month, and the profit was 12 percent, a huge improvement over the previous year. We still owed Gene ten grand on her investment and Alice's parents $296. But with $5,000 in the bank, things were looking up!

The '66 Little Red Dart: A Day in the Week of a Chef

My week would begin on the day it ended, the one day we were closed, Monday. First I would look to see if we had any money. Then I would look at the menus for the coming week, which I had written for posting to the public on the previous Friday. The Panisse regulars knew I would change much of the menus depending on what I found in the market that day (or what foragers brought in) but that I would try to stick to the main courses. Then I'd make up purchasing lists and call purveyors to alert them to what we would be needing. With luck there would be a few hours left to do personal things before the stores closed and the bars opened. Then I'd be off to Oakland's Trader Vic's to collapse into a martini.

Very early Tuesday I would head off in Alice's little red car to buy the food for the day and snoop around for the week, since the real inspiration for the menus came from wandering around the markets. The trip to San Francisco was a logistical nightmare because the car couldn't go up hills. It was an ancient, battered, powerless, ugly but faithful Dart, a car which at its age and decrepitude should never have run but which never broke down.

First stop was Chinatown, for ducks, fish, shellfish, and the occasional vegetable far fresher than I could get from other suppliers. I would watch the little old Chinese women blow air up a chicken's anus to see if it was fresh; I would also watch the vendors sneak ice into the boxes of fish before weighing—and remove it, with much gesturing and laughing in Chinese, when I called them on it; I would ritually confront the parking meter "dykes on bikes," then head over the Bay Bridge to Oakland.

By the time I got there the pressure was on, since I had still to get back to Berkeley and cook lunch for sixty by myself. In Oakland there was one beef and veal "jobber," where whole animals, hanging by their feet, would whiz past me down steel runners from huge trucks into the warehouse. As they swept by I would stand at the end of the ramp with my bucket and grab the sweetbreads and kidneys. The Sicilian workers, covered in dried blood and specks of animal fat, wondered aloud why I didn't just go into the freezer and pick up boxes of already butchered meat. And they were really fascinated, in a Hammer Films sort of way, when I rolled up my sleeves and got shoulder deep into the big drums filled with the blood and livers of calves. I wanted only the blond ones, since they had the mildest flavor and reminded me of foie gras. No one, not even the old geezers, knew what I was doing, and I didn't have the energy to explain. It was too long a story if you didn't know the short one: Buy fresh, buy the best.

I did get a lot of respect for my beef project—aging the New York sirloin strips on the bone for twenty-one days in a refrigerator with no moisture. Those Sicilians hadn't seen anyone do that since the old days. Plastic shrink-wrapping in Cryovac, they soon learned, was a dirty word to me. The blood from that packaged beef smelled dead. My dry-aged beef smelled like mown grass (with a lot of mold thrown in), and that, I knew from my childhood visits to English butcher shops, meant perfect steaks.

From the butcher's I would have to hit the dangerous section of Oakland, and here that old red jalopy came in handy. The door locks had long since failed, but the poultry and fish blood that had leaked into the spare tire well in the back of the car and congealed, raised green-hazed aromas in summer that kept thieves away. It also drove off valet parkers, who'd retch and refuse to park the car.

I had to make my peace with that car, since the only deliveries in those days were of what the companies had to send—the lowest commercial-grade stuff, usually frozen. Spices, extra-virgin olive oil, and decent cheeses were unavailable anywhere except Italian specialty stores, which didn't deliver. It fell to us all to find what we needed, and to me to devise menus around what we could find.

If I hadn't come up with enough fish in Chinatown, my last hope for live crab, fresh shrimp, and still-kicking Baja (Mexico) spiny lobsters was the commercial fish market in Oakland or Berkeley's Spenger's, the Bay Area's biggest restaurant, which had its own boats and wholesale fish business. But detours to both meant cutting into lunch-preparing time.

With luck I'd make it back to Chez Panisse with two hours to cook—although I still hadn't figured out what Berkeley people wanted for lunch. My spirit had been badly shaken the first Christmas season, when I proudly served some of America's first fresh black Périgord truffle–stuffed omelets. I knew that charging ten dollars was asking for trouble, but not the kind that showed up: The first customer ate the eggs but carefully piled the truffles around the edge of the plate for me to see. I felt trapped in a barbarian land. The second order was completely eaten, but the plate came back with a butter-drenched fly on it. "Flies in December?" I shrieked to the waiter. "Give me a fucking break!" I needed every penny from that omelet to cover the exorbitant cost of the truffles. Next Christmas the fly came back again, and I swore I recognized it as well as the customer. Did he keep flies in his freezer to get free lunches? I made him pay me for his omelet personally.

The midday meal was usually a bit of a blur, since my mind would be already on overdrive about dinner. There was a huge amount of work and only two of us to do it—although the dishwasher and a busser would help out in a pinch, a collaboration that turned out happily over the years, with several (like Steve Sullivan, who went on to open the famous Acme Bakery) becoming cooks themselves. Another reason for anxiety was that, despite the published menus, I was unsure what we were cooking until the amateur foragers showed up with the promised wild mushrooms, octopus, or hand-harvested mussels.

At two Willy would come in, and while I was finishing off the last lunches I would go over the evening's menu, telling him what the planned vegetables were and how he was to cook his dish. I had two dishes and he one, usually something that he'd never done before. It was by necessity of time a rushed and inexact conversation, and then Willy would wing it. I prayed every day for an easier, less harrowing way.

Finally, at six, the guests would arrive, and sometimes we'd be ready for them, although with tempers frayed and nerve endings as raw as the bloody livers I was cutting up.

One of my more talked-about intemperate moments came when a busser carried food out of the kitchen with his fingers still in the plate, and I banged my spoon down on the table in fury. "What is it about 'keep your fingers out of the food' that your little cockroach mind can't grasp?" I yelled over the blaring Puccini. He blanched but held his ground. Then he said, "I am a person too, you know."

That was too Berkeley for me.

"So what's your point?" I asked.

That was only the beginning of the evening. An hour later Tom Guernsey, the very sweet upstairs manager and a partner in the restaurant, came in with two plates that guests had returned. "Bugs again," he said with a sigh. Sure enough, two or three little red centipedes were swimming around in the cream sauce on fresh morels gathered that afternoon in the hills above the restaurant by our mushroom man. "Jesus *Christ!*" I yelled, picking out the insects and re-plating the food. "Don't they know this proves they're eating the only fresh morels in America?"

A fresh and even louder scream was heard above the Maria Callas tape, freezing staff to the spot and curdling the food that had just hit diners' stomachs. A dishwasher staggered out of his corner, blood spurting through his fingers. Some idiot had put a knife in the pot sink.

In a restaurant as small and understaffed as Chez Panisse, everyone is critical, and we'd just lost both the dishwasher and the employee who had to rush him to the hospital. I was frantically putting lobster claws in four different bouillabaisse pots and plating six others when the phone rang in the kitchen and a voice on the other end demanded, "Where is the finger?"

Two anxious waiters, shifting from foot to foot like racehorses eager to get out of the chute, were drafted to finish plating the bouillabaisse while I tiptoed over to a sink full of water as gray as my face, pots, and—evidently—one knife and one finger. I wasn't certain which I wanted to find first. "Do fingers float?" I asked Alice, now looking over my shoulder. I rolled up my sleeve and gingerly reached through the congealing inch-thick layer of grease, coming first upon the knife, then upon the severed member, which I slipped into a zipper-lock Baggie and handed to our last remaining busser, who dashed out the door and into a waiting taxi.

By then there was a serious backlog in the kitchen, but the guests would have to wait. It was a champagne moment. I opened a bottle of Clicquot, drained a glass in one long and sensual draft, and went back to cooking.

The scream had softened up the customers, who by now must have figured that any more food coming out of the kitchen would be a miracle. So after catching up with the orders, I knew it was time to visit the dining room. First I reassured the guests that the injured man was well cared for. Then I showed Californians how to get lobster meat out of the claws. A waiter had spilled the beans that the bouillabaisse contained a wolf eel, and the news had traveled around the dining room as fast as that scream; I explained that wolf eel was not poisonous and that it really did give the broth a wonderful punch of authenticity. I informed one group that the salad oil was not "weird" but only "extra-virgin," and that the fresh California goat cheese did not smell or taste like the rear end of a billy goat because the milk came from a dam with clean udders. That sent a neighboring table into paroxysms of giggles.

More champagne.

Just as we were getting back to a kind of normalcy in the kitchen, a waiter announced with great self-righteousness, "I am not serving that prick!" I recoiled and looked up: it would take something very rare indeed for a waiter to talk like that to a chef. With all that opera blaring, I hadn't heard the wait staff's powwows about the politically undesirable "shithead" in the dining room. It was H. R. Haldeman.

"He's paying, isn't he?" I told the waiter. "Take the food out *now*."

The mutinous staff stood firm. H.R.'s food was getting cold. Then Gerry Budrick, the headwaiter and another partner, stepped up to the plates and said, "I'll take them. But for this you owe me big time."

Haldeman was dining with his daughter, who was graduating from Berkeley—a schooling choice I thought a bit off-the-wall, if not downright dangerous. Alice was with the staff on this one, but I was adamant that the man would be served and served well. As somewhat of an outcast myself, I sympathized.

I noticed all the phone lines on my wall phone blinking. Most of the customers and half the staff were trying to call out—to reporters or for reinforcements, I was not sure. I went back to cooking, hoping Gerry would handle whatever came through the front door. Then I heard Willy say "motherfuckme"—or words to that effect. I looked up to see him staring—false teeth at snarling half-mast—over my shoulder, at Haldeman, who was advancing on me with a smile and an outstretched hand.

The best part about English public school training is that, when all else fails, your manners take over. Mine did. So I watched my hand as it rose slowly to clasp Haldeman's.

"Thank you," he said. "And for my daughter, thank you for that."

He was nice.

Somewhat blessedly, Alice and the staff did not speak to me for a week.

On a normal night we would be finished and cleaned up by about eleven—as long as Alice had not overbooked the room. If she had, Willy and I would do the loaves and fishes act, not always as successfully as the original. Then Willy would once again pull off his apron and threaten to quit unless Alice promised never to do it again, a vow that came off her lips as easily as Willy accepted her cooings and proffered glasses of old Chambolle-Musigny. The time I spent holding both sets of hands (no one wanted Willy gone) was time I needed for planning the next morning's sorties.

But I was not entirely out of sync with Alice on the subject of late walk-ins. They were almost all profit (who had heard of overtime?), and the sales were always needed.

The rule, though, was that she had to check with the kitchen around ten to make sure there was food for those late diners. When she didn't it would be cause for panic, since she would always seat her friends, the famous, or any filmmaker. Nick Ray, Fassbinder, Pasolini, or Francis Ford Coppola were brought in late by Alice's ex-boyfriend Tom Luddy (of the Pacific Film Archive), and there would always be a table for them somehow. But the most disastrous night for Panisse was when she seated, without checking, her current lover, Robert Finigan, who was also the Bay Area's most powerful restaurant critic.

As we were getting ready to clean up the kitchen, the order came in for the first course, triggering what I knew would be a crisis with the now finished main course, leg of lamb. I looked down with dismay at the plastic buckets with lamb leg bones bare of servable meat. All that remained were the "souris" (little mouse) part of the shanks—that and some crisp bits that tasted delicious but were totally unpresentable to paying customers. The waiter was dispatched to ask if steaks would be acceptable instead. The answer was a firm no. He wanted lamb and Alice had told him he could have it. In those days I thought it improper for a chef to go out and talk to a local restaurant critic, so Finigan and company got what they asked for. ("Inordinately gristly," he would write.) The plates came bouncing right back, the waiter (a friend volunteering for the night) announcing they'd demanded better lamb.

"Tough shit," I said. Then: "Where's Alice?"

"At the table."

In an instant Willy flung his apron down, his brows and beard twitching. "Get Tiny now," he growled.

I searched the buckets for lamb I knew was not there and looked up to find Alice, red-faced and shedding not her usual crocodile "please forgive me" tears but genuine ones, of rage. "How could you?" she said.

It turned out that the volunteer waiter had repeated—in violation of a cardinal rule of the kitchen—my offhand comment; he'd told Finigan, "The chef says tough shit."

All of this led to an hour or so of recriminations over many drinks, and we left around midnight, so that I could try to be asleep by 1:00, up by 6:00, and into San Francisco's Chinatown by 7:00 A.M.

It never occurred to Alice to consider the role she had played in bringing about this embarrassing episode. In a 1978 article on the history of Chez Panisse, she typically shifted the blame to someone else. "I almost died," she said. "Jeremiah just got fed up. It was not amusing at the time."

She never bothered to tell the reporter why I'd been fed up and how less amused we were in the kitchen to serve unpresentable food.

Finigan explained it nicely: "Had I not been visiting Chez Panisse in a professional capacity [with his lover the owner sitting with him], I might well have decorated the waiter with the gigot rôti and then set out for the kitchen, but instead I cooled my outrage with sips of the remarkable 1972 Mt. Eden Pinot Noir."

Alice may have nearly died, but I was more worried about the customers and if any were now in convulsions after having eaten American white truffles. Linda Guenzel, Panisse's most devoted customer, had brought some from Texas, where she found squirrels digging them up in her mother's front lawn. We found out at the university that they were *Tuber texense*, but there was no record of anyone eating them. Certainly not serving them in a restaurant. I had called England's culinary encyclopedia, Alan Davidson, and for the first and only time, he was stumped. He knew about *Terfezia*, the North African dessert truffles so beloved by the Imperial Romans, but Texas? White Oregon truffles had not been heard of yet, so he cautioned me to try one first and wait a day. But there wasn't time; we were to serve them that night. Alice thought I was mad—if not criminal.

Chefs have a reputation for bad behavior in part because they have to play so hard to counteract the daily pileup of tension and fatigue, and that play didn't mean yoga. For many of us, it was about how many oysters and great wines we could fit into a few hours and still get some rest before the work began again. The dilemma in my few hours off was how to recharge my batteries instead of depleting them further. The mental onslaught was never-ending, even in sleep (restaurant operation nightmares are famous in the industry). And drugs were easier to organize than sex, unless it was casual, which usually meant with one another. Who else would put up with us?

Temporary oblivion was what we sought. So on my one day off and before a four o'clock lunch with some of the staff, I would head off to the Japanese baths for a long soak. In later years, when I was a bit more flush and certainly more famous, I would be invited out, sometimes by San Francisco's elite restaurateurs. But in those early and not so well funded days, it was either Trader Vic's in Oakland for its tandoor oven–cooked food and expert bartenders, or Vanessi's in San Francisco for tomato and anchovy salad, tortellini in cream, a great filet mignon cooked on charcoal, and zabaglione for dessert. We ate like pythons coming out of a long sleep. As cooks we had not really eaten during the week, just tasted and picked. And after sixteen hours of shopping and cooking, I couldn't look at food for at least two hours. That meant if we ate at all, dinner would start at one in the morning, and that I'd have only four hours' sleep before heading back to Chinatown to sniff the bloody gills of fish and hold down my rising gorge.

So it's no surprise looking back that one night I wandered into the dining room, empty except for Alice and some staff sitting around a bottle of old Burgundy (most likely Le Corton from Doudet-Naudin since the son and heir was "working" for us—as in getting away from his arranged fiancée), and burst into tears. All my strength and discipline were gone. The months of a relentless attempt to make it all work with so few hands had done me in. "I am out of here," I told the astonished group. "See you in a week." I added, "And, Alice, you will just have to do the menus."

She did, and took over the kitchen for a week. A photo of her and Willy from when I was away tells much: Alice is dipping her finger in a container of sauce, hesitancy and doubt pervading her face, and Willy is looking on with the scolding frown he reserved for her alone.

The most creatively lonely places in the world are beaches, and it's on warm ones that I do my best thinking. Thirty hours after leaving the staff open-mouthed in the Panisse dining room, I was sitting on the white sands of Yelapa, down the coast from Puerto Vallarta. (One look at Vallarta and I was out of there, my opinion of it perhaps clouded by being stoned by small boys, their instincts for an animal wounded and down, barrio perfect.)

I was the only guest in the "hotel" (actually a hut) on a beach visited every day at lunch by a boatload of tourists from Puerto Vallarta. When the boat arrived I would retire to a hammock in the trees, to which my soon-trained waiter would bring perfect fresh ripe lime juice margaritas every fifteen minutes. I managed a lot of thinking while sipping those drinks, some of it brilliant (between the first and third margaritas) and a lot of it junk (thereafter), but I returned to Panisse ready for battle, snippets from Sun-tzu's *Art of War* still buzzing in my brain, my tactics outlined and ready to put into action.

I had already come up with the idea of culinary festivals to promote the restaurant nationally, starting with the regions of France (using Curnonsky, Austin de Croze, and Jacques Médecin). But when I got back, I decided to move on to the classical greats (Escoffier, Prosper Montagné, Pellaprat, and Urbain Dubois), and then lead up to the present, with Elizabeth David and my pen pal Richard Olney. First, we would look back so that we could go forward.

Listening to my tape of Sidney Bechet's soprano sax on the beach, I remembered that he was as famous for never sticking to the score as he was for his excuse for being always three days late for work: "The taxi driver got lost." I figured I'd never be famous by sticking to the score, so I might as well do big, outlandish, nontraditional things based on traditional principles. If and when I got into trouble, if the revolution failed, I could always continue to Hawaii.

A chance to do something "out there" came when Michael Palmer reminded me that it would soon be the one hundredth anniversary of the birth of Gertrude Stein. For the Stein–Alice B. Toklas dinner, I selected dishes from the *Alice B. Toklas Cookbook*, Michael wrote the menu text, and Willy Bishop designed the menu card with a drawing of an old-fashioned stove that was Gertrude; in the oven was Alice.

> Dining. Dining is west. **Mushroom sandwiches.**
> Upstairs.
> Eating. Eat ing.
> Single fish. Single fish single fish single fish,
> **Sole mousse with Virgin Sauce.** I wrote it for
> America.
>
> Everyone thought that the syringe was a whimsy.
> Mousse and mountain and a quiver, a quaint statue
> and a pain in an exterior and silence. **Gigot de la
> Clinique** a cake, a real salve made of mutton and
> liquor, a specially retained rinsing and an
> established cork and brazing
>
> **Wild rice salad.** She said it would suit her.
>
> Cake cast in went to be and needles wine needles
> are such. Needles are. **A Tender Tart.** That
> doves have each a heart.
>
> Nobody ever followed Ida. What was the use of
> following Ida.
>
> **Cream Perfect Love.**
>
> February 3, 1974

On the strength of Michael having invited his good friend the poet Robert Duncan to read from *The Making of Americans* for after-dinner entertainment, an audience eclectically more diverse than our usual patrons showed up. The room filled with high-minded Berkeley street poets, the

Birkenstock brigade of both sexes, hunched-over academics from the university, anyone haunted by Gertrude, and the usual troublemakers, like my sister. When Robert seemed out of his element reading from Stein, my sister took his place. As she sat down, she unconsciously took the posture of Gertrude in the portrait by Picasso, and a hush fell over the room. It was a warm and unusually light-filled audience, even for Berkeley. My sister described to me, years later, those hours: "I have never felt so free, so comfortable and secure, so lovely, and surrounded by acceptance. It was a wonderful evening—a magic dinner."

The year before I had contacted James Beard in New York. Since he was the most powerful food journalist in America, and the high priest of American food, I invited him to the restaurant, and in his annual widely syndicated reminiscences column he called Chez Panisse "fascinating." But even with Beard onboard, no national press responded to my notice of the Stein–Toklas dinner.

We did better locally: For the first time since it opened, Panisse appeared in the top San Francisco press. I invited Herb Caen, the Walter Winchellian gossip columnist for the *San Francisco Chronicle*, who telegraphed his regrets—"Jeremiah: Would that we could be there for the signal event but alas, it is impossible. Much luck, merci mille fois-gras, and vive le Gertrudinus one. T'jours, Herb Caen." But he mentioned the dinner twice in his powerful daily column. So started an alliance that would boost my career as much as anything else. Later, Caen would put Stars in San Francisco at the top of the list of places to be.

I didn't have the nerve to put hashish in the after-dinner cookies, although not for lack of supply. I had learned to steer clear of it. The problem with smoking marijuana is that all food tastes just wonderful and that cooking to a schedule becomes meaningless. We learned that lesson during the Moroccan Regional Dinner, when for atmosphere we burned some marijuana stems in braziers under kitchen tables and got so stoned that instead of the smoke our burned best efforts went up the flue.

And I didn't like it much by that time anyway, since the really good marijuana from Hawaii and Jamaica was a far cry from the low-grade stuff that in college I could smoke all night. One night a Panisse friend handed me a cigar-size joint as I was cleaning up. I smelled the powerful resin from the new "Maui Wowie" or "sensimilla," and said, "No thanks." But the waiters kept pestering me as I was trying to get by them to join Alice and a group of eight food journalists, so I had one puff, pushed open the swinging doors to the dining room, took three steps toward the writers' table, and passed out. When I came to I heard Alice screaming I was dead and Willy telling everyone to calm down, cancel the ambulance, and get me a glass of champagne.

A few months later we were all at a late-night party celebrating the opening of a local bakery when someone handed me a cigarette with black resin on the end. It was opium. I had tried it once with a blind Moroccan boyfriend, who parlayed all sorts of resinous substances in a village in the hills outside of Tangier, and preferred to stick with the mediocre hash. But I smoked the proffered cigarette and quickly knew the most perfect moment of my life: I was fused emotionally, physically, and mentally in one perfect state—and I knew within seconds I must never use opium again or there would be no coming back.

Later there would be nitrous oxide canisters in the kitchen and a case of them at home. One night I was gazing fondly at a poster of the SS *France,* which I'd hung across from my bed so it would be the first thing I saw in the morning and the last thing at night: It stood for my planned escape. After taking several little canisters of gas, I completed an entire crossing without leaving the room.

But these substances were diversions. The only drug friendly to the restaurant business is cocaine. It was cocaine that became the fuel for the energy that changed the way America dines, and for the high-profile and all-consuming peripatetic schedules that launched the superstar chefs.

At Chez Panisse it started on the restaurant's third birthday, in 1974.

We planned an open house at five dollars per person (wine included), so we needed something cheap to serve. And I had to come up with it fast since there was a poster for the party (Alice idealized and in her signature vintage clothes) in production by David Goines, one of Alice's lovers. I grabbed a favorite cookbook, Jacques Médecin's *La Cuisine du Comte de Nice,* and saw a recipe for something called, aptly enough, "Les Panisses," a flat pancake type of thing with something boring on top, which I knew I could improve upon. Excitement caused haste, so I didn't read the recipe carefully. I wrote the menu—

Chez Panisse

Menu for 3rd Birthday

28 August 1974
6 p.m.–12 midnight

Hors d'oeuvre Variés

Panisses

Salade Verte

Glace de Fruits

Demi carafe du Vin

$5.00 tout compris

—and sent it over to David at his St. Hieronymus Press for printing.

Soon the day arrived for me to tell everyone what a "panisse" was and to order the ingredients. The recipe called for chickpea (garbanzo bean) flour to be mixed with water and fried in olive oil. I drove down to my Italian delicatessen in Oakland, bought all they had, and made a "panisse." It was disgusting. So I decided to lie. When anyone asked what a panisse was, I said, "Basically just a little pizza." Alice and everyone else was happy with that. So pizza was what it had to be.

Since we had no ovens that would cook regular-size pizzas, individual ones were the way to go, and what went on top had to be cheap and easy—and novel. I decided on a fresh California goat cheese (still new to the world in those days) and Sonoma beefsteak tomatoes, a fine idea until a hundred or so people more than we expected showed up and the cheese and tomatoes were all gone. In our walk-in refrigerators there were still fresh ingredients from the previous night's bouillabaisse (clams, prawns, squid, crab, lobster, onions, saffron, garlic, and fennel), so I decided to scatter everything on top. What came out of the oven changed every hour depending on what was left, but little bouillabaisse pizzas they were.

These searches for ingredients caused delays, and soon a line formed to get into the kitchen. I was flagging a bit, and everyone was buying me champagne, which slowed me down even more. Word went out that the chef needed a boost. In sauntered a friend of one of our waiters with a black-leather-coated accomplice. Flashing a gold toothy smile as he glided by me, he pulled a plastic bag out of his coat, then dumped a pound of white powder on top of the chest freezer at the back of the kitchen. He cut it into lines and handed me a straw fashioned from a rolled-up twenty-dollar bill. In an instant, I was back at the stoves, and then a conga line formed (this time not for the pizza), snaking out through the kitchen, into the dining room, and up the stairs into the bar.

The demand for pizza—and any other food—soon evaporated, but there was more cocaine and more champagne. The night was a huge success, premiering three new trends: individual pizza, the freedom to use any topping one wanted, and the drug that made all the long hours possible, then impossible, in the kitchen.

The same person who supplied us that night did business with many of the restaurant staff for the next three years, until he was murdered. No one was ever charged for the crime, but the rumor flew around the restaurant that the perp was someone known to all of us.

When our cocaine intake got out of hand, I would write impossible menus or think someone on the staff was in love with me; Willy would be stone broke and more interested in scoring than cooking; my partner waiter Tommy would spend the whole night at the Stud and, after hours, the gay baths in San Francisco; and Gerry would shoot up the telephone with a friend's .38. Alice disapproved of using cocaine, partly the result of her New Jersey suburban background and partly because she knew it interfered with the proper running of the restaurant. Still, inasmuch as she knew it was a release from the mad pressures of maintaining and improving upon an increasingly famous restaurant, she turned a mostly blind eye. Lindsey and Charles Shere never partook: they regarded us as naughty children, with Charles stentorially pronouncing doom for all.

I don't know the source of the dispute that got our original dealer killed, but he was replaced by another waiter's friend, along with a few new runners. All was peaceful, in the drug world that is, for a few years, until Willy stabbed someone in a bar in San Francisco for hogging the coke lines in the bathroom and was carted off to the state penitentiary— but not before we had cooked hundreds of marvelous meals together. Panisse somehow survived our love affair with champagne and cocaine.

Drugs had not dulled our ability to create a wonderful restaurant, or my instinct for public relations, so in 1974, well into the French regional dinners using old texts, it was time to liven up the menus with some contemporary culinary giants. Though fairly unknown to the United States, Richard Olney was my first choice. We had finally met a year before at Williams-Sonoma. "Yes he is what I hoped and expected," I wrote in my journal. "Could easily spend some time with him, and cook. He knows I will see him again. That eye understanding was established." I put in the back of my mind that, before the year was out, I would go to France and cook with him.

I was able to think about more time-consuming menus now, since I no longer had the killing responsibility for both lunch and dinner. We had hired a lunch cook. Her name was Lilly Lecocq, and she was, in her words, "just a peasant from the Savoie," but said in the kind of way that if you agreed with her you'd never be forgiven. She reminded me of her peasant heritage every morning, when I returned from market with all the things she said she'd love to cook but couldn't. I had a very trying time with her. Lobster Bordelaise she couldn't do, but with a potato gratin Savoyard she was a genius. Not so much of one to make up for her constant nagging about the glories of peasantry versus my less worthy ancestry, but enough for me to forgive her mustache, her nasal whine, which sounded like a slowly opening warped cupboard door, and her flirtatious looks, intended to make me like her. All I knew was how helpful it was to have her at those stoves when I was shopping and gearing up to cook eighty dinners.

And in crises I could draw assistance from Alice or the staff. One night, when Willy bowed out early and the waiters were lined up, their desperate sighs audible over the blaring *Rigoletto,* I asked a fifteen-year-old dish-washer named Joshua to come over and watch me make a sauce. "Now taste that and remember the taste," I said. "Then duplicate it." He did. Very well. So I said, "Do it again, and quickly." As the waiters looked on hopefully, Joshua made the sauce even faster and better. He was a natural. I kissed him, work resumed, and we had a fifteen-year-old cook.

By now I had located, grown, or imported a lot of ingredients that a year before had not existed in California, and the kitchen had a new assurance. So midyear I decided to push the envelope again. A menu from June 1975 included the classic, expensive, very time-consuming, and now rare dish of shelled crayfish tails sautéed in Cognac, covered with a cream and crayfish sauce and gratineed; duck consommé with pureed red cabbage and sliced red cabbage cooked in walnut oil; marinated loin of pork roasted over a charcoal fire with fresh herbs, fresh herb butter sauce; and salad of spinach wilted in olive oil and sherry vinegar.

Other dishes were Oeufs Knapik, dites Alice B. Toklas (coddled eggs with a fresh basil, lemon, caper, mustard, and garlic sauce, an example of Alice Toklas's love for "corse" or forthright food), and Filet de boeuf Nantua (beef grilled and served on a crouton spread with mushroom duxelles with a cream, crayfish butter, and vermouth sauce).

Another successful menu was the Sauternes Dinner, inspired by my favorite childhood Russian, Count Cheremetev, and his stories of Prince Yusupov, and conceived for drinking Sauternes throughout the meal. *The Chez Panisse Menu Cookbook* (1982) prints the menu in English, but the original was in French:

Jambon de Virginie aux pruneaux

Colombines de saumon Nantua

Entrecôte de boeuf

Pommes Chez Nous

Salade Alice

Tarte chaude de fruits

Blanc Manger

Noix caramélisées

After this dinner Alice thought I walked on Sauternes. She said the meal was "revolutionary, but magnificent in effect" and that it was a turning point for the restaurant. I could not have done it without Lilly cooking lunch, without the five co-owners' willingness to provide service for a meal with four added courses, without Alice's gift for explaining our mission to the guests in the dining room, and without a new confidence in the kitchen that we could cook the food correctly and on time. It did feel revolutionary: A dinner in which sweet wine could be drunk from beginning to end was surely a first, and this one followed Olney's principle of keeping the palate fresh, teased, surprised, and excited.

Alice's phrase "revolutionary, but magnificent" implies the concepts for her were mutually exclusive, whereas I believed there was no oxymoron. Although the food at Panisse was no longer what would restore the soul after a romp with the police in People's Park without compromising one's principles, it did make a political statement. The revolution from radical to radicchio that started with the college dropout Alice Brock in the Back Room in Stockbridge, Massachusetts, was, as Arlo Guthrie sang and told us when he dined at Panisse, all about fresh, healthful food. But while half my gaze was still on France, the intent was to use American ingredients for themselves rather than as substitutes for unobtainable French ones.

But we had still the already-planned French culinary regions festival to finish, and when I ran out of regions, ended up venturing farther afield, first with Morocco-Tunisia and then with Corsica. The Corsican menu pushed me over the edge. The first course, of Strozzapreti or "quenelles of summer greens," I had never even heard of. I called them "Hommage à Darrell Corti" because I had to call this culinary genius (of the Corti Brothers specialty food stores in Sacramento) and ask what they tasted like. The next course was U Pestu or Stocaficado à la Corse. Caught up in a frenzy for authenticity, I found the "real" stockfish—dried-out cod as hard as an air-dried plank, and just as palatable. But since salt cod was second nature to me, I was not worried—until I cooked this version. The dish was authentically inedible, and the one Alice remembers as my low point. I could feel I was nearing the end of slavishly French cooking but could not give up overnight. I needed a break. A surreal holiday in Mustique, where Lord Colin Tennant tried to persuade me to stay as Princess Margaret's chef, gave me an idea.

On my return I wrote a festival of menus from the cookbook of "The divine Salvador Domenech Philippe Hyacinthe Dalí for Gala," warning the public they were about to see their favorite (they thought by now predictable) restaurant take a surrealistic leap. The first week was "Dinners for Gala," the second, "Galas for Dalí." Among the dishes were "Un délice petit martyr sans tête," a toast of avocado, brains, almonds, Mexican liqueur, and cayenne, and "L'entre-plat drogué et sodomisé," a leg of lamb "sodomised" with Madeira and brandy. One diner wrote to me, "My god, that dinner last night was more memorable than a Dalí crucifixion and a lot less painful to contemplate," but reported that others—like "the pillow-breasted shrike" who demanded a green salad and soup in the old style of Panisse—were not so happy. If the unhappy ones had seen me sticking or sodomizing legs of lamb every day with huge syringes full of tangerine juice, Madeira, and brandy, they might have been even less confident.

All these challenging menus called for more ingredients than we could find. Our attempts in the last two years to have Francis Coppola buy the Niebaum-Inglenook estate for a Panisse country inn and farm had not worked out, but the idea seemed still our only way to find the ingredients we needed. The list of what we couldn't get seemed endless. When I hauled out my college notebooks filled with garden and country inn projects, I came up with some new ideas. I reread my notes on Robert May's seventeenth-century *Accomplishd* [sic] *Cook* and found old recipes for salads calling for Alexander buds, or black lovage, and put the salad of watercress, sliced oranges, lemons, currants, and pears on the menu—without the buds. Then I read a 1950s *Farmers' Weekly* section on "Farmhouse Fare" and made notes to grow elders, mountain ash (for rowan or "rodden" berries) to flavor vodka as my Russian uncle had shown me, and whortleberries for stuffing game birds. We had bought some goslings and taken them up to Sonoma so they would be ready for the fourth birthday, on August 28. I cooked a lineup of cassoulets with real confit of goose, to such public acclaim that I was now under pressure to make more cassoulet nights, and I nearly fell back into the comfortable lap of French bourgeois cooking.

The plans to make our own culinary region was not so much then a conscious movement as a race to have quality fresh ingredients available in enough quantity to keep up with more and more ambitious menus. To see if I was on the right track, I needed a reality check. In mid-October, after serving our first in-house smoked California salmon, I put a side of it in my luggage and headed for Paris to join Richard Olney at a special dinner at Lucas Carton given by the Club des Cents for the legendary Madame Decure, the head of *Cuisine et Vins de France*. From there we journeyed south to Sollies-Toucas near Toulon, to his little house on the hill above the town. The place was still fairly primitive, unfortunately for bathing but fortunately for cooking since we did a lot of it in the fireplace, over coals that burned twenty-four hours a day to keep the house above freezing.

After we got the sex part of our affair out of the way, we got down to business. The long winter nights were filled with single-malt whiskey, old French music-hall records, and talks about food. I had never been to Chez L'Ami Louis (I couldn't afford it), so I listened in awe to Richard's stories of the ortolans cooked in butter, the perfume of premortem Armagnac anesthesia still lingering in their bodies; of the huge slabs of duck foie gras served with raw country ham; of the woodcock in the fall and the tiny legs of lamb for two at Easter. We shared stories of L'Hôtel de la Côte d'Or and of Alexandre Dumaine, particularly his adaptation of Lucien Tendret's L'Oreiller de la Belle Aurore—a "gros pâté" intricately cross-sectioned in a mosaic of (in Richard's words) "pistachio-speckled dark and light forcemeats, alternating with striped layers of dark game and white meats, punctuated with fingers of red tongue, white back fat, and black truffle." He promised to make it for me, but an exploration into the glories of the Bresse chicken and his whiskey-soaked stories took over. He talked endlessly (I wouldn't let him stop) about his first days in Paris and later in Grasse cooking for a bunch of opium smokers, including the head of a well-respected travel guide. Dinner had to be ready by ten o'clock, but sometimes the group didn't sit down to table until two in the morning. Richard was forbidden to get caught up in the opium, but he didn't mind since he was too busy fending off (he said) the most famous chef in France at the time (Georges Garin), who was in love with him while Richard was in love with a male black Folies-Bergère dancer introduced to him by James Baldwin. Listening to the stories of the look on the dancer's face when he saw the broken-down hovel on the Sollies-Toucas mountainside that he was supposed to exchange for the makeup mirrors at the Folies, I knew in a bizarrely comforting way that Richard had been as mad as I had.

In 1975 Richard was trim and still youthful. He was not beautiful, but the sight of him walking fully tanned around the vegetable garden in a turquoise cotton bikini, a bottle of Krug chilling in an ice bucket under the grape arbor behind him, could be thrilling. His under-the-surface melancholy for past grandeurs and true loves I minded not at all, nor did he mind my simultaneous reverence for the past and obsession with the future. After a couple of glasses of champagne, we were in perfect sync. All this talk of eating and love made me want to do a festival at Chez Panisse in celebration of his new book, *Simple French Food*. But first he gave me a lesson in ingredients.

I waited patiently in line at the neighboring town fish store, admiring all the varieties of fresh sardines and anchovies that I couldn't get in California. One particularly intrigued me for its freshness. I asked the woman behind the counter what it was. She ignored me. I asked again, only to be ignored again. Finally I turned to Richard, who asked her. "*Ils sont étrangers*" was her disdainful reply. Foreigners? I wondered. I asked Richard if I had heard correctly. He laughed and explained that the fish were caught more than twelve kilometers from the shop, so they were "foreign" and not fit for selling to him. "Wow," I said to Richard, since the fish looked better than any I could get in California. "If that's the standard, we're sunk."

To complete the lesson he took me to lunch at Domaine Tempier in Bandol. The wine was unavailable in the United States at that time, and Richard thought that since we were going to cook his food in California, I should have his favorite local wine to go with it. We tasted all the wines from barrels, then sat down to sea bass cooked on a fire of dried vine cuttings served with a sauce of its roe made in a huge marble mortar, spit-roasted leg of lamb, and deeply ripe and perfect apricot tart.

I asked Richard if we could write menus together for a two-week Olney festival for spring 1976 featuring "simple French food." I also wanted his feedback on menus inspired by his *French Menu Cookbook* for an upcoming California Zinfandel festival. We wrote while listening to Mistinguett, Freyel, and Piaf, and drinking Niagaras of Krug, other great wines, and the ever-present Glenmorangie. The original paperwork shows we changed our minds at least four times and constantly reworked the order of dishes and the sequence of evenings so that Saturday night would be the crescendo. I had sent him my preliminary ideas and menus before I arrived at his house, and final versions weren't ready until after I returned to Berkeley.

Back in Berkeley, I tasted the Tempier wines with my friend George Linton, the brilliant eccentric vet who had started Connoisseur Wine Imports; and by April the first cases of Domaine Tempier arrived. I was eager to proselytize on behalf of the Mourvèdre grape that made Tempier's wines so good, and was able to commission and help blend a nouveau style with Joseph Phelps Vineyards in Napa to go with Richard's menus. The menu read: "Three Richard Olney Autumn Menus to Celebrate Gold Rush Zinfandel from Amador 1975 County Grapes of Frank Dal Porto Vineyards Produced at Joseph Phelps Vineyards" and included dishes like "rich pork stew garnished with vegetables, pigs' ears and tails" as well as "French moussaka with watercress" and "fresh white goat cheeses."

The year 1975 ended with a menu of French food influenced by rereading the great Lucien Tendret's *La Table au Pays de Brillat-Savarin*. I'd found a hundred-year-old salad very similar to the one I had seen in Escoffier's 1908 magazine *Le Carnet d'Epicure* and which Richard and I had seen at the great Jacques Manière in Paris. It was the "salade gourmande" or "salade folle." The green bean puree was an homage to Georges Garin, the turnip puree was Richard's Puree Blanche, and the rest was elegantly easy. But no one except Alice understood or appreciated it, and over a few glasses of yeasty champagne, I suddenly had the feeling that I'd gone about as far as I could go at Panisse.

New Year's Eve Dinner: Chez Panisse

December 31, 1975

Salad of lobster, chicken breasts, black truffles, squab breasts, mushrooms, and shrimp with a mustard vinaigrette

Prime sirloin of beef with truffles, roasted and served with a truffled Madeira sauce

Puree of green beans and puree of turnips, leeks, and potatoes with garlic

Champagne sherbet

Fruit tartlets

Bonbons Chez Panisse

Many thought I'd gone mad charging twenty-five dollars per person—and I almost did when the truck carrying the fresh truffles and foie gras hadn't arrived from the airport until 6:15, fifteen minutes after the first guests had been seated. That one had me sweating. We couldn't charge so much without the truffles, although even at that menu price we were hardly making any money. It was truly time to reassess what we were doing.

A Region Called California

The instrument of change arrived in the form of the 350-pound James Beard, who came to Panisse for dinner the day after Christmas in 1975. The menu started with a trio of oysters: one an oyster soufflé with shellfish sauce, the others Escoffier's "favorites" with cream and black truffles, and cold "natives" on ice. This was followed by filet of beef with beef marrow, and then California goat cheeses.

I showed him the press we had been getting that year. The pieces were a paean to the accomplishments of our little band of amateur owners. They are worth repeating to see how much difference a few years had made with the food press and how they felt now what the nature of a "serious" restaurant could be.

James Beard had said that Panisse had become "a superbly authoritative restaurant." A Bay Area critic reported the now familiar quality moniker "unrelentingly superb quality in food preparation, innovativeness in menu planning, purchasing only the finest ingredients, and resolute attention to even the smallest culinary details." Caroline Bates in *Gourmet* magazine (October 1975) summed up what I had achieved: "Jeremiah honed his palate at an early age and now, like many creative young chefs in France today who have turned away from the pretentiousness of *la grande cuisine*, he strives for the simplicity and directness that characterize French regional food with its emphasis on fresh ingredients and the integrity of each taste." So why did I tell Jim that I was still not satisfied?

I moaned to him that size of the profit line was still a vital question for me; that places like Ireland and England, not to mention Italy and France, still had better ingredients, and that they had the courage to put food on the plate without much interference from the chef. I told him that I had not turned my back on "la grande cuisine" in its purest and most perfect form (as in Tendret's book) but that I was beginning to doubt a three-star French restaurant could ever be had at Panisse prices.

Jim gave me the smile he reserved for young men he held in favor. "Darling," he said, "keep your mouth shut about all that. You have a good thing going here, you're on the right track. Just stick with America." I promised to reread his wonderful 1972 book *American Cookery*.

The next morning at the Stanford Court Hotel, where Jim's own court was held each day, I bandaged his feet (devastated by lack of circulation), giving his devoted servant Marion Cunningham a rest from her daily chore. His robe had been left open where it "fell," exposing a belly as vast as Yosemite's El Capitan, which swept down to reveal what he could have been proud to reveal were Jim not the exception to the rule that large fingers are also a measure of the family jewels. Jim did have very big hands. This was a morning ritual, exposure to which I had long since become familiar and with which I'd grown comfortable over the years I'd known him. After a little fondle, we talked about my career, about Alice, about Marion, about *Gourmet*, saying it was fine not to make money. We talked about Delmonico's and the time, a hundred years earlier in New York, when the great restaurants listed the provenance of their ingredients on their menus. And about the great William Niblo in his Old Bank Coffee House in 1814 serving ingredients with their origins called out on the menu: "Bald Eagle shot on the Grouse Plains of Long Island." And The Four Seasons in New York, where Jim had consulted starting in 1959.

Jim had rethought his earlier position. He asked me if I wouldn't be happier in New York, since the local press had begun to see me as "pretentious," "autocratic," "royalist," and so on. "Perhaps you should start wearing Birkenstocks to work," he quipped. "Whatever you might think, there is no love lost for you here." I showed him a letter in the Berkeley *Gazette* that complained of paying ten dollars for "pork and beans"—meaning the cassoulet I'd made from a confit of our own geese! He also read a *Bay Guardian* article from November, in which Alice said the restaurant had reached a "plateau." She complained that the telephone lines were always clogged and that 60 percent of the customers were now from out of town instead of the East Bay regulars. "It's extremely frustrating," she concluded.

I wasn't frustrated so much as impatient to go to the next level. Jim knew that Alice's ideas of success were going to conflict with mine, and sooner rather than later. "Jeremiah, they're jealous," he said. "And if they aren't now, they will be. Get out."

"But, Jim," I protested. "I have to work. No one wants an underwater architect!"

We pondered this for a while.

"How about a restaurant of your own?" he called out as I was almost at the door, motioning me back with that huge, effete hand from which his gold wire bracelet hung loosely.

I reminded him of his recent comment that if he had to go back to four restaurants in the United States they would be Tony's in Houston, the Coach House and The Four Seasons in New York, and Chez Panisse. I hadn't been to Tony's, but I knew it was "Continental" and red plush. The top famous restaurants in San Francisco at that time—L'Etoile, Ernie's, and La Bourgogne—were similar: They had severe dress codes and even more severe headwaiters, who would flick open menus half the size of the table and call you "Madame" even if you weren't.

We talked of food in San Francisco and the rest of America. Locally there was Dungeness crab, Petrale sole, and abalone at Sam's and Tadich Grill, and a great mutton chop at Jack's. Trader Vic's had surprisingly forward-looking ingredients (mahimahi, fresh mangoes, and tiger prawns). In Los Angeles you could eat simple and direct food (if the cooking was often heavy-handed) like sand dabs, more Dungeness crab, and prawn cocktails (Chasen's), and even crabmeat baked in papaya with cream (Il Padrino), which always sounded better than it was, and it didn't sound too good. You could get Mexican lobster tail (frozen) with California avocado in La Jolla (Top of the Cove). In Baltimore there was Danny's with its Chesapeake Bay blue crabs, crab soup, and perfect fresh lump crabmeat that I adored and that was a favorite of my Russian uncle when it was made "Imperial." In New Orleans there was Commander's Palace serving softshell turtle stew; Le Ruth with frogs' legs, oysters and artichokes, and French fried parsley long before it became a fad in the eighties; the Bon Ton had its fried soft-shelled crabs; and Maylie's, my favorite fried oysters and soft-shelled crab po'boys. In Detroit there was the legendary London Chop House with its menu of Americana, Continental cuisine, and English grills. In Boston, Locke-Ober, the scene of my twenty-first birthday dinner, had its famous baked oysters, as well as a lobster dish from a century earlier in New York. The Union Oyster House was where I had spent most of my college allowance on scrod, codfish cakes, clam chowder, and oysters.

This was all very appealing, but you couldn't get these ingredients except in their locales, and even then they were often frozen. The age of airline shipping of fresh food would not arrive for at least a decade.

I had brought along one of my favorite books, a 1958 *Picture Cook Book* that listed the great American city restaurants of the day. Of the nineteen selected, we saw that only five served American-ingredient-driven menus, and they were all in either San Francisco or New Orleans. Of the photographed specialties from eight "America's Inns," only one—"devilled crab"—was American, and only the southern and Texas establishments had menus derived from regional ingredients. We decided that, seventeen years later, the two notable American restaurants (rather than Americanized European) were the Crown Center American Restaurant in Kansas City and The Four Seasons in New York, and Jim had consulted on both. We laughed about the former's Swiss German chef, who could just not resist the old European sauces (grand veneur) and garnishes on indigenous American ingredients like Montana elk, Columbia River salmon, Olympia oysters, South Dakota pheasant, and smoked Minnesota turkey.

When Joe Baum, Jim Beard, and Restaurant Associates created The Four Seasons, an American benchmark was established, albeit at staggering costs. The menus were huge. A dinner had eighty items, not including the twenty or so dishes listed "as a Dinner Accompaniment" (no garnitures here), which might include "Nasturtium Leaves," a "beefsteak tomato, Carved Tableside," and "Broccoli Flowers." In block letters was written, "OUR FIELD GREENS ARE SELECTED EACH MORNING AND WILL VARY DAILY." Under the separate "Vegetables & Potatoes" section it said, "Seasonal gatherings may be viewed in their baskets."

They were obviously mad.

I could not get mallard duck or Jersey poularde, or frogs' legs. And I'm not sure how many of those ingredients were fresh and in perfect condition anyway. When I posed that question to Jim, he lifted what was left of his eyebrows in reply. Those brows over the years did a lot of rising and falling.

But the menu fascinated me. It was mainly in English and in its scope reminded me of an article called "Recent Menus" from an English publication named *The Epicure*. I had filed it years before under "Regional Dinner ideas," and I showed it to Jim; it featured a banquet "recently given at the California Hotel, San Francisco, the object of which was to prove the possibility of making up an extensive menu solely from the products of the State." No date is given for "A Californian Banquet," but a supper menu that follows, for three hundred at the National Skating Rink on London's Regent Street, is from 1896. Of the hundred or so dishes (some were just things like "puff crackers") I underlined Artichokes; Lettuce, Egg Sauce; Bear's Meat; Striped Eels, fried in butter; Spiced Pickled Cantaloupe; Black Halibut; October Strawberries; Frozen Watermelon; Figs White; Figs Black; Grape Fool.

"It's like Delmonico's," said Jim, "and from the same era."

"So how about an American restaurant!" we chimed in together.

I fell into his large arms and onto his even larger belly and gave him a big kiss before heading off to Panisse to cook dinner, proving Marion Cunningham wrong when she claimed that Beard was incapable of loving anyone. "And don't forget California wines," he bellowed as I was going out the door. Apart from Panisse, the only restaurants I knew pushing premium California wine were The Four Seasons, the Wooden Angel outside Pittsburgh, and Tampa's Bern's Steak House.

On the taxi ride home, I thought about the complexity of Jim's personality. He was like an erratic elevator car, one that could take you up fast but sometimes, when you stepped in, wasn't there. Like all the great men I had met, he had two parts. The big jolly one and the big-tempered one. One could never claim to know him until one had seen the temper-induced flapping and flying of his weighty and ponderous jowls, their quivering a preface to an even more serious seismic body event and a stentorian roar. I'd seen it for the first time a few weeks before in a Nob Hill restaurant. I had finished bandaging his startlingly black and maroon legs, had massaged the even worse feet, rewrapped the bandages, taken tea, heard the latest gossip, seen on the coffee table the latest unreleased cookbooks and endorsement proposals, and listened to what was going on in the cooking world and its satellites. Then it was time for my taking him to lunch in the new restaurant of his choice. We were oiled to the table by the maître d.' The owner's prostration made Jim nervous from the outset. Nothing went well. The food was mediocre, our guests fidgety. Jim's already pink face turned even redder, splotched with streaks of purple. Those jowls started to quiver, but he held himself back. When his espresso arrived the jowls went into full swing. "Who asked for lemon zest in the coffee?" he roared. The waiter looked as if he might make a puddle; I hid. Soon his cane was found and he launched himself, Robert Morley–like, into the foyer. "And furthermore, the coleslaw was terrible."

I stretched to a new height and said, "OK, Jim, but whose coleslaw is better? Your uncle Billy's or my aunt's?" Jim looked at me fiercely. His body stopped heaving and began to roll; tears appeared and he roared again, this time in laughter.

A month earlier I had my thirty-third birthday lunch with Jim at New York's Maxwell's Plum. There was something coyly in the air, and it wasn't until after our hamburgers and a magnum of Dom Pérignon (I was paying) that he offered the usual advice: write a cookbook and take on the job of chef there—in no particular order. After lunch he called his editor, Judith Jones, at Knopf to set up a meeting about doing a Chez Panisse cookbook, and we looked at the kitchen at Maxwell's Plum. It was far too small to make all the dishes on the menu, and I could see why the chef wanted to leave. There were four-foot-high mounds of bus tubs packed with food oozing out of them and spilling down the narrow stairs. When I left I stopped to wipe my alligator shoes. "That's New York, my dear." I gave up on the idea of moving to New York and redoubled my efforts to capture America.

A few months later in 1976 I was hit with three bombshells, one professional and two culinary. After the glowing *Gourmet* review, Willy quit. He could not stand the idea of "food weenies or trendies," who float from restaurant to restaurant, like the one out in the dining room soon after the article who kept demanding dishes we didn't have but had served weeks before. That lone diner had a copy of that *Gourmet* open on his lap under the table. The first culinary bombshell was Jim Villas's article in *Town & Country* called "At Last, A Table of Our Own." The second was the Gault and Millau article summing up what was happening in France in a way that was to catch the imagination of all Western food chefs and writers. In their *On the Town in New York*, Michael and Ariane Batterberry put it well: All unnecessarily complicated cooking was to be dumped. In order to "reveal forgotten flavors," cooking times were to be reduced, and the new style was designated a *cuisine du marché*, cooking inspired by what is found in the marketplace and reliant on the freshest seasonal produce—a proposition that would lead to collaborative efforts between chefs and breeders of livestock, cheese artisans, vegetable and fruit growers, to secure the finest. Domineering sauces were to be discouraged, especially any thickened with flour; game was to be served fresh and not high from hanging; regional dishes would be reexamined; technological breakthroughs like the food processor were encouraged in the interests of convenience, speed, and virtuosity; long menus, once the hallmark of "Grand Hotel" or "Continental Cuisine," were to be discouraged. I recognized that a less formal in-house printing job could mean that the chef could finalize a seasonal market menu honoring the day's best fresh produce mere hours before the meal service.

Villas's article was about "the possible existence in the United States of a slowly developing formalized American cuisine, a stylized native cookery that might one day rival the European and Far Eastern culinary traditions." He mentions the Bicentennial "American Culinary Festival" that Hilton International was holding around the world during the summer of '76: "Sea Bass with Ginger," which Jim described as Californian; "Berkeley Banana Fritters" (in Tehran!); and "Peanut Soup," "Black Bottom Pie," and "Shoo-Fly Pie" (in Hong Kong!). I knew the Hilton chefs were fishing in unchartered waters: bananas from Berkeley? Perhaps just menu alliteration.

My notes from Villas's article read: "Duck with Quince Puree; Walnut-Macadamia Nut Crepes—make crepes with cornmeal; Sweetbreads with Crayfish Ragout; Oysters with Green Chilis Vinaigrette with Meyer Lemons; California Cheeses; think Thomas Jefferson." None of those dishes had been cited, but the article was so provocative I started making up my own.

But I had still some work based in France and its great traditions that I needed to finish.

Finishing France

As 1976 opened, Alice and I were starting to go in different directions. We were equal partners in the restaurant, and up to this point had avoided confrontations. But she didn't agree that great restaurants should have cafés attached to them. I believed that revamping the upstairs of Panisse would be its financial saving, as well as bring in new, younger, and less affluent "starter" customers. And we needed nonreservation seating, since our fame had brought also the ruinous phenomenon of no-shows.

The fact that I was living temporarily in her house made the arguments turn final. Alice had recently been assaulted there and didn't want to stay alone, and she didn't regard Willy, before he quit, living in the garage with his paintings, as protection. It was not long before the close quarters became claustrophobic. It had been a while since Alice and I had sat on the terrace of Venice's Gritti Palace in the moonlight sipping vintage Krug champagne, or stayed with friends on a romantic trip to Nice. Both were wonderful memories, but I was newly seeing, and in love with, someone else. One night I did not come home when I said I would. Moreover, I had forgotten my keys. She met me on the steps, screaming loudly enough to bring out the neighbors. "It's my house!" she shrieked (which was true), "my car [the restaurant's], and my restaurant [she owned 10.4 percent]!" It was such a preposterous lovers'-tiff performance (a woman scorned) that all I could say was "May I have my toothbrush?" I took "her" car.

The next day while eating the last of the crystallized fruits that Alice and I had bought at Vogade in Nice, I decided to take a break and think. Or quit. But whatever, it was time to find myself again.

I left a note for my love saying that the only difference between caprice and a lifelong passion is that caprice lasts a little longer, and sent a roomful of parrot tulips to Alice with an apologetic note. "Like Lord Henry's wife," it said, "she was usually in love with somebody and, as her passion was never returned, she had kept all her illusions." I told her I had drafted a cookbook called "A Matter of Course," taken from Zuleika Dobson: "As the homage of men became for her, more and more, as a matter of course, the more subtlety was necessary for her happiness."

I fled to Paris, only to run out of money two months later and terrify myself with lots of nights alone in the Île-St.-Louis apartment above Marc Chagall, which I rented from Pavel Tchelitchev's former lover Charles Henri Ford. My thoughts turned back to California and employment. In Paris I no longer felt starved of educational intellect as I had in Berkeley, "a soul exhausted by concealed thoughts." I shrugged off my latest obsession, the young and godlike godson of the Queen of England who said of the Bay Area, "It's a pleasant euphoria, but not for me," and thought of how to get back. I returned to a frugal little abandoned motel room in Berkeley, and put up the poster of the SS *France*.

Alice felt abandoned by my leaving, but while I was away she had my wonderful sous-chef Jean-Pierre Moullé, who had long since given up his first notions that if food was not French, lobster, or filet mignon, it did not make for a serious restaurant. The menus from the time I was away were mostly the dishes we had done in the past, leaning heavily toward Provence, the Brittany Regional Dinner menu, and the dishes that I had brought back with me from Richard's house in the South of France. Emotionally bruised by French bureaucracy and shopkeepers, I looked around California with a new glee, even a little love.

I remembered all the conversations I'd had with Beard about my career, and all the doubts I had about California were transformed into a new focus as I reread Charles Ranhofer's cookbook from Delmonico's, *The Epicurean*. I realized I had been improvising for years, so why fret any longer about authenticity of "French" ingredients for French regional food? Why not just go shopping in Northern California and call that the region? I wrote a series of menus called "a week of the Cuisine of Charles Ranhofer, Former Chef of Delmonico's," including a dish called "Crème de maïs à la Mendocino." What in the world, I thought, was the chef of New York's most famous 1890s restaurant doing thinking about dishes local to small regions of California? Once again it was the soup that kick-started my future.

I was all fired up with new plans for Panisse even if I felt I was numbering my days. I told my partners all the ideas I'd come up with in France: an à la carte menu for Panisse downstairs, including four menus starting at the low end of ten dollars (as in a menu touristique) to the high end of twenty-five dollars (menu gastronomique with California Country ham, oysters, spit roasted quail), a café menu, a list of "dishes available on command one week in advance" (Tripes à la mode de Caen, Lobster bordelaise chez Denis, Choucroute garnie Brasserie Flo, et cetera), and a new statement of our philosophy for the menu: "If there is ever a dish on the menu that is not available, it will be because of the caprices of the weather, the fish themselves, the transport services, and our own limitations. We would rather buy sometimes scarce first-rate good ingredients and run out of them than compromise standards and disappoint ourselves and the customer."

Alice was dead set against the ideas, though not the philosophy; only the headwaiter, Gerry Budrick, and I were in favor. I decided to stay until the end of the year and let them all buy me out.

After I said I was leaving, the board listed Chez Panisse at a price Herb Caen reported on May 26, 1976, as $500,000. Now that the restaurant "has made a big splash with the critics, the owners are tired," he wrote.

Meanwhile, the first reviews saying that Panisse was becoming pretentious appeared. I felt we were not pretending to do anything but actually trying and most of the time succeeding. My partners were unnerved. They felt I was taking them down a path they did not know.

Reviewers wondered if we had our anchor out. Some guests wrote. A Robert Scheer complained that Panisse at ten dollars per person was "expensive" (untrue) and a "hangout for drug pushers" (true). I replied that Panisse was a victim of uninformed "radical-chic liberal veneer," since now the food was taken for granted and critics were focusing on things like us not having senior citizen discounts. One critic complained that Panisse was in a converted house, another that we were not expensive enough to survive.

And on it went, making me more determined than ever to keep from being defined—made or unmade—by the press. I was a bit defensive about our old house, which I'd redesigned three times. We now had heat, a chilled wine cellar, a carpet, and a pleasant atmosphere. It was also "world famous," because the great chef Jean Troisgros had actually asked if his nephew Michel could work with me in the kitchen. I was aghast. Troisgros was one of my heroes—I said it was I who should be studying with them. "Au contraire," he said, "you may not know what you have here, but I envy you and admire what you are doing with the food. I am jealous of your freedom to do what you want, to make the customers want what you do. I have to cook what the customers expect, and if I were to do it again I would do what you are doing."

Michel arrived and was part of the cooking team that took over from me with Jean-Pierre Moullé as their leader and executive chef. Mark Miller and Fritz Streiff, who had worked in Paris with Jacques Manière at Au Pactole, were the others.

Alice herself was now getting the hang of special festivals and events. Her main interest in 1976, others than friends' birthdays, was a benefit she did for Les Blank and his "Louisiana Playboys" to raise money for a film. Although I had a deft hand with gumbo and other dishes I'd learned in my culinary travels through Louisiana (our very first regional dinner at Panisse had been Creole), Alice imported a certain Creole "madame" to "authenticate" the food. She was hardly a madame, and she dealt a fair blow to that always-difficult concept of authenticity when she boiled twenty pounds of beef lung in our big soup pot, without salt, producing a mess so stinkingly ugly that even our resident tomcat, Blackie, hissed at it. We threw it out, and at the last minute I had to cook the whole meal.

"Authenticity" took on less meaning after that, and we all now saw it as a verbal and mental crutch. Its kissing cousin, "purity," raised even more hackles in my kitchen. Whenever I heard a cook say, "I am a purist," I knew that bean sprouts were only a moment away, and that his or her pets were fed macrobiotically. Despite our using Big Sur trout and California pigs, no one challenged the authenticity of my menu for an Alsace dinner we did later, which Alice called "one of the highlights of the last ten years":

Pigs' ears breaded and grilled, mustard sauce

Alsatian vinaigrette salads

Live Garrapata trout cooked in court bouillon, butter sauce

Munster cheese

Tart of dried fruit with a coffee cream

This was the last of the French festivals, since my mind was on America in my last year at Panisse. But I summoned up the energy for one final push, returning to the lessons of past masters in order to understand the forces that had shaped the current ones—even if only in reaction—and so create a foundation for the future. I announced we'd be educating both ourselves and the public with menus to "celebrate a great master, a great pupil, and their followers." The "master" was Escoffier, the "pupil" Olney, the "followers" the young French Turks Bocuse, Michel Guérard, and the Troisgros. Then I became caught up in the idea of educating the public and expanded the masters to include Carême (1784–1833; "I want order and taste"), Urbain Dubois (1818–1901; "a new order"), Prosper Montagné of *Larousse Gastronomique* (1865–1948; "Miracles? No, simply good food"), and Philéas Gilbert (1857–1934), who persuaded Escoffier that Montagné was right in a "reform" of the classic cuisine and service. I wrote a two-page history and handed it out to the public and staff.

The "Curnonsky Week" (regional French food) at Panisse two years before had been a huge success, and resulted in our first featured magazine article. But the roar of success from the Escoffier week—five days of my adapting menus from *Le Guide Culinaire* and *Ma Cuisine*, with a menu printed in side-by-side French and English—was heard for miles. Darrell Corti sent us a funeral wreath and a note that said there was nowhere to go except down after this little death moment of success.

That week was followed by two of the Olney menus, ending with one from Olney's Paris teacher, Georges Garin, that included a duck boned through the neck and left in one piece so it could be presented whole but sliced right through.

There remained one region: our own.

I was encouraged to take on America by an act of daring at The Four Seasons in March 1976, at the "First Annual California Vintners Barrel Tasting Dinner." The menu was in English with French terms only for those now accepted in American grand dining.

The dinner started with

Snapper Tartare

Fresh Foie Gras in Aspic

Medallions of Salmon

Quenelles of Shad

Velouté of Crayfish

Spring Chicken in Riesling (Phelps)

Risotto of Mussels

The wines were Wente, Château St. Jean, Freemark Abbey, Parducci, Mirassou, Phelps, and Beaulieu for these courses.

The dinner went on for several more courses, including

Émincé of Young Rabbit

Pâté of Pheasant

Veal and Morels in Cream

Stuffed Quail with Pistachio

Tournedos of Beef with Marrow

Sliced Breast of Duck Bigarade

Essence of Fennel

Duck Livers with Apples and Cabernet

Sweetbreads in Brioche

Roast Rack of Spring Lamb

French Cheeses

Mignardises

This menu seemed wonderfully way over the top, but the language was elegantly restrained, a combination I thought was perfect. I wondered if any of the diners knew just how New York it was, in the Astor fortune and Diamond Jim Brady grand tradition.

I loved the daring of this menu and now wanted to have our own new region at Panisse. My menu, in English, was a celebration of our new sense of place, of where we lived and ate.

The Northern California Regional Dinner

October 7, 1976

Spenger's Tomales Bay bluepoint oysters on ice

Cream of fresh corn soup, Mendocino style, with crayfish butter

Big Sur Garrapata Creek smoked trout steamed over California bay leaves

Monterey Bay prawns sautéed with garlic, parsley, and butter

Preserved California geese from Sebastopol

Vela dry Monterey Jack cheese from Sonoma

Fresh caramelized figs

Walnuts, almonds, and mountain pears from the San Francisco
Farmers' Market

In his *The Last Days of Haute Cuisine: America's Culinary Revolution*, Patric Kuh predicts that this night at Panisse "would be one of the great switching points in American gastronomy." I didn't have such high-flying sentiments then: I was more concerned with writing a whacking good part for myself, as Noël Coward said about the high "morality" some saw in his play *The Vortex*. All I knew at the time was that for me there were only three months to go. So I amused myself with a series of menus to amuse everyone else: for the "Society of Grand Stomachs"; one "For the Spirit"; a "Black and White"; and some old favorites that spanned a century or so.

The menu on what was meant to be my last night, New Year's Eve 1977, was ambitious. Paul Bocuse's truffle soup (which he did for the president of France at the Élysée Palace), roast fresh quail on a bed of watercress (au vert pré), California cheese, chocolate cake with nougat ice cream, bon-bons, and a croquembouche for every table, all for twenty-five dollars per person.

At the end I was standing by myself at the pastry table in the back of the kitchen while everyone else was celebrating the passing of the old year, still making one- and two-foot towers of pastry-cream-filled prof-iteroles stuck together with hot caramel. I remember laughing bitterly at the irony that I should have my arms and hands burned by the hot caramel in order to fix this most festive of French desserts—when Amer-ican chocolate cake would have done just as well. My French-American schizophrenia was dead after that night, well gone by the time the burn scars had healed. Beard was right. Love for me had been lost, but then I had been a fickle lover.

The Final Bow

I did return once more to cooking at Panisse. It was at the end of 1978, after I had worked at Ventana in Big Sur for six months in 1977, and with Richard Olney at Time Life books in London. Alice wanted to take the last three months off and did not trust the kitchen team headed by Jean-Pierre to hold the fort—especially when she heard that Beard would be coming back after Christmas. The previous nine months of dishes had been pretty much drawn from the material we did when I was there, with more Richard Olney menus; another Alice B. Toklas dinner; and menus like huîtres natives, crêpes bretonnes, porc braise au cidre, salade ou fromages, fruits of which Alice was proud, since she included that menu in the 1982 Panisse cookbook. The menus she left me with to start off the ninety-days' absence were "The Best of Chez Panisse." It was very familiar territory, so I left most of the work to Jean-Pierre and the others while I busied myself trying to launch an American restaurant in San Francisco. I would write the last few weeks of menus and go out, again, with a bang.

There was a bit of tension in the kitchen, however, since I was there for no particular reason other than to soothe Alice's nerves. Michel wanted to show the latest beurre blanc from Troisgros. Mark was inclined to think he knew everything already. And Fritz had never forgiven me for laughing at him when, during an important wine tour with Olney and a group of American journalists, he returned to our hotel room in Strasbourg with a bloody nose—having been attacked in a public men's room.

After the Best of Chez Panisse festival was finished, I did a week in honor of cooks who had influenced Panisse menus the most: "Richard Olney, Prosper Montagné, Auguste Escoffier, Elizabeth David, and My Russian Uncle." For the last week of the year I asked Mark, Alice, Jean-Pierre, and Michel to take a night each and write their own menus. All of them had so much difficulty deciding what to cook that I took over their menus. My Saturday night menu was:

Fresh select Tomales Bay oysters on ice with lemon and Pernot

Poached fresh sturgeon with caviar butter

Capon stuffed under the skin with truffles Lucien Tendret (homage to Alexandre Dumaine)

Crêpes Suzettes in the original manner of Auguste Escoffier at the Carlton Hotel in London

What would be my very last Chez Panisse menu coincided with Beard's visit: "The Orlando Dinner: Following the Last Hundred Years," a four-course affair with Carême (ragout of vegetables in a puff pastry, which he called "Moderne"); Escoffier (his oyster "favorites" with black truffles); Point and Dumaine (white veal loin with cream, truffles, and fresh noodles); and then "New and Future" (fresh fruit with creamed chilled papaya yogurt with macadamia nuts). But I never got to do it. When Alice returned and saw that Beard was coming to dinner on December 27, 1977, she condoned a palace revolt. She said that the chefs wanted to cook for Beard by themselves. And with a different menu.

I saw Jim at his hotel as usual that morning, and told him I would not be cooking. "I guess they don't want me to know you have been holding their hands." He giggled.

"Do you think I should force the issue?" I asked him.

"Jeremiah, you have already done that. If I were you I wouldn't ever go back. You should have never agreed to fill in for Alice in the first place."

The next morning he called me early.

"Well, that was god-awful," he bellowed, with just a tinge of accusation, as if had been my fault.

"The duck was inedible," he said, then went on to scold me for every dish as if I had been there cooking it. "At least that reviewer [Merrill Shindler] said that the public noticed your food when Alice was gone, even if she called you 'oft-crazed.' But don't do it again."

I went to his room to kiss and make up, and then went home to reread Alice's farewell letter, which she'd written on a piece of yellow-pad lined paper. "Dear Jeremiah," it started, and then expressed how hard it was for her to accept the fact that I wanted to leave Chez Panisse before going on to say that our relationship and the restaurant would not be so vital after I left.

I would not go so far to say, like Ford Madox Ford, that "there is no man who loves a woman that does not desire to come to her for the renewal of his courage, for the cutting asunder of his difficulties," but Alice did some of that for me originally. Now this private Alice showed it was the same for her still.

But the public Alice had another face: By my last year she had already begun being circumspect with the press, editing what she could about where credit in the kitchen and the success of the business should fall. If that is what she needs to do, I felt in 1978, so be it: What harm could it do to let her have the limelight? After all, we had been partners and equal co-owners, and I had always given her credit and told her when photographers would be around (a gesture she did not return). I knew that there was plenty of room for everyone. But within the next few years I was beginning to be a bit edgy about the extent of her editing.

Alice gave her first interview from Panisse after I had gone in *New West*, and her faults became mine in print. She talked of the garden to be founded in Amador County, and so began the myth of the gardener with the little sun hat and Provençal basket full of wild mushrooms and little lettuces. She said that she was the chef, flying in the face of "old conservative menus." Linda Guenzel, who wrote *The Chez Panisse Menu Cookbook*, wondered with me over the telephone about that comment, and agreed this was pretty funny given the Dalí menus and their leg of lamb "drogué et sodomisé." But Alice believed in her role so much that when it leaked out in the press that Jean-Pierre Moullé was really the chef, she wanted me to fire him even though I had not been his boss in months.

The press began to believe Alice totally.

When later they said that Alice was tired, that there were too many fingers in the pie, that Panisse was now just a case of the emperor's new clothes, Alice described herself not as the chef but as the "orchestrator." She lamented that it was very difficult to be so successful "and not have people upset." She was referring to Linda Guenzel. At least of me she said, "I would never consider him a protégé of mine."

When Robert Finigan wrote in 1983 that dishes poorly executed and badly served were coming out of the café and main dining room with alarming frequency, Alice said he was nitpicking and just looking for something to write about. Jean-Pierre Moullé had gone back to France, and the general press feeling was that Panisse had lost it. One article said that even though Alice wanted a one-star restaurant, by 1983 it had no stars at all.

In 2001, the thirtieth anniversary party was a national event, lauded by everyone. Reading all those accounts of the party, I thought Alice could replace all those little lettuces in her arms with both arms full of awards—and sit back for a well-earned rest.

Paul McCartney summed up our relationship when talking in 2001 on American TV about his with John Lennon: "We had a war in the newspapers."

CHAPTER 4

A Region Called California

The Second Great American Menu

"DEAR JEREMIAH TOWER" is how my second letter of employment read. "Your salary will be $22,000 gross . . . and the starting date will be July 15, 1977."

Actually, I didn't start until a few months later, because the Ventana Inn in Big Sur was in a mess—had I known how much, I would not have taken the job. But in that halcyon beginning, both the general manager, Lee Ivey, and I thought that a great American restaurant in the middle of several hundred California coastal acres—a wilderness of frozen vegetables and chef's salads—would bring us national attention and fill up the Inn.

So I set out to write the Great American Menu.

I went to my collection of American menus from the past and dug out my Massachusetts farm plans for a country inn fruit and vegetable garden. The first menu I found was from the "Southern Pacific Special Train" in September 1959 that took "Nikita Khrushchev and Mrs. Kruscheva" from Los Angeles to San Francisco: Caviar Frappé, Omelet with Walnut Jelly, Strip of Bacon, Fried Young Chicken, White Wine–Flavored Au Sec [sic], and so on. No wonder there was a Cold War! This was boarding-school food, not what I knew America could do better, and a long cry from America's first luxury train and its dining car, the Delmonico. I looked at a menu that René Verdon, the ex-chef under the Kennedys, had given me from the 1962 White House. The language was compromised French, like "Pommes Chipp," but then I remembered the Kennedys and the day I was drinking Jack Daniel's in my Boston "Champagne Palace" when Jack was shot, and put the menu aside.

Perhaps further back in the past was the clue to the future. A 1936 dinner menu from Yosemite's Ahwahnee Hotel began with the usual appetizer, a flat glass dish of celery and olives, as well as the ubiquitous first course, Grapefruit with Honey, broiled or not. Then the standard prime rib "au jus," Virginia ham (it wasn't), and Broiled Half Spring Chicken, Spiced Blue Plums. It was a September menu, but it had no hint of season- ality, so I put that aside as well.

A 1941 pre–war rationing San Francisco Western Women's Club menu seemed more promising, though not with Lemon Ring Salad with Seedless Grapes and Stuffed Figs, which reminded me too much of my New En- gland grandmother and her grape peeling. But Sliced Avocado, French Dressing, Crab and Grapefruit Louis seemed likely to please the rich ladies of Carmel and the Pebble Beach Club, and Broiled Sweetbread au Beurre Noir, Crisp Bacon would please the serious eaters.

A souvenir menu from the "SS *Morazan*" of the Standard Fruit & Steamship line (with my mother and sister aboard) encouraged me more with its Calf's Brains Vinaigrette and Sauté of Lamb Kidneys, and bowled me over by including a place on the menu for autographs—a bit of public relations I copied immediately. But it was a 1961 menu from the Mon- tecito Room at the Clift Hotel in San Francisco that sealed my determina- tion to update the future with a bit of grace from the past. The food was pointedly seasonal (Fresh Cracked Crab Now in Season), and there wasn't a French word in sight. It included even Grand Central Station Oyster Stew ($1.75), for which I made a pilgrimage every time I visited New York. On the back it invited diners to "Mail this menu to a friend"—and paid the postage. An eminently stealable idea.

That was the past; now I had to look around at the present. When Cecilia Chiang, America's greatest Chinese restauratrice, told me that momentous things were afoot in Los Angeles, I knew I had to take the tour. It was early 1977, and her itinerary listed her new Mandarin, Mr. Chow, Le St. Germain, La Scala Boutique, Rex, Le Bistro, the Palm, Le Restaurant, L'Ermitage, Chaya, and the soon-to-open Michael's in Santa Monica. The black-and-white decor at Mr. Chow's was daring; Rex was all homage to Art Deco; The Palm was interesting but couldn't hold a candle to New York steak houses; there was nothing new about the Italians; and the French restaurants were new only in that their owners were young, ambitious, and of a generation not quagmired in preconceptions. What were new, and already resonating with the drumbeat of revolution, were the restaurants created by young Americans steeped in the traditions of France yet just beginning to express their California background and lifestyle in food, attitude, and decor.

The three restaurants that in the late seventies gave birth to the "Cali- fornia" look were the West Beach Café in Venice, Michael Roberts's Trumps, and Michael McCarty's Michael's. The first was a single room, its bar featuring glass shelves that held fifty single-malt whiskeys and cognacs. It took my breath away, then breathed into me the courage to banish red plush ("serious restaurant") forever. I loved the irony that the most avant-garde and trend-setting "first" hailed from that roller-skating little beach town named after an Italian city, and I loved even more the stark white concrete decor that changed every few months depending on the arrange-ment of the sand sculpture around the dining room cornice. Sitting at its concrete bar waiting for my lunch guests to arrive, I felt immediately that this look was going to be the new restaurant establishment.

Trumps was pure Michael Roberts, insanely individual, almost uncom-fortable in its concrete bunker style of chic, its menu in the new California colors of white and beige, ferociously spare in its English ("cold lobster pesto," or "grilled swordfish"), the whole place daring in everything from its lack of flourish to its new Italian glassware.

Michael's food was basically French bistro, but the interior and exterior were a new version of Mediterranean (Vergé's Moulin de Mougins) that was a whole new California style. At my first lunch, I had a grilled chicken with pommes frites and watercress that was the perfect spirit of French bistro cooking, but better than most in France could do it. The chef was the young, bushy-haired American Jonathan Waxman. Out front was Michael McCarty, in azure tie, slicked back hair, and Susan Bennis–Warren Edwards ocelot loafer-slippers. The waiters, the umbrellas in the open garden, the curtains, the walls, the tablecloths, were all the color of Michael's suit—off-white toward cream. We sat at a garden table. Marion Cunningham was along and chattered away, but I could barely talk. Cecilia knew why: I was choked up by seeing and sitting in the future.

I knew what I had to do, but jobless, first I had to make enough money to eat.

Richard Olney had written that he'd been hired for a Time-Life series called *The Good Cook*. The twenty volumes were to be heavily illustrated with how-to photo spreads, and to keep the costs down the recipes had to have been previously published and in the public domain. That meant surfing the last four centuries of cookbooks for material. The French and Italian recipes had to be translated, and all the recipes had to be usably formulated: Would I come to the South of France, he wrote, look after his house whenever he was in London, and translate the old texts? I called him when the Ventana negotiations bogged down, and by April I was liv-ing with Richard, surrounded by dictionaries, lexicons, chickens, and an old Corona typewriter.

While translating old French cookbooks into English in his little farmhouse in Provence, I reveled in the local ingredients from the markets and the garden, cooked, ate out, and continued to plan the second great American seasonal menu (the first being The Four Seasons's in New York). So when I had lunch at Roger Vergé's three-star Moulin de Mougins in the June heat of the French Riviera near Nice, I was amazed at how unseasonal the menu was. It was 1:30 on a Sunday afternoon, boiling hot, and I had the best table in the house, looking out at the garden. After some cool white wine I stared at the huge menu card and felt ill: It was, in effect, a dinner menu for February. Was there nothing light, cold, refreshing? I asked. The waiters stared. Not even a salad? Non. My friend John Sanger and I shared a grilled lobster because it was the closest thing to something cold. A chicken and foie gras terrine was superb—but foie gras should be outlawed in the South from May to September. After seeing the bill of $140 for two, I could not blame the poodle at the next table for biting the waiter when he served it a $40 lobster salad under the table.

The next morning, despite the insanity of the Mougins chefs putting sugar in their sauces, I felt unexpectedly nostalgic for the restaurant business. Since rumors were afoot that Richard was up to something and, for the first time in his life, in the chips, a flurry of the famous came through the little house on the hill above Toulon. Naomi Barry, at the top of her form in *Gourmet* and the *Herald Tribune,* told me over a May dinner of zucchini flowers stuffed with green fresh almonds (and after the first bottle of Cheval-Blanc 1948) that I should go to New York to find my fortune. A week later the collector Mary Guggenheim, and the writers Edouard Roditi and Philippe Jullian suggested Paris. The novelist Sybille Bedford, over several bottles of Krug, said I should try London. Over a lunch of oysters and "pourpres," Michael James of Robert Mondavi Cooking School fame and Julia Child's *Mastering the Art of French Cooking* coauthor Simca Beck said nothing that wasn't petulant. Julia was without any advice at all. I wrote the general manager of Ventana and said that I was hot, tired, and mentally exhausted after two days of Simca, Richard, Julia Child, English writers, unbelievable Côte d'Azur rich lesbians, and U.S. Cuisinart salesmen, but ready to return. Then Richard said I should forget the whole terrible nonsense of running a restaurant and live with him, but first he wanted me to join him in London, meet the Time-Life editors, and apply for the job of creating *The Good Cook* with him.

In London, Rudolf Nureyev said I should live with a dancer, which was the only sane advice I received until Elizabeth David advised me to have another glass of white wine. "Oh dear," she said, "oh dear," her voice trailing off into memories of when she was young and beautiful. "If you must" (go back to restaurants), she went on, "let's go and look at Boule-stin's. Perhaps you could revive that. And the Dufy's, even if a bit faded, are very pretty."

I have hardly ever been as happy as when having lunch with Elizabeth. Not so much because of the restaurants of choice, in which anything could go wrong and the hours could be filled with more "oh dears" than eating. But the conversations—which would come to life after the second glass of wine and continue until she'd called it quits in her Chelsea kitchen at around seven in the evening—were spectacular.

Mention of James Beard elicited two further "oh dears" before a long pause and the observation "He could be very sweet, but what about all those rather louche boys?" Certainly there had been enough queens in her life—that was not the point. It was more about Jim's scholarship: Could he really concentrate on the culinary matters at hand, she wondered, while obsessing about rent (as she saw them) boys? Was there perhaps just too much of Oscar in Beard?

Of Alice she said, "She *does* mean well"—although she wondered why, if Alice regarded her as the first inspiration for Chez Panisse, she'd never actually bothered to contact her. But she was flattered that someone should pay her such homage for so long. Elizabeth was far from ungrateful, and later, while visiting her friend Gerald Asher, the wine writer for *Gourmet,* in San Francisco, she met Alice and became very fond of her.

Before she came to know Richard Olney well, his name provoked an "*oh dear*" and a very long silence. In the beginning she thought Richard a bit of a bombast and a snob about wines. She hated his restaurant scenes, when invariably he would call over the waiter and tell him to plunge the red wine (1947 Cheval-Blanc at the Ritz one lunch) in an ice bucket. He was quite right to, of course, since those wines tended to be a too warm dining room rather than cellar temperature. Later, when the great wines flowed and flowed, she became more tolerant—but we did stop going to restaurants with him.

After a long Saturday lunch at our flat in London, I would take Eliza-beth home at five and we would dig into quite a lot of Chablis to reestab-lish her sense of reality. Both of us would feel a tiny bit guilty as I got up to open the third bottle, but Elizabeth would inevitably sigh, "Well, if we must." Then we would continue talking about whatever latest scholarship possessed her. Perhaps how the Romans transported ice to chill their creams, and did I know anything about New England icehouses? Did Richard as a boy really have chilled oysters brought in by train as late as May in Marathon, Iowa?

I adored her.

It was time to go only when we both got teary-eyed over some past and improperly forgotten glory—such as restaurant service in the fifties, or how a real sole Colbert or côtelette Milanese should be cooked. Then she would wipe away the ever rebellious strands of wispy gray hair, her Garboesque former beauty now glorious only in its suggestions of past magnificence, and lift to my face her robin's egg blue eyes, now clouding over with fatigue and old age. As I kissed her good night, my heart would break at the delicious sadness of her brilliant mind in a body so gracefully tendered into frailty.

Back in Richard's house in France, alone and consoled with a twenty-year-old Côte Rotie with whole lamb kidneys encased in their fat and cooked very slowly in earthenware in the embers of the kitchen fire, with wild thyme from this Provençal hillside above the house, I thought sadly of the ingredients I was used to. The best American produce was still in Southern California, but could I live in Los Angeles? I thought not.

The next morning over a plate of Tunisian oranges sprinkled with sage-flower sugar, a double café au lait, and a tartine slathered with Normandy butter and wild fig jam, I wondered why I would ever leave France. But I wrote a list of food to serve at Ventana, even if we had to grow our own.

Suggestions for a Lunch Menu

Virginia ham with California fruits

Smoked local Big Sur trout

A devastating green salad with our own fresh herbs, and herb flowers

"Fruit salads" with sauces like watermelon vinaigrette

Pickled shrimp

Chicken and pheasant hash

Paso Robles peaches in local red wine

Shad roe on toast

Chicken pie Delmonico

Wild boar, walnut vinaigrette

Scrambled eggs with sweetbreads

Macadamia nut cream pie

Cathy Simon's Blackbottom pie

It was mid-1977, and California was calling. Old Rhônes, a perfect butcher in the village owned by the "Mouton" sisters, five-dollar white wine made by local priests, original Piaf records at four in the morning as the mistral blew through the terrace cork-beaded curtains (each cork a memory of a perfect meal), Richard in sweat-soaked and revealing gardening bikinis—none of these could delay my return. I'd have to get on with it. Back in Berkeley I packed up Alice's old house, where I had lived; filled the car with wine, the cat, and Gregg; and drove to Big Sur.

The three of us moved into the little cabin on the highway, the hundred-year-old Pfeiffer homestead of this original landowning Big Sur family. From the beginning it was filled with the feelings of Big Sur, which, stories of UFOs and ghostly magnetic fields aside, is one of the most magical and spiritual places on earth. No matter what horrors happened up in the restaurant, the mornings on the back porch with my Earl Grey tea in the light of the rising sun reflected on the honey-colored hills, looking at my usually spooky Abyssinian cat now cross-eyed with contentment, were as happy as any this side of France. If up at the restaurant I felt like a UFO myself, in the cottage I have never felt so at home.

My Mexican restaurant staff was a godsend, their jefe a dream. But even then I needed help. Ventana's restaurant in the summer was a seven-day-a-week, 250-seater, serviced by a three-man cook team. The bad habits that had set in after a long period of neglect could hardly be eradicated by one person. Then there was the INS's habit of rushing in at the busiest times and sending the Mexican cooks scattering into the fields below, their white hats high in the air and aprons fluttering after them—all very amusing to the guests, until they figured out the relationship between disappearing cooks and nonappearing food.

In addition to preparing the menus, I oversaw the inn's and the store's baked goods from our shared pastry shop down the hill. This little fiefdom, like the rest of the operation, saw me only as a disturber of the old ways. Nothing I could do would convince the pastry chef to get rid of the cream fillings that needed no refrigeration for months on end. I was desperate. Marion Cunningham, in a break from washing Beard's feet, offered to help. She sent me three ideas on a piece of foolscap paper: rhubarb with crème anglaise, a rhubarb ring with strawberries, and baked bananas. The American public then wouldn't touch rhubarb, and I hadn't gone near the smell of cooking bananas since my time on that Italian ship from Australia. Hearing Marion's ideas, Beard snorted. "Well, my dear, she's great at cookies." From then on Marion would be known to us as "Cookie."

I called Panisse and a few friends and begged for help right after I started. To my surprise, everyone showed up, with Alice leading the caravan. Then the sensible ones decamped after a week; only my old pal and sous-chef Willy remained. He had as much disdain as I did for the man who claimed to be the owner, but Willy stayed on.

After one of Pebble Beach's richest women refused anything but chef's salad made with the frozen canned cheese that I had inherited from the previous kitchen administration, I had a talk with Lee, the general manager. My confidence was shaken. Together we reviewed the rest of my original menu ideas:

Excellent steaks (a ranch connection in Santa Barbara)

All grilling to be done on wood or real charcoal

Vodka in a block of ice—small individual bottles

Aquavit the same way (do our own herring)

All fruit and vegetable juices done to order at the bar

Lillet with champagne

Juleps

Fiuggi water only

I was getting carried away, I told him, so went back to the grilled food:

Roast duck with Big Sur blackberries or green walnuts

California real chicken with Napa Valley olives

Beef cheeks in bread crumbs

Charcoal grilled tuna steaks with our fresh herb butters

Live trout

Oysters out of our tank, on a bed of ice, with our own lemons

Deviled ribs

A wonderful boiled dinner, beef, chicken, and duck, vegetables, salt pork belly, little cornmeal dumplings

Parsnip cakes with watercress salad

Pigs' feet or sheep trotters on johnnycakes

Whole fish grilled over wild fennel branches and rosemary

Smoked Big Sur lamb

Bread and butter pudding with pears

Syllabubs

Turtle Cay bananas in rum with mango ice cream

Tangerine sherbet served in the fruit

"And let's change the menu every two months, and do the breakfasts with everything raised on the property—the honey, the jams, stone-ground flours, Indian cakes, espresso machines in every room," I said.

"I realize this is only a list and not menus. What is American food, let alone Californian?"

"Let's go for it again," Lee said. We did, and almost everyone hated the food. I lasted less than a year.

But there was one menu left in me before I took my American menu on the road again. Beard was in San Francisco, and I invited him down for a dinner in his honor. Amongst the group of twelve were Alice Waters in Victorian black lace, a black ribbon at her throat holding a gardenia; Marion Cunningham in denim; an impeccable Cecilia Chiang in Mandarin clothes, pearls, and emeralds; and Darrell Corti in English tweeds. Jim loomed large next to Emile Norman who, I had told Jim, had introduced me to the glories of drinking great wine, naked, in the countryside of Big Sur.

A Dinner for James Beard, at Ventana, Big Sur, California

January 7, 1978

Perrier-Jouët "Flower Bottle" 1971

Seafood service

Paiusnaya caviar blini

Consommé of Big Sur chanterelles

Petaluma pheasant salad
Chappellet Chardonnay 1974

Steamed Périgord truffles & potatoes
Château Haut-Brion 1970

Wild herb-roasted Wisconsin veal loin
Chalone Pinot Noir 1971

Fresh & aged Lafler Canyon goat cheeses

Troisgros "Opus Incertum"
Monterey Vineyard botrytis sauvignon blanc 1974

Entrance of the mandarins
Delamain très vieux Cognac du Grande Champagne
Corti single vintage Cognac selections

The tables were set with big glass globes full of water holding goldfish and sprays of cymbidium orchids. For the "entrance of the mandarins," an homage to Cecilia Chiang, we wheeled in an orange tree covered with mandarin oranges hanging from gold wires, to the overture of *Coppelia*. The waiters snipped the wires with fruit shears, and each guest was presented with an orange filled with a sorbet made from its own juice.

The gesture caught the breath of the guests, and the eyes of Ventana bugged. Now they thought I was truly mad. Later, when I posted the gushing letters of thanks from the famous, Lee and I were heroes.

No letter was as warmly written as the note from Alice.

"I will never forget a single moment," she wrote. She told me that every moment of the meal was unforgettable, and none so much as the black truffles, the moment when Darrell Corti read from Lucien Tendret's story of the "overindulgent nuns and their craving" for crayfish. Alive loved the sea urchins, the taste of the sea in the mussels, and the fact that the caviar on the blini was so thick that she could hardly see the little pancakes. She loved the entrance of the mandarin tree, and wondered, looking into what she said were my "sad, Escoffier eyes," what that look was all about?

I hoped Jim Beard would do for Ventana what he had done for Panisse, but we both knew it was too late. A few weeks later a fire burned most of the countryside and nearly the Inn. We were packed, our car engine running, the cat screaming at the prospect of leaving paradise—but the flames stopped a few hundred yards on the crest of the ridge above the cottage. Then when the rains followed the fire and washed out what was left of the village and our supply route from Carmel, charm of the countryside turned to nightmare and, given the Inn's nonexistent cash flow, I knew it was time to go.

So when four days later Richard Olney called from London and Time-Life's *Good Cook*, explaining that he could not handle both the photography studio cooking and the writing now that a book was due every two months, and asking, Would I come to London to cook? I felt that travel itch again.

London's *Good Cook*

Richard and I lived in the center of London, above the food photography studio and around the corner from the Time-Life offices on Bond Street. The schedule was rough but no worse than at a busy restaurant.

At seven every morning we'd review the day's shooting and the next day's writing. Then I would cook in front of the camera until 7:00 P.M., crawl upstairs to nosh on leftovers, drink some Lynch-Bages '66, and go over the next day's shoot until midnight. The late-night Scotches were soon relegated to Saturdays, which were devoted to finding and translating more recipes, outlining and writing the next books, and reviewing what we had done the previous week. Sundays, if not devoted to more of the same, meant lunches at the studio with writers, publicists, journalists, and friends. I made sure to put the sexy food on Friday's studio shoot. Nothing like a little leftover goose or suckling pig with a pumpkin and black truffle gratin for keeping the soul together.

I cooked for all of my London writer heroines, including the very English, large and wonderful Jane Grigson, whose presence in a room made one feel like taking off for a country cottage and cooking there forever. She was the woman whose book on charcuterie had helped me put Chez Panisse on the map. I had been dying to meet her. This lunch as recorded in my notebooks must have come during the making of "Beef and Veal," since the loin of veal was already roasted.

Lunch with Grigsons, Elizabeth David, Sybille Bedford, Richard Olney, Jill Norman (Penguin Books), Chez Nous, Conduit Street, London

July 9, 1978

Smoked salmon
Chablis, "Mont de Milieu" Pic 1975

Cold stuffed loin of veal with Montpelier butter
Château La Pointe 1971
Château Lafite 1962

Cheddar
Château Rieussec 1975

Goooseberry, Red Currant, Almond Fools
Château Filhot 1969

It must have been all the superb Sauternes, because somewhere in the end of that lunch, it was decided unanimously that we all go to Bordeaux for a weekend. So when the Comte and Comtesse de Lur-Salaces sent us an invitation to lunch at their Château d'Yquem, within days Richard and I were off to France with Sybille Bedford and the ex-wife of the director John Huston. Elizabeth did not go, thinking that more than two on the road was too much. The Yquem lunch lived in all our memories for all the obvious reasons, but for two that stood out: the taste of Sauternes with a crayfish sauce and the subsequent story of the Sauternes dinner at Panisse a few years before, and the red wine served in a plain carafe in the middle of the table but never offered. For years afterward we all wondered what one of the greatest men in the white wine business would offer for red wine in Bordeaux. I was restrained from asking, so we never found out.

We started the meal with Pommery & Greno champagne, a very old-fashioned gesture. Then:

Filets de sole au coulis d'écrevisses
Château de Fargues 1970

Caneton farcis
Vin rouge en carafe

Jardinière de légumes

Fromages
Château d'Yquem 1969

Frangipane
Château d'Yquem 1937

The dessert frangipane was a puff pastry with almond butter cream slathered in it, and it went perfectly with the '69 d'Yquem, which though not as famous as the '67, had more guts and held up to the cooked flavors of the puff pastry. The '37 seemed older than expected with a very deep color, but it was still bright. *Polite* and *round* were the words the others used. For me it was almost too polite. But it did have the infinity of a great Yquem.

After a tour of Latour, a tasting at Mouton with every wine from 1971 to 1976, and a lunch with the director of Lafite, it was back to London, reminded again how magnificent it is to taste wines that have never left the places they were born. Then my sister, Mary, rang from San Francisco with two pieces of news, one that was a devastating closure of the past and one that blew open the future. My mother had just died, and Mary had found a site for my new restaurant.

I was devastated that I would never share with my mother a grand hotel suite overlooking the Quirinale Palace, or a beach in Ceylon, or see her face seized in frozen politesse when a young plover was brought to the table at the Connaught smelling more like Pont l'Evêque than like perfect game. Starting with the huge and great parties in Sydney with people dancing until dawn after staggering buffets, and continuing on that ship from Australia while stopping at wonderlands of fresh pineapple, shops full of rubies and Egyptian gold necklaces, deep-carpeted Roman couture houses, and sea-urchin-filled seafood restaurants floating on the then clean Bay of Naples, my mother had shown me how to live.

Still dealing with losing my mother, I went to see the site Mary had found, a now run-down restaurant called Bacchini's, a version of an Old World red-plush Italian restaurant in the scary Civic Center part of town that only we believed would be great again. The owner of the space was polite if skeptical: I wasn't Italian and was far too young (thirty-five). That and the fact that when I walked into the restaurant, on its last day of business, it was so dark after the strong California sun that I tripped over the potted plants and fell into a jungle of plastic leaves and fronds. As I picked myself off the floor, the Sicilian attorneys rolled off their barstools and turned to me with eyes rock still. The only noise in the vast room was the sound of the owner's artificial leg scraping against the once-plush carpet, now slick with decades of grime. No expense had been spared when the restaurant was built, in 1961, but it took a starry-eyed optimist to see even a trace of that grandeur now.

Yet I was breathless, and not just from the air, which hadn't been clean filtered in twenty years. It was the perfection of the setting. When my eyes grew used to the dark interior, I saw not the swarms of cockroaches eating the grease in the kitchen or the dirt-encrusted walls but a perfect stage setting for a grand American brasserie. I envisioned a place evoking the staying power of Delmonico's and Rector's, the food of Le Pavillon, and the ease and comfort of San Francisco mahogany-lined restaurants like Jack's, Sam's, and Tadich—but with new air tinged with the cordite smell of the California food revolution.

I saw it all as I dreamed of how to make again the powerful synergy between restaurants and freshly harvested ingredients, just as Delmonico's had done with its own truck garden in New Jersey in the nineteenth century. But I would keep that added expense to myself as I spent the next two years wooing, gaining, and losing investors in places as far flung as Alexandria, Virginia. I took any job that came along, and I continued my stint with the *Good Cook* series while giving parties for Eartha Kitt and Geoffrey Holder's rich friends and sponsors, for the younger sons of mainland Chinese warlords laundering money in the restaurant business, and for anyone else. To pay for the wonderful lunches and dinners, I accepted also any invitation to do cooking classes. The most lucrative were at Carole Steele's cookware store in Scottsdale, Arizona, the most fun with the bored of New York in Nantucket. The best were with Ken Hom in Berkeley.

"East Meets West" in Hot Fusion

In 1978 Ken was a long way from the *Independent* magazine's 2001 description of him as "a Buddhist monk in Gucci shoes." He was barely getting by, living totally unrecognized as one of the best cooks in America.

To make ends meet, he gave cooking lessons in his house in Berkeley. We used to cook together, his Chinese and my Franco-Californian food side by side. In 1977 he began teaching at the California Culinary Academy, from where some pupils, among them the now famous Chicago chef Charlie Trotter, went on to great success. Ken was a Chinese traditionalist—killing live chickens in the kitchen after showing how Chinese cooks tell if a bird is healthy by blowing the tail feathers away to inspect the anus—but a modernist as he combined French and other cuisines' principles with his Chinese cooking. So when Belle Rhodes, then doing public relations for wineries like Mondavi and Phelps, suggested in 1979 that we do some classes together in Napa, we agreed with enthusiasm.

She named the four days "East Meets West," an oft-used phrase nowadays but original at the time. She invited local and national press, a few bankers (for me), cooks from Panisse, and the cream of Napa Valley "society."

My notes show the design for the fruit and vegetable day:

Jeremiah	Ken
Ragout of vegetables	Vegetable stir-fry
Wilted salad with duck	Chicken skin steamed with spinach

Eggplant timbale with vegetable sauce

Fruit purees: raspberry soufflé, blackberry ice

Olallieberry sauce

Vegetable mu shu in pancakes

Bean curd with green onions

The first dish started off as planned, but then I began to covet Ken's Asian ingredients. And since Ken knew, loved, and cooked Western food, he coveted my Western ingredients right back.

I took some fermented Chinese black beans and salted duck for the wilted curly endive salad. He took my fresh herbs, vegetable purees, and extra-virgin olive oil. By the end of the first day, we were filching each other's mise en place at a furious rate, and the students were as fascinated as we were.

The second-day fish-and-shellfish menu morphed into a kind of cooking that no one had seen before, unless one had been to Richard Wing's surreal The Imperial Dynasty in the Central Valley's Hanford, where the menu featured things like tripe consommé garnished with various glandular parts of live Chinese frogs. Ken and I kept to the dishes on our list, but the printed recipes were virtually useless except to see the themes on which we cooked variations.

Jeremiah

Fish stew with artichokes

Sea urchin soufflé

Bouillabaisse

Zephyrs of fish mousse with fish soup

Ken

Sweet and sour cod with fruit

Scallion steamed fish

Sizzling rice shrimp

Blue crabs

My bouillabaisse turned into a fish stew with whatever was on the table, adding a flourish of Ken's sizzling shrimp. Ken set my artichokes and foie gras on his steamed fish, and some of the strawberries ended up in the sweet and sour cod. And so on it went. The next day he put his squab in puff pastry and I found a use for his noodle cakes. At the end of the last class, Belle said, "Jeremiah, something amazing happened here. Something really has now changed forever."

One student spoke for all: "There was a time when I would have been totally intimidated because I didn't have a specific recipe to follow. Now it's just a pleasure to watch them work and learn new rules." And the *San*

Francisco Examiner's Harvey Steiman opened his account with a boxing ring metaphor, with Ken in one corner and me in the other: "At the sound of the bell, Tower starts applying the techniques of Carême, Escoffier, and the French housewife. . . . Hom uses the centuries-old methods of Chinese chefs—and housewives." But this was not a war between two conflicting cuisines but an exploration of a spur-of-the-moment "market-basket" approach to cooking and menu making. In "the battle of the ducks, no winner was declared."

Back to the Chalkboard

Foie gras was not covered by our rather minimal food budget, so after the Napa event I was broke again. In the nick of time came a call from my friend Ron Batori, dean of the California Culinary Academy. Would I provide an antidote to their usual European classical recipes and sometimes worn-out techniques? I would have total freedom, he said. Ken had horrified the students by blowing up chickens' butts before killing them in the open kitchen. After that precedent, he said, my hands were free.

After I toured the Academy's kitchens, I called Ron back, shocked by all the carts piled high with five-gallon tins of Maggi stock and sauce bases. And those frightening canapés covered with industrial gelatin, made Tuesday to be served on Friday: What was that about? I told him the air was thick as a skunk's den with old-guard Swiss and German professional jealousy and suspicion when I walked in. Perhaps, I said, he didn't want me making trouble.

"That is exactly what I do want," he said. "Just don't kill any chickens!"

As far as I knew, the students were satisfied with their old Swiss masters and their mummified canapés. But to win them over to what I thought was the way to cook, my first classes focused on ingredients. I explained that new techniques in air transportation guaranteed arrival in the marketplace in good condition, and that these changes were a challenge to completely rethink the concepts of "fresh," "local," and "quality." Fresh fish in San Francisco had always meant from the Bay or outside the Golden Gate. Now, I told them, sometimes that fish is three days old, while the Norwegian farm salmon was only eighteen hours from the water to the kitchen. So "quality" had new boundaries now that "local" did not now always mean "fresh."

I took them to a new San Francisco import company that with my encouragement was now bringing in fresh European ingredients such as mascarpone, buffalo milk mozzarella, and real Reggiano Parmesan. Then it was on to blind tastings of beer, rum, chocolate, whiskey, cheese, pepper, coffee, bottled water, dried meat, smoked fish, and every possible oil coming in from France, Spain, and Italy. Each student had a form to grade each product according to appearance, color, odor, taste, and overall quality; all were astonished by the results. Before we blind-tasted the beers, I asked them to name their favorite. "Budweiser!" came the resounding cheer. Not when they couldn't see the label. Much to their horror, 85 percent preferred the Czech Pilsner Urquell.

At Panisse I showed them dessert wines and the lesson that the dessert must always be less sweet than the wine served with it (if the wine is not to taste sour); with Darrell Corti we tasted single-cask cognac and whiskey against blended ones; with Linda Guenzel, who wrote *The Chez Panisse Menu Cookbook*, we tasted chocolate, which became the ultimate lesson in quality—and why one shouldn't mind paying more for it. The differences between Hershey's and Lindt was profound, but not merely because one was European. The Swiss chocolate was "conched" 40 percent more than its American counterpart, with the result that it was smoother, richer, and much more satisfying—the extra work in making it clearly worth the extra money it cost. They found they could taste the difference between a mass-produced product and a hand-crafted one. They were now willing to accept that excellence is not just a personal "matter of taste," that one can commonly perceive and measure a standard that can be agreed upon as "the best."

Now we were ready to cook. It's hard to believe now that, until the late seventies, the ingredients we started to cook with at the Academy were not available throughout the United States: extra-virgin olive oil, nut and grape seed oils, cured meats like bündnerfleisch and wood-smoked bacon, gravlax and smoked salmon, real Roquefort, goat and Val d'Aosta fontina cheeses, red and green peppercorns or real saffron, fresh herbs, salad greens, white veal, haricots verts, snow and snap peas, radicchio and Treviso, American caviars, fresh paprika, Belgian endive, fresh ginger, fresh Asian vegetables and spices, ripe true tomatoes, Jerusalem artichokes, sherry vinegar, fresh tuna, yellow bell peppers, foie gras, wild mushrooms, truffles, or fresh and great quality dried pasta. With these, at the beginning of 1980, we cooked the following menu for the public at the Academy's restaurant:

Salmon tartare with deep fried salmon skin and chive flowers

Tricolored bell pepper salad with crayfish sauce & tails

Baby green bean salad with Treviso, whitefish & steelhead caviars

Buckwheat pasta with goat cheese and onion flowers

Bayonne ham with ripe Farmers' Market figs

Provimi veal carpaccio with fresh ginger, mammoth capers, salted anchovies, and Key limes

Grilled squab with fresh raspberry vinegar

Sole "fingers" with Muscat Beaumes-de-Venise

Salmon stew with Szechuan pepper, artichokes, and kombu (a seaweed)

Grilled duck with blackberries, cloudberries, blueberries, and Jerusalem artichokes

Duck with mangoes & fresh lychees

Fresh albacore with Mexican limes, avocados, red torpedo onions, and olive oil

Santa Barbara white peach salad with basil and rose peppercorns

Unlike at Ventana, the food we cooked was a big success with the public and, more important for me, with the Academy's main benefactor. When I accepted the job I was not unaware that he was also the Bay Area's richest and most influential man: Cyril Magnin. Would this legendary food lover fall in love with the idea of a great American brasserie? Ron Batori thought so. He made the introduction, and Magnin was taken with the proposal. He especially loved the thought of saving millions by using CCA students in the kitchen. I chose twenty of my best students, made them my executives, drew up a staff list, and called the bank with the good news.

Then Cyril Magnin died.

Once more I was staring unwilling bankers in the face.

And more teaching.

"Connecting the Source"

Teaching was in the air, and I was fascinated to read a letter to me on the Fourth of July 1979, from John Ronsheim, a professor of music at Antioch College in Yellow Springs, Ohio. "Richard Olney has suggested that I contact you: finally I got the faculty to accept that I prepare the College for a new program to give a B.F.A. in the Culinary Arts. It will be the first."

It took my breath away to think one could get a degree while working on a farm that provided ingredients for a college dining room: what a departure from the diet of bread-margarine-marmalade at my English boarding school, or the chipped beef in flour sauce on Wonder bread at my New England prep school, and the lime Jell-O with bacon and marshmallows (a feat of architecture, if not cuisine) there and at Harvard!

This Antioch idea could be the beginning of a national awareness about food in all parts of our lives, and I was convinced that school food, no matter how young the students, was the place to start. Since Panisse, America had learned that California no longer meant Pebble Beach Club Salad of canned peaches and cottage cheese, and the press had trumpeted the idea that the movement had meaning for the whole country and its national culinary identity. With professional cooking schools and the new-found fame of star chefs started by the Young Turks of France (Guérard's *Cuisinières de Roanne* was published in 1977) and continued by the California style and a few chefs, restaurant work no longer needed an apology. It was no longer a second-class profession. Now it would have a place in serious academic thought.

I called John Ronsheim and told him I had visions of my favorite eighteenth-century architect, Claude-Nicolas Ledoux, who spent his life designing an "ideal town" to be called Chaux. Perhaps we could have a modest "ideal town" of our own, with working farms where students could track a single ingredient—say, milk, from udder to butter to cheese to the final dish. Ohio would become just as prolific in perfect ingredients as the Île-de-France. Perhaps, I went on, we could do everything from reproducing Thomas Jefferson's kitchen garden and vineyards, or Louis XVI's private dining room to teach service, to serving thousands of students three times a day. Even mad John was quiet on the other end of the phone.

"Couldn't we just start with making wine?"

The Antioch staff was scared half to death, but I wrote everyone in the United States, Italy, and France who I thought would be interested enough to raise money, drew up the board of advisers, and created a budget. I set up files on experiments such as the new Picart Snail Factory in Santa Rosa and Aquatic Farms for oysters raised on land in Maui's Waihee Valley.

In February 1980 John's letters to me struggled with questions such as "Does Mimi pose a problem?—call Jim Beard." I did. He said she did. And "Andy temperamental. Madeleine Kamman—great response. Has Alice asked Coppola?" At a West Coast meeting, Janet Trefethen gave a dinner and I presented the board of fifty-one I'd recruited, which included Jim Beard (reluctantly), Joseph Baum (founder of Restaurant Associates and The Four Seasons restaurant in New York), Craig Claiborne (*New York*

Times restaurant critic), Darrell Corti, Elizabeth David, Sybille Bedford (famous English novelist), M. F. K. Fisher, Gael Greene (restaurant critic for *New York* magazine), Pierre Franey (partner with Craig Claiborne), Barbara Kafka (cookbook author and restaurant consultant), Jane Grigson, Robert Mondavi, Richard Olney ("The art of the table will be very much at home with the Humanities, and this program cannot help but rapidly influence and humanize the food of America"), Joseph Phelps (of the Napa winery), James Villas (*Town & Country* food writer), Chuck Williams (of Williams-Sonoma), Hugh Johnson (English wine writer), Cecilia Chiang, and Sri Owen (English cookbook author). Jane Grigson wrote, "I think your idea of connecting the source with the final dish is admirable."

The 1980 East Coast Meeting lunch for this board, which was to have been sponsored by the "21" Club, ended up as a two-thousand-dollar tab handed to me by the headwaiter. Now my funds were as exhausted as I was. I told John that we could not keep up the pace and money required to get this off the ground on one coast, let alone two. But the idea had been launched. The Antioch East and West 51 Culinary Arts Advisory Panel evaporated, but it soon reentered existence as the American Institute of Wine and Food, a name which took at least a case of Dick Graff's (founder and chairman of Chalone Winery) Chalone chardonnay for a small group to decide whether it should be "food and wine" or "wine and food."

There is a moment in all revolutions when the bureaucrats take over, and since the Robespierres were on the horizon, I was out of there—happily resigned to handing over the reins to Dick Graff and Julia Child, both of whom had a great deal more tolerance for such bureaucratic perambulations than I did.

Dick had the administrative services of the Chalone offices, a private Cessna to fly us down every two weeks for six months across the turbulent Ojai Valley updrafts to meet Julia and the provost of U.C. Santa Barbara (Julia had convinced him to donate some land to the Institute near her winter headquarters). The site we picked smelled of the crude oil spillages just offshore, but it was free and on the beach. As I enthused about the possibility of bringing surfers into the organization, some of the board members began to look at me the way John Ronsheim had the year before. So when my negotiations began in earnest in 1978 for a San Francisco restaurant site, I was relieved to be out of the world of food politics and back in the more familiar territory of cooking.

Enough people did stick around to keep the organization alive, especially the wealthier wineries of Napa Valley, led by Lila Yeager of Rutherford Vintners. The AIWF went on to promote and celebrate American gastronomy, and was a necessary first step for the formation of the James Beard Foundation (a center for showcasing emerging chefs in the United States) in New York and the Robert Mondavi culinary center in Napa.

"The Fixer"

In 1978, while I was teaching at the California Culinary Academy, Mark Miller, who had been one of my sous-chefs at Panisse, opened the Fourth Street Grill in Berkeley with the ex-Panisse hostess Susie Nelson. Because the decor was modified California as started by West Beach and Michael's, and the food a variation of Panisse (with Mark's beloved southwestern flavors perfectly introduced), it was a smash hit. Heady with success, the pair opened another restaurant up the road in the old Santa Fe Railroad Station and called it the Santa Fe Bar & Grill—the name a bow to traditional San Francisco restaurants like Tadich and Sam's, but the food a new vision of southwestern tinged with California. The place was a hit at first, despite its location too far away from the Bay (and Fourth Street) and not close enough to Shattuck (and Panisse), in an area more comfortable for prostitutes and drug dealers from Oakland than for Volvo and Saab drivers from the upper Berkeley hills.

One night right after the opening, I was sitting at the Fourth Street bar trying out their margaritas and lamenting the paucity of investors for my restaurant, when Susie—whom I had once approached to be part of the new restaurant but who had grown tired of waiting for me to get the financing—gave me a lead. "Why not talk to Doyle Moon, our new partner?" she said. "He has money and knows the bar business," referring to his once hugely successful Balboa Café in San Francisco.

The Balboa was located in the singles' bar battleground off Union Street called the "Bermuda Triangle" after so many customers' girlfriends had disappeared into the arms of other men (or women). But now the Balboa had reached a state of neglect where no one cared who disappeared, having gone from being packed with singles to being half empty with people who always would be. When I called Doyle Moon, he saw an opportunity. If I wanted access to his bankers and credit line, I would have to give the Balboa a quick fix.

The Balboa Café had been one of the first "fern bars" after the legendary Henry Africa's, but what I found was the look and smell of vintage testosterone stuck in dark corners. The food was hamburgers and Iranian. The "fix" obviously meant freshen, so on the first day, in 1979, I showed up with my car full of flowers, which I made into free-form English "country" arrangements that the few diehards at the daytime bar immediately pro-claimed "faggoty." I installed women bartenders ("treason," "queer," "they must be dykes"), white tablecloths on the tables ("too fancy"), and long white aprons on the waiters ("effeminate").

Soon the disapproving barhounds were gone, replaced by the likes of the socialite Ann Getty and her friends eating hamburgers and pasta next to actors, real estate moguls, and restaurant workers on their day off. And soon, on any afternoon, you could hear the two or three regulars who refused to decamp giving anyone who'd listen their critique of the day's flowers and taking credit for the idea of female bartenders. We'd succeeded.

After nine months, just as everyone was getting bored, things came to a boil across the Bay. Doyle and another Balboa owner were owners of half the Santa Fe Bar & Grill and, known to Doyle but not to me, the Santa Fe Bar & Grill was broke as well as under surveillance by the Alcohol Con-trol Board (the ABC). Oakland dealers were ensconced at the bar drink-ing free Baileys Irish Cream and selling drugs and firearms. Loss of liquor license, foreclosure, and arrests were imminent.

Within minutes of calls from the bank and the ABC, Doyle Moon and I were in his new top-model BMW speeding across the Bay Bridge to Berke-ley. My queries about our destination and mission were answered with uncharacteristic coyness by this Apache in Hugo Boss. When he pulled off the freeway into the avenue on which I had driven for years to Panisse, my stomach turned. But when he pulled into the parking lot of the Santa Fe, I knew it was another fixer: Save it or kiss the bankers good-bye. I nearly threw up.

My horror yielded to mixed emotions as soon as I walked in. My fatal attraction to underdog once-beautiful spaces kicked in. Like that of Black Beauty, the restaurant's body had been racked by neglect and cruelty, but the soul was still there. I was charmed. Just as I had never been able to resist the allure of a neglected but once great garden, I was challenged. Here again was the tired, unfiltered air, the walls and carpets stained with grime, the peeling paint, the coke dealers at the bar. They were not like the first rather jolly dealer at Panisse's third birthday party, who took to my Billecart-Salmon rosé like a fish to water. These guys were grabbing shot glasses of Goldwasser and Amaretto in hands heavy with gold.

"Those have got to go," I announced, cocking my head at the bar cus-tomers.

The Balboa was making money now, so Crocker Bank confirmed that, if I cleaned up the Santa Fe, we'd get a $350,000 loan for the new restau-rant. Not a bad deal for three months' work, I thought.

Despite their ownership of 50 percent of the Santa Fe, Mark and Susie seemed to have no say in the ensuing makeover, but by now they were barely speaking to each other anyway. It was Crocker and Doyle calling the shots. As we stood in the bar surveying the situation, Doyle told me Crocker wanted the place redone in four days to be ready for the evening before the Berkeley-Stanford game, with its guaranteed cash flow.

I was stunned. I was even more stunned when I said, "We'll have to close the restaurant immediately," and Doyle said, "Fine."

How had I gotten here, on the end of yet another banker's strings? Every money man I'd ever "taken care of"—the ones who'd wanted special favors at Panisse and discretion at Ventana Inn (one from a major financial services company liked to keep young men in his suite back in the canyon)—had told me I had "no track record." I knew this was one of life's lonely moments. Would I do the healthy thing and walk out the door? Or follow my troublesome preference for the slim chance? It was midafternoon in a near-empty restaurant, a good time to act, if I was going to. My gut told me I was dealing with the Devil & Company, but I was willing to make that bargain if I could just get on with my own San Francisco restaurant.

I turned to the leering jerks at the bar and announced that the restaurant was now closed. Then I told the staff to be out in ten minutes and to come back the next day to reapply for their jobs. Then I called a locksmith. Then I called my best students from the CCA. Then I opened a bottle of champagne Grande Dame. Within an hour we had new locks and keys, and my students had assembled. "We have a date with destiny," I told them—a better line than the one I was actually thinking, which was "Welcome to the final circle of Dante's hell."

That was Tuesday. The place would have to reopen on Friday before the November 1981 game, to catch the first wave of fans.

And suddenly I couldn't walk. Muscle cramping—brought on by the tension of having to come up with a restaurant menu and philosophy in a few days—had me confined to a massage table in the bar. From there I addressed the wide-eyed new staff.

"We open in three and a half days," I said, "and I want to finish what I started at Ventana, continued at the California Culinary Academy, and lay the foundation for a Great American brasserie."

"What about the Southwest?" someone piped up. "We have the name 'Santa Fe' and an Indian chief logo. Won't the public expect chilies?"

Thank God for my mother, I told them, and all those Sunday morning huevos rancheros and chiles rellenos. If she could, in the thirties, drive from Connecticut to Mexico City with my two older siblings in a Model A

Ford, I could do this and conjure up all I remembered of my childhood Mexican food and barbecues in Australia at my parents' friends' hacienda. The allusions confused everyone.

For the food, I told them to remember the dinner that Mark Miller had done for the Académie Internationale du Vin and Richard Olney a couple of months earlier at the Chalone Vineyard. That meal, cooked outside and served on white-clothed tables on top of a wilderness mountain, was southwestern-infused yet truly Californian in style, the next generation after my California Regional Dinner of 1976.

"And we," I said, "will create the generation after that."

As for the facilities, they could be surmounted, I told them, feeling a bit like the commander of the fleet in *Sink the Bismarck!* who encouraged his staff in the face of impossible odds.

"Is it going to be that bad?" they asked.

I recounted one of our most delirious moments: when my Balboa cooks and some CCA students had prepared an elaborate dinner in the de Young Museum without any facilities at all. It was a fund-raiser to create the Philharmonia Baroque Orchestra of the West. The museum had promised us a back room and kitchen, then made us work on the floor of a corridor filled with priceless twelfth- to fourteenth-century triptychs. I got the go signal a half hour ahead of schedule, when my cooks were all in the parking lot taking a last-minute break before service: It fell to me to plate 250 salads by myself. I was madly tossing the contents of four twenty-quart bowls when I heard a gasp from three cooks who'd just walked in and looked up to see leaves of baby lettuce and rivers of vinaigrette rolling down tens of millions of dollars of Flemish altar paintings.

"Get a towel, say nothing, and plate the fucking salads *now!*"

The seventeenth-century dinner had been a triumph, and we hadn't, somehow, altered the course of Bay Area art history.

I hoped that this sermon would inspire the staff and give the hosts a sound bite for the public when they came in the door for the first time. But it seemed to be making things worse. Finally my star pupil, Mark Franz, said, "Let's cook good, simple food, not make fools of ourselves."

That put a lid on my ramblings. Everyone understood and knew what to do.

Lawyers representing other partners showed up the next day, but I told the staff not to bother with them. We had a menu to write. And since the reality is always determined by the layout of the kitchen, we set about ana-lyzing the setup, how many people it would allow to cook at one time, and what kind of food we could do in quantity without compromising quality.

The kitchen layout was the kind that comes from an initial budget close to zero: nowhere near enough space to plate cold first courses, and an obstacle course to run with the hot ones. This was not going to be pretty. The grill was a monster six feet long and three feet deep, guzzling fifty pounds of mesquite charcoal at a time. If you were slightly crazy and a firebug, you could cook fifteen or twenty orders of fish and meat at once. Steven Vranian was the man to do it: unfazed by multiple burns along his forearm flesh from being sizzled on the grill's front (a sound you could hear over the noise of the kitchen), and sanguine about the .22 bullets that occasionally exploded in the charcoal. The waiters became adept at ducking without dropping plates—the knowledge that bullets travel faster than sound perhaps mercifully repressed. We all felt charmed. Young and untouchable.

There was neither time nor space for advanced sauce making, so we opted for salsas and simple compound butters that took no time to do and could be made at the last minute. Their beauty was that if we ran out of, say, Key limes for a lime-cilantro-cumin butter (and we would run out of things often, as our fame spread), there were always tangerines or mandarins or Meyer lemons to dip in mint oil and roll around on the grill (to toast the oils in the skins) before throwing them into the food processor with butter, salt, and chilies or pepper. As for salsas, we started with the fresca (tomatoes, red onion, cilantro, lime juice, olive oil, salt, and sometimes garlic) that was always chopped by hand. When this ran out we'd invent (because the tomatoes had to be time-consumingly peeled) salsas based on whatever was in the walk-in refrigerator and easily assembled.

There was another reason for our reliance on salsas and butters. The majority of the main courses at the Santa Fe were grilled, and it makes no sense to create a crisp skin or surface and then douse it with something that leaves it a soggy mess. So out of one restaurant's necessity came— after the Newport Astor Mansion lunch for the food press—a national fad. Eventually salsas would be one of the clichés of California Cuisine. In 1981 they made total sense.

We never made the Friday evening as planned because I was still on the massage table and the utilities inspectors hadn't signed off. But the day of the Big Game we did—to great success. Within days the drug dealers had found greener pastures—replaced by the usual free-spending foodies and the critics, including Robert Finigan of the infamous Panisse lamb incident. He'd been about to publish a scathing review (with the restaurant business as soap opera, using an account of the fallout between Mark and Susie), but in the face of the new regime, he changed his mind. "Enter

Jeremiah Tower's team," he wrote, "all dressed in chef's whites and fresh from transforming the Balboa Café into one of the city's most popular bistros." The Santa Fe, he continued, is "much cheerier now . . . and there is a comfortable air of informal elegance about this place and the seriousness of the kitchen is immediately evident." He praised the smoked Oregon trout and sturgeon, the wild Bélon and Pigeon Point (Sonoma) oysters, the black bean soup and cake, the squab marinated in raspberry vinegar, bay scallops, Rex sole, and other local ingredients. "Tower delights in devising and executing menus like this one, emphasizing freshness of ingredients prepared with that extra twist of inventiveness which distinguishes the great chefs from the useful ones. . . . See to what levels apparently simple conceptions can be taken in the hands of a master."

I was ecstatic that our first review was so positive. But I'd have to spread the word if we were ever to get back over the Bay to San Francisco.

America's Culinary Regions

I had moved from Berkeley to San Francisco in anticipation. One night, early in the Santa Fe era, I was sitting in my Bernal Heights rosebush and vegetable garden, drinking champagne with my college friend Philip Core. He had just finished his paintings of famous people who'd traveled the Santa Fe Railroad for the restaurant's walls, and had then rendered the likes of Escoffier, Marlene Dietrich, Richard Olney, Gary Cooper, Johnny Hard-On, Clare Boothe Luce, and Truman Capote on my dining room ceiling. He was bored. As we moved from champagne to a bottle of '27 Taylor from the cellar under a trapdoor in the dining room, he said, "Let's do a TV show. Or a book. We'll call it 'Stars in Your Eyes'"—I guessed from the stars on the room's ceiling—"and it will be all about the food and culinary regions of the Americas. We'll travel around on the Santa Fe Railroad and have them pay for it."

Into the second bottle of Taylor we did an outline, with topics like "Combination of heritages—roots of American eclecticism; reworking tradition—the bounty of nineteenth-century America; harvest as menu—the new eclecticism as the garden and market come full circle; European principles established in America; the American outdoors— localization and ease of preparation, the directness of Texas, redefining the frontier." The symbol of the show or book would be a dining car with people looking at a menu while the American landscape speeds by.

I couldn't cope with much of Philip's inspired madness while still in the opening phases of the Santa Fe. But he did give me an idea of how to promote the new American Bar & Grill. I would restart the regional dinners we had done at Chez Panisse, but using the culinary regions of America.

I started with the "Florida State Dinner" in March 1983 as a benefit for the American Institute of Wine and Food:

Tarpon Isle rum cocktail

Salty dogs

Florida backwood biscuits

Gulf stone crab claws with Key lime "Old Sour" sauce

Palm Beach crabmeat salad with avocados

Key West conch stew

Roast Appalachicola oysters

Tarpon Springs fish and shellfish soup with salt cod dumplings

Cross Creek French fired eggplant with "guspachy" sauce

Pompano en papillote

Grilled rum-spiced Gulf shrimp with creamed onions

Turtle Cay bananas with mango ice cream

Guava pecan pie

After the dinner a *Metropolitan Home* writer asked, "Is this really Florida food?"

"No," I replied. "But it should be—and with your help it will be."

This dinner was such a hit that we followed it immediately with another at the Santa Fe, this time inspired by my visits to my mother's San Antonio spice-vendor friends, called the "Texas and Spanish America Dinner":

Grilled Appalachicola oysters with 1883 Catsup

Broiled Spanish onions cowboy style with B-B-Q sauce

Gulf shrimp and bonita in escabeche with avocado

Rabbit chili with mole sauce and peppered mangoes

Smoke-grilled red snapper with fresh sea urchin roe sauce

Goat stew with hominy, cilantro salad, and smoky chili sauce

Hot pecan pie with chocolate ice cream

The national press was now paying attention, so when we did a "Michigan and Midwest" dinner, the governor of Michigan actually attended. His presence did nothing to ameliorate the hurt pride of my friends in Napa and Sonoma, who were aghast that I'd do regions of America with no indigenous winemaking. I told them, "Soon there won't be any."

In late 1982, in an article in San Francisco's *Focus* called "Withstanding the Taste of *Time*," Liz Lufkin had written that "until recently, no one paid much attention to California cooking." Although Spanish Jesuits had planted orchards of pears, peaches, plums, apricots, cherries, and oranges, a variety of anything other than fruit was nonexistent, and the accounts of miners and settlers about California food in the 1830s are famous for their enthusiastic disgust. It made me laugh to read that Liz felt sorry for a priest who "back then lunched on only an ear of corn roasted over coals" as we were making our living to re-create those haunting flavors not interfered with by an overenthusiastic chef. She went on to say that cooking in California was coming into its own: "Indeed, some think it's a trend that will sweep the country and change the face of American cooking." Six months later our Newport lunch proved her right.

Meanwhile, we honed our skills with the help of another journalist, Pat Brown and her "Cuisine Game" in *Cuisine* magazine. Pat gave a group of chefs a market-basket list of ingredients and then asked them to come up with a menu and recipes. Our ingredients included lamb shoulder, trout, American caviar, coconut, asparagus, salt cod, rhubarb, and pine nuts. I decided to serve the pine nuts toasted with champagne, then continue the champagne with a tartare of trout with asparagus. The rest of the menu we submitted was this:

Raviolis of salt cod with American caviar

Braised lamb shoulder with garlic cloves

Fried goat cheese with shredded romaine lettuce salad

Rhubarb soufflé with coconut custard

When the contest was published, our customers immediately wanted that food, and once more a restaurant that had started simply was pushing its limits to live up to what had been promised in the food press. In August 1982 we cooked a menu for the birthday of *Gourmet*'s wine columnist, Gerald Asher, using local wild salmon we smoked ourselves, served with Sacramento River sturgeon caviar processed by Narsai David, another Berkeley restaurateur. Following the salmon were

Garden herbs, flowers & black truffle soup

Ravioli of brain puree with sweetbreads

Mesquite-grilled partridge with chervil butter

Laura Chenel Sonoma goat cheeses

Figs poached in Sauternes with rose petals

By the time we cooked a dinner called "Future" for a promotion for Berkeley's sportswear company The North Face a few months later, New York was watching. I began with trays of champagne and pills—a joke on the futurist idea that all food will one day be in pill form. But the courses that followed were "real" and included melted Sonoma cheese in a ramekin lined with Meyer lemon leaves and Lunar Free-Ranging Rabbit Stew with Crazed Mushrooms.

But it was the menu for the Napa Valley Wine Symposium that whetted Jim Beard's appetite:

Fresh Berkeley morels stuffed with duck livers fattened for the
Santa Fe Bar & Grill

Poached wild striped bass with chervil butter and nasturtiums

Sonoma squab smoke-roasted over cabernet vine cuttings

Warmed goat cheese dipped in violets

Winter fruit compote in Napa Riesling

The squab's breast meat was served in its juices, the leg and thigh meat chopped into a puree with sage leaves and served on grilled garlic toasts. "If that is not new American food, my dear, it should be," said Jim, impishly parroting my Florida dinner line. The food seemed awfully French to me, but I kept that thought to myself.

By mid-1983 the word about "California Cuisine" had spread. Wolfgang Puck had given up his job at Patrick Terrail's very French Ma Maison and opened Spago on Sunset Boulevard. It picked up on the theme set by Michael's a few years earlier: simply done, all white, great lighting, and a bedazzlement of highlighted flowers, a style now known as "Californian."

Word spread as far as that hotbed of trend Hong Kong. The Mandarin Hotel, wanting to transform its old-boy Mandarin Grill, called to persuade me to come and introduce Santa Fe Bar & Grill's "New California Cuisine." As I talked to them, I could feel the starched heavy linen sheets in the suite with its own butler. I needed a rest. I sent them a list of 150 dishes, some of which were

Cornmeal blini with three American caviars

Anaheim chilies stuffed with California goat cheese, Chinese black bean sauce

Warm avocado salad with shiitake and lobster mushrooms

Palm Beach crabmeat salad with pomelo

Duck prosciutto with pear and spiced pecan salad

Grilled oysters with barbecued duck

Gumbo with crayfish and smoked duck sausages

Grilled sweetbreads with sea urchin cream sauce

Buffalo steak with BBQ sauce

Cranberry-glazed lamb loin

Turtle Cay bananas in rum with durian cream

Tropical fruit compote with coconut ice cream

"Inspired by the superb natural produce and wines of California, and fresh Pacific seafood, Jeremiah Tower is leading a revolution in American restaurant kitchens with a highly inventive, highly personal style of cooking, giving new flair to ethnic and regional dishes, whilst maintaining their basic simplicity"—that's what the Mandarin's press release said. "Dishes are brilliantly eclectic blends of wholesome 'country fare' and exotic imported ingredients such as blood oranges, Maui onions, Oregon morels, nasturtium flowers, stone crabs, quail eggs, American caviar, and garden tomatoes." I thought garden tomatoes were going to be a challenge in Hong Kong, but the Mandarin assured me their import company didn't know the meaning of unavailable, that we could get whatever we wanted in Australia.

I burst out laughing. The land of flathead and carrots fit for pigs would supply us? "No way, mate," I said.

"Check it out," the supplier replied. "You'll be surprised by what's going on down there."

All I knew about Australia was that anyone who could live somewhere else did. My childhood playmate Brett Whiteley was now Australia's most famous painter, and he lived in London. As did all his Australian pals.

At the Newport event in 1983, where the love affair between
the American food press and California cuisine began.
COURTESY OF OXSANA CZUCZMAN

Unless otherwise noted, all images are courtesy of the author.

At six in Australia, trying to eat the barracuda the old Aborigine Nick
had taught me to roast over a coconut-shell fire on the beach.

My father, Sheldon "Pete" Tower.
He was the same age here as I was
when I started at Chez Panisse.

My mother, Margaret Tower. She threw
lavish garden parties for which I often
had to take over the cooking.

My sister, Mary Tower, the eldest of the children. She would later help me find the location for Stars.

My older brother and later Green Beret, Jonathan.

My Philadelphia socialite aunt Mary (Slattery) Zakhartchenko, who wrote me constantly when I was a teenager with recipes and cooking advice. She and her Russian husband sent me to Paris at sixteen to eat, learn about, and buy them truffles.

My Russian uncle Constantine Levovitch Zakhartchenko, a celebrated (presidential medal winner) aeronautics and rocket inventor for the American armed forces. He taught me and my college friends to eat blini with vodka.

Postprandial summer lunch cigars with Michael Palmer at my house in San Francisco.

Alice and I worked together, but in different realms, she in the dining room and I in the kitchen. Here we are two years after I left Chez Panisse at a picnic in the Chalone vineyards, given by Richard Graff for Richard Olney. *PHOTO BY EDWARD R. GAINES ©1981*

Alice with Willy Bishop (*right*), my Beatnik menthol-cigarette-chain-smoking English-atomic-mint-sucking sous-chef at Chez Panisse.

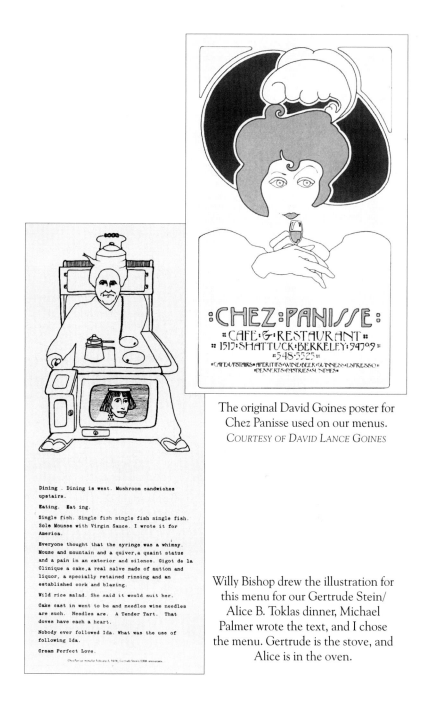

:CHEZ:PANIƧƧE:
:: CAFE·&·RESTAURANT ::
:: 1517·SHATTUCK·BERKELEY·94709 ::
::·548·5525·::
::CAFE·UPSTAIRS·APERITIFS·WINE·BEER·GUINNESS·ESPRESSO::
::DESSERTS·PASTRIES·SUNDAES::

The original David Goines poster for
Chez Panisse used on our menus.
COURTESY OF DAVID LANCE GOINES

Dining . Dining is west. Mushroom sandwiches
upstairs.

Eating. Eat ing.

Single fish. Single fish single fish single fish.
Sole Mousse with Virgin Sauce. I wrote it for
America.

Everyone thought that the syringe was a whimsy.
Mouse and mountain and a quiver, a quaint statue
and a pain in an exterior and silence. Gigot de la
Clinique a cake, a real salve made of mutton and
liquor, a specially retained rinsing and an
established cork and blazing.

Wild rice salad. She said it would suit her.

Cake cast in went to be and needles wine needles
are such. Needles are. A Tender Tart. That
doves have each a heart.

Nobody ever followed Ida. What was the use of
following Ida.

Cream Perfect Love.

Chez Panisse menu for February 3, 1974, Gertrude Stein's 100th anniversary.

Willy Bishop drew the illustration for
this menu for our Gertrude Stein/
Alice B. Toklas dinner, Michael
Palmer wrote the text, and I chose
the menu. Gertrude is the stove, and
Alice is in the oven.

As a friend, James Beard convinced me
to leave Chez Panisse and to run my
own restaurant, my way.

A publicity shot with my trademark
glass of champagne at Stars, San
Francisco. *PHOTO BY FRED LYON*

The entrance to the original
Stars, San Francisco.

The interior of Stars Singapore, which we opened in 1996.

The main Stars team of managers, catering the fiftieth anniversary of Beaulieu Vineyards in Napa *(from the left)*: David Robins, Noreen Lam, Steven Vranian, Mark Franz, Emily Luchetti, Loretta Keller—and behind more staff, Charles Thompson and Larry Doyle.

The Peak Café in Hong Kong, which opened in 1990.

Speedo 690.

All of us chefs at Chez Panisse—Jean-Pierre Moullé *(center)*, who took over when I left, and Paul Bertoli, who took over when Jean-Pierre did.

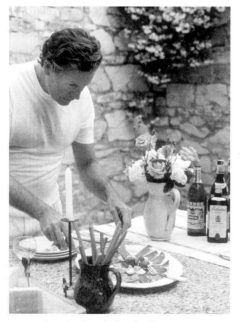

Serving lunch for the Stars managers at our villa in Tuscany.

The always present magnum of champagne.

With James Beard and Denise
Hale at a fund-raiser in San
Francisco.

With my friend Rudolf Nureyev.

With the incomparable Richard Olney and Stars chef Mark Franz
in front of the restaurant in Paris that inspired me to do Stars.

With the great Mario Batali in the early days at the James Beard House kitchen. *PHOTO BY CAROL GILLOT*

With master chef and good friend Jacques Pépin.

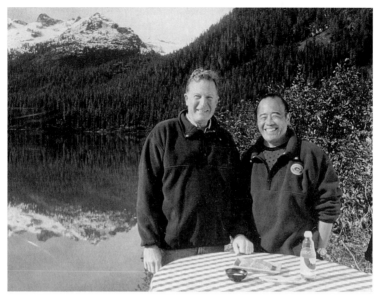

At a glacial lake in British Columbia for the BBC with my great friend and show host Ken Hom—also my partner in the first "East Meets West."

With Robert Mondavi.

Bon Appétit! Julia Child

With Julia Child at Stars celebrating our *Cooking with Master Chefs*.

With Wolfgang Puck at a Citymeals-on-Wheels event at
Rockefeller Center in New York.

Smoking with George Hamilton at Stars for the debut of his new line of cigars.

Luciano Pavarotti at Stars.

Jessye Norman at Stars. *PHOTO BY BRUCE FORRESTER © 1993*

A glossy from Barbra Streisand from the wall of the VIP section at Stars.

With Sophia Loren at the dinner we cooked for her at the Italian consulate in San Francisco.

With Tipper Gore at the Stars Café in Napa Valley.

Robin Leach of *Lifestyles of the Rich and Famous*,
presenting me with the James Beard Foundation's
Best American Chef Award in 1996.

A 2001 portrait of me, drawn by Willy Bishop,
for Mark Franz. COURTESY OF WILLY BISHOP

Alice and I celebrating at the party at Chez Panisse for its twenty-fifth
anniversary in 1996.

I knew the names of Tony and Gay Bilson, who would open the amazing and Panisse-like Berowra Waters, of Phillip Searle, Neil Perry, Peter Doyle, and Serge Dansereau at the Regent, all of whom were said to believe that California chefs lived by the motto "If we can sell it, someone will produce it." Serge said that in Australia restaurants had to drag, cajole, and coax their suppliers into producing anything other than mass-market ingredients. I was not optimistic.

But the ingredients from Australia turned out to be marvelous, and I made a note that I must soon return to the land of my culinary awakenings—both wonderful and horrible.

In Hong Kong we cooked fifteen hours a day. I ruined two pairs of Italian loafers running up and down the stairs in the usual multilayered hotel kitchen, wowed the local press, filled the Grill with locals loving California food and, dying from food later at a floating restaurant, was pumped in my behind with an amphetamine–vitamin B–antibiotic cocktail such as only Hong Kong could provide. That got me onto the train to mainland China, where I revived myself with a huge bowl of fresh pink ginger and goose soup. In the Canton markets I saw that "freshness" and "local" still held their original relationship: everything was alive, and in its skin (including for my morning pick-me-up of cobra blood mixed with Chinese wine). Giant salamander, eagles and owls, civet cats, puppies, and snakes were in abundance, if menu challenging, but the richness of choice was an inspiration.

The success of the Astor Mansion event a few months earlier had made the Hong Kong promotion easier, and I could hardly wait for the next one. So when I got a call from Jonathan Waxman and Larry Forgione (of New York's An American Place) saying they were organizing a charity dinner, in either New York or San Francisco, using American chefs, I felt another great moment was upon us.

The Region Called America

When the list of chefs arrived, I saw it was made up of East and West Coast friends of Larry's and Jonathan's, with no one new and no one between the two coasts. I pointed out that if this were to be a truly American festival, we should cover the geography of the nation. What about Paul Prudhomme from New Orleans's K-Paul? What about Bradley Ogden of the American Café restaurant in Kansas City? Or Jimmy Schmidt of the London Chop House in Detroit?

The list was finally decided, and the dinner was held at the Stanford

Court, then owned by James Beard's West Coast angel (in every way), James Nassikas. My copy of the menu for the 1983 dinner is inscribed top and center by Dick Graff: "Hooray! The American Institute of Wine and Food." Barbara Kafka wrote, "Laugh a Little."

This menu celebrating regional America says it all:

Cultured Olympia oysters from Puget Sound, Washington

Bélon oysters from Tomales Bay, California

Portuguese oysters from Vancouver Island, B.C.

Terrine of three American smoked fish with the respective caviars
Larry Forgione, River Café, Brooklyn

Red pepper pasta with grilled scallops
Jonathan Waxman, Michael's, Santa Monica

Garden salad
Alice Waters, Chez Panisse, Berkeley

Blackened redfish
Paul Prudhomme, K-Paul's Louisiana Kitchen, New Orleans

Marinated grilled quail with poblano chili, cilantro, and lime sauce
Mark Miller, Fourth Street Grill, Berkeley

Roasted rack of lamb stuffed with Missouri greens & hazelnuts

Gratin of wildroot vegetables, fiddlehead ferns & cattail sprouts
Bradley Ogden, American Café, Kansas City
Jimmy Schmidt, London Chop House, Detroit

American Cheese Selections

Pecan puff pastry with chocolate & sabayon sauces
Jeremiah Tower, Santa Fe Bar & Grill, Berkeley
Balboa Café, San Francisco

After-Hours Party

Spago pizza
Wolfgang Puck, Spago, Los Angeles

Tripe Gumbo
Barbara Kafka, Star Spangled Foods, New York

The donated wines were the best of Napa and Sonoma: Schramsberg, Jordan, Beringer, Iron Horse, Acacia, Robert Mondavi, Joseph Phelps, and Domaine Chandon, with a little South Coast—Chalone and Sanford—thrown in.

Prudhomme's blackened redfish cooked in white-hot black-iron skillets would produce thick clouds of impenetrable and eye-stinging smoke, so he was banished onto the fire escapes, where he wouldn't set off the alarms. But the hundred-foot-high pillars of fish and spice smoke were just as impressive on the outside. Soon every alarm was ringing and every hook and ladder in the city was on its way to save the Stanford Court.

My photographs of us all eating Wolfgang's pizza after the main dinner show faces filled more with relief than with awareness of a momentous occasion. The look of slowly forming elation that history is being made, that the burgeoning American food movement had come together for the first time, is on only a few. We had made history.

Jimmy Schmidt wrote to thank me for the opportunity of participating, as did Bill Wilkinson from Campton Place for inviting Bradley Ogden to San Francisco, where they met and Bill offered Bradley the job as executive chef. Bradley arrived to take up the job at the same time Masa Kobayashi and Hubert Keller were starting at Masa's and Sutter 500 with Roger Vergé, so I gave a lunch for them to meet the local press, restaurateurs, and my suppliers.

Bill Rice from *Food & Wine* wrote me about a panel discussion we had all participated in before the event: "As Barbara Kafka said, it's too bad Julia [Child] couldn't have been there to realize there really is an 'American' cooking/cuisine." Harvey Steiman in the *Examiner* wrote that Alice was not sure it was an amazing event, that she suggested it was more about novelty than about the actual quality of the food. But most of the enormous amount of press that covered the event agreed with the headline in *Revue West*: "American Cooking Comes of Age."

Now it's common for famous chefs to get together to cook for charity, but at the time this was unprecedented. However, after all the press coverage of new trends and food at the Newport event, the press was primed for this event. The leaders of the burgeoning American food movement had come together for the first time. The coverage was immense, and it set off an appetite for reading about chefs. Very soon came *Newsweek*'s "Palate Power in the New Berkeley" proclaiming: "Twenty years after the Revolution, eating well is the radical's best revenge." Before the student revolutions of the late sixties, the article goes on, a great restaurant in Berkeley was as rare as a doctoral candidate who finished his thesis in less than five years. But by 1983 good restaurants were so commonplace that when Chez Panisse was named one of the seven best in America, one jaded Berkeley gourmet sniffed: "It may be the seventh best restaurant on Shattuck Avenue." Panisse was credited as the source: "It does not matter if [Alice Waters is] a good cook or not. She educated her customers."

"Berkeleyites can even tolerate a royalist like Jeremiah Tower," said *Newsweek,* "because of his unstinting emphasis on quality."

In that article there is a photo of Paul Johnson, the "hands-on supplier" of fish and shellfish for all these winning restaurants. Only ten years earlier he had knocked tentatively at the back door of Panisse's kitchen, holding a salmon he had caught as a "boat boy" on the return trip of a fishing charter. Seeing how fresh that salmon was, I'd told him I'd take anything that came out of the sea or bay.

The changes were almost complete.

On December 1, 1984, I resigned from the Balboa Café, since I no longer had time for it. I kept the Santa Fe only one more year. I sat one last time at its bar, where I had asked the drug dealers to leave years earlier, and wondered at how far we had come. Halfway through a bottle of 1971 Dom Pérignon, I let the kaleidoscope of memories pass in front of me in this restaurant that had launched us to national fame, it seemed, without our even knowing it. For my part, it was a fame nearly cut short when the local restaurant union decided to use me as a stepping board for recruiting new members. None of my staff was inclined to join their lines, especially after someone from the crowd on the sidewalk shot at me through the windows. I was used to flying bullets from the Mexican charcoal, but someone trying to kill me because I was famous did rouse a few worries in my head about the path I had chosen. I had used state police to bust the picket line, making everyone realize what I had known for years—that Berkeley was just not for me. Other and more warming memories filed through my head: making sandwiches for the firemen who left the kitchen arm in arm after a kitchen fire; the lunches I gave there for chefs like Hubert Keller, Masa, and Bradley Ogden to welcome them to the Bay Area and to introduce them to the local press, share our supplier lists, and have them meet local personalities like Alice Waters, Mark Miller, Cecilia Chiang, Jim Nassikas, Gerald Asher, and Barbara Tropp.

But what I thought would be six months had turned into nearly five years, and it was time to go to San Francisco.

Second Interlude

Cooking in California

AT CHEZ PANISSE menu writing had become the task of creating a new one for every night a week. Foie gras and "turtle fat" couldn't feature on those $6.50 per person 1973 menus, but I still needed to let out the Cecil Beaton in me, so I loved cooking outside the restaurant. At home, at Alice's, or at friends' houses, I could splurge. Sometimes the menu was over the top (even if the food was simply prepared), and sometimes the wine.

One dinner was both.

An Alice B. Toklas Dinner at Fern Canyon for Von Thurn und Taxis

May 29, 1974

Ten people, ten bottles.

I cooked this menu for some friends at their palatial Mill Valley house on top of Mount Tamalpais. The menu was written mostly in French, because in 1974 that was the language Chez Panisse was using, and the friends wanted a Panisse menu—if Alice (B. Toklas) inspired. The dinner was a big success despite the guest of honor, the Prince von Thurn und Taxis, declaring as he looked at the first course, "All you need in life is birth-control pills and hundred-year-old Cognac." I agreed about the Cognac.

The prince turned out to be a fake, but no one and nothing else was.

Pâté de foie de volailles
Lillet

Quenelles de saumon, sauce Nantua
René Lalou 1966

Pigeoneaux rôtis
Richebourg 1959

Glace d'asperges

Gigot de la clinique
Château Montrose 1932
Puree de topinambours

Brie de Meaux

A Tender Tart
Château Suduiraut 1955
Château Suduiraut 1928

Nitrous Oxide

Cocaine
Roederer Cristal 1966

Here the cumulus-cloud-light salmon quenelles with a cream crayfish sauce were followed by plain roasted pigeons stuffed with herbs, because after the quenelles, I wanted something not too rich but substantial enough for the great big rich Burgundy. I don't like sweet fruit sorbets between courses (the sugar spoils the palate for anything else), but an unsweet sorbet of asparagus was the perfect precursor to the very rich lamb, which had been injected every day over a week with a mandarin-orange-and-spices concoction and cooked for seven hours. A wonderful Brie finished off the rest of the red wine; then the rich but not too sweet "Tender Tart" from Toklas's cookbook was accompanied by two aging Sauternes. Nitrous oxide sent all to their "postprandial pleasures" on a high and me back (now uncaring) to my little one-room apartment in Berkeley.

～

Another dinner was all about the wines that Darrell Corti (Corti Brothers wine and food in Sacramento) and Ron Batori provided for this dinner at a large old farm mansion along the Sacramento River Delta. My notes of the time say that the wines show the wonderful madness and deep knowledge that Darrell had, and his willingness to share it by the shovelful. Ron Batori was the dean of the California Culinary Academy and had invited first Ken Hom, and then me, to teach at the school.

Ken and I cooked.

Dinner with Darrell Corti, Batori, Hom et al.

February 15, 1980
8 people

Jeanmaire Brut en magnum

Smithfield ham
Pol Roge en magnum 1973
Tokaji Furmint 1975
Tokaji Szamorodni 1973 dry
Tokaji Aszú 3 puttanos 1973
Tokaji Aszú 4 puttanos 1973

Grilled Delta sturgeon
Joseph Phelps, chardonnay en magnum 1977

Duck breasts and legs with kumquats
Château Margaux en magnum 1960
Château L'Evangile 1971

Cheeses
Château de Pommard 1972
Réserve de Chèvre Noir 1934

Pear tarte Tatin
Tokaji Aszú 5 puttanos 1973
Tokaji Eszencia 1969

Ken and I decided it was important to keep the menu as clean as possible across from the almost (but not quite) overwhelming lineup of wines, particularly the progression of the very heady and rich Hungarian Tokaji, going from the driest to the beginning to be sweet (three puttanos) to the sweetest at five puttanos and then the Eszencia itself. I love old Malmsey Madeira, or semisweet sherries with ham, so to taste the progression of dry to sweet Tokaji with the Smithfield ham (soaked, poached, cooled, very thinly sliced) was an education in the level of sweetness that was perfect with salty, rich ham.

Ken cooked the duck Peking style for the breasts with seeded kumquats stewed briefly in duck stock and red wine, and we poached the legs in duck fat to make confit before grilling them to be served with endive salad.

❧

For a dinner at the Joseph Phelps winery to celebrate Joe having amassed a huge cellar of wines from auctions in London and the arrival of a lot of new fresh products onto the California marketplace, I wrote and cooked this menu for Joe, his then manager, Bruce Neyers, and a bunch of visiting chefs like the great Frank Stitt from Highlands Bar & Grill in Birmingham, Alabama.

Dinner at Joseph Phelps Vineyards

Friday, October 10, 1980

Beluga caviar
Billecart-Salmon en magnum 1975

Great Lakes whitefish gold caviar

Chicken breasts with fresh Oregon morels
Château Gruaud-Larose 1962, 1937, 1934

Rack of lamb grilled over vine cuttings
Château Gruaud-Larose 1945, 1929, 1926, 1918

Autumn vegetable stew

A basket of California goat cheeses on a bed of vine leaves
Coulommiers

Salad of warm fruits, Guatemalan cream
Steinberger Riesling, TBA 1959

Roasted Italian chestnuts
Cockburn port, vintage 1950
Unknown port, perhaps Warre, vintage 1920

I don't remember what the Guatemalan cream was, but at that time I was very excited about the newly arrived (in the marketplace) fresh tropical fruits, and I think this cream was all about fresh guavas.

I was stunned to be able to taste a sequence of one of my favorite red wines, Château Gruaud-Larose, over a forty-four-year period, let alone to taste one harvested at the end of the First World War. But my excitement was to convince everyone to serve a white wine with the cheese, a crusade that to this day has been only partially successful but that I still fervently believe in as a better pairing than cheese with red wine. With white wine one can taste to their fullest both cheese and wine; with red, the flavors of both cheese and wine are dulled. (Try rich cheeses with a high-alcohol, high-extract California chardonnay served after the red wines.)

The superb woman of wine, Martine of Martine's Wines in the Bay Area, shared a passion with me for the wines of Burgundy's Fixin, as well as for the wines of Leroy and the Domaine de la Romanée-Conti, which she represented in California. So when I wanted to cook a dinner at my house for Alice and some of the staff from Chez Panisse (including Pat Curtan, who later did all the drawings for the Chez Panisse cookbooks) a couple of years after I left the restaurant, Martine supplied the wines.

So much for the so-called feud.

Dinner for Panisse Staff Chez Moi

May 19, 1981

Salad of California smoked sturgeon
Bourgogne blanc, René Manuel 1978
Chassagne-Montrachet, Château de Maltroye 1967

Spaghetti with sun-dried tomatoes
Hermitage Rouge 1976

Sadie Kendall goat cheeses
Fixin, Clos La Perrière 1964

Platter of Indian mangoes & strawberries
Château Doisy-Védrines 1964

Cooking in France

In 1975 Richard Olney wanted to introduce me to the Bandol wines of Domaine Tempier owned by his friends Lucien and Lulu Peyraud. He knew I would be bowled over by a day there with the kind of hospitality that the Peyrauds offered so well, and would find someone to import their wines again to the United States (they were imported by the *Gourmet* wine writer Gerald Asher, when he had his own wine company in New York).

Lunch at the Peyraud Family Table

Rosé 1964

Fresh striped bass with fennel grilled over vine cuttings.
Sauce of its roe and liver
Rouge 1973, 1972, 1970, 1960

Tomates provençales

Lamb's lettuce with garlic oil

Frommages de chèvre
Rouge 1961, 1968, 1964

Fruits

Coffee
Marc de Tempier 1961

My notes are all about the wines (since Richard and I with Lucien had tasted twelve or so from casks before lunch), because I knew the food would be forever etched in my memory after I saw Lulu stocking up a fire of vine cuttings and dried wild fennel branches outside the back door of the kitchen for cooking the bass. I had not seen her making the off-white sauce that appeared on the table in an off-white sauceboat. But when I tasted the sauce I knew it was one of those few life moments at table that I would never forget.

She had ground up the liver and roe of the bass with a mild, fruity extra-virgin olive oil and lemon juice, perhaps a bit of fish stock, lots of freshly ground white pepper. It did not look like much, but spooned over the moist, white, flaking flesh of the perfectly fresh and perfectly grilled fish, flavored by fennel and the lemonlike acid of the smoke from the vine cuttings, it was heaven on earth.

After all that wine, the coup de grâce of the marc (think French grappa), and a two-hour drive over the mountains back to Richard's house, I was more dead than alive but, oddly enough, a few hours later a bit peckish, as one can be after a long day of food and wine. Richard then, casually and with sleight of hand, produced a dish that, for the second time that day, created a memory which is perhaps even stronger now than the moment, perfect for its time, when I ate it.

Bread and Water with Richard Olney, 1975

We went out into the garden in the fading light of the evening and picked potatoes, onions, and thyme.

Soup of water, potatoes, onions
Puligny-Montrachet 1971

We added chunks of stale bread and French butter to the soup, salt, and ground pepper. A lifesaver!

❧

Cooking for James Beard

The guests were Cathy Simon, Michael Palmer, and my brother, as well as James Beard. His command had been to keep it simple, but that he felt like some great French wines (he had heard I had a decent cellar), and that he was pining for the fresh and chemically untreated bay scallops I had been bragging about now being able to get in San Francisco.

I knew he would love the caviar and would understand my serving the pressed or paiusnaya, apart from the fact it was all I could afford. And beef was always safe when served with Lafite.

Dinner for James Beard, My House, San Francisco

October 19, 1979

Caviar paiusnaya & toast
Jeanmaire, Blanc de Blancs

Pasta with bay scallops
Corton-Charlemagne, Louis Latour, 1970

Roast beef, Jerusalem artichoke puree
Château Lafite 1955

Cheeses
La Tâche, Domaine de la Romanée-Conti 1953

Fruit compote
Wehlener Sonnenuhr Auslese, J. J. Prüm 1950
Cockburn 1950

Jim wouldn't hear of putting a white wine with the cheeses, but after a precautionary tasting of the old Prüm, and the comments were "faded from opening—should have been aperitif, overpowered, badly placed," we put it with the cheeses and drank the La Tâche, which turned out to be truly a great one, afterward and before the port.

Two months later I cooked another dinner for him at my house, a menu to revive tired palates after a season of feasting.

Post-Christmas Beard Dinner, for Tired Appetites

December 27, 1979

The guests were Cecilia Chiang (of the great Mandarin restaurant in San Francisco), Marion Cunningham (Beard's San Francisco factotum and minder in those days), Robert Finigan (restaurant critic and wine writer, now speaking to me after the lamb incident at Chez Panisse several years before), Alice Waters, my companion and rose grower Gregg Lowery, and a friend from Nantucket, Ken Duprey.

I must have found some money from somewhere to pay for the sevruga.

Pol Roger, Cuvée de Blancs de Chardonnay, 1971

Caviar sevruga blini
Pol Roger, or Akvavit frozen

Smithfield ham in Madeira
Pol Roger, or Malmsey 1920

Salad "Alice," Chinoise

Compote of tropical fruits
Pol Roger, or Rieussec 1975

The salad was adapted from Escoffier's *Ma Cuisine* (curly endive, lemon juice, walnut oil, olive oil), which I made "Chinoise" for Cecilia by using fresh water chestnuts. The compote was fresh mangoes, papaya, and stewed quinces, flavored with an essence of roses from Gregg's garden.

Cooking for Lovers

There is nothing like past and present relationship tensions and appreciations to spice a meal with friends. Alice Waters cooked this dinner at her house in Berkeley for two pairings: hers with Robert Finigan, and mine with Gregg Lowery.

I brought the wines from my cellar. The wine everyone was poised to taste was the sweet white wine made by Beaulieu Vineyard from botrytis grapes in the thirties. It was the gold color of a middle-aged Château d'Yquem, stunningly good, but turned out not to be sweet. It was more like a Château Grillet, or a vin de paille. It was a bit oxidized, but beautifully, if you have that English taste. My notes say it "would have been perfect early in the meal—with fish. Memorable, *haunting* wine."

As was the evening. Mine with memories of Alice with me in the moonlight at the Gritti in Venice, of her coping with Gregg's existence, and of several stories Bob related about Alice, funny only by the time we got to the Mount Veeder.

Dinner with Alice and Boyfriends

May 26, 1980

Baby lettuces
Meursault Genevrières 1970

Grilled lamb chops
Beaulieu, Georges Latour Private Reserve Cabernet
Sauvignon 1974
Mayacamas, Cabernet Sauvignon 1969
Mount Veeder, Cabernet Sauvignon 1973

Asparagus

Coulis of strawberries
Beaulieu, "Château Beaulieu" 1930s

Dinner with Alice and New Boyfriend

October 27, 1980

This was a meal I cooked for Alice Waters and a new boyfriend who was not yet twenty-one—to celebrate their first being together. He was a wonderful guy, very good looking, but very complicated. They both were very nervous about the occasion, so I invited old and common friends (to Alice), Cathy Simon and Michael Palmer, as well as Gregg, to show that we were not against the new one just because our common good friend Bob Finigan had been at the altar before him.

Vouvray Mousseux, Brut 1970
Veuve-Clicquot, Brut NV

Fettuccine with white truffles
Château de la Maltroye 1967

Mixed green salad

Sonoma goat cheeses
Les Forts-de-Latou, en magnum, 1970

Dried fruits and nuts
Gonzalez & Byass 1970

Abundant white truffles have a way of conveying that all is right with the world.

Balance may be everything.

CHAPTER 5

Stars in Our Eyes

"EAT AMERICAN!"

That was the opening of a 1985 *Time* cover story called "The Fun of American Food." The cover image was the Renaissance-style head of a chef with an asparagus neck, romaine lettuce shoulders, a sea bream forehead, tangerine cheeks, and shrimp lips. On his head was a star-spangled chef's hat.

Two years earlier, just after the AIWF's "American Celebration Dinner," the *San Francisco Chronicle* asked some of the personalities involved for their idea of "an elegant meal." Sautéed foie gras and fresh truffles with asparagus and Madeira sauce, said Julia Child. "Fresh rabbit cooked étouffé style," said Paul Prudhomme. Michael McCarty, always the up-to-date showman, said first caviar, followed by pasta, and then by "quail grilled over mesquite coals, served with a salsa of fresh cilantro, jalapeños, and triple virgin olive oil." Alice Waters wanted Chinese food from Cecilia Chiang's Mandarin restaurant. Larry Forgione cited the menu he was cooking for the Brooklyn Bridge's centennial: "Sixteen courses based on American recipes from 1880," among them soft-shelled crab glazed with beach plum jelly and "oysters and sea urchins sharing a shell." I wanted American woodcock and wild strawberries, although not together.

We were all over the map. So what was American food?

Time said it started on the West Coast and was more or less interchangeable with "Californian," with its "dedication to lightness and freshness and its celebration of vegetables, herbs, and fruits." A *Life* article of the same period agreed that California had a profound effect on the new cuisine, and named Chez Panisse as the formative influence, crediting me as "the innovator" who still dreamed of a farm-restaurant that would produce its own "butter, honey, jams, vegetables, chickens, trout and hams. . . . Tower is already trying out tastes newer than radicchio, miniature vegetables, and fruit vinegars, and pushing the next trend: Southeast Asian flavorings like lemongrass and fermented Chinese black beans."

The writer wondered if that mix was un-American. "Nope," I was quoted as replying. "The cuisine of the United States, like its population, is an amalgam, taking ideas from abroad and, in pure American style, mixing them all together."

Jonathan Waxman added, "You can fool around"—this time not meaning only sex and drugs.

In the recent past the de rigueur gastronomic pilgrimage had been to France for the latest three-star food of Paul Bocuse, Michel Guérard, and the Troisgros brothers. But now the magazine recommended a summer trip "with equal zeal" through the United States to "sample the highly publicized creations that make up the new American cuisine." As the restaurant becomes "the new American theater," said *Life*, even Julia Child (the reigning Francophile) was courting the young Americans, and travelers sought out Paul Prudhomme, Larry Forgione (An American Place), the Ivy in Los Angeles, Chez Panisse in Berkeley, and me at Stars in San Francisco. In Boston, America's best woman chef, Lydia Shire, believed that "the average diner is very much aware of 'new American cuisine,' which is really the creative cooking of good simple food, using American products while infusing some kinds of classical preparations"— like her smoked Massachusetts partridge under a cloche.

Almost as important as ingredients, said *Life*, was the new esprit de corps. Waxman credited Larry Forgione with giving him so much help with suppliers that his restaurant Jams should have been called "Another American Place." A full-page photo shows Jonathan looking embarrassed in a pond full of ducks, Top-Siders hanging over the edge of his dinghy. How I agreed to get into jodhpurs and Hermès riding boots for my photo I don't remember, but I do recall hauling myself and a goat to the top of a hill above Paso Robles for a reluctant (the goat) kiss.

Waxman's Jams was a shock to New York, if a delightful one. The prices were electric, and the decor an eye-opener for New Yorkers who hadn't seen Michael's Trumps, or the West Beach Café. How could a "serious restaurant" with a "famous chef" be so plain? None of the "frog-pond" great French restaurants had white walls. And the elegance of The Four Seasons (the only other American restaurant mentioned) was indeed very formal. The co-owner of Jams, Melvyn Masters, explained: "I hate the theatrics of pseudo haute cuisine—the kind where you need a torch to see the menu." He opted instead for bright walls with works by modern artists and a kitchen open to public view—where diners could watch Jonathan again prepare his trademark dish of "free-ranging" chicken cooked over mesquite charcoal and served with French fries.

Time claimed that the new cooking was in "an intellectualized, even esoteric style, characterized by the use of fresh native ingredients." Now I would add that since one cook's esotericism is another's poison, the term "California Cuisine" was brought to its knees by overenthusiastic combinations of ingredients known only for their newness. Kiwis were piled on top of blueberry vinegar–infused reductions that were loaded into squirt bottles lined up in front of restaurant cooks just waiting for some poor squab to come along, probably paired with foie gras, scallops, and balsamic vinegar–drowned baby lettuces.

But that was later. For now California was the media darling: It had the freshest ingredients in the land.

Stars in the Carpet

With that Californian cornucopia, conceptualizing the food for my new restaurant was the least of my worries. Panisse was all about food, as was the Santa Fe Bar & Grill. But now I wanted to make a restaurant statement, about the greater challenge of being a restaurateur rather than just a chef. On my mind was whether Americans were ready for a new take on the brash elegance of old New York and San Francisco. I loved the callused-hand-with-a-manicure elegant roughness of Tadich and Sam's. I loved Clark Gable in the gold-paved San Francisco with Jeanette MacDonald. And I worshiped the photograph of Gable, Gary Cooper, Van Heflin, and Jimmy Stewart in white tie at Romanoff's in Los Angeles. I carried that photo wherever I went: as in "Someday it will be regained." I wanted a place where the young princes of Ken Russell's *The Music Lovers* could rub elbows with bankers and dancers and musicians from the arts center a block away, where fur coats could be flung aside with the seeming carelessness of Dietrich onstage. In short, a place that was charming and perfect.

In early 1981 I had sent my Green Beret brother a letter that included the proposal for the restaurant, telling him it would be a brasserie like Flo, Lipp, or Pharamond in Paris, but modernized and adapted to San Francisco. My sister had found the location in late 1978, and in mid-June (I wrote) we'd finally close with the bank and start construction. My two partners, I said, had experience and assets, and seemed "normal and honest."

Stars would not open until July 4, 1984.

It had been a maddening six years. The promised group of ten investors had come and gone like dance partners at a dateless prom. The owner of the ghostly old Italian restaurant had panicked several times, forgotten to renew his lease twice, and died once. After our lease was signed and various lawsuits settled, my partners decided to savage each other. One of them, an accountant, had distinguished himself by delivering Balboa's annual report on a cocktail napkin. He was soon history. I should have known to leave for New York then, to take glamorous offers from Windows on the World or Le Plaisir, or with the head of Air-India to buy The Royal Palms in Scottsdale. But my sister, who as one of many equal partners had seen firsthand the way I chafed, advised me not to worry: I'd be working with grown-ups in San Francisco.

In March 1981, I led James Beard, Barbara Kafka, James Villas, Jim Nassikas of Stanford Court, Danny Kaye (fresh from an affair with Laurence Olivier?), and several awestruck investors on a tour of the deserted site. I warned them to pause just inside the front door to let their eyes adjust to the deep gloom. The fixtures had been illegally removed and the place was gutted. As two remaining forty-watt bulbs responded to my flipping on the circuit breakers, the hushed group tried not to notice that Jim Beard had taken a swing with his cane at a large rat. A little bit of light was worse than the darkness. Now they could see the remains of the gold-flecked black mirrors on the walls, but dominating the view was a geyser of water, which spewed eight feet above the kitchen floor from a faucet ripped out of the wall. My friends tiptoed gingerly through the mirror shards, damp-eating fungus, and rat droppings.

"Jeremiah, it's a disaster," cracked Barbara.

"Really, dear . . . ," began Jim. Then words uncharacteristically failed him. His huge hand waved limply in a gesture of hopeless dismissal.

Danny Kaye gave a glass-shattering whistle to test the echoes.

It was all so awful that I had to fight off a fit of giggles.

Jim Nassikas saw only the expense and privately withdrew any thought of investing. All I could see were pale lemon walls, mahogany wainscoting, shiny brass, huge Chinese tubs holding oversize flowers and entire wild rosebushes, and a deep, star-covered Wilton carpet, from which the restaurant would take its name.

Everyone emerged from the site quite shaken. Perhaps worse interiors had been successfully remodeled—though doubt hung heavily in the fetid air—but my choice of site was thought downright suicidal. Although the restaurant was in the heart of the Civic Center, itself the political and cultural heart of San Francisco (City Hall and the mayoral offices were across the street, the ballet, symphony, opera houses two blocks away), the area was a mess. Drug dealers, criminals, and the homeless moved amid the blowing garbage. The only visitors by day came to beg or bribe for building permits. At night the visitors arrived in chauffeured limousines or held their noses against the smell of urine as they hurried out of the Civic Center garage to the opera or symphony. But no one was as shaken as my partner Doyle, because the answering machine for days recorded messages he didn't want to hear: the site is hopeless, the facility a mess, and that man (Doyle) downright dangerous.

I saw a different future, but with doubts. Breaking the rules at Chez Panisse and the Santa Fe was lauded, but would the public understand our choice of site even when I constantly voiced that I had no doubts about its future? I knew that a state government building would soon go up down the block, that plans for renovating the Civic Center with new museums and a new symphony hall were in the works. I saw a restaurant to which you would drive up, give your car to a valet, come in for a drink or oysters, walk a block (escorted by my staff) to the performance, walk back two hours later with the crowds, have dinner or a snack or dessert, then pick up your car and leave. I knew people would come to see beautiful dancers or famous opera or ballet stars, so I would subsidize the young dancers and court the stars. I wanted people to feel as if they owned my restaurant, as if it had everything for them rather than something for everyone. San Francisco didn't need another "special occasion" restaurant, it needed another "regular"—a home away from home, a place one could casually drop into for a glass of champagne, a business lunch or dinner or meeting in the bar, or a four-hour gourmandizing meal. I had visions of a place full of lawyers and city politicians selling us all down the river at lunch, afternoons at the bar full of glad victories or unhappy defeats from the law courts next door, the cocktail hour with all the office workers in the area, the pretheater crowd, a full house for dinner, and then post-10:00 P.M. the restaurant full again with the stars of the performing arts eating oysters and drinking champagne, with fans coming by to ogle the lithe young bodies of the corps de ballet. Filling the place four to five times a day was the dream. Reality was the pro forma at the bank that said three, and "best possible" gross at $3 million a year.

Meanwhile, there was a restaurant to build.

Pushing aside the lawsuits against my partner (with often me co-named) as thick on my desk as the rats had been on the floor of the abandoned Bacchini's, I got to work. The sheer weight of our press (from the Newport Astor Mansion, the AIWF festival, and many other Santa Fe national and international events) was enough to convince the Crocker

Bank to set a meeting to sign loan papers. Then our banker left Crocker, sending us into a scramble to find another who would hand over $350,000. Our ace in hand was the very favorable—and therefore valuable—lease that I had negotiated before I met Doyle. Then a lawsuit from our third partner (and one of Doyle's other partners) forced a public auction of the lease, our only asset. Few showed up to bid, and those who did were scared off by Apache Doyle in his Eddie Bauer sunglasses, which he wore throughout the session. His expression in victory was not one of joy but one of bloodlust. "If we ever have a problem," he assured me, "I am more than willing to step aside or buy you out." His long list of victims, he promised, would stop at me.

The problems began at once. Doyle evidently had no use for my master's in architecture from Harvard or the successful remodeling of Chez Panisse and Santa Fe. He insisted on managing the project himself—which would have been all right, I suppose, if he didn't habitually show up on the site an hour before the workmen left for the day. The pace of reconstruction was painfully slow. So I took over the decisions. And it was one scorching battle after another.

Looking at the mess of construction every day, I would have to remind myself of the wonderful dignity of trains like the 20th Century from New York to Chicago, of what it was like to dine in those mahogany-and-nickel cars as they flashed through the countryside of the United States. I'd think of the great ocean liners; of the grand old restaurants of New York, New Orleans, and San Francisco; and of Lucius Beebe, my hero since college days, who had dropped dead in his Turkish bath a few miles south of San Francisco only a few years before I arrived. His column in *Gourmet* called "Along the Boulevards" described a life I wanted to re-create, and the terms on which I wanted to re-create it. "If anything is worth doing," he once said, "it is worth doing in style and on your own terms—and nobody goddamned else's." I wanted to be as James Villas described him in a *Gourmet* article called "Lucius Beebe: The Last Magnifico": the randy and dandy boulevardier, the "eminently polite, generous, witty, and kind gentleman, who was not out to impress anybody and simply relished a civilized evening on the town over 'a hot bird and a cold bottle.'"

Eventually the spirit of this millionaire bon vivant prevailed. But the opening of the restaurant was a nightmare. The stakes were vastly higher now than they had been at the Santa Fe Bar & Grill, and I was about to be hoisted on my own press petard. The staff and public actually thought I knew what I was doing, so I had to act like it.

The sound of Birkenstocks slapping across the bare boards of the old

Victorian in Berkeley, or up the tarmac drive to the Santa Fe, was to be replaced by the sound of Manolo Blahniks swishing across a soft and star-filled Wilton carpet, but there was no carpet. A week before we were to open the restaurant, it wasn't finished by the stretch of anyone's imagination. So I turned the press lunch into a tongue-in-cheek "construction" one. We couldn't let the workmen stop, so we made them part of the scene. Remembering Cocteau's playful tables for Picasso (he used toys from the boulevard hawkers), we set a long, plywood-and-sawhorses table with nails, colorful electrical wire, hammers, and drills in the carpetless main dining room. The only other decor was a massive bouquet of flowers in the one completed corner, so that *Vogue* could photograph the "finished" restaurant in the tradition of the great Dorothy Todd, who changed fashion magazines into lifestyle when in 1924 for English *Vogue* she photographed the revolutionary new Boulestin's in London. Barbara Kafka reminded me how thin a limb she was perched on by writing that the restaurant was already a great success. She said she'd kill me if that wasn't the case by the time her article was published.

The press was poised to be enchanted, but their Caesar-like thumbs hovered between up and down. When I told the champagne-swilling crowd that the menu might veer from their printed ones because the gas had not been turned on, all the little Caesars looked around to see if I had invited the president of the utility company. While the cooks fired up the grill and I prayed there were no bullets in the charcoal, I told the story of the grilled dessert at the Astor Mansion lunch a year before. I downed a glass of champagne and relished the adrenaline of the moment.

"Right," I said to the cooks who had been with me at Newport, "line me up ten sauté pans." Hearing the cheers of the press as I juggled four pans at a time over the fire, I wondered why I hadn't thought to stage the whole thing. I relished the thought that events beyond my control always seemed to produce the most powerful results.

The public was less forgiving. And who could blame them? On opening night, bare bulbs were still hanging from the ceiling. We didn't even have chandeliers: Doyle had been promising that his friend in Napa would finish and deliver them the next day—for the last six months. We had promised glamour, and here was only gloom and confusion. What customer in those first two months could be expected to know, walking in the doors for the first time, what the place was going to be?

On opening day, the hostess ran up minutes before the doors opened and urgently inquired: "When the customers ask what kind of restaurant it is, what kind of food, what shall I tell them?"

I madly tried to think. "Tell them . . . American brasserie," I said, then muttered to myself, "whatever that means."

"Oh," she said. "That's fine"—as if I had replied "Italian bistro."

After lunch I asked her what people had made of the "American brasserie" tag.

"Oh, no problem, they got it."

Which was certainly more than we did at first.

But soon we did get it, and as we all pulled together as a team, we felt that Stars could be what the new American restaurant was all about, more than just a California style.

Not that I thought Stars would ever win the best food in America contest: It was too big, and I couldn't supervise it all, all the time. What Stars did best and uniquely was measured in the breadth of the food, offering everything from lobster gazpacho to scrambled eggs with black truffles, to what the *San Francisco Chronicle* columnist Herb Caen called a "superb $3.50 hot dog with sauerkraut or the $7.50 hamburger which is probably the best in town."

Robert Finigan had wondered what we could do that we hadn't done at the Balboa Café and Santa Fe but now wrote that the food "resting on its raw materials is at once harmonious with Tower's latter-day style, familiar from Santa Fe and Balboa, and yet more exploratory and adventurous. Once you glance at the Stars menu, you will see how far the offerings range beyond 'California cuisine' clichés (sun-dried tomatoes and goat cheese), even those which seemed so new when Tower and his colleagues developed them." He lists a few favorite dishes: the Iced Oysters with Spicy Lamb Sausages ($6.75), which "are truly sensational in the truest sense of that overused word"; the hollowed-out Brioche with Marrow, Lobster Sauce, Poached Garlic, and Chervil ($7.50); the Blanquette of Veal with Summer Vegetables and Crayfish Sauce ($15.00); and an "exquisite" fattened Duck Liver on Grilled Bread ($12.50). He loved the huge champagne list, the long list of innovative cocktails, all the flavored frozen vodkas, and urged his readers not to miss "being present at the creation of something very special indeed."

The kitchen was but one element in the overall experience. As San Francisco's version of Walter Winchell meets the *Post*'s "Page Six," Herb Caen wrote in his column the morning after I introduced him to Rudolf Nureyev and Makarova, "Thank God for Stars, which honors the city's legendary reputation for kick-up-your-heels liveliness." He found Stars "the perfect place" to wind down after a show: "Stars looks terrific"— going on to describe the fifty-two-foot bar, the illustrations and posters crammed on the walls, the various eating locations, the café effect in the center of the room, the chandeliers and paneled walls, the wide-open kitchen, and the grand piano presided over by Mike Greensill. "And then," he continued, "there's the energy and electricity. You feel it the minute you walk through the doors. It's enough to light the city of Bakersfield." A couple years later, Herb gave me an even more sparkling quote about Stars's "unique mixture of fun, vitality, throwaway elegance, and wide, beautifully done choices." Then he said Stars blessed San Francisco as a world-famous hangout. "That puts Jeremiah Tower right up there with Coit Tower as a beloved landmark."

Whether you came in for Herb's beloved hot dog or a sixty-five-dollar truffled three-pound lobster cooked in the wood oven, you had to come Clark Gable–in–San Francisco style, up the steps from the alley into the pulsing main room filled with three hundred guests, sixty of them at the fifty-two-foot bar in the center of the space along a wall facing the oyster bar and the open kitchen with its ten cooks.

Finigan said the kitchen, bar, and patrons were the principal decor, while dishing the namesake carpet, which looked to him as if it belonged in the office of the president of Paraguay. He was right about the powerful punches that created Stars's ambience. It was not just that we didn't have money to spend on expensive fixtures. It was also that I didn't believe (and I still don't) that a restaurant should outdress its customers.

Jim Beard got immediately that Stars had "caught the spirit of its time." He loved its welcoming informality, comparing its look to a "quality that one sometimes finds in a nineteenth-century restaurant that has lived on" and its hustle-bustle to Paris brasseries like Le Vaudeville and La Coupole (which had actually been my part of my inspiration).

Caroline Bates in *Gourmet* got it too. She remembered my telling her that Joe Baum's motto "new-old food in a new-new setting" would be Stars's and reported that the food was provocative and satisfying. The feeling of the restaurant captured "the times so surely that some day it may be looked back on as the restaurant that best defined the tastes of the eighties."

"Throwaway Elegance"

I told the staff on opening day that the Stars motto was "Everything from black tie to blue jeans." That it would be dining for people of all incomes all in one place. In Stars you could see types in formal dress (Mayor Dianne Feinstein looking better now that she had let her hair turn from

basic black to gray) squeezing in next to types in jeans (the left-wing diners with Daniel Ortega), and everybody getting along just fine: the way
San Francisco was meant to be. One magazine caught the crowd in amber:
tuxedoed men and ball-gowned women from performances, students and
stockbrokers and Sacramento car dealers, old money and borrowed
money. R. W. "Johnny" Apple of *The New York Times* called Stars the only
truly democratic famous restaurant he had ever seen. Stars was Paul
Bocuse's favorite, "the kind of restaurant that every Frenchman envisions
an American restaurant to be," so it was not surprising that, for Jacques
Pépin, Stars was "the most exciting place in San Francisco."

Within four months *Travel & Leisure* recognized that le tout San Francisco had adopted Stars, and we were soon doing three times our best-case
scenario, filling Stars five times a day. *Metropolitan Home* used the word
superchef for the first time and gave six full pages to photographs of the
food. The articles were great for morale and business, but my favorite
response to Stars was written on a cocktail napkin: "Dear Jeremiah, Ahh-
hhhhhhhhhhhh!! We've been to Paris, England, Berkeley, Germany,
Yugoslavia and Livermore etc. and this is #1. Thank You."

Needless to say, there were dissenters, not all of them lipstick limousine
liberals who told *The Boston Globe* that California cooking had started
when Alice Waters built her pizza oven. Some distrusted the story of
where the restaurant got its name, some felt uneasy with all the signed
photos of stars on the walls, and some Berkeley critics just decided to build
a wedge between Alice and me.

Trouble was in the air.

In the *Chronicle*, the Birkenstock-clad old hippie Stan Sesser, with
whom I had much-publicized rows, hated everything about Stars and, of
course, me—a stance later inherited by a restaurant reviewer for the same
newspaper, Michael Bauer. Sesser repeated his peeve: "Tower's weakness
has always been a lack of consistency, an inability to control the kitchen so
that everything comes out just right." How unable, or not, the years would
show.

At the time, however, I listened more to the averages than to Sesser; I
knew that in feeding six hundred people a day there might be casualties.
But most of the complaints turned out to be of the "high" prices-"small"
portions variety. And then there were those who felt that a superstar chef
should "always be in the kitchen."

My "patrician" accent and stories of storms with a soon-to-be iconic
Alice turned up in a few East Bay reviews. One important national review
opened with me hearing an airline promo in my car on the way back from

Napa and capriciously jetting off: "Seizing the moment Tower thought 'why not' and twenty one hours later was lunching at Alain Senderens' Lucas Carton in Paris and then, after shopping for supplies for the restaurant, in less than forty eight hours was back cooking in his own restaurant." On the flight back I had read all these reviews. What I read made me want to head right back to Paris—and to decide never to read anything but the helpfully negative reviews again, and then only the ones about Stars itself. Wide open to the press, who were either fawning, lapdogging, or on the attack, I felt that Stars and I were getting too vulnerable for comfort.

But nothing made me feel as vulnerable as assassins at my door.

Who Is Killing the Great Chefs?

Around four on a Tuesday afternoon in 1984, Lawrence, my self-styled general manager, gingerly handed me an envelope, apprehension on his face. "Another fan who wants me to father her child?" I asked.

"How did you know?"

Its Freddy Krueger–like writing made me recoil and drop the envelope on the floor. The contents were even more scary: details of a murder of Masataka Kobayashi, the fabled chef and co-owner of San Francisco's Masa's. Then, in what sounded like acid-fueled rantings, it spoke of our taking the insurance money, getting married, raising kids, and sailing off into the sunset.

"You had better call North Station [the police] just in case this means something later," I said. "And put the case number on file as usual." The police were used to these threats and loyally sent an officer by to pick up the letter. He had his usual hamburger and coffee and left. Two hours later the front-desk phone was for me.

"Stay right where you are," a voice said. "Do not move. Don't leave the building, we'll be right there," which sent me over to the bar for a fast champagne. A second glass was cut off by my sight of flashing police car lights in the alley.

A captain and two officers made a beeline to me.

"Jeremiah, we want you to get out of town, and don't pass go. Be gone for four or five days and tell no one but us where you are. Here's the number for a private line to the mayor's office and to North Station."

"What the hell is going on?" I asked.

"Masa's been murdered. We found his body today, but he was killed probably on Sunday."

The captain handed me the envelope with my name on it. "Look again," he said. "Note the postmark."

I looked: It had been mailed on Friday, two days before the actual murder. I dropped the letter again, this time in the captain's hands, and had another glass: a double Polish vodka.

The officers were to see me to the airport. But I knew I would stick out a mile at any California resort, whereas there is nothing so anonymous as being at a local hotel under a false name, cash deposit on account, and making sure to be in the bathroom when room service shows up.

While one officer got my car and another took keys to get things from my house, which would be off-limits to me for at least a week, I called a pal who managed the city's most luxurious small hotel, told him that I'd have to enter anonymously, that no one could know I was there, and that I'd be using cash. I told him nothing else, and the tone of my voice upset him. He said no. I went anyway, and let the police take me there. After a club sandwich and bottle of La Tâche, I calmed down, thought the whole thing ridiculous, even if the coincidence that the night before Masa was killed was the end of the season run of *Who Is Killing the Great Chefs of Europe?* gave me pause, and went home. After immediately ordering a sophisticated alarm system to be delivered in the morning, I watched horror movies all night with my cat, Boy Burma. The cat had never shown fear of anything and loved the all-night session.

After the alarm—with its silent panic button to signal the police station—was installed, I finally slept. The next evening police, very angry at not finding me at the hotel, found me at Stars. A van had been discovered at the base of my street in Bernal Heights, the interior soaked in human blood with hundreds of little pieces of paper, torn up from larger ones with my home telephone number written on them, stuck to it.

I got out of town. Boy Burma and I went to a friend's house in Inverness, a place so quiet at night that he growled at every sound and scared me half to death.

Back to Bernal Heights.

Two days later I was still alive and went back to Stars. The night of the second day I heard a noise downstairs. The thing about sharks in the water is that you often think you see one, but when they're there you know it. It's the same with burglars. When someone is actually in the house it's unmistakable—no matter how much you try to wish the realization away.

I wondered why the intruder was talking to himself. Then it hit me: there were two of them.

I swallowed my fear and guessed that once you cry out and turn on the lights, burglars will run away. So I yelled that I knew they were there and turned on the lights. They didn't run away. Now they knew where I was and could see where they were going. I hit the silent panic button along with the horns that would wake up everyone for miles.

As the men came up the stairs, I threw on a pair of briefs, even at the time thinking that hiding nakedness was a stupid reason to die. I searched for a weapon and found only my twelve-inch seventeenth-century sterling silver English letter opener. I grabbed it, then tried to scoop up Burma, who had taken a bulldog stance at the top of the stairs and was growling at a huge volume, his raised hair now making him three times his size. Urging him on, I ran through the guest room and out a window on top of the entrance roof.

"Freeze!"

There were policemen everywhere—three with guns pointing directly at me. Later they told me I had been an immeasurable moment from being blown away, because all they could see was a silhouette against the lighted window holding what looked like a huge knife.

The back of the house was under construction, so the two intruders dove through the plastic cover, fell into my vegetable garden below, and dashed down an overgrown gully into the projects at the base of Bernal Heights, where they disappeared.

It was time for more late-night television, expensive Burgundy, and cigars with the two handsome cops, who stayed with me until dawn. They left, saying to tell no one of the incident.

The next day I called a real-estate agent and explained my needs for the next place I would live. She showed me various plush apartments but had the same reaction to my security concerns that people have when they read about rock and roll or movie stars and their "necessary" bodyguards. Sure enough, the gossip columns a few days later had me arrogantly demanding security that no chef could possibly need, no matter how famous. The next night another chef, still clad in his white jacket, was ambushed as he got out of his car in the Sunset district and stabbed through the head with a large chef's knife. His murder shut up the real-estate agents and gossip columnists for a while, at least about me—although one columnist did speculate that I might be next. Wishful thinking.

Meanwhile there had been a funeral and lots of newspaper coverage about the murder, the fact that Masa had no money, and that his widow and children were penniless because Masa had died four months before his life insurance policy would have automatically reverted to him (and his wife). The principal beneficiary was said to be his partner Bill Kimpton, then in a heavy expansion mode. The newspapers and police were fascinated that the murderer or murderers had shown up when Masa's wife and children were out of town, on his night off—and that they'd evidently been welcomed, since there was no sign of violence, other than Masa's being dead. So it looked as if the murderer was no stranger. But where was the motive?

The list of people Masa knew and trusted was small, and no, I told the police, he did not have boyfriends. Find someone who could benefit from his death, I said. I could see the list going through the captain's head, processing the list of potential suspects. A few weeks later, I called, as usual, the private number at the mayor's office; the woman on the other end said she had no idea what I was talking about. I cited the case number and got the same response. There was no record—it had been expunged. Someone had gotten to it.

I felt a connection with Masa. In early 1985, Herb Caen had reported I was about to put Santa Fe and Stars up for sale and open a place all my own in New York. I had planted that story, and had even gone to New York to look at sites, to get my partner Doyle's attention. Certainly nothing else did, unless it was time for lunch or a cocktail waitress. During this period I turned down the job at Stephen Spector's Le Plaisir, despite Jim Beard handing it to me on a plate. Why not use the sous-chef Masa, I had said. Then, when I turned down the job as chef of the Auberge du Soleil in Napa, Claude Rouas, whose top San Francisco restaurant L'Etoile was put out of business by Stars (some said), hired Masa. We thought we were stalking each other. So when I learned his widow was penniless, I decided to act.

I gave a fund-raiser at Stars one Sunday morning to send Masa's widow and children home to Central America or, as her thank-you note to me said, to "ensure a stable future for my children." Bill Kimpton and his two cronies had always seemed cold to me, but they showed up briefly for the event. After a few minutes Bill approached me, his eyes as dead as the fish we were serving. "Why would you bother to do a thing like this?" he asked. I was speechless.

Later I decided that it was all what Lord Peter Wimsey or Hercule Poirot would call a "red herring," and that the idea of serially killing chefs had been borrowed from a famous book, movie, and TV series. I meant nothing—and neither, probably, did the chef who was knifed in the head in the Sunset. Nothing like leaving too many clues to get away with murder.

Which is still "unsolved."

Saying Good-bye—and Looking Ahead

Soon after Masa, Jim Beard died on January 21, 1985. At the age of eighty-one, he was a testimony that if you stay vitally interested in life, it does not matter what you eat. Or how much.

Of course Jim's body didn't keep up with his desires, and there were long hospital stays, since the vast quantities of animal fat he had eaten in his life tended to stick around, occasionally in his arteries, but especially in his legs and feet. But he managed to leave this planet to go organize another with most of his dignity intact, and a life full of pleasurable culinary moments.

A few months before he died he called me to New York. The instructions over the phone were vague, but his voice held no room for refusing. I arrived at his house on West Twelfth Street in Manhattan around ten in the morning. He offered no coffee or anything to eat, so I knew the business was serious, even when it took him almost ninety minutes to get to a point.

"Jeremiah"—his voice steely velvet—"you know you still have an enemy out there?"

Stunned, but not surprised at the statement, I waited to reply. Only one, and one so important to have to say it to me personally and in private?

"Of course it's not Alice, because that would be stating the obvious, and you wouldn't have called me all the way here to tell me that. You are not going to tell me who, are you?"

He snorted his agreement.

"But it is someone whom you consider a close friend."

Then there was silence. A long one.

"I guess I can't buy you lunch" was all I could muster, especially since I knew the conversation and visit were over. How could any conversation follow that?

He was in the downstairs library, sunk into a huge chair. It all seemed so formal. I leaned over him and did not avoid the old-man unevenly shaved, bristly wet lips.

"Good-bye, darling" were the last words he ever said to me.

I thought I had now found safe home ground in the Bay Area by opening Stars, but Jim had said I had enemies, and not ones I could keep close. And I always listened to what Jim had to say. I liked my enemies out in front—this one was obviously more of a terrorist hiding in the gloom.

On the plane I had a premonition that I would not see Jim again, and I thought about him the entire way back to San Francisco. How I would sum up what I thought then was best expressed by one of Australia's greatest impresarios, Leo Schofield, critic and food writer for *The Sydney Morning Herald,* a year later. His article "California Cuisine" in Australian *Gourmet,* a magazine I read religiously, said Beard was the person who "liberated American cooking from Gallic shackles." He mentioned chefs whom Beard had influenced, among them Wolfgang Puck ("combining European traditions with chutzpah," photographed in Spago drinking champagne with Stevie Wonder), Bradley Ogden ("the wunderkind from San Francisco, via Traverse City, Michigan"), and me. Puck told Leo that Beard was more important than *The New York Times*'s French classicist Craig Claiborne, "who thought one had to go to France for ideas." Schofield mentioned that my link with Beard was particularly strong because of my love of nineteenth-century regional American cooking. My favorite story that I told Leo was of the sun-ripe cantaloupe melons filled with hundred-year-old Madeira chilled to perfection down a well. Leo said I "combined a romantic streak with extraordinary practicality." I told him he had it the wrong way around, for me and for Beard.

From Beard I said I learned—and here my old Australian slang was coming out—that American cooking is about "letting the cooks have a go." I continued, "Americans have never been ones to hold back. They go at something and it's that straightforwardness of personality that really helps in cooking. If someone puts lemongrass in a sauce and the next thing you have is Lemon Grass Beurre Blanc. It may not work, but at least they will have a go."

Sometimes this American quality was lauded. In me it was increasingly seen as the "arrogance" of a "megastar."

"One Litigious Bitch"

Star or not, any romantic needs dreams to go forward.

When asked by a reporter about my future plans in early 1985, I said the first thing I would do was raise my salary. Because my disputes with my partner in Stars had now turned into a full-scale war of litigation, my salary was frozen and I was still paying myself fifteen thousand dollars less a year than my chef was earning. But my ambition was to retire as soon as possible with as much money as possible. And that had been my thought from the day I started. Then I could open a restaurant in Monte Carlo.

The war had started after the "civilized" conversation we had agreed one day might be necessary, but which when we had it, didn't work. By the piano one afternoon thirty-six days after we opened Stars, my throat, guts, and heart in a tangled mess, I sat down with Doyle and his wife for that chat and our promise to part amicably—one selling to the other—if the partnership was no longer working.

"Tough" had been Doyle's reply, the two of them smirking at my astonishment while the bartenders leaned over to hear why I was so alternately red and white in the face.

Our differences were no secret. The previous night Doyle and his wife had come in at prime time to a packed Stars. He complained to me that he had been waiting for two hours for a table. "Let them [the walk-ins] wait," he said, so that he could have a table. I knew then that we were truly different animals: I could no more have commandeered a table that night in my own restaurant than have told the cooks to burn the food. Owning a restaurant meant one thing to me, another to him. The next morning I looked at my Gault-Millau magazine filled with photos of the Côte d'Azur and wrote, "I plan the way out, a coup, or just sell out." The following night Doyle pulled his own coup.

That Sunday evening was the first benefit for AIDS research in San Francisco and the United States at which world-famous stars and socialites thought it safe to be seen in public for such a then socially unacceptable cause. Terry McEwen, director of the opera and a rather grand queen of great style, had the idea of bringing the world's top musicians and singers to the San Francisco Opera, with our very chic mutual friend and mentor Denise Hale ensuring the social turnout and its press. The musical evening brought tears to all but the most hard-bitten, and the after-performance party across the road at Stars was both triumphant and socially safe: Suddenly raising money for AIDS at social gatherings was fun—and acceptable. The only fly in the ointment was my partner.

Since it was a Sunday night, the staff was surprised to see Doyle, especially in his Napa farming clothes for a black-tie affair—although no one was surprised to see him sitting at the bar downing drinks. He seemed quiet enough, but I could see the usual chip on his shoulder slowly growing back into a tree as the more and more famous and bijou-bedecked socialites assembled around the bar before dinner. It did not sit well with Doyle that we were giving away the evening, "losing" probably fourteen thousand dollars in gross sales. It never occurred to him that the staff were donating their time and the food and wine had been donated as well. The next day our headwaiter, Rick, who was gay, was incensed when he described Doyle's reaction to the event and his comment to him. According to Rick, Doyle said something like, "If it weren't for you faggots, we would not have to do things like this." That was shocking enough for Rick, but the fact that the comment could easily have been heard by the opera director (gay), the mayor (straight), and a major opera star (gay), all standing within earshot, was even more damaging. Rick said that since Herb Caen had not heard Doyle, he told him.

The next day Herb called to ask what I was going to do—before, the implication was, he told the entire city. Two days later the story was out, and, inflamed by in-house gossip, so was the staff. They assembled in the alley outside the restaurant after calling me at the Santa Fe. They would return if I insisted, but they wanted my assurance that I'd do something, and fast, about my partner.

I drove into the alley at Stars and persuaded the staff to go back to work. When I asked the managers if they wanted to work for Doyle, the answer was a resounding "No!" It was obvious that he should now manage the Santa Fe and I, Stars, so I posted an announcement that I'd be taking over 100 percent of the operations, and that Doyle and his wife would no longer be coming into the restaurant except as equal owners, with all those carefully defined privileges. Within the hour, the staff of the day at the Santa Fe showed up at Stars. I sent them back, and then several of San Francisco's most expensive lawyers began working overtime.

A superbly ruthless attorney understood my predicament in under an hour of conversation: "You want me to put his neck in the gutter and stand on it." With his help I kept my partner and his wife out of Stars long enough to calm the restaurant down. But I knew that the trouble was just starting.

I had the restaurant to myself now, so I decided to go for the big deal. And fight for it. But there was still the Santa Fe Bar & Grill.

On New Year's Eve 1985 I was supervising dinner at both Stars and the Santa Fe—alternating one hour at each. Hurtling back and forth over the Bay Bridge without a driver on New Year's Eve, I wondered if my divided loyalties and responsibilities would get me killed. On top of that, Santa Fe was in chaos under Doyle's control. He had promoted a mediocre waiter to manager, where he was less competent, and when I arrived at 6:00 P.M. on the biggest night of the year, he was having a leisurely dinner in the office. The staff looked lost, and Doyle was nowhere to be found. No one knew if he'd show up at all.

When my attorneys filed a suit to appoint a receiver for the Santa Fe, Doyle countersued. When asked by a reporter for his take on all this, Doyle said, "The restaurant business is intense and complicated and often inspires disputes." I laughed when I read that, since if Doyle had known as much about the restaurant business as he did about intensity and disputes, we wouldn't have had a problem. I publicly shrugged off the countersuit: "I don't own anything personal except a cat, some clothes, and a lot of cookbooks."

But I was worried. This was much more dangerous than Alice standing on the steps of her house and screaming, "It's my house, my car, and my restaurant." A lot more than the tensions inside her Panisse kitchen described by one of the staff: "We were told that we were a family, but it was more like we were the ugly stepsisters and Alice was Cinderella." More than Jonathan Waxman saying you could never really know fear until you'd heard Alice's footfalls on the stairs. This was Doyle's last stand, and he had a pit bull lawyer.

After much binding in the marsh, we agreed finally that the Moons would run the Santa Fe and I would run Stars. But that created a management vacuum at the Santa Fe. After a kitchen fire that was the direct result (or so one of the kitchen staff told me) of no one having set maintenance schedules, Doyle alleged to me that the staff had left the flues dirty to make him look bad. I knew that he was paranoid and that our arrangement would never work. I agreed at last to put the Santa Fe up for sale in 1986.

One partnership down, one to go.

I also agreed to list Stars with Sotheby's. I knew no one would buy it without me or a noncompete clause, but if the opening bid of $3 million was met, so be it: The Côte d'Azur hadn't gone anywhere. Of course no offers were made, so Doyle and I entered the next phase, in which we could bid against each other for 100 percent of Stars.

We needed to be at the attorneys' office first thing on a Monday morning with a down payment of fifty thousand dollars in cash; the remaining balance (whatever it came to) would be due in ninety days. I did not have anything more than a Mercedes payment to my name, so we'd have to go to the bank. As it happened, however, a manager, Steven Vranian (from our now famous Newport lunch in 1983), had missed the three o'clock Friday bank closing, so we took the cash from the restaurant. I was later sued for fraud for that ingenuity, but it worked, even if all weekend I was terrified of the illegality. Fortunately, I had much to distract me that weekend, including a celebrity appearance at an Orange County March of Dimes gala and an article to finish for *Vogue*. On Sunday night I opened a magnum of vintage Krug and looked for a bad movie on TV to put me to sleep. The only option was *Attack of the Killer Tomatoes!* and that seemed somehow quite fitting.

At 9:00 A.M. sharp on Monday we were in the attorneys' office, ready for more drama than a high-stakes craps game in Vegas. As usual, Doyle was half an hour late: To save a few bucks, he'd searched for a parking space instead of putting his $60,000 car in the building's garage. After the Moons arrived, it took six hours to set the rules. The bidding started at 3:30. The Moons' attorney tossed the 1889 silver dollar, the wife called, and I won—it was my opening bid of $500,000. I was so nervous I forgot the agreed-upon floor and wrote $550,000. Doyle immediately topped it. The poker game had begun.

One had to have this money in hand, and I did not. What I did have was a secret weapon. Tapping a San Francisco source would have given Doyle a shot at finding out how much I had to spend. So I'd gone out to my international contacts. Sitting in the foyer was a man whom I had not introduced. But he could never have been mistaken for poor. Benjamin Bitanga, a friend from the Philippines, and I had an understanding: He would guarantee me up to $1,250,000, over which I promised not to bid.

As the bidding reached $1,000,000, rivulets of sweat rolled down under my shirt. I could not remember how to write the numbers that add $50,000 to a million, and after almost bidding $1,500,000, I pulled the note back and told my lawyer, "Here, you write it, you know what I mean."

What was the restaurant worth? While there are mathematical formulas for working this out, the spread of multipliers is so great, the variables so numerous, and the psychological and emotional forces so powerful, that establishing the monetary value is more art than recognizable science. Commonly understood practice is to multiply the annual net by a number ranging from three to eight, depending on the intrinsic values of the lease, the location, the staff performance, and the goodwill of things like the central figure staying on or not, or anything else that will affect the future viability or earnings. So to Doyle the restaurant was worth a good deal less than it was to me. If he bought Stars, it would be without me, goodwill, or the top staff. But this was poker. Bluffing would get me to pay him more than I wanted to spend.

When the bidding hit $1,250,000, Doyle, his wife, and his attorney left the room. I was used to his tactics. His rigor mortis smile meant nothing. The sweat pushing out from the armpits of his Hugo Boss suit did. I had him, but I was at my ceiling, so he had me, too. He returned with another fifty grand, which I topped with money I didn't have to reach $1,350,000.

Doyle shot out of his chair and said to his lawyer, "Let's take a walk"— which I took to mean they were walking away from the game.

Champagne bubbles floated in front of my eyes. I called the restaurant and told them to put the three cases I had in my car (in the event I lost) on ice, and to serve them to the hundred or so regulars in Stars waiting for the outcome.

"You have not bought anything yet," my Asian friend said coolly.

He was right. I called back to tell the restaurant to put the champagne on hold, but I knew from the uproar on the other end of the phone I was too late. The chefs had had their résumés ready in case of my defeat; now they were ceremonially tearing them up. I told my attorney that if the Moons returned with another bid, I'd have a choice between slitting my wrists and jumping out the office's thirtieth-floor window.

"Your aces beat my kings" was Doyle's concession as he came back into the room and looked pointedly at my wild card Filipino friend.

I called the restaurant and confirmed the outcome of the shoot-out. When I returned to Stars, I saw that the evening's menu bore the inscription "All Our Love and Support." I was going to need it.

The opposing attorney later said that Doyle had been "very much a buyer." I wondered where he'd gotten the money—if he had it at all. We later heard an eerie rumor that it was Bill Kimpton and his group. In any case, it was by no means clear who the "winner" had been. The Moons had put $57,000 into Stars; I thought their getting $1.3 million would satisfy their appetites (2,300 percent annual return should satisfy anyone) and whatever sense of honor they had. But how hurt was their pride? With my first partner I had ignored the power of a woman scorned; now I had denied the power of a dishonored Apache.

Heaven at Last?

Now that I owned and had Stars all to myself, I had to face running it. A typical day started at six in the morning. I would stop at Stars for a coffee and to check how many of the flowers had to be replaced. I was doing the arrangements myself because flowers and the flower market brought me peace and sanity. Also I wanted to find out how much labor and cost it took to install the five arrangements: two six-foot-tall and four-foot-wide beauties that reached from on top of each end of the bar to the eighteen-foot ceilings, and three other restaurant-size ones.

That day the espresso machine fouled my cappuccino, so I left a note to the opening bartender wondering what it was in his job description and checklist that he didn't understand about flushing the machine every day with cleaner. Of course my note was written in state-of-the-art California human resources language rather than mine. I didn't want a pouty and whiny bartender when I returned for my nine o'clock coffee.

I bought twelve-foot-long wild rose runners, massive magnolia and just-fruiting fig branches, and twenty dozen cut flowers. After a fast gossip with a couple of the less discreet vendors about which restaurants were not paying their bills, I stuffed all the flowers in the van and drove back to Stars. As I walked through the doors, the bartender forced a smile and held out a new cappuccino. As soon as the flowers were done I visited the basement and greeted the Latino-Tibetan-Vietnamese prep crew. These were my favorite employees, and twenty minutes with them could have been the last really good moments of the day, depending on what I would hear at the morning managers' meeting at ten. So I savored the time talking about washing lettuce by hand and showing them again how to peel fava beans (never blanched) and peel and cut the cardoon for a lobster dish slated for one of that night's private parties. Without these little teaching sessions (which worked both ways), and sometimes despite them, the day—which could last from then to two the next morning— could go really bad.

I checked on the toilets, the homeless outside, the basement pumps, the carpet, the "take" from the day before, and sat with my chef, bartender, assistant, private dining manager, dining room manager, sous-chef, and bookkeeper. We knew it was going to be a rough day, so I canceled my day-time once a week bartending and called in the spare: the mayor was in for lunch with a new girlfriend and so was his old one with someone else, so seating in the preferred section was going to be delicate; our most regular couple, and also our most demanding, hated the mayor and, when drunk (every time) would go over and tell him why his lack of Irish ancestry left him less than a man, and they too were booked at the same time as the mayor; Joan Collins and Barbra Streisand were booked at lunch for the same time and the same table and, knowing restaurateurs never have the benefit of coincidence, I wondered aloud if one of them was for the same time the following week—either way I would be asked to sit with both after lunch; Herb Caen put the pressure on with a note saying he hoped we did our usual eleven out of ten for "Baby Denise" that night; *Parsifal* was opening at the opera, which meant starting an hour earlier— lunch would be frantic to end early; San Francisco's top socialite was giving a party for Zubin Mehta, leaving us a little more than the usual fifteen minutes to turn "The Club" from regular seating into a fairyland of special decor that would have strained London's Ritz when there were four staff members for every two guests; Carol Channing was with that party, and her antiallergy lunch box taken from her the moment she entered had to be kept at the maître d' stand so she didn't worry it would be contaminated; Godfrey, the hostess's chauffeur, was to be there at 5:00 with her pink light-bulbs, the candlestands, tablecloths, and napkins. All the special plates, glasses, decor, and flatware would have to be polished (by 5:00 P.M.) and put in the hallway out of sight because we would have only minutes to set up her party. I told the bartender to make new special ice cubes with Evian for the host, and to leave a note for the evening bartender to have the Water-ford glass, little tray, and two pieces of bread ready for his arrival by 7:45.

"It's your neck," I reminded the dining room manager, and continued briefing.

The security guards for the jewels worn would have to be fed; the piano had to be moved and tuned in place for the reception, then moved back (it took eight people); chilies had to be crushed for Zubin Mehta no earlier than 8:00 P.M.; cookies set aside for the chauffeur; the North Station guys alerted that another guest was wearing the two-million-dollar-each Graff twin diamonds, one on each hand, and her Dior dress cost $150,000, so no waiter was allowed near her, the red wine would have to be poured only by the manager, and she needed a special stool because she could not sit down; our insurance company had to be alerted about the jewels and the dress; there was to be a special cake, which Mrs. Mehta was bringing, arriving by private jet from Los Angeles by six o'clock—and an alert was to be sent out if no one had seen it by then.

There were two private dinners that night other than Denise's, one for twenty-five in the Grill Room and one for forty in JT's. The chef reported all the food had arrived or was about to; the late-arriving wine steward said he'd checked the wines and one selection of the parties' wines was missing. He would call to find it. The flowers were being supplied by the hosts of the parties. I reminded the manager about our 10 percent service charge for that. And to make sure Denise was not charged for the cake Mrs. Mehta was bringing.

"Whatever you do, if I am busy, make sure the security guards have the homeless out of there by seven o'clock." I heard a shout from the men's room as one of the bookkeepers ran into a particularly scrofulous homeless man taking a bath from the sink. We threw him out, and the dishwasher cleaned up the piles of wet old newspaper that had been used as under-wear. With concealed rage I reminded everyone to keep the front door locked until 11:00 A.M. and told them to reclean the room. Then I went up to my office.

The first meeting there was about the ever-mysterious and always emotional annual health insurance policies; the monthly financials; the bank loan payment, now at $35,000 a month; cash flow, and the cash for my trip.

The second was with my assistant about my seven-day round-the-world press trip in two days' time.

The phone rang with Denise: she would be late for the late-afternoon decor meeting because her red dress being flown in by Gianfranco Ferre had not yet arrived. But the new fragrance presents for her guests, Fendi, had. Her driver would drop them off if she couldn't make it.

I told my assistant to copy the letter from Barbara Lazaroff after we had launched Wolfgang and her frozen desserts in San Francisco, and put it on the staff board for all to see: "For my darling adorable * talented * #1 boyfriend—it was fabulous. See me for the other list of adjectives in private!" And to post Ken Hom's letter saying how "fantastic" we all were.

The other letters to be answered included one from Frank Stitt at the Highlands Bar & Grill wondering if he could come and observe the kitchens for a couple of days; from Diana Kennedy with "abrazos" suggesting a trip with Alice Waters and Dick Graff (AIWF) to see her in Mexico; thanks from restaurateur Danny Meyer for his "fabulous" dinner at Stars and offering jobs in New York to any of my staff; from chef Jasper White loving the Stars's excitement; from chef Jan Birnbaum scolding me for not offering him a job, forcing him to take the Quilted Giraffe job instead; from Bill Rice at *Food & Wine* saying I was one of the first to be nominated for the "Dining Hall of Fame" (I noted to post that letter on the staff bulletin board); from Willy Bishop, now in the North County Jail, saying, "I don't know what the fuck is happening here . . . but I need money"; from *Cook's* magazine's Chris Kimball saying he needed by the next day my nominees for their "Who's Who" (I wrote in Joe Baum, Marion Burros, the Chino Ranch, M. F. K. Fisher, Judith Jones, Diana Kennedy, John Mariani, and James Villas); from Bruce Neyers at Joseph Phelps's vineyard saying the previous week's trade tasting at Stars "was quite simply the benchmark against which we will undoubtedly compare all future tastings"; and from the chef Micheal Chiarello, then at Toby's in Miami, saying that the Stars crew was the "most intense, totally committed group" he had seen. He wanted "to be just like you when I grow up."

I answered those and letters from the Soviet ambassador about my proposal for a culinary exchange between "our two countries"; from *New York* magazine's Gael Greene saying how beautiful our fish had been at the Citymeals-on-Wheels at Rockefeller Center and asking me to do another; from Martha Stewart about her supper at Stars after we judged a March of Dimes together; from Elaine Whitelaw asking me to do a March of Dimes in Houston; and from amfAR's Mathilde Krim and fourteen other organizations inquiring about donations.

I dictated letters to the chefs Alain Ducasse and Gérard Besson (always my first lunch stop in Paris) to thank them for coming to Stars; to Jacques Pépin and Madeleine Kamman for saying Stars was their favorite restaurant in San Francisco; to Julia Child for our breakfast together; to Terry Durack and Jill Dupleix, my favorite Australian food writers, who wanted to fly to Stars from Sydney for the night; and to Coudert Frères, from whom I hope to buy the Grand Restaurant Colbert in Paris. Then there were the hate letters.

One woman was "very angry" at having spent ninety dollars for five people in Stars Café, which had butcher paper on the tables. She accused me of "fraud" for calling a salad of mixed greens with oil and vinegar a "green salad," a dish which she said was defined as having vegetables in it. And she said that if a steak could not be cut with a fork it was not a steak. She called me a "cheat," so I penned in return very politely what a salad was, what made up a great New York steak, and advice that she should get new teeth. Another letter hated the noise and the color of the walls, and insisted I was a "screw up." I asked that customer to give us another chance.

Then it was time for lunch service. So I blew up a page from a profile on James Beard in *Gastronome* in which he is questioned on food fads ("Chacun à son mauvais gout") and hung it on the cooking line. There were three appetizers, seven salads, one soup, four sandwiches, seven grills and main courses, and six desserts for me to taste—a teaspoon each. After that I just wanted to go home. Six hours into the job, and ten to twelve more to go. After the lunch service was over and I had said hello to half the 225 guests, I sat down to my own—a salad. The fork was about to enter my mouth when I heard an urgent, if not desperate, "J.T.!" My chef, Mark Franz, had arrived, and he was gesturing from the door down to the basement—with its offices, wine, and food storage, and a sump pump.

"The drains again—backed up big time."

There was a scream from the ladies' toilet as something gray and uninvited came up through the floor drain. I looked into the kitchen and saw the same. If it was not stopped in a few minutes, theoretically Stars could be closed for twenty-four hours by the health department, and they were fifteen feet across the alley from our entrance. The opera started in three and a half hours, and Denise was due in twenty minutes for the third of many meetings about the lightbulbs to be changed for her party.

I ran down the stairs, back into the farthest reaches of the basement. The water was an inch deep. Around the large-oil-drum-size five-foot-deep hole in the floor, now overflowing with what looked like the bottom of San Francisco Bay, were gathered two dishwashers, two sous-chefs, and some prep crew, all gawking. The faces turned to me signaled a silent but very clear "do something." It was clear that this was something they could not be asked to do. It was a job for the one with whom the buck stopped.

I flipped off my now-soaked Italian loafers, peeled off my French cashmere jacket, and jumped in. There was no time to remove the Egyptian cotton shirt, or the Chinese silk tie. Having to not breathe underwater meant I had only a minute or so. I bent over double in the confined space filled with sewage water and pulled out a cook's towel that had been sucked into the pump. The group hauled me out, and burst out laughing. A tampon was lodged on my shoulder, and a piece of onion skin was stuck to my forehead as a third eye. They wrapped me in garbage bags so I could get home without ruining the Connolly leather in my car.

An hour later I returned, pink-skinned from all the scrubbing and disinfectant, and had all the bar-hound regulars bowing to me. A few curtsied. For a moment I thought I was a sewage hero. It turned out that San Francisco's most important magazine, *Focus*, had come out with its annual awards, including "Classics of San Francisco," which included the Opera House, M. F. K. Fisher, Levi Strauss, and Jeremiah Tower: "self-proclaimed monarchist who overthrew the ancient regime of Continental chefdom, ushering in a new era of endless experimentation, American regionalism, and California cuisine." After the ribbing I needed a tetanus booster shot from a Stars doctor who had been alerted and, bribed with a glass of champagne, plunged the needle in while suggesting we reroute the sewage away from the sump.

In the hour before the bar filled up with operagoers, we had the afternoon managers' meeting to go over the details of the rest of the evening again. The topics other than the night's events and its overtime costs were Halloween (no leather chaps with bare asses or nipple rings this year); the policy again that managers may not take employees home with them when they already have someone there; the ongoing and never solvable problem of staff meals; the annual closing for cleaning; the location of the thirty-three bottles of Leroy wines (in 1987 valued at $1,000 each) for Lalou Bize's tasting in two weeks and where to store them; and the right message to the managers about the details and extravagance of my press trip. They knew already that, like James Beard, I was "born with an airline ticket in my mouth."

Then I tasted wines with the Joseph Phelps manager Bruce Neyers, who always showed up around martini time; with the liquor salesman

"Fast" Eddie Cayson, changed the house vodka, and with the wine rep Madeleine de Jean, changed the champagne by the glass from Billecart to Clicquot; gave a lesson to the staff on what "corked" wine really is and tastes like; met with the ADA inspectors and refused to talk to the Channel 4 TV crew who were checking measurements in the men's room again; heard with deep shock a favorite (five days a week at the oyster bar) young customer tell me he had AIDS and ask if I could pay for his AZT; still reeling from that, was therefore not shocked when a naked streaker ran from one door through the restaurant to the other screaming protests at the Public Utilities inspectors lined up at the bar, who were at their usual (12:00 to 2:00 P.M. and 4:00 to 6:00 P.M.) barstools drinking so many Sapporos that I was practically a Japanese national hero.

By 5:30 the flowers for one of the private parties had not arrived. The dinner was at six. I ran to my office and grabbed some flowers, took them down, and made four centerpieces, delivered to the tables as the hostess walked in. "Just checking them myself to see they are perfect," I lied. She adored the lie. For the other private party thirty minutes later, one of the reserved wines had not arrived. I took the host to the wine cellar and let him pick wines from the right side of my private collection. The wine was on me. The Mehta cake had not arrived, but I got a call from the pilot of the Lear: they were about to land. I checked on the homeless at the front door. It was raining, so they hadn't moved. My nemesis was shouting he wanted to kill me and chased me inside Stars. I hit the panic button at the podium, and when the North Station guys showed up and moved the homeless down the street, some of the customers cheered and some called me a fascist.

The evening was right on schedule.

Our most regular customers, the O'Deas, arrived, already smashed, and told me they were not moving from the table until they got to see the Mehtas, to whom they were going to give several pieces of their now-blurred minds about the Three Tenors.

Denise arrived and, bathed in the light of the hastily installed pink lightbulbs, wondered aloud if they were the right color.

"Well, here comes Zubin, so they had better be," I said.

"Remember," she whispered in my ear, "the Haut-Brion is for me and Zubin. All the others get the Jordan."

At that moment, Sally Jordan walked in and asked what wine we were drinking tonight. I told her the usual, and the usual: hers and the bottles wrapped in napkins. She looked at me, and the corners of her mouth twisted into an unspoken "That Denise!"

"I guess I'll have to have the Jordan."

This is what the guests saw on their menus:

Scallop Hash with Lobster Sauce

Black Truffled Braised Beef

Cèpes Mashed-Potato Timbale

Passion Fruit Stars Cream with Raspberry Sauce
Jordan Chardonnay 1988
Jordan Cabernet Sauvignon 1987

Halfway through the dinner I saw the waiter had let the napkin fall off the mystery bottle. I couldn't have Denise busted, so I raced to the table and told everyone that the Haut-Brion was my gift: I just wanted to see if the host and hostess liked it before I offered it to the group.

That really cost me.

The cake arrived in the arms of the hosts' chauffeur.

Meanwhile I ran between the two kitchens attached to the private rooms to cook and help serve. Since I was cooking also for the Mehta party, the three menus became confused in my head, and I directed one of the dishes to the wrong room, though, thank God, not to Denise. I went out to the hostess and lied that I had not liked the fish I had recommended a few days earlier and changed it at the last moment. Of course I would not charge her for the dish.

That cost me.

She loved that I was cooking.

I was summoned over to the edge of Denise's party. One of the guests, almost as smashed as the O'Deas, who were now glowering at the Mehtas, told me that her Oscar de la Renta (he was at the head table) had been ruined by water in the ladies' room, and that the "water" was not water. I would have to pay for the dress ($3,500). On checking out the cause of the dampness, my maître d' whispered to me that perhaps the woman had peed herself since there was no "water" on the floor. I sent a note to her on my card saying Stars would be happy to pay for the dry cleaning—even when, as she informed me, it would have to go to New York.

The day was becoming expensive. I wondered if I could send the dress in the Mehtas' plane to New York.

The wife of a famous local rock star grabbed me on her way back from the ladies' room. "Darling, the light in there is bright enough to sear the makeup right off a whore's face!" I tilted my head at the manager to check out the lights. "And, furthermore, the counter is wet, so I lost all my fucking coke."

That I didn't have to pay for, thank God.

The bathroom bulbs were indeed white. The dining room hosts had forgotten to change them to pink. I hoped that Denise didn't have to pee before I could get one of the staff to find the bulbs (I prayed the procedure to keep them at the podium was in place) and put them in.

The dining room manager then told me that Denise was ready for dessert, and that Mrs. Mehta did not want the planned forty wild strawberry soufflés we were about to put in the oven—only the cake.

That cost me several hundred dollars in ingredients and lost revenue, since it was now too late to put the soufflés on the supper menu or offer them to the private parties and charge a supplement.

The waiters hauled out the cake to the table draped and ready. Denise and Mrs. Mehta got up, came over to the cake. Then Mehta handed me the knife and asked if I knew how to cut cake. She thrust the meat carving knife delivered with the cake into my hands.

"Use this," she said.

Visions of sinking it into her head instead of the cake temporarily unbalanced me, but a quick nip of champers at the bar put me right. Then back at the table, sticking the knife into the cake nearly broke my wrist, and trying to pull it out nearly dislocated my back: the cake was still 90 percent frozen. Now I was standing there in front of forty of America's finest with Excalibur in my hand. The look on my face brought a couple of managers running.

"Get Mark [the chef] now!"

Somehow, and against the adderlike whispers of Mrs. Mehta that it had to be cut right there and right now, the cake was removed to the kitchen and sawed into pieces. I retired to the end of the bar farthest from the party for a breather before they left. Then I shook hands good-bye with the sixty-odd private dining guests after a speech in each room and went back to the bar. My stomach felt as if the sump pump was getting its revenge, so I pushed the champagne away for a Fernet-Branca. It was almost midnight.

I shook hands with everyone from Denise's party and saw her glare. After all had left and the flowers were being put in her car, she showed me her bill. She never paid them at the moment but always wanted to see them. The computer had automatically added a cake charge even though the waiter had written: "Cake—comp JT."

"Frank," I said loudly to the dining room manager, who had been at both meetings, "come over here and kill yourself." This was one rap I was not going to take. But the party had been a success because Prentis, as usual, had the last word.

"Well, what do you expect from a chef? They're all goddamn cheats," roared Denise's tycoon and patrician husband, whom I adored.

"If I were, Prentis, I would be as rich as you."

He roared with laughter and went down the corridor on his cane. "And don't forget to get the goddamn ladies' room fixed." I saw them into their car and waved good-bye. I needed some oysters and Le Montrachet. I had earned it. A little voice behind me said, "J.T.?" I recognized one of my favorite people at Stars, my Ethiopian head valet, Solomon. I turned.

"J.T. We have lost a car."

I was then momentarily distracted as Gianni Versace walked in with some of San Francisco's socialite switch hitters, and I showed him to the best table in the house. He had just come from the opening of the opera, for which he had designed the costumes.

At the bar, someone male, young, Asian, and handsome motioned me over. "Would you tell Mr. W. with Versace that I am here? My name is Andrew Cunanan."

I did, and Andrew sat at their table.

Meanwhile, it seemed to Solomon that I had forgotten his valet problem. "It's not just any car, J.T. It's a new Mercedes 560 SEL."

I went to the front door and saw a couple standing there on the sidewalk. I asked Solomon how in the hell that could happen. Had he looked everywhere? After as little fussing as I could manage, and no sign whatever of the car except for the owners' valet parking stub, I told Solomon to give them my keys. I told the extraordinarily patient customers that my 560 would be there in two minutes, and did they mind it was silver, and could I have their telephone number? I gave them Solomon's number and prayed the car had enough gas in it.

Solomon drove me home, and I told him to leave a note on the opening chef's desk to say that I might be a little late in the morning, and for him not to call me if the customers in my car ran out of gas in Mill Valley!

The next morning I was to leave on the trip I had put off for Denise's dinner, but I decided to hang a right to some tropical island first. I took my first extravagant, nonworking vacation since I'd started at the Santa Fe, four years previously. I went to Bora Bora at the recommendation of Mark Franz, who had gone there the year before. Ever since that glass of pineapple juice in Fiji forty-six years earlier, tropical air and food had always been a guaranteed way of nursing myself back to life. Extreme hotel luxury helped. While I was sitting on the white sand in front of the azure waters, sipping a forty-year-old Calvados after a lunch of still-kicking rock lobsters, the future of owning Stars on my own came into focus: get back to the real business of running restaurants, and back in the biggest possible way.

It had taken me eighty-six of the allocated ninety days to come up with all the money for Doyle, and now I was committed to a killing payback. It was going to take a lot of grilled fish and hamburgers to pay off the $5 million of principal and interest that would accumulate after the buyout. At least, I comforted myself as I wrote my new cash-flow projections from the veranda of my tropical villa, I was free from the ten-thousand-dollar-a-month attorneys' fees I had been paying for the last four years.

When I returned from vacation, there was a huge stack of "discovery" demands on my desk. Sued again. The shock was as big as my delusion that everything was going to be mine, and mine in peace. Leaked to Herb Caen, the Moons' new lawsuit made headlines. To the press it seemed I was incapable of letting a year go by without going to court. And they were right: In the past twelve years I had spent almost a million dollars on attorneys and costs for the privilege of being a partner in restaurants and then a sole owner. One column quoted someone calling me "a litigious bitch." Only my attorney, Richard Collier, knew that I had actually initiated just one of those lawsuits—the Santa Fe one that moved Doyle to the negotiating table.

Now the Moons wanted to see every receipt, guest check, letter, and memo that had been generated since the day we opened: several hundred thousand documents, including some 800,000 guest checks. The cost of compiling those records would have choked a billionaire. The only—if extremely painful—answer was to let the Moons back into Stars to search and do the copying themselves.

Doyle knew better than to waste his own time, but his wife was possessed. Now she had a more significant role to play than being locked up in their country house by her husband. She would be the Sherlock who'd find evidence of the $985,000 they claimed I had stolen from Stars and Santa Fe.

After a year of this, we ended up in binding arbitration. But it meant once again putting the restaurant on hold. Now the ninety-hour weeks I had slated to resurrect Stars were filled with amassing the answers to the Moons' hundreds of allegations, and searching through the dusty basement storage area for documents now in disarray from their blind gropings.

Finally, it was time to head over to the arbitrator, a retired judge. He turned out to be a white-haired septuagenarian of the old school—

definitely someone to relate better to me than to Moon, however expensive Doyle's shiny new suit. But the list of accusations was so vast that, if only a quarter of them proved true, I should have been thrown in jail and the key thrown away.

As sins going back ten years to Santa Fe were recited, I would reach down and pull out a folder of explanatory records and put it on the table under the gloating eyes of the Moons. At first the judge was enthralled. On the third full day of their accusations and my comprehensive answers, he fell asleep—a good sign, given the vividness of my alleged crimes. When, across the polished rosewood table, the burly and bellowing Moon attorney failed to rouse him but my patient and quiet response did, I knew we had won, but for how much, I didn't.

On my way back from Napa to Stars one afternoon, I called my attorney Richard Collier for any news from the judge. First I told him about the little café I had just seen in Oakville with a "For Sale" sign outside (later to become Stars Oakville Café) and then remembered to ask if there was any news.

The judge pronounced: The Moons received the price of my ticket to Tahiti. In my shock upon returning from the beach to find the foot-high stack of lawsuits on my desk, I had forgotten to reimburse the travel agent, who had then billed Stars. This was the only time in eight years I had not kept perfect records, down to my smallest reimbursement check for $1.75, which so inspired my white-haired justice.

The results of the hearing were not publicized, so I remained a crook in the old boy capitalist eyes of my richest customers. But to reassure the staff, all capitalists themselves, I walked up Van Ness Avenue and returned forty minutes later with a new BMW 750 IL.

Now I could finally turn to the business of Stars. And it worked.

Ann Bramson, one of America's greatest cookbook editors (then at William Morrow, but she had done *Jeremiah Tower's New American Classics* for Harper & Row), described Stars better than anyone: "It has an energy and spirit and a come-hither quality that makes you feel just plain better the minute you walk through the doors. It's a high to be there. Unlike any other place I've ever been."

Now I just had to keep it that way.

My Best Shot

Herb Caen reported my vow "to give Stars my best shot now," saying I should be encouraged by the framed letters from famous lovers of Stars on the walls. The one that amused him the most was from his pal in crime Harry de Wildt, the man who had asked fifteen years earlier to be moved from next to me at table when he found out I was a chef. His note saying how wonderful Herb's seventy-seventh birthday had been reprimanded me: "Next time, you must join us and *Sit Down*." My favorite was from someone not massively famous—yet. "You looked great, and so did my favorite restaurant in the world, Mario Batali. P.S. Barbara Kafka won't come into my new restaurant [1993] without you, so get out here [New York] soon!" Others were already famous: "Still fresh and exciting, as if it has always been there" from Jasper White; from Georges Blanc a postcard said his French chef pals wished us "très fidèlement à bientôt"; Robert Parker thought his Sonoma rabbit loins wrapped in pancetta better than any in France; the "Lettuce Entertain You" genius Rich Melman from Chicago thought Stars "wonderful"; Australia's wine guru Len Evans adored Stars because Ernest Gallo had fallen in love with him there; and a message from the Archbishop of Canterbury said Stars was his favorite restaurant in California. The great Johnny and Betsey Apple loved the buzz in Stars that was just like his favorites and mine—"La Coupole, Bibendum in London, George Lang's in New York [Café des Artistes]"; Anne Willan got right to the core, saying Stars's "sophisticated good eating reminded me irresistibly of a picture of the Savoy in London in Escoffier's time—and now Jim Woods [*San Francisco Examiner*] tells me you were brought up in the Savoy shadow—so perhaps it's not just an accident"; and from Julia Child: "You have such a flair. . . . Gastronomy is not dead chez vous." Now that all these compliments were in print and in view, we had the public challenge to live up to them.

So my managers and I outlined a battle plan at the same time that the press heaped new attention on the restaurant. Germany's *Die Welt* spoke of our "kalifornischen Meisterkoch." *People* magazine had a full-page victory photo of me lounging on the star-covered carpet stairs, a glass of champagne on the upper step. *Members* magazine, for the rich and famous, named Stars one of the world's best brasseries, with Harry's Bar in Venice, Da Bice in Milan, and Le Caprice in London. The mayor of San Francisco, citing the restaurant's community and charitable work, declared a "Stars's Day" in 1988. What to do to pay off our debts seemed clear: more of the same.

I told the managers that success in the future meant building press away from the melodrama and hubris of the "superchef" to focus on the restaurant. We had not strayed irretrievably far from that priority, so now we could steam full ahead without diversions.

The Charitable Road Show

One of the best tactics for restaurants promoting themselves in the eighties was their role as fund-raisers and providers of high-profile press coverage for national and local charities. Our first AIDS research fund-raiser and the 1983 AIWF "American Festival" dinner had proven that a lot of money could be made by giving the rich an amusing time while they ate—and the press loved to watch. A fifteen-page 1987 cover story in San Francisco's *Focus* magazine explored this increasingly big business through the prism of an event called "AID & Comfort," which a thousand people paid $250 apiece to attend. According to the article, Alice Waters charmed her way through the crowd, "lending her glamour, her name, her star appeal. Back in the kitchen, as Jeremiah Tower was quietly putting the finishing touches on one of the evening's culinary triumphs—tuna carpaccio—one of the local restaurant mavens cracked, 'That's the way it's always been, Alice out front, getting all the glory, and Jeremiah in the background, cooking great food.'"

But most chefs felt it was always about teamwork with enough publicity to go around, and everyone made out splendidly from the new charitable bashes. In addition to the Meals-on-Wheels extravaganzas, there were various AIDS fund-raisers, Open Hand, Share Our Strength, and others. My personal road show was Elaine Whitelaw's March of Dimes (which *The Washington Post* called "the Munch of Dimes" in 1988).

On our first extended show on the road we learned a precious lesson. When we arrived at the site of an event in Maui, we found the Austrian chef in a severe depression, sitting alone in his glass-walled office high above the empty kitchen, chewing the end of a three-foot raw kielbasa coiled in his lap, wondering who I was and why I was there. We were supposed to work with him and a team of six cooks he had promised us. No one appeared, so we got to work. After staying up all night cutting nine cases of red, gold, and yellow bell peppers into very fine slices, I swore on my bleeding hands that I would never be dependent on another chef or restaurant again.

After that miserable experience, I increased the number of staff on the road show team, and I insisted they be put up in the same hotels as I. When this was viewed as "demanding," I had a momentary lapse of resolve. But after landing in New York in the middle of an ice storm to find our donated transportation—for six chefs and two thousand pounds of luggage and food—missing, and our Hotel Pierre reservations nonexistent, I decided a different future was starting that night. As we stood in the Pierre lobby with our mountain of luggage, the person behind the front desk masquerading as a man finally agreed to let me use his phone. I called my favorite, Plaza Athénée, and explained I needed four rooms and my usual green suite—this on a Friday night in the middle of New York's tourist season.

"Really?" gasped the manager. There was a long pause. "Come right over."

Once I was in my suite and the staff was bedded down, I wondered how I would explain this expense to a judge—since the trip was just before the last arbitration with the Moons. As I sank into the Irish linen sheets and watched the snow falling outside the greenhouse on my penthouse terrace, I didn't care. I vowed we would now pay for everything, and to hell with the evanescent donations and freebies.

Some of the disasters, of course, were of my own making. I thought it would be cold for one October Meals-on-Wheels in L.A. under a tent in the parking lot of Wolfgang Puck's Spago, so I decided to do suckling pig with a white truffle sauce (one dramatic food and one expensive) to show us off and grab press attention. As one of the longer lines gathered in front of our Stars sign, I realized the first gasps were of not pleasure but disgust. Most of the guests were Jewish. Some asked how could I have been so stupid? Even my usually loyal staff were shaken at my naïve miscalculation. The turkey-necked and pearl-throated squawks from some of the older matrons in orange capri pants finally unnerved us all, so we left early to get back to the Westwood Marquis. Over the first Ladoucette Pouilly-Fumé, we discussed our next road show. I promised that we'd serve "safe" food, and that the only drama would come from the props. "You will notice," I said, "that none of the chefs is doing anything to decorate their booths. That's our way to glory."

The next Citymeals-on-Wheels was a year later at Rockefeller Center, and this time I was ready. I pulled rank well in advance to get a prime location on the rink, across from the steps down to the fountain. I had noticed at past events that no one could see the food once the sun had gone down, so that was my focus, and we had our travel pack (lights, tools, electrical equipment, French tablecloths, first aid kit) with everything we'd need to be independent of the local support staff.

On this June night at Rockefeller Center we set up a ziggurat of ice behind our well-lighted table (also of ice) for a huge shellfish bar. I lit the ice from behind, using the same colors as in the huge golden-figured fountain beside us, and when the guests arrived at the top of the stairs, they saw first the fountain and then us. It helped that we were spit-roasting a whole head-on swordfish over an eight-foot-long mesquite-charcoal grill, something no one, including us, had seen before. So when *Lifestyles of the Rich and Famous* arrived, the fish caught the camera. With that publicity, the five thousand mid-eighties dollars it cost us to do the event would have been cheap at ten times the price.

A Ruth Reichl story in the *Los Angeles Times* about a Meals-on-Wheels on the terrace of L.A.'s "Blue Whale" Pacific Design Center was called "Chefs as the Star Ingredients." The lead photo shows me arriving with my "Travel Pac." Wrote Ruth, "They roll into town like rock stars, roadies in their wake. They stay in the best hotels, are wined and dined in the finest restaurants, and when show time finally comes they are interviewed, photographed, and besieged by autograph hunters. They are 'The Celebrity Chefs.'" She went on, "Chefs used to send a check, a recipe, or a dish to charity. Now they send themselves with such regularity that some of them have regular road crews." One of the guests said she came more for the show than for the food. "I just wanted to come and look. . . . I guess you call me a food groupie. But isn't he handsome?" Another fan passed up what was said to be the best food of the night, from Avneer Samuels of Dallas's Hotel Crescent Court. "I've never heard of him," she sniffed, and went searching for whoever was being filmed by *Entertainment Tonight.*

I was already a victim of the travel bug bite, but all this touring and cooking had such an invigorating effect on the staff and the tourist business at Stars that I rarely turned down an invitation to any exotic or educational spot. And I thought up a few on my own when morale was sluggish. Several times I took deserving staff to Paris or London for the weekend, most memorably for the breakfast at Paris's Crillon hotel. The hotel alone cost seven thousand dollars, but it was worth every penny: It inspired changes at Stars that became trademarks later, like the traditional European seafood service stands and the round paper covers imprinted with a star logo that covered the butters on the table.

But as much as the road-show promotions brought new press and new customers, any restaurant has to look after its locals and regulars if it is to survive. So I installed brass plates at the regulars' tables and barstools, giving them a recognition for which others would soon fiercely compete. Eager wanna-bes were soon smuggling in screwdrivers to remove a plate or two to make room for their own. I formed a "Brassplate Society" and held annual lunches for the original members—whose deaths were anxiously anticipated by those who wanted in. Everyone knew my list was the only thing at Stars that could not be influenced by money, power, or politics. I loved the fact that there were local shopkeepers and lower-level bureaucrats drinking up my champagne and Cognac while rich socialites looked on wondering how such a mixed crew got to be such stars in Stars.

But this showy democracy did not cause as much ruckus as the three-day event in the summer of 1989 I held to welcome the Kirov Ballet to San Francisco, as requested by Jeanette Etheridge of the famous Tosca Café, and her mother, Armen, who had been Nureyev's all-forgiving mother figure since he first landed in the United States.

This was before perestroika, and the dancers were still surrounded and contained by KGB. It was my job to get them out on the town. First there was a party at my brand-new Stars offshoot, Speedo 690. I had been warned that the dancers were coming by bus and, always hungry, would want to eat right away. So I created a buffet that featured a stack of twenty wooden farmers' market boxes of ripe peaches, melons, grapes, figs, and apricots. The hundred people arrived at the door with military precision. The young dancers gasped at the sight of the food, while we gasped at their beauty.

They all sat down, but then nothing happened. It was totally quiet. I went over to the male star, Andreas Liepa, a twenty-one-year-old of world-challenging magnificence, and asked what was up. He pulled my ear down to his mouth and whispered, "KGB." The head honcho was a porkpie-hatted Brezhnev look-alike who introduced himself through an interpreter as the Minister of the Interior of the Soviet Union. With that kind of authoritarian rank in attendance I knew I was in trouble. So I called Armen, who rushed over. The hulking senior men had resisted any of my frozen vodka tactics to jump-start the party, but a few moments after Armen had ensconced herself at their table I heard the old guys shout a toast in Russian, knock back their vodkas, and yell for food. Instantly the ninety other Kirov staff and dancers plunged into the food.

I asked Armen what she had done to get the old geezers off their cheap-suited behinds. "You see this pin I am wearing?" she asked. "Well, it's a Soviet army medal. The minister asked me how I had got it. I told him I had to fuck a general." The roaring laughter of the generals had been the noise that launched the party.

I was bowled over by the natural style and the elegance of the young Russians, who came from a society described as "impoverished." Each table made a centerpiece of fruit that would have done Maxim's proud, just so they could eat the fruit with their eyes before devouring it. The magnificent star pulled me onto his lap and told me he'd seen a peach or apricot or any fruit like this maybe twice in his life. Dodging the KGB, I managed to steal him and five of the dancers for a spin in my new BMW.

The car phone grabbed their attention, so each called his boy- or girlfriend in Leningrad or Moscow—except the star, who gave me his hotel room key, a palliative for some heatedly disapproving local press accusing me of loving "Rooskies." They weren't far wrong.

The Press Goddess

As Louis Auchincloss said of Ruth Draper, "You can get away with absolutely anything, if you are a success." So the carping of the right-wing press had no effect on my social standing locally after I was seen with the blond Russian superstar on my arm, giving me the lesson I had learned with Malcolm Forbes, that two celebrities are exponentially mightier than one. Surrounding myself with the famous was both armor against the media and oil for our business machine. "Tower promotes himself and his restaurants tirelessly," said one article. "'It is bone-crushingly exhausting,' he admits, 'but it certainly is much better for the business to be constantly in the public eye.'"

Certainly once Denise Hale adopted Stars as her venue for Italian friends like Gianfranco Ferre, French friends like Givenchy and Frederick Chandon, Hollywood friends like Billy Wilder, Kirk Douglas, George Christy, Dominick Dunne, and the Reagans, and New York friends like Oscar de la Renta and the Kissingers, we were "it"—and then everyone else came to watch. Denise's list extended to the Gettys, Rex Harrison, David Brinkley, and the King of Spain. She threw parties for all of them at Stars. The laconically flamboyant Berkeley critic Charles Perry wrote that I was paying too much attention to fame and not enough to food: "It's too bad that celebrities can't be eaten, because the way many California restaurants are going these days, the promise of hobnobbing with the wealthy, famous, and powerful is almost as big a drawing card for them as their menus." He had been to Spago as well.

Charles was early Berkeley, so David Webb paste diamonds around surgically enhanced necks would have been difficult for him to swallow. But he had a point. At a party for the U.S. Ambassador to Mexico (the toweringly handsome John Gavin), such was the power of Denise that tout San Francisco came out on a rainy Sunday night when they would usually be home in their TSE cashmere sweats secretly watching *Tales of the City.* All the newspaper barons were there, the Hearsts and the Thieriots, Danielle Steel with a few million in Rajasthan jewels studded into her gold maternity jacket, corporate giants from Syntex and the incomparable helicopter-flying Al Wilsey, the gloriously beautiful and impeccably dressed

Urania von Ristow, the Safeway Magowans and the winery Jordans. It was heaven, gushed the gossip columnists, and the two hundred others who came to have dinner and watch agreed. All except Charles Perry. Stars was proof that if you open such a place, all the world will come to see each other; he would rather they came for the food. He reproached me with early days of Chez Panisse. He was reliving them, and I was not.

Gerald Asher from *Gourmet* gave his view of my appetite for the press. "The press, especially the Eastern press, loved Alice—this little girl who'd started a terrific restaurant with no experience was a good story. Why should she argue? It would not have helped if she had been a shrinking violet. When she was cast as the Joan of Arc of California cuisine, Jeremiah probably felt like the Dauphin." Now I was ready to be king.

Constantly in society's eye, chefs moved from socially unpresentable to socially necessary. I had never been comfortable telling my old-school grandmother (with her staff of domestics) that I cooked professionally after all that money she spent sending me to Harvard. Now working in a restaurant kitchen became not only respectable (sort of) but glamorous. "Talking to Tower," one reporter wrote, "you realize the days of the semi-literate hash slinger are over, and that the men in white hats are, well, white collar as well." By the time the press was giving me "as much press as Meryl Streep," damaging controversy started to rule as much as door-opening fame.

The end of the eighties saw the maturation of the chef as superstar, until it picked up again around 2000. But the first seeds of discontent were sown, and not just from Berkeley writers who had not been invited to sit with the likes of the King of Spain or America's best-selling romance novelist. I had stopped reading about myself, but the regulars at Stars never resisted the latest silliness in the columns, like my "Ronald Colman" voice and "Ivy League" airs, or my being called "the Cary Grant of the cuisine scene."

When a paper as far away as *The Maui News* reported that I looked "like an Americanized Michael Caine, curly blond hair and skin flushed from the tropical heat," it was obvious that more than food was involved. Which came first in this love affair, I wondered, and who will be blamed when it falters? One reporter talked of my "auburn" curls, another of my "blond" ones, and yet another of my "long English locks": I vowed to get out of the business while I still had hair.

When the reporters got to my old friends, I knew it was time to reassess my love affair with the press. They found Michael Palmer. "Were the stories of flying blancmanges true?" they asked. "It never came to blows," said

Michael. "Jeremiah does have a temper and doesn't hesitate to make demands. He does have a certain verbal outrageousness."

Asked if success had tainted his old Harvard cooking buddy, Michael laughed. "No, he's the same old perverse Jeremiah."

Yes, I had done more than my share of the wooing, but even as I worried that my obsession would backfire on me, I found it impossible to resist saying yes to every offer to put myself out there. I was in national magazines and on billboards as a Dewar's poster boy: the billboard outside Spago on Sunset annoyed Wolfgang Puck with its huge caption "Jeremiah Tower: Chef to the Stars." (He said *he* was.) I particularly loved *Focus* magazine calling me a "nouvelle Napoleon spreading the revolution."

In 1988 *USAir*'s magazine exaggerated that I was "arguably America's best-known chef-restaurateur." What was more true was the statement that Stars (I would have included Spago) "has introduced diners to a new way to appreciate dining out." In an article called "Drugless in L.A.," the blowup quote beside a photo of Elizabeth Taylor said, "Most people would just as soon meet a chef like Jeremiah Tower as Warren Beatty." The next day the story went around that I had been at the Betty Ford clinic with Warren and Liz. A *Chronicle* piece called "Jeremiah Tower: The Star Behind Stars" noted gratuitously, "He is not insufferable." And if I couldn't get into trouble enough by myself, some reporters started currying favor by taking sides that were not even there. One said that Wolfgang Puck, "the over-hyped proprietor of Spago . . . couldn't pull it off. His bars are little more than overpriced queues for patrons praying for a power table, whereas Jeremiah Tower . . ." and so on.

I wondered how long it would be before a writer unable to get a table at Stars would turn on me.

A Carmel newspaper wrote: "Some call Jeremiah Tower aloof, a snob. They say he doesn't take telephone calls." I wondered who had not reached me on the four phone lines at my desk, my car phone, or my cell phone—at which I was available seven days a week. Who had I jilted without knowing it?

With all this, I again made a vow again not to read favorable publicity anymore: I knew that disaster was the only possible result of believing one's publicity. I would have my assistant hand me only the negative items—things that we could do something about. There was nothing I could do about the fawning and swooning and lapdogging. I knew I had to build a buffer against the press or go mad.

Or maybe it was time to get out of Dodge.

So I made a plan to sell Stars a year after the $1,350,000 (now, with interest, more like $5,000,000) was paid to the bank by 1992. Without the outstretched bankers' shovels, the cash flow would be great enough in one year to set me up, and the sale would let me live well. By 1993 I would be in Brittany—or back in Sydney with a house above Bondi Beach near Neil Perry's Blue Water Grill.

Then the earth shook.

The Earth Quakes

I had just popped an ounce of beluga in my mouth to chase a large shot of buffalo grass vodka when the phone rang. I had rented a house in Sea Ranch on the Mendocino coast north of San Francisco for a much-needed week away from everyone, so I thought of not answering the telephone. But it had to be Stars, since no one else knew where I was. I looked at my watch and picked up the phone. It was 5:20 P.M.

"J.T.—there's been an earthquake."

It had happened fifteen minutes before.

"Stars seems fine, and the windows are still in Speedo [my new restaurant around the corner from Stars]. At a fast look it seems we have lost only a few bottles of liquor. But the power is out, and everyone wants to know what to do."

I told them to turn off the gas and water, lock up, and leave. That was my first mistake. There was no earthquake-business interruption insurance (now available), so we should have left the gas on since we did have fire insurance. My second mistake was trying to get on my motorbike after two vodkas, thinking that the bike would be fastest not only on the winding coast road back to San Francisco but through any backed-up traffic leading into the city. After the first hairpin turn, however, I went back to the house and approached the 750 Beemer as I might a great eighteen-hand hunter after too much prehunt sherry. I told it gently that somehow it had to get me back to San Francisco in record time and in one piece.

I set off with visions of a Beirut-like scenario of smoking funeral pyres and police barricades at the Golden Gate Bridge, but there was not a patrol car anywhere in sight. Now quite sobered with adrenaline and fear of what I would find (the radio did not work on that mountainous coastal road), I arrived on the bridge to see that there was nothing out of the ordinary except for a total lack of traffic, and a plume of smoke over the Marina area at the San Francisco end of the bridge.

The Marina itself was blocked off with motorcycle cops, so I drove up into Pacific Heights and down into the Civic Center. The only people I saw were gathered at corners, just standing in silence. I stopped the car for a minute and listened; the city was totally quiet except for distant sirens. After the telephone call, it was not a surprise that the huge storefront windows on Speedo were intact, but it was a relief nonetheless. I had expected the sights we had all seen from Afghanistan, or China, or South America, with buildings down everywhere and bodies in the debris. It all looked normal, though the silence was powerfully eerie. I tiptoed gingerly into Stars, and sure enough, there were the five broken liquor bottles on the bar with a note to me saying that everything else was intact. Incredibly relieved but somehow still very worried, I went over to Speedo 690 to find some gathered managers waiting for me with cold champagne. At least the ice has not melted yet was the first in-shock thought that came to mind. We laid out a plan of action for the next day and went to our apartments to see what was left of them.

My house, even the dining room's painted ceiling, was intact, although Barbara Stanwyck's already lined face had a few more cracks. As I looked at the newspaper I saw it was October 17, and at the irony of having opened Speedo 690 five months earlier to the day, I felt superstition sliding into my unease. Every day closed would cost Stars several thousand dollars in profits, and I wondered how much we were going to lose. I knew Speedo's infant but successful cash flow could not take a big hit.

Nineteen eighty-nine had been normal until that day in October. We poured the new slab for Speedo on April 1 (Speedo came about because some friends had bought the old Speedo 690 carburetor building around the corner from Stars, and putting a restaurant in it seemed like a good real estate idea to them, and a good cooking opportunity for me, since I was dying to try out a new cuisine using all the fresh Asian ingredients just arriving in the markets). We had picked up our usual awards from the *San Francisco* magazine party; we had already served about 150,000 meals at Stars, including hosting several winemakers, like Masteroberadino, Gaja, Maurizio Zanella of Ca del Bosco, Jordan, Bernard Hine, Pierre Lanson; had hosted an Open Hand charity dinner; had greeted the usual Australians like top food journalists Jill Dupleix and her husband, Terry Durack, who flew in for the night from Sydney for Jill's birthday; had hosted Condé Nast, the Gunds, Bronfmans, Sotheby's, *Newsweek*, Grace Mirabella, Gianfranco Ferre, and Rose Marie Bravo for Saks Fifth Avenue, the Kirov Ballet and its KGB shadow, Carter Brown, Liza Minnelli, Danielle Steel, and Jean-Louis Palladin; had finished a two-year court case brought by a cocktail waitress who allegedly mis-served some customers and then sued me and Stars; had ended up in court with the

Speedo corporation when they sued me for using a diver logo for Speedo's beach theme decor; had survived Denise Hale's birthday week of at least twelve parties; had seen Stars on *Lifestyles of the Rich and Famous;* had snuck the annual case of Stoli to Herb Caen for his birthday; had attended world championship boxing with the mayor; had cooked at the Meals-on-Wheels in Los Angeles again; had got a call from Hong Kong saying we had very surprisingly won the government lease tender for the old Peak Café (and had started commuting there in late July); had made a video of life at Stars; had taken a private jet to Bangkok with the Hales; had yet again fought off rumors that I had AIDS when Philip Core, my great college pal and painter of my dining room and the 150-foot "beach" canvas at Speedo, had died of AIDS; had done a photo shoot at Denise Hale's for the Tiffany *Entertaining* book—all of this before the earth quaked in the longest ten seconds anyone could remember.

At 5:04 on Tuesday the city had shut down. Now I had a gut feeling that nothing was going to be quite normal for a while. Had I known how un-normal, and that those few minutes would end up costing me a million in expenses and nearly $12 million in lost sales, I would have taken that match down into the basement of Stars during the aftershocks and gone up with it to more heavenly stars. All I knew then was that the city was without electricity, that the gas was off, and that the president of the utilities company—a great customer of Stars for whom I had done favors—was not answering my telephone calls. We had Paul Bocuse coming in for dinner in a few days, the *Aïda* cast party on Sunday, were hosting the special Olympics on Monday, a *Cook's* magazine shoot on Tuesday, a Nissan convertible commercial on Wednesday, a trip to Hong Kong Thursday, and an International Wine and Food Society dinner at the Hong Kong Hilton and press lunch at the Regent Hotel a few days after that.

By the next day it was clear that when we would have utilities again was quite unclear, so we took the perishable food down to the Red Cross and Open Hand headquarters in the Marina Middle School. Finally the PG&E president took my call, and four days later we were up and running again. My purchasing agent stopped me on the kitchen stairs and asked me if I wanted anything special since Julia Child was coming in the first day.

"We're open, that's enough" was all I could say. And open just in time to greet Julia and serve Bocuse his usual meal of steak tartare and large New York strip steak.

Stars recovered, but we did have to close Speedo a year later, since pouring more capital into damaged San Francisco seemed not a very good idea to my investors (they had all seen the endless television coverage of the fires and broken bridges). To deal with Speedo's payables (I was the general partner), I sold my shares in the young but fabulously successful Peak Café.

Now I was without both restaurants where I could cook using the new fresh Asian and Indian ingredients, and was tempted to change the food at Stars. I did replace the pizza oven with a tandoor, but other experiments just confused the public. It was time to take stock of what kind of chef I was going to be in the nineties. As the decade opened, America was still looking back at Chez Panisse and California for clues.

CHAPTER 6

Culinary America's Mid-*Life* Crisis (1985–1995)

The Chef

THE NINETIES WAS the decade when I sat on a cow for the Milk Board, Wolfgang Puck put his coffee in cheap hotels and did a bad raisin commercial, and there was lineup of naked chefs showing hairy bodies somewhat the worse for gravity and booze, hiding their genitalia with electric food mixers, when everyone preferred the real "Naked Chef." All this made a clothed Jonathan Waxman ten years earlier lying in a pond with ducks for *Life* look tame. *Rolling Stone* tried to define what kinds of chefs we all were: Alice was called "Chef as Doyenne" and I, an "Entertainer." André Soltner, the doyen of French chefs in America, called us "soup merchants."

An eighties Living section cover in *The New York Times*, by Marion Burros, called "What Alice Taught Them: Disciples of Chez Panisse," documented the state of thinking about restaurants and food in the United States at that time, saying that if Henri Soulé at Le Pavillon "can be credited with igniting the explosion of fine French food in America in the 1950s and '60s, then Chez Panisse deserves similar recognition for revolutionizing American cooking in the 1970s and '80s." And the photo of the chef was of a face behind the veil of Alice's antique hats.

Mark Peel had said, "I wanted to work at Chez Panisse in 1980 because it was a major force behind the return to our culinary roots . . . but it was not highly organized. There was never-ending confusion." Jonathan Waxman, at Panisse in 1978, was quoted while still chef at Michael's in Santa Monica as saying he applied at Panisse because of Alice's reputation, but "quite frankly I didn't understand what it was all about. But I learned that you don't serve a dish unless it's perfect." He lauded the use of fresh herbs and of "going through sixteen cases of fresh lettuces to find the finest." Mark Miller was inspired by Panisse to use "native ingredients," and Judy Rodgers of San Francisco's Zuni Café credited Panisse with the "obsessive pursuit of perfection" in raw ingredients. Judy said that Alice was "the kind of cook who is visceral instead of one who quantifies" but that she "used to get three cases of green beans in order to find enough tender small ones for a single meal." At least I taught Alice something.

The *Times* went on to say that in the early eighties Alice acted simply "as a consultant to the restaurant and spends only two days a week there, one cooking and one working in the dining room." Alice mused to Burros in 1984 that she might go back into the kitchen—"I'm curious to cook up coq au vin right now"—and mused further about the difference between her and my kitchen styles: "Jeremiah was not hesitant. His cooking is more elaborate than mine, more flamboyant, but I was fascinated by his combinations, things I wouldn't have thought of." And my comment? "'Mainly,' Mr. Tower says, 'we had fun together. Alice has a wonderful sense of how to eat," as I well knew from our travels alone together.

As I told *The Detroit News*, I remembered an evening in September 1980 on the terrace of the Gritti Palace in Venice, under the moonlight, drinking Krug with Alice, when she admitted "that without you, there would be no Chez Panisse or me." I didn't mention that Alice and I, enjoying our on and off again affair, and on our way to lunch at Harry's Bar, sent a telegram the next morning. It was to her new beautiful boyfriend back in Berkeley for his twenty-first birthday:

> FUNGHI, UCCELLINI, GRITTI;
> SEPPE, FRITTI, HARRY'S—
> A HARDONNA! MADONNA (PARDONNA)!
> KRUG '59

Nor did I mention his vacation with me in Hawaii.

After I left Chez Panisse, it was undeniably still the unquestioned influence, and would be even in 2001, when the restaurant garnered first place in *Gourmet*'s best restaurants in America issue. After reading that piece, I wondered what made up a chef of America's best restaurant. I asked the original so-called disciples themselves at a dinner to honor Alice in Los Angeles, where they made it quite clear that no such across the board real "teaching" had gone on during their tenure with Alice. Even Alice, now as "co-chef" of Panisse, admitted she hadn't cooked in eighteen years. When I asked her if that meant she was now "emeritus," she laughed. That night, surrounded by all the former chefs of Panisse, I asked Jean-Pierre what the term "*co-chef*" meant. He was not sure it was even true. We laughed about the night in 1978, while he had taken over from me as chef, when Alice had called asking me to fire Jean-Pierre because he had been mentioned in the press as "chef of Chez Panisse."

So if Alice had not been cooking as a chef since 1983 (Jean-Pierre said not since I left in 1978), what was the lesson or lessons here about the nature of a chef, great, famous, or otherwise? As Alice said in a 1986 interview with *Restaurant Business*, "It's hard to balance your own feelings as an owner with the necessity of putting someone else in charge" of the kitchen. Looking back on our equal-owner status, I wondered if that was how she had always felt with me.

The Yellow Brick Road

The eighties press had done its job, and the public was primed to eat new American, to see chefs as stars, to think that cooking was a new form of theater and part of the entertainment industry. So caught up was the nation in this new food fantasy pastime that there was hardly any dissent. The pendulum swing of disillusionment with this culinary flash dance was still a few years in the future, if a handful of writers, used to identifying trends still in their fetal stage, did speak out. *Town & Country*'s James Villas, writing a few months before the Astor Mansion lunch and the American Festival, said, "I am up to my neck with all the phoniness and abuse and elitism and celebrity. All this business is really getting out of hand." Perhaps he was sore still (in 1983) at Alice having threatened, a few years before, to call the police over his smoking ("that military state called Berkeley"), or was it because Alice, now a celebrity, had spent the end of an evening in his lap at Georges Blanc's restaurant (outside Lyons) before sliding to the floor?

But no one else in the now fascinated public was fed up or thought anything had gone far enough. John Mariani took several pages to extol the "Regional Favorites" in his *Playboy* list of the nation's best restaurants, even if only eight of them served "regional" American food, including Larry Forgione's An American Place in New York, Stephan Pyles's Routh Street Café in Dallas, Jasper White's Jasper's in Boston, and Frank Stitt's Highlands Bar & Grill in Birmingham, Alabama. Some reporters talked of the new "stars" of the culinary world, and some, like the "Question Man" in the *San Francisco Chronicle,* featured chefs instead of taxi drivers as "the regular Joe on the street." One can't blame the chefs for being a bit confused.

Trying to figure it all out, the Australian critic Leo Schofield talked to the "megastars" of the West Coast chefs to find out what was happening, and which "new directions" the revolution was going in 1986. Leo predicted that chefs were faced with a choice of two wells of inspiration—new ingredients (and cooking them) or money (and spending on expensive decor). Was a chef to believe, as did Bradley Ogden of The Four Seasons in New York, that "style and decor are more important than food"? Which road was a chef to take?

The food/decor question highlighted awareness of the tension between the now famous American hero chefs' belief in authentic simplicity, and our steadily increasing bank accounts. This and my crise de coeur were nowhere more evident than in the 1986 cover story for *Restaurant Business* magazine titled "Chef Celebrities." The five cartooned chefs include Prudhomme holding his pan for blackening fish, Larry Forgione running after a chicken, and Alice Waters in overalls holding a rake. "Flashbulbs are popping and the video-tape is rolling. Moviestars? No, chefs. Suddenly, working in the kitchen is a glamour occupation, and a new generation of aspiring chefs is entering the ranks, making American cuisine truly world class, as Americans have become food-crazy." In this same article I was held up as a prime example of the new dilemma facing chefs because of my maintaining a heavy schedule of public appearances, charity events, travel, and interviews with the press, my life reading, it said, like a script from *Lifestyles of the Rich and Famous*. Five years earlier, "Jeremiah Tower's appearances would have been limited to two choices: the front of his restaurant (dining room) or the back (kitchen)."

But in the mid-eighties the superchefs knew that not to use the mantra of food as their leading public voice was unwise. The point is that this picture was not all about food. The chefs made their lives public like any major star in Hollywood. *Rolling Stone* warned of this emerging crisis in new America's cooking, incredulous that the *Los Angeles Times* devoted the entire front page of the food section to photos of the wedding vows not of a movie star but of the chef Michel Richard. The magazine notes that the epicenter of all this weirdness was Northern California (with its edible flowers, its sound of Birkenstocks slapping on Berkeley's pavements, and homegrown snails), where eating had taken over from sex as the preferred form of sensual gratification. "We can't have sex anymore because of AIDS, and we can't do drugs because of Ed Meese's storm troopers," said one of the chefs, "so what's left?"

But drugs were still around, and cocaine was still fueling the overtaxed schedules of famous road-running chefs. One night in Miami with the March of Dimes we had been to a bizarre and huge estate patrolled by armed guards mingling with the guests. All that day had been TV and radio appearances for me, so by eight o'clock, when the curtain was ready to go up on our performance in black tie for five hundred of the Boca, the Beach, and Coral Gables classic swells, I was beat. I simply could not go on. In my hotel room for a minute to splash cold water on my face, I wondered whether all this was worth it and whether I would just rather be at home in the arms of a great white Burgundy. The telephone shrilled.

"Come on down to my room," a familiar voice drawled. "I have something for you."

A champagne thirst surged through my body as I hung up, but since the voice was that of a chef who had a reputation for cramming the divine white powder up his nose, my body waved then with a certain peristaltic rush instead.

Sure enough, when I walked into his room's short corridor with its built-in dresser, the top ten inches below nose level, I saw four white powdery lines, each the size of a small python.

"Two are yours," he said.

And two I took. Within seconds I was myself again, or some newly energetic version of it, mentally fit for the press and all the smiling and clinging fans. The second round four hours later was laid out on the thick marble counter of the men's room, setting off a panic in me for a second as, my eyes only two inches from the counter, the white lines in the thick black Italian marble momentarily camouflaged the drug. We needed this round before going into the bar to face the event's sponsor's new vodkas being passed around in long-stem martini glasses the size of goldfish bowls. Glamorous "New Society" was embracing "New American Cuisine," or was it the other way around? Lucius Beebe, who had invented "Café Society" fifty years earlier, would have looked around the room for Cole Porter and the Murphys and seen only chefs—albeit courted by gun runners, drug dealers, and slinky trophy wives in Armani beaded couture.

By 1998 there was some backlash: Was it the twenty-eight-dollar price of chicken at the California temple Jams? Did the public agree with *Rolling Stone,* that what we were doing was really "ambitious gardening followed by crude mixology"? One classically trained French chef called California pretentious: "Its cuisine consists of things you don't normally hear of going together, like alligator fritters with a parsnip sauce. The alligator tastes like chicken, and the parsnip tastes like turnips. It's frightening." In the hands of a hack, and one who probably had no experience of great family cooking or a classical kitchen, the results were indeed very often frightening. But in the hands of a classical principles–inspired new chef, the mixology often made wonderful and exciting food that, at its best, was indeed "new" without being solely for newness's sake. Some visionaries looked forward and said that the new tradition would be remembered not for certain dishes like the ones made famous by the previously established cooking— tournedos Rossini or chicken Cordon Bleu—but for our "attitude."

Rolling Stone had Alice Waters put the background of this new cooking into a nutshell: "At first we wanted things to be like in France, and we called everything by French names, then all of a sudden straining to do so—like huîtres de Bolinas instead of 'Bodega Bay oysters.' It was absurd." Both Alice and the reporter pointed out that my 1976 California Regional Dinner at Panisse began Berkeley's second revolution, the first having been the political one of the late sixties. *Rolling Stone* thought Alice was still stuck in the first one, even if the Volvos parked outside Panisse were new and the bumper stickers no longer rooted for the Black Panthers but for the lifestyle of "Living well is the best revenge," a suggestion from the reporter that left Alice on the defensive.

No such defensiveness about this lifestyle was heard across the Bay at Stars. *Rolling Stone* could not help but be fascinated by the difference between the clienteles at Panisse and at Stars. "Jeremiah is equally comfortable with the rowdy Beastie Boys and Run DMC who Tower shooed successfully out the door just as the baroness de Rothschild showed up with a reservation for the same table." Using this event as an example, the article somehow made the point that, whereas I had kept evolving my style, the one at Panisse had stayed the same. And that this "split" in styles had created two camps and an atmosphere on which the new young chefs were "neatly skewered."

And nowhere was the conflict between choosing whether to be a private or a public chef more evident than in the institution of the chef-driven benefit banquet, the proliferation of which the reporter blamed me for. The motives for participating were under suspicion: Were they self-promotion or charitable concern? "There is something that sticks in the craw about the average gourmet benefit," said *Rolling Stone*.

For me, they were publicity opportunities waiting to happen. At a Rockefeller Center Citymeals-on-Wheels, Robin Leach was looking around for material more interesting than Wolfgang's spit-roasted ducks in flames, or Bradley's lamb chops on the grill in the interior kitchen threatening to burn down the tallest building. He spotted Malcolm Forbes and me spotting each other. As Forbes walked over and put out his hand, I introduced myself. "I know perfectly well who you are" was the reply caught on tape by *Lifestyles of the Rich and Famous* as Forbes took my arm. All this intrigued Leach so much that he later filmed Stars for a show that aired for years afterward all over the world, one in which the public remembers Leach saying that "Stars is the best restaurant in the world," even when he said no such thing. After that event any chef who did not have a publicist or handler got one. The relationship of the superstar chefs and the press was a symbiotic marriage made and consummated on the battlefields of charitable work, and definitely not in church.

But the benefit that *Rolling Stone* really choked on was for a whole new cause. It was held in San Francisco in 1987 and called "Aid and Comfort." AIDS had hit the California restaurant industry as early as 1984, just as Stars opened. Two of our dining room staff fell fatally ill within the year, both events that were ten years later to turn me from local hero into a San Francisco pariah. At this time, however, the charity-going community was fresh and the party a huge hit, if a bit staggering and foreboding. I was quoted at the after-event party for the volunteers as saying I thought perhaps we were flying too close to the flames, but no one else seemed worried or even noticed. After all, we had raised a lot of money for AIDS research and hospice support in a town where a thousand waiters had died of AIDS since the early eighties. The evening's very success bred a proportional amount of hype, and what some saw as enthusiasm was already being seen by some press as opportunism. By the end of the food service, Alice Waters said she had no control, "as she was relegated at that point to picking up cigarette butts off the floor of the wharf, and no less than fourteen HYC [Hot Young Chefs] had muscled their way into the kitchen, as the whole thing had come to look like the biggest photo opportunity of the season." The chefs weren't stupid.

"The Hot Young Chefs have arrived," screamed the *San Francisco Chronicle*'s food section a few days later. And André Soltner (Lutèce in New York), the dignified and beloved older chef of our profession, who was seen (quite oddly) as having no penchant for public relations, was interviewed about all these carryings-on. "I blame you . . . the press," he said. "If you glorify a young guy at twenty-four, good for him, beautiful, but if you don't help him at the same time, you spoil him. We cannot forget, even if we are celebrities, who we are. We are cooks, but soup merchants too."

The point is that we chefs were not just soup merchants or celebrities with heads too big to see beyond the latest press clipping. The problem was a misdirection in some of the new chefs. Since they knew the origins of the changes in culinary America only from the press, most felt the first part of the American food revolution was the realm merely of legend, and since they had not been at the beginning of the second part, which started with the press events of 1981 through 1983, they were not grounded in what inspired it either; they had only the terminology of "fresh," "organic," "local," and "California." Were they all finding the origins and essential meanings of these concepts or living them only in the press, cooking magazines, and the floodlights of fame? How many of them had ever gardened or been on a farm? In general the question was not answered until the end of the century, when the new chefs like Ken Oringer of Boston's Clio; Thomas Keller of Napa's The French Laundry; Terrance Brennan of New York's Picholine; Mario Batali of New York's Babbo, Lupa, and Esca; Eric Ripert of New York's Le Bernardin; Tom Colicchio of New York's Craft; and several others (and their sous-chefs) found and held their own true ground and the entire revolution reached its full fruition.

In 1987 Vis à Vis explained that the freedom I had achieved by changing the way people eat instead of cooking according to what people like to eat was possible because of the fame, but it was a fame that brought temptation also. "Offers pour in daily: A Stars in Los Angeles. Another one in New York. Restaurants in Paris [Le Grand Colbert in Galerie Vivienne]. Hong Kong. London [a takeover and rehab of Boulestin's in Soho]. Tokyo [a partnership with Sapporo]. More cookbooks. Even T-shirts." My response? I would be out of my mind not to do it, but I would be more out of my mind to do it. Stars was what made it all possible, but if I ignored Stars, it would all come crashing down. "Every six months I get ten projects on my desk and I say 'Yes,' and then I get my chefs and we go out and have dinner. And we will have a good cry and decide that, for one more year, it's going to be the quality, not the money."

The Crossroads

Every chef in the industry adored and revered André Soltner, judging from the reception he received for Lifetime Achievement at the James Beard Awards when he retired, even if several of the new chefs on their feet may have been wondering why. Not even Julia Child ever got that kind of standing ovation. But between his saying we should not forget that all chefs are cooks and soup merchants too, and the seminal backlash in the national culinary press, any chef attuned to the pulse must have thought about which path to take, especially since the restaurant business was a lot of work, and if fame alone as a payback for all the exhaustion seemed not enough, who could have blamed any chef for looking beyond the glamour for something that was worthy? A big bank account seemed the obvious answer, since it was now clear that fame only indirectly paid the Visa or MasterCard, and the obvious way to achieve that fat account seemed to be to add more projects to the income stream.

The choices were basically two: stay where you are in your first restaurant (or redo it) and take care of business, or take care of business by opening some more. Many might have thought that a single restaurant was a beast insatiably devouring one's life, so how much more could another be? Many were to find out, and some even succeeded in handling more than one restaurant. The big dilemma was the food. Could the same food that made the chef famous in the first place be offered in multiple locations? Did it matter? Maybe that's what publicists and handlers were for: To publicize the food in ways other than how it was cooked in the restaurants.

So regardless of whether you stuck to your original guns, or your publicist told you that the publicity machine needed more fuel, every chef saw that, to be taken seriously, you needed your name on a cookbook. This trend escaped no one's attention. The success in America of promoting a whole new style or presentation—as the publisher Laffont's late seventies illustrated editions of the Young Turks did for "nouvelle cuisine," the kind of legitimization that Alice got in 1982 with *The Chez Panisse Menu Cookbook,* or the kind of publicity that I received for Stars with *Jeremiah Tower's New American Classics* in 1986, when I got to be seen, heard, or read about by over 15 million Americans—was well documented, so across America creativity of the menu was temporarily halted while every famous chef wrote a book.

In 1981, at the tenth birthday party of Panisse, Alice gave me a copy of the manuscript of what was to be *The Chez Panisse Menu Cookbook.* The next day, as I looked at the manuscript poolside in Napa, I noted with shock the lack of acknowledgments. Alice had taken sole credit for the most important events in Panisse's history, among them the Gertrude Stein dinner, the blue trout of the Champagne and Alsace dinners, the Louisiana dinner, the whole Escoffier festival, and even the California Regional Dinner. When I read on page 297 of the manuscript, "For some ten years now, I have faced, every Thursday, the weekly dilemma of planning" the menus, I nearly fell off my deck chair. That claim was unconscionable. Did she think she had done the menus all those years because she had typed them? I reached for my cabana phone to ask the author, Linda Guenzel, if she thought I had never existed.

"I asked Alice about that as we were taping our notes," Linda replied, "and she said it wasn't necessary to include your name everywhere after you had been mentioned once in the credits [as having been a chef there]."

Then I called Alice and said her approach was beneath her, and downright dangerous to her reputation if the book were published without some important changes. I then wrote Alice that I had finished reading the manuscript and that I was happy to read the note she'd handed to me at the Balboa Café, asking me to write down the changes I wanted "before anything happens. I really do want it to be right with all my friends; I hope you believe that. I should have sat down and talked to you first—but it was such an afterthought to do it." I told her, at the risk of sounding condescending, that giving proper credit and telling the truth could only reflect more credit on herself, that all the book had to do was "to honor all those people involved in the history—most of all yourself. Though a scandal might be fun, it is probably best avoided."

When the book appeared in print, I saw that some menus and events that were so obviously mine had been removed, and that the "for some ten years now" had been changed to "for some years now." She just could not go all the way.

On the back cover, Richard Olney's quote characterizes the book as "wonderful—funny, instructive, and rich with common sense," which describes Alice's contribution to Panisse, and "eccentric and passionately serious, full of an air of celebration," which describes mine. The woman who actually wrote it, Linda Guenzel, was all of that. She told me that she had done the book out of love for Panisse and Alice, but also so that Alice would introduce her to the Random House editor Jason Epstein, for whom she wanted to write a book on chocolate. At the book launching party at Panisse, Linda reminded Alice of her promise. I had not been invited to the party, so I called Linda the day after. She was in tears; Alice had introduced her to Jason as "the typist."

Obviously typing in some cases was more important than in others.

On the inside cover Linda inscribed my copy, "For Jeremiah—The inspiration, the raison d'être, the creator on these pages—without you, there would be no Chez Panisse, no cookbook. Truth shall triumph. Much love, Linda. August 10, 1982."

The Panisse cookbook set the personal tone for a chef's cookbook. And personal is what came out in the next wave of books from American chefs, perhaps the most idiosyncratic being Jean-Louis Palladin's Jean-Louis: Cooking with the Seasons (1989), a book that probably did not sell a huge number of copies, but that all chefs in America bought if they could afford it. Chefs who were nine years old when my book came out in 1986 tell me now how influential my book has been for them, a wonderful and heartwarming compliment whose specifics are still unclear to me. But there is no doubt that Jean-Louis's book created a style of presenting food that has

chefs in an even firmer grip now than it did a few years after it was published. And the photography of Fred J. Marron set a style that dominated
half the market and would have been the whole were it not for the 1990
publication of Marco Pierre White's *White Heat*. Its cinema vérité style
made the chef and staff of the restaurant as interesting to photograph as
the food.

Jean-Louis and Marco wrote the second generation of American chefs'
cookbooks; the third and current generation is a mix of what Palladin did
(the *Farallon* cookbook) or Marco Pierre White (Charlie Trotter's books).
The culmination of the two styles combined with Thomas Keller's *The
French Laundry Cookbook* and Eric Ripert's *A Return to Cooking*. They promote the chef and the restaurant, and some even pay off the credit cards.

Chasing Our Culinary Tails

If you couldn't or didn't want to write a book, there was always the world
of cooking magazines, even with its danger of who was wagging whom—
who was the tail, and who the dog. It was one thing for a chef to be
inspired by Jean-Louis's food from original material like the book, since it
looked exactly as it did in the restaurant, but another when the chef's
food, as featured in a cooking magazine, was prepared by stylists who had
probably never met the chef, tasted the food, or been to the restaurant. So
when aspiring chefs (or bored and creatively stuck ones) or students at the
CIA or CCA would look at the magazine photographs, they thought they
were seeing the chef on the page. When they took those photographs
back to their own restaurants and cooked from them, the original source
material was at best twice removed. What happened in America then was
that within a week of a magazine featuring a famous chef, his or her food
was being reproduced three thousand miles away in a manner light-years
from the original. Charles Palmer's fantasy of caramel at Aureole in New
York looked like Indian astrological temples, and was soon all over America. The only problem was that most of his imitators, experiencing it only
from glossy photographs, had never tasted it, and thought it was all architecture with no flavors. Imitations of these imitations were soon imitated
in their turn, leaving Charlie's new pastry chef trying to stay ahead of the
field, imitating himself. All this could take just a year, putting the eighties
right back into the arms of nineteenth-century staged foods and pièces
montées, from which we had all fled so righteously in the previous forty
years. And without even knowing it. So happened the worst sins attrib-
uted to California Cuisine.

Letting the Dice Fly High

Books paid the MasterCard bills and helped fill the restaurants, but they could not do it alone. The press had to be fed in order to keep one's restaurant full, and the cost of a publicist and a personal assistant to deal more and more professionally with the press seemed best amortized over more than one property. Whether to concentrate on increasing the quality of one's only restaurant while trying to squeeze more profits out of it or to open more was the single biggest decision facing the leading famous chefs in America in the second half of the eighties and into the nineties. We had seen a few amazing flops, like Wolfgang Puck's brewery restaurant, which closed after less than a year, and I wondered with marvel how Jonathan Waxman could open Bud's and Hulot's in quick succession after Jams without even being there except (it was said) on opening night. So it was claimed years later when *The New York Times* said his absence at his own restaurants was because he was too busy attending the openings of other people's, but no one questioned the quality at Jams while wondering what had happened at the other two.

By the late nineties, quality and value were on the public's mind, as the glitter of chef stardom became like last year's Christmas ornaments, and a recognizable reputation at a restaurant became a given for its customers, both regular and first time. So now a chef had to stand out from the crowd. I remembered the wine merchant George Linton teaching me the difference between truly great and just great. He would use very expensive and truly very expensive wines as examples, asking if Romanée-Conti from the Domaine was worth two or three times as much as its next-door neighbor La Tâche (also from the Domaine de la Romanée-Conti). It was a tricky question, given that sometimes La Tâche tasted better than the RC in a certain vintage when they were "young." He asked me to draw a quality graph from 1 to 10, ten being the ultimate. The first thing that came to my mind was an equally calibrated line from 1 to 10. Then George drew a vertical line six inches tall, put 1 at the bottom, and 9 an inch above 1. That left five inches before getting to the ultimate 10. "Anyone can measure from and talk about 1 to 9," he said, "it's that other space that is the mystery. That's where Romanée-Conti lives when it's better than La Tâche, and La Tâche never gets beyond 9." I have always used this measure.

Lack of quality in a restaurant was not as simple as a chef just not being there, although we hoped that our presence in the restaurants was what made them good. And until Las Vegas came along, one could fairly accurately predict who would stay with one restaurant, and who would go out and make more. I looked at Las Vegas as early as 1988 at the request of the Howard Hughes company, and when Wolfgang opened his Las Vegas Spago and my sous-chef went there as chef, I looked again. After a couple of trips with my dining room manager, Tony Angotti (dying to take on a restaurant in Vegas), I knew that I could never stand to be there more than three days, so I called Wolfgang about my problem. "What do you care? You don't have to be there," he replied. I was elated, then remembered the brewery, though not for long enough. Nor did others.

Michael McCarty came a cropper over a hotel project in Santa Monica, a disaster he overcame with true grit even with forest fires burning down his beautiful Pacific Palisades house and earthquakes shaking his confidence; Jimmy Schmidt and Michael tried the Rattlesnake Club in Denver, and its initial huge success soon turned to a closing; the Jams in London was the breaking straw, and Jonathan Waxman lost all of his restaurants; Paul Prudhomme went on a road show that left his New Orleans operation strung out enough to serve compromised crawfish étouffé at one of Wolfgang's Meals-on-Wheels and to have cigarette butts floating in the andouille "cooling off" in the iceless water of the bus tubs on the floor of his Café above K-Paul's; Larry Forgione soon realized one restaurant was enough after some attempts at multiple ones; some like Texas's Café Annie chef and owner Robert Del Grande stayed local and flourished, as did Scottsdale's Robert McGrath; and some stayed single, like Alice Waters (well, there was her Café Fanny) and Jean-Louis Palladin (sort of).

When Danny Meyer opened Union Square Café in Manhattan with California inspiration, and soon was able to open others, my penny dropped. Maybe it was only famous expansion-minded chefs who were hoisted on their own petard of fame. No one but regulars expected to see nonchef "owners" in the restaurant, because no one else knew their names or faces. The fabulously successful Rich Melman in Chicago could open one wonderful restaurant after another, and no tourist even knew his name or asked him to come to the table. Had anyone ever seen the other restaurateur genius, Keith McNally, at Balthazar or Pastis (New York)? Other successful groups like the Bay Area's Real Restaurants were also faceless to the nation, as was anyone from New York's Restaurant Associates, or the Flo Group in Paris.

So when the offer to redo the Peak Café in Hong Kong arrived, I thought it would be a perfect and safe absentee owner situation. I looked at the 12 percent labor costs and the one-time 14 percent income tax, and drooled. Stars Café had been a huge hit, so when in 1990 the telephone call came saying that the governor of Hong Kong had awarded us the tender (government lease), another café seemed a natural move. I was on the first plane.

Like a lot of restaurateurs around the world, I had lusted after the old Peak Café since I first saw it in 1983. At a lunch at the end of the Santa Fe Bar & Grill promotion at the Mandarin Hotel, I had joked with the general manager that if the lease ever came up on the café, we should do it. Several years later, we did.

It became my favorite restaurant of any I had ever done, and not only because its 125 seats generated over a million dollars cash a year to be distributed. But also because I was able to continue the "East Meets West" culinary exploration that Ken Hom and I had started eleven years before, in 1979. I added Indian food to the menu as well (especially breads) with some Thai (salads), some Chinese (dumplings), some pure California (salsas), and some a fusion of all of these.

The Peak Café was one indulgence that paid off handsomely.

The Food

A crisis of identity was looming in the growing community of flashbulb chefs and their mostly adoring press. But what about the food? What was American food really as we searched our way in 1990? To find an answer, I think it's worth looking back first at the lessons of Panisse, and I agree with Marion Burros that they are "manifested in different ways." They were seen as an inspiration to embrace "the principle of simplicity and impeccably fresh ingredients that you must be prepared to highlight, rather than mask"; as well as to write menus that are "not too esoteric, not too intimidating. Sort of straightforward and, at [their] best, surprising." These were the lessons established twenty years before and made into a philosophy picked up by the press and therefore the rest of the country. But was it inspirational Californian as claimed and, as such, still inspiring to a new generation of chefs as well as to a few established and older ones? A 1978 menu from Chez Panisse after I left reads:

Gâteau Crespeus

Poissons en Parchemin

Cadillac Grille

And another, still in French:

Blini au saumon fumé

Ragoût d'Été

Côte d'Ours Grillé

Of the six dishes, four were either mine or Richard Olney's, which he showed me in the South of France and I took back to Panisse. Nineteen years later, in 1997, though the menu is in English, it still has dishes written as "Maiale arrosto con prugne secche." Italian at a "California" restaurant!

By the mid-eighties, California and America had embraced the values and philosophy of Chez Panisse, but the food had moved on, evolving under the influence of both the tradition of Japanese, Thai, Chinese, and the Asian and Mexican-Spanish food that all chefs like to eat, and the tradition of the new products and fresh ingredients of all these cuisines turning up in the marketplace. Chez Panisse stayed itself, marched to its own drummer, and the food stayed the same, a goal not to be sniffed at by anyone. But a leader in food, however delicious, Panisse was not. California cooking as "New American" bedazzled the American press, but in reality the change toward the national cuisine was led by most of the same people who had been at the Festival of American Chefs in 1983 and a host of newcomers who could see beyond the mantra of California to be inspired by their own regions; even if in the process they did beat the word *local* to death, and even if such regions now encompassed the world's marketplace ingredients.

The lineup by 1990 was Lydia Shire and Jasper White celebrating New England and New America in Boston; Michel Richard, Wolfgang Puck, and Michael Roberts in Los Angeles basking in the riches of farms like Chino Ranch and L.A.'s amazing Farmers' Market; places like Mustard's Grill in Napa Valley under Cindy Pawlcyn; a few glimmerings this early from Joachim Splichal, who brought an amazing elegance to this emerging food; the ongoing festival of the French South at Commander's Palace (the divine Ella Brennan having brought forth Paul Prudhomme and now Emeril Lagasse in New Orleans); an extraordinary explosion of international foods and restaurants in Chicago by Rich Melman, king of American restaurateurs; Waxman's Jams and Forgione's An American Place in New York; Frank Stitt's Highlands Bar & Grill in Birmingham, Alabama—he never forgot the tastes of the bounty of the rural South and the tastes of his mother's food; a huge Texas, Arizona, and Southwest movement lead by Robert Del Grande, Stephan Pyles, Robert McGrath, Dean Fearing, and Mark Miller at the Coyote Café in Santa Fe; and oddly enough a European: Sirio Maccioni at Le Cirque, who presided over a strict casual elegance, as had the great Jean Bertranou of L'Ermitage in Los Angeles, the greatest chef in the United States in his time, who actually did raise those ducks and set standards that others just talked about; a few scattered country restaurants across the country, some stirrings in Hawaii, and Stars in San Francisco.

This regional explosion could happen because it was more than ingredient driven. The two-income-family cash (or credit)-rich nation was changing in many ways socially as well, with more women working and having no time to cook the family meal at night (even if anyone was there to sit down to it); greater information was available about food and its nutritional values; a revolution in transportation and delivery of national and international fresh ingredients, increasing the quality and quantity of choices; a far greater spectrum of the population was traveling abroad, eating well, then returning and demanding at least as good; the redesign of supermarket produce sections and the rise of food markets specializing in fresh produce; and farmers' markets being allowed into the city centers. In short, food was taking on a kind of appeal generally saved for sex.

I am sure that people have always cared for how food looks, but now the press made a national case out of it as they weaned themselves from the juicy stories about "nouvelle cuisine" and created the "New American Cuisine." Even *The Wall Street Journal* carried articles about cooking and food. "It's spread like wild-fire," Larry Forgione told one of its reporters, "and the notoriety of the young chefs has helped fuel it." Some of the fires were fairly soon extinguished, as the public did not take too long to figure out that a single scallop on a white plate with a dollop of white sauce was not worth twenty-five dollars. Or that someone was being made a fool of by the language of the menu, though whether the chef or the paying public was not immediately clear. The *Journal* lists one of John Sedlar's Manhattan Beach restaurant dishes as a "Navajo Mosaic" of California Vegetables, which must have left any Arizona or New Mexican Native American a bit confused, and was certainly not the kind of contemporary American cooking inaugurated in 1959 at The Four Seasons restaurant in New York. So what was contemporary American cooking after Panisse?

In the first six months at Stars, we cooked for thirty American food editors, serving them Alaskan Pinto abalone with lime butter sauce as well as portobello mushrooms in the center of which nested Gaspé ortolans, a dish I begged them not to talk about unless they wanted me in the Fish & Game penitentiary. For Pat Brown's *Cuisine* magazine we cooked a Virginia ham-stuffed saddle of rabbit with chanterelle-filled pasta shapes, and for New Year's that year we served dishes like truffled salt cod puree ravioli with crayfish butter sauce, black truffle mascarpone-stuffed polenta with wild mushroom ragout, Muscovy duck breasts with chestnuts and persimmons, and California figs cooked in Zinfandel and served with truffle cream. Whatever we cooked it had to conform to the list of food items available according to the month of the year that I handed out to all the chefs, a then cutting-edge list which included seasonal cheeses, edible flowers like violets, fuels like vine cuttings and fruitwoods, and herbs. The list was fanciful, given that the explosion of ingredients we'd started in the seventies was now in full roar and the months started to blend in with one another, but the list's variety does tell how much had changed since I was looking out the back door of the Panisse kitchen hoping some amateur forager would walk in with a huge salmon or basket of chanterelles. The three hundred then rare ingredients you could now easily get on-line, on a trip to a farmers' market, or on a jaunt down to your new fresh foods supermarket.

We had started to make the things that we could not get, like duck breast prosciutto. The Stars chef, Mark Franz, built a special refrigerator in the basement (well out of the way of any health inspectors) for air-curing meats, and that is where we kept the game sausages, salamis, duck breasts, hams, and ribs of beef. By 1985 we served smoked Russian boar, our own gravlax and smoked salmon. The revolution starting in air transportation of fresh food meant that in 1985 we could serve for New Year's a dessert of Satsuma mandarin orange, Meyer lemon, and Australian fresh young ginger and pineapple sorbets with ripe passion fruit sauce; that we could celebrate three fresh American caviars for a dinner at the Imperial Bank in San Diego; and at the California Wine Perspective dinner, after we had survived the evil treatment at the Hotel Pierre's front desk, that we could serve braised sweetbreads with fresh Côte d'Azur violets, nasturtiums, and sage butter.

These dishes and others, like wild boars' head galantine with truffled mushroom vinaigrette, or lobster risotto with monkfish, worried me that Stars had moved from California into a personal style that was made up of classical disciplines dressed up in new clothes. Did that mean we were looking fashionable? And if so, was it acceptable as a style? I compared it with what the other chefs were serving at the time, like Wolfgang Puck's Gulf snapper with red onion sauce, and Bradley Ogden's pheasant with smoked bacon vinaigrette. Certainly the sea bass carpaccio with lobster vinaigrette and caviar that I served to debut Wolfgang Puck's frozen desserts in Northern California was not classical. But by the time we got to wild boar ham with grilled sweetbreads (lentils & foie gras) in 1987 for the AIWF with Dick Graff, I thought perhaps I really had relapsed to the menu I had in 1965 in Paris at the retirement of Lucas Carton's chef:

Oysters

Minced pike

Roast lamb

Hare pie

Woodcock

Cheeses

But when I remembered the dinner's radical futurist pairing of 1955 Château d'Yquem with the oysters, and the wild strawberries in the pastry for the hare pie, and drinking the 1929 Bollinger and 1911 Clicquot with the cheeses, I knew we still had a long way to go.

I thought I was getting dangerously close to reverting to a grande cuisine American style, so when I was asked in early 1987 what the future trends would be in America, I said I had no idea. "But why not take Cuban cooking, easily one of the most mainstream of America's regional cuisines, give it a breath of fresh air, and turn it loose on the U.S.A?" I asked *The Miami Herald*. The reporter loved that fact that I answered my own telephone. "I would die to have time to do for Cuban and Indian food what nouvelle cuisine did for the grande cuisine of France. Rework it, make it smaller, lighter, more lively with less heat." When he asked me if this was Florida cuisine, I told him it should be. After saying this, I still needed to look around for a jolt of inspiration.

That's when the phone rang from Sydney.

Later in 1987 the two-week California promotion I did in Sydney's Regent Hotel with its chef, Serge Dansereau, was the jolt I needed. The fish and shellfish abundance and perfection, which I had seen before only in the fifties in Italy, the seventies in France, and at Neil Perry's Blue Water Grill, as well as the time I spent alone thinking on the beach of Lizard Island after two weeks of hell in the kitchen, brought sanity and a flood of ideas. Australia was just beginning its love affair with Asian ingredients and Thai flavors, and I picked up the scent with my old dog nose of a new revolution about to happen. All these elements and Neil Perry's genius new casual style set all my wheels going, and my love of the tropical and exotic moved them into high gear. The photo I have of one of our dishes (mussels,

Moreton Bay bugs or slipper lobster meat, fresh tiger prawns, and pieces of barramundi fillet on a plate sauced with shellfish-saffron butter sauce, with a drizzle of Thai basil cream and a tiger prawn head standing up proudly in the center of the plate) is still my all-time favorite.

But meanwhile, Stars had become institutionalized, meaning that every regular customer, every food magazine editor, and every restaurant critic was the only one who knew what should be on the menu and how much it should cost, so my most personal statements were no longer on the Stars main menu. I built the private rooms at Stars so that I could cook for forty instead of four hundred and then, in another corner, a thirty-seater called JT's. There we could cook the kind of food I wished we had time and space for in the main dining room of Stars, and there I could get a higher average check. In 1992 Stars's average per-person check with drinks and wine was forty-nine dollars; this with a gross just over $9 million with only two hundred seats not including the bar, meant the main kitchen was cooking as fast as they could. My JT's black-truffled salt cod puree fried club sandwich with lobster sauce and steelhead caviar would have raised screams in the main kitchen because of all the steps required. It was in these other venues where we could let our wings stretch out in the nineties.

For San Francisco's most wonderful couple and Stars's favorite customers, Urania and Bruno von Ristow, I cooked a white Oregon truffle custard with Jerusalem artichokes, chervil sauce, and more Quinault River steelhead salmon roe; in JT's there was one night a capon breast stuffed with fresh Berkeley morels and steamed over lovage leaves, served in a lobster sauce; at one of the James Beard Foundation dinners I served smoked sturgeon with deviled quail eggs and lobster rémoulade followed by roast capon broth with ginger, foie gras, and Chinese fermented black bean custard; and for the great wine collector Barney Rhodes's seventieth birthday, to accompany magnums of 1864, 1870, and 1874 Château Lafite, we served a puff pastry individual pithiviers-like shape filled with goat cheese and duck and goose cracklings; at the Florida Winefest for the wine importers Wilson-Daniels (Marc Kreydenweiss, Kumeu River, Biondi-Santi, and the Domaine de la Romanée-Conti wines), smoked wahoo carpaccio with grilled fresh Florida frogs' legs; for British Columbia's Mission Hills winery, arctic char with lobster mushrooms; and with Barbara Tropp at Stars in Singapore a lightly smoked sea bass with lentils, minced Chinese pork, lobster, and more duck cracklings. That's what we were doing.

The new guard, represented by chefs like Charlie Trotter, at the 1993 Napa Valley James Beard Foundation benefit dinner served dishes like his hand-harvested sea scallops with olive-oil-poached tomato, artichokes, caramelized shallots, vegetable juices, red wine essence, and veal stock reduction. Drew Nieporent and his chef from Montrachet, Debra Ponzek, served Pacific sea bass with chanterelles, spinach, and lobster au jus, and Stars, a mussel and potato timbale with herb-huitlacoche shellfish sauce. For "A Taste of the Nation," Ritz-Carlton's Gary Danko offered a warm caramelized onion, goat cheese, and morel tart. Bradley Ogden at the Celebrity Sports International event at Squaw cooked a bit of England-California with Zinfandel jam on lamb chops, some Southwest with a black bean cake, and a taste of New England with his lobster and salt cod stew. Wolfgang Puck had both Asia (his restaurant Chinois) and California cum Germany: Chinois chicken salad and apple-cranberry relish on foie gras. Obviously we were all over the map. The country was inundated by famous chefs cooking in what seemed to the press like a dizzying spectrum of individual styles that were not easily legible as a single style, so they called it New American Cuisine.

Edward Carter's magazine of the best restaurants around the world said the Stars food "epitomizes what is now known as 'California Cuisine' by its freshness of ingredients, clean-ness of taste, utter simplicity of flavor and texture that can't be faked and are unpretentious." I thought it was New American, but his analysis is not a bad beginning to define California cooking not fallen off its tracks, which was about the same thing.

California Cooking

The California style is a bear to define but, as long as one stays away from potshot lazy thinking, not difficult to describe. Making fun of a few grains of corn on a huge white plate with some minuscule dollops of sauce is fine as long as one doesn't think oneself a dragon slayer, because there was no dragon, just a lot of enthusiastic mistakes. But a legion of writers and journalists in a frenzy of smiley-faced thinking in the late eighties threw the baby out with the dishwater, and led the public to think that California cooking could be defined by bashing the food. Paula Wolfert in *Cook's* magazine goes on about how her father used to cook tuna in his backyard, so doing it in a restaurant with a seasoned butter was no big "advance," pointing out also that California cooks didn't invent coriander butter. On the defensive, she misses two points: that recipes do not develop in linear progression but are historically cyclical, and that what "advanced" the United States on from Continental Cuisine, whether an advance or not, was not tuna, or butter, or mesquite alone, but a vision that allowed a new simplicity to be recognized and welcomed as being as important as the temples of red-plush French, old Italian, and Continental American food and restaurants beloved by previous generations. My response was that the new vision was strong, clear in what the food should taste like, and cutting edge and trendy as it was, had a purity and simplicity that indeed made it classic.

Throwing "a few aging pansy petals on a one-note salad" does not make a cuisine, as one journalist scolded. I told everyone at Stars that the food should be done up but not overdone. But the debate whether there even was a styled California cuisine had raged since 1981, when the *Chronicle*'s Harvey Steiman and a bunch of us gathered at the California Culinary Academy with Julia Child to debate its existence. She stopped all conversation with "When I first came to San Francisco, the height of gastronomy was cinnamon toast and artichokes," a mind-boggling statement until everyone realized she didn't mean together. Marion Cunningham said she thought California cooking existed in "fresh, pure, and seasonal"; the Academy's French chef said that it was all about regional cuisines that developed around the availability of the raw materials and the genius of the cooks working with them; Alice Waters said, "It's very exciting to be in kindergarten," meaning (I think) that we had "advanced" no further than that. Harvey put up with everyone rattling on and said California was the only place in the United States with a great abundance of fresh ingredients. He said that was the point. When I reminded everyone that in 1976 there was no such bounty, I met only blank stares, as if I had said that the Pope wasn't Catholic.

Of course it took someone outside Californian tunnel vision to nail it all down. When Sydney's Renaissance man and critic Leo Schofield walked into Stars, he wrote that he felt he was witnessing the death of the old culture as defined as an evening spent out with a three-course meal. Stars, he said, was not old-world dining but a new style that said, "Here it is, just pick out what you feel like eating and we'll get it for you—either just a salad or a five-course meal if that is what you have the time for." When the lifestyle caught on in the East Coast, he said, for obvious marketing reasons, the food could not be called "California," so it became "nouvelle American." Leo's last evaluation is a bit bitchy, but there is a hint of truth in that it was the East Coast press who determined first that California was the leader (after the deluge of national press over the Astor Mansion lunch) and later that America was in the lead (after the American Festival in San Francisco the same year). *Newsday* wondered where "America's Nouvelle" was headed, asking Larry Forgione, Dean Fearing from Dallas, and me if we all agreed it was "an evolutionary process." An evolution toward "Liberty Cuisine," as *The Detroit News* called it. Alice Waters said, "There is no set way of doing things"; Jimmy Schmidt was driven by his love of experimentation; Paul Prudhomme yelled, "Just freedom"; and Len Allison from Huberts in Manhattan spoke like a true chef: "The challenge is to create a harmony, to be inspired by the past but allow it to be an inspiration, not a ball and chain."

A February 2000 listing in the *San Francisco Chronicle* of restaurants categorized by cuisine put Panisse under California along with Spago, a brotherhood too wild from any outlook, particularly since Panisse menus a year later contain dishes like Pissaladière, Grand Aïoli d'Hiver, Brandade Croquettes, Lasagne Bolognese, Choucroute Garnie la Panisse," and "Djej Ma'ahmar" as well as "Larsen Farm Pork Loin with Fig Sauce and Savoy Cabbage." Panisse was leading again, though this time, ironically, backwards. It had become a "Continental" restaurant in the old and highly respected world of famous restaurants like the Pump Room in Chicago, Ernie's in San Francisco, and the two Tony's of St. Louis and Houston, which took famous dishes they loved from all over the various continents.

Spago had always been Californian of a kind, with no really European-dominated dishes on its menu; rather Whole Red Snapper with Grilled Fennel and Sonoma Baby Lamb were the norm, not Chez Panisse's Maiale Arrosto. Eighties New York's The Four Seasons continued a celebration of American food from the past with a new vision; even New York's Maxwell's Plum—the Maxim's of hamburgers—was changed under the menu execution of Mark Peel and Nancy Silverton, whose one European dish was Black Pepper Fettuccine. The Santa Fe Bar & Grill had featured at the Mandarin Grill in Hong Kong Chili-Braised Rabbit with Peppered Mangoes. In an originally California-influenced Australia, by 1990 Neil Perry's dishes were Spicy Baby Octopus and Jerusalem Artichoke Mash Salad or Blue Swimmer Crab Ravioli with Burnt Butter and Yogurt. In 1987 a dinner in Sydney to honor my crew from Stars cooked by another Australian leader, the Regent Hotel's chef, Serge Dansereau, saluted us with Blue Eye Cod with Coriander (Cilantro) Vinaigrette and Chinese Black Bean Cream, Roast Hare Loin with Sweet Potato Puree; we saluted them with snapper hash with chili cream and coriander, prawn salad with Cajun eggs rémoulade, and slipper lobster with peppered mangoes. This was California cooking. The question remained for me what kind of restaurant was the best way to showcase it.

CHAPTER SEVEN

Falling Stars

Cafés: A Survival Plan

A BIG PART of wanting to do the Peak Café was to have the cash reserve for Stars, given what we knew about the near future of the Civic Center. It had taken the city government a year to assess all the damage to the Civic Center buildings after the 1989 earthquake, and to announce the plans for its future. Some buildings, such as the state building next door to Stars that produced about $300,000 a year in bar business and the same in food, never opened again after that fateful afternoon, but I knew from the mayor's office that the Civic Center would close in its entirety in 1994. The government would be moved elsewhere, the opera, ballet, two other performing arts halls, the library, the museum, in short 40 percent of Stars's business, would be gone, and it was the 40 percent that attracted the rest of the business. Stars had brought life to the center of San Francisco; now the Civic Center was going to suck the life out of Stars.

A ray of hope appeared in the form of developers who wanted to raze the block on which Stars stood, taking the state building abandoned in 1989 and everything else, and turn it into a 6-million-square-foot city offices and law building right next to a huge new courts building. So when I realized that a spot around the corner from Stars was coming available, and that it was the only corner in the Stars block that was not going to be razed, I held a meeting of the restaurant's board, now made up of the top managers, and told them the plan. We could sell Stars to the developers for their proposed $3 million in cash, void the current lease, write a new one with the city, and come back in three years to operate Stars as the major tenant in the new city offices building, designed and fitted out at their cost; or we could wait it all out while they built around and above us. All we had to do was figure out how to keep the name alive in the community, so that when we reopened the Stars name would not fall on ears now filled with whatever other new restaurants were coming along with Wolfgang Puck,

Drew Nieporent, or the Kimpton group. So I proposed to the board that the way to keep the Stars name operative in San Francisco while waiting for the new Stars to open was to move and franchise the Café to that corner, and look at moving Stars as a franchise to the up-and-coming Palo Alto. There I would plan a whole new concept, along the lines of 70 percent Stars Café and 30 percent Stars. That formula, I told them, would survive any recession.

That business plan was to have a building with a main restaurant and a café, each with its own kitchen. The Stars part would have ten in the kitchen, a large menu, and serve sixty seats, the Café would have five in the kitchen, a small menu, and serve two hundred seats. Stars would have the cachet and reputation, and would be the training ground for all the cooks; the Café would be the cash flow, kept full by Stars's reputation and recognizable value. We would have gross sales similar to those we'd had before, but with a million shaved off our currently almost $3 million payroll.

I told them that the reconstruction was backed by the mayor, and that the only snag could be the Board of Supervisors. They had said they were in favor, but I knew what a nightmare that board could be. I had just seen the current president, as she presided over the highly emotional smoking ban hearings, flipping through a magazine, berating smokers, and then out in the corridor bumming a cigarette. In San Francisco anything could happen, and if it was self-righteous enough, it usually did.

So all faces were turned to me in the Stars boardroom, silent after I asked them to make a decision. Perhaps the silence was because of my closing remark. I had said that if we were to proceed as planned and then down the road sometime the supervisors negated the entire deal, leaving us to operate isolated in all the construction, we would be screwed. "Royally!"

We decided to go ahead and move both Stars and the Café. I followed up with Jim Baer, the Palo Alto developer who had lost Wolfgang Puck as a first choice to open the restaurant—a piece of news that I listened to since I was pretty convinced that Wolfgang did not do bad deals. I called Wolfgang to ask about Baer, and he said nothing was amiss. I wondered later about that judgment when the Napoleonic-size and driven Baer made his only truthfully heartfelt comment, "I have never made anything less than a perfect decision." I should have headed for cover, but by that time the franchise deal and management contract had already been signed. It took me a day or so to realize that his statement must have meant also that he thought me incapable of even flawed correct decisions, and I wondered if this would be where we would receive the royal screwing, and not in San Francisco after all.

Meanwhile the franchised Café was not doing well. It didn't help that I was traveling a lot.

The Travel Bug

The new decade had opened with the Peak Café, so I began commuting to Hong Kong, and looking around for buyers in southeast Asia just in case the plan for a closed Stars and later a new one did not get signed. Stars was still very profitable in the early nineties, so why not find someone who would not mind paying himself what so far had been a guaranteed 15 percent return? I looked at a site in Bangkok (next to the Oriental) and Sydney (next to the Opera House). And I stepped up all the public relations I could get my hands on, no matter how much it kept me away from Stars, which after all, was soon to move to Palo Alto. One such trip in 1996 was a true PR marathon. I flew to Saint Martin in the Caribbean to join the maiden voyage of a Viking Line ship that was to host two hundred American food journalists on a three-day voyage to Miami. First I did a demo for some press at Cap Juluca in Anguilla, then caught the ship, survived the press dinner the first rough night out, did cooking demos the next day, and managed to cook the press dinner the night before docking in Miami. From there I went straight to New York to see the new Michael's before getting on a plane that night for Berlin for the three-day In Flight Catering Association conference. There in front of two thousand delegates I gave a talk on the style of California Cuisine, setting off a small flood of German press like *essen & trinken* (calling me the Voodoo-Priester of American cooking) and *Die Welt* about Stars over the next five years. I flew on to Hong Kong, where I cooked a press lunch the day I arrived, introducing them to how a Californian would cook Hong Kong's so mei (the greatest fish in the world), had dinner with some Australian press, and flew that night to San Francisco, where the evening of the day I arrived, I cooked for the Academy of Friends. Three days later we cooked a lunch in Napa for a hundred of Beaulieu Vineyard's friends and press, and the next day to Las Vegas to check out an offer from the Howard Hughes Corporation.

Just as I was lining up a buyer for Stars, San Francisco changed mayors. Our deal was dead. We would have to survive the emptied-out Civic Center in isolation except for the hordes of homeless, mentally ill, and drug dealers who poured in to fill the unsupervised void. The area was no longer civic, and it was the center of nothing. What was to be a wait for our 1997 triumphant victory march return now turned into a long wait for that year to arrive. I had thought I could sell Stars to a Japanese group, perhaps to the new Stars groups forming in Singapore and Palo Alto, or at least to Canadian Pacific Hotels, for whom I was consulting. But now the dangers of the Civic Center would be obvious to all. When San Francisco's old guard Prentis Cobb Hale died, that inner part of me that lived happily in the old order vanished. With Prentis gone there was no one to tell me how full of shit I was, when I was. I started to make real mistakes.

The first ones came from listening, in an attempt to understand the changing times, not to my instincts but to my "handlers who ruled the times": publicists, insurance companies, and human resources experts. But I continued my international search for a buyer for Stars. My business card, which in 1990 read Twinkle, Inc., the Turk Street Group, and Freedragon, Ltd., in Chinese as well as English, in 1996 had a single name, Stars, in English only, and even that was soon being fitted for the emperor's clothes.

My Peers

For ten years my team at Stars had been my soul mates, but now there were signs of fatigue, of hairline cracks in the bonds—the bonds that had held us together even through all the partner disputes, the drama surrounding our meteoric rise to success, and the lawsuits.

It didn't help when, in 1993, we were sued (again) for wrongful termination.

"Oh, that," I said carelessly.

And AIDS discrimination.

"Oh, dear."

When I first met the lawyer who had drummed up the charges against Stars, Kafka's *Trial* and *Metamorphosis* somehow conflated; he had the same kind of beady-eyed greed as the sewer-loving bugs I saw in the garbage left by the homeless in the urine-filled parking garage of the Civic Center. But the charges could hardly be taken seriously, and thinking the usual exterminators would do the trick, I called the lawyers.

The plaintiff had been terminated a few years before. I was out of town when human resources, the dining room manager, Tony Angotti, called me to say that a waiter had lied to some customers, given them what they said was compromised service, tampered with the guest check to cover up his errors, and lied to his supervisors about the incident. My final permission was required to help protect us against wrongful termination suits, and to prevent any ganging up by the managers against one of the staff. I asked if they had processed this potential firing by the book: Were there a minimum of three documented discussions and counseling in his file? More than three, they assured me, with witnesses, and co-signed by the waiter himself. They insisted the action was deserved, just, and with respect to the labor board rules, watertight. I consented, and then double-checked the file when I returned.

Three years later the waiter was hospitalized with full-blown AIDS and the family needed money. So who better to sue than the perceived closest, easiest, and—they thought—deepest pockets?

There was always someone around trying to extort money from Stars, and this case—like so many others before it—was thrown summarily out of court. And thrown out again at another hearing. I remember a note from the lawyer saying that he knew he had no case, and that if he ever got me in front of a San Francisco jury, he would destroy me.

Some months later, in November, he did his best.

During that time the California State Supreme Court ruled (somewhat retrospectively) that all wrongful termination suits had to be heard in front of a jury. Now that meant me.

I was told on a Wednesday that a trial was set for the following Monday—rushed because the plaintiff was dying.

My hastily called deposition was no good: I simply could not remember a three-year-old incident that had taken ten minutes of my time on the phone from Hong Kong. As for all the staff and customers of Stars who had died of AIDS since we opened in 1984, those memories were well buried. Unearthing did not come easily.

I got my initial whiff of danger when, on the first day of the trial, a large photo of the dying waiter with tubes up his nose was left in the courtroom for all to see. Sitting in the courtroom were my protector Richard Collier and regular customer Jim O'Dea, himself a legal hit man for Boston's more dubious Irish politicos in older and rougher days and now a seasoned plaintiffs' lawyer. Having him defend me would have been like having Mayor Daley as an attorney in Chicago, and I considered asking him to take over the case. But a sense of fairness tripped me up, and I didn't switch.

The list of my alleged sins was long: I had cared nothing for any of the staff and had brutalized them—particularly the gay staff—for years. I was flabbergasted that the opposing attorney was allowed to repeat these lies in court, that both his scribbled note and the previous judge's having dismissed the charges twice were inadmissible.

I sat for four days as the waiter's lawyer spat insults at me and ruined my community and social reputation, charging me with arrogance and an "uncaring" attitude. To an extent the charge was true: I *didn't* care about this at best mediocre waiter who was now trying to extort $13 million out of me. I'd barely known or talked to him—a fact his lawyer twisted into proof that I cared for none of the staff. Why would I care to pick on a waiter, I wondered, if I did not care for any of them? And there was a catch-22: I was accused of looking in an employee's private file (illegal) but of not looking long enough to discern that his serial absences were the consequence of AIDS. I must have known he had AIDS, they said, because he was gay—but it was in fact illegal for me as his employer to have concerns he was gay!

Called to the stand, I was an ineffective witness. I was overwhelmed by the long list of gay male waiters I had allegedly pilloried, starting with our first fatal cases of AIDS: both I had supported privately, paying two thousand dollars a month out of my own salary for AZT. The memories paralyzed me: I couldn't talk, could only stare in horror at the human sewer in front of me spewing obscene charges that I had sent these men to early deaths. I broke. A few months before, a friend had died while on the phone with me as I was telling him I would be right over with his Stars's hamburger. When I choked at that memory I knew I had to get out of the room; as I rose, I saw the gloating smile from the opposing attorney, the approaching bailiffs, the incredulous faces of the people in the courtroom, and the mixed looks of believers and unbelievers in the jury box. I wondered how I could have let things come to this.

The bill was finally coming due for every sin I had ever committed: every sarcastic remark; every hour not spent counseling an employee who had broken the rules or screwed up; every flashbulb moment not shared with one of my chefs too late for the shoot, every huge bonus that was not big enough. Prosecution witness after witness (all ex-employees) testified that I had not taken them to New York or London or Paris, that I had played favorites. And that I never had taken employees who were on probation or consistently late for work. Only in San Francisco would this make sense to a jury, and it did.

The trial started on my fifty-first birthday and went for two weeks. When I heard my friends botching their best efforts to protect me, and others—who had done very well out of Stars and gone on to big jobs in the United States and abroad—exaggerate and outright lie in front of that impressionable jury, I felt cut off from everyone and everything. All I could think of were my Burmese cat and my BMW motorbike—give me a tank of gas, and I would be out of there—with the cat. No wonder the jury felt I was "distant."

Herb Caen had taken care of the verdict the week before the trial when he printed that I was getting my just desserts. Only in San Francisco could political expediency take precedence over years of personal loyalty. The politically gay activists, who for years had been "fed" by my hand, joined Herb and were now ready to bite it. Suddenly I was political death in San Francisco. After the prosecution lawyer opened the trial saying that the million dollars I had raised for AIDS research and hospices had been to hide my alleged antihomosexuality politics, a rumor went out that ACT UP was going to come in and trash Stars. No one knew where to hide, but it certainly was not behind me. I called my pals at the North Station, all good Italian and Irish cops. They knew what to do. The moment the ACT UP clowns started Brown Shirt tactics in Stars, the police were there to arrest them. Now I was even more a pariah.

The closing arguments were on the Monday before Thanksgiving. Everyone knew a verdict would come in Wednesday afternoon, since the jurors wouldn't want to be back in court on Friday. While they were out deliberating, I attended the punitive damages hearing with the judge and the smugly confident opposing lawyer, who doubtless had visions of moving from his apartment-office in a seedy part of town to a downtown suite, where he could put out a brass plaque commemorating the defeat of Jeremiah Tower.

Then he discovered that I owned nothing. Nothing worthwhile to him, that is, and nowhere near the punitive $13 million that he saw in his dreams.

He went ballistic.

Stars without a noncompete clause and still paying off the bank was worthless; the cat wouldn't have him; the apartment was leased, as were the cars; my cookbooks (worth a hundred grand) seemed like just so many *Joy of Cookings* to his eyes. All they had asked for were records—those I gave them. But my best Cheshire cat smile drove him over the top. A sweet moment.

The jury filed in and sat down without looking at me, and at that moment I knew for sure. My attorneys moved one step back and to the side of me.

"We find for the plaintiff."

As the verdict was read out, only two of the jury did not give me looks of hate. I had nothing to say to them or to my counsel. I reached into my jacket pocket and caressed the first-class one-way ticket to Hong Kong that I'd bought the day before; I wondered if I could get out of town in time to use it. I expected a sheriff with handcuffs and an orange jail suit for me, but no one appeared except the reporters, whom I had kept fully employed for two weeks. The room seemed weirdly still immediately around me, but outside that cocoonlike realm there was a chaos of camera lights and microphones on gaffs shoved into my face. Finally a reporter's scream got through my daze: "Any comment?"

"No thank you very much" were my only words—ones widely reported the next day as evidence of my unrepentant arrogance.

On the jury was a Presbyterian spinster minister who had frowned on me with disapproval for ten days. When the award came in far less than demanded—approximately one four-hundredth of the $13 million requested—it was because of this woman, who spent all her time and money taking care of transsexuals with AIDS. Only in San Francisco could I have been so reviled and then so oddly saved from bankruptcy. It turned out that the jury was split ten to two, the other dissenter being Penny Alexander, an executive search consultant. She later told the *San Francisco Chronicle*, "I was amazed at how ineffective the system is. I always assumed that it worked, that it was fair. But it's amazingly unfair and in no way gets at the truth of anything. There is no such thing as a trial by your peers."

I was hissed at by my peers at an ARC benefit a few days later. Later, the San Francisco AIDS Foundation would withdraw my selection for the Community Service Award, bestowed on an individual "who has made hastening the end of the HIV/AIDS epidemic an urgent priority in their life." They wrote they were sure I would understand.

I did perfectly.

"You are so dear to us," they added. The "so" suggested not dear enough.

A month after the trial the California Supreme Court revised the decision that had landed me before a jury.

One of my first post-trial crisis management acts was to take down from the wall in the VIP section of the dining room all the photos of fading stars and put up new ones of younger, cooler, and hipper ones. Gone was the large photograph of Robin Leach and me engaging in the sport of champagne drinking that was captioned "The mediagenic master of faux familiarity has fashioned a career out of celebrity voyeurism." The line referred to Robin but was printed on top of my image—an irony I'd enjoyed until people believed it of me.

But I knew I had to keep up a front: that I was the same, and that Stars would be the same despite the Civic Center exodus. I leased a new big Mercedes.

The Emperor's Clothes

We kept up appearances, but nothing was ever the same again: Confidence and loyalties had been stretched to the limits, and the original team started to fall apart.

Mark Franz had been my star pupil at the CCA and, after a stint cooking for fishermen in wilderness Alaska, had run the kitchens at Santa Fe Bar & Grill and Stars. Mark was the one who knew my palate, and no one could see inside the soul of my food the way he could. Also Mark was one of the boys, and the leader to whom the testosterone-driven young cooks could relate when my role to them may have sometimes seemed other-planetary. Steven Vranian (the one who got lost in Manhattan in the van on our way to Newport in 1983) had been our great grill chef. Now he was in charge of buying and storing the food; no one could organize a storeroom or walk-in refrigerator as maniacally, or knew better that a restaurant's food could never be truly great without those controls, and that keeping track of and properly storing newly arriving perfect ingredients was the only way to prevent them from turning into ordinary ones. Noreen Lam, also from the CCA, was in charge of Stars Café. No one could set the standards with prep cooks as could Noreen; her infinite patience and her willingness to take the time to teach and create perfection never lagged.

Others had come and gone, but these managers were the core, the conscience of Stars's philosophy and its quality standards. They were the ones who trained any newcomers, managers or line staff, in what it was all about. For a long time we all got along swimmingly.

I am not sure which came first: their doubt that they wanted to go on managing Stars, or my doubt that they could manage Stars with their conflicting emotions about staying. Money was not an issue since I had been paying them huge sums (for the time). It would have been deserved and practical to make them partners in Stars, but before 1988 the stock was not mine to give, and after that—at least until 1993—its ownership would have been encumbered with lawsuits, potentially huge punitive damages, and enormous capital gains taxes.

In my heart I knew that different bones thrown to them probably would not work, but I still hoped they would. Mark had always said that he was in my shadow, a place we both knew he found, at least for a while, more comfortable than being on his own. I hoped a good compromise with him was a country restaurant that he could call his own. Feeling guilty about not making him a partner, I bought and gave him Stars Oakville Café in Napa and my BMW 750 IL to go with it. He probably didn't want either, so things became even more complicated. With those kinds of emotions the year before he left, we often passed like ships in the night. A few years later Mark told a reporter what it was like working for a man who he said was unpredictable, moody, and an unrelenting perfectionist. "You never knew if you were going to get your ass kicked or what. You could really get roasted for doing the wrong thing, but he was always a gentleman with me."

Steven had always said that he wanted for his children the same kinds of advantages that he had had as a child while traveling around South America, so I hoped that Stars Singapore would be what he wanted. I knew that Noreen's hometown, Honolulu, was calling strongly to her but hoped that she would want first to travel amongst the new Stars, including the Peak Café in Hong Kong, to teach her dedication to perfection to new staff.

As I had never let personal relationships stand in the way of adventure, I missed an increasingly important point. Single when we bonded at the Santa Fe Bar & Grill, the team members were now married, soon to be, or in lasting relationships. They needed a stable future, and one that shed its own light on them. When they realized that the kind of drama that surrounded us at Stars was not inevitable, they looked further than the light shining from it, a light still visibly shining, but originating perhaps in the past, as if from a now dead star.

I knew Mark was in trouble when one Sunday afternoon, as I was setting up to cook the menu I had chosen for Jacques Pépin that night, Mark more or less demanded that I step aside because he wanted to show Pépin that he could cook without me.

I should have said no.

I knew that there was something more wrong than just this dinner as I saw him bring out more and more bottles of Sapporo. He was well into the beer by the time Jacques arrived. Without me he could cook magnificently, but that night he self-parodied both in his choice of menu and in how he served it.

After the Pépin dinner, Mark and I were a bit leery of each other, wondering how two people who trusted each other with their lives could find it so difficult on any given day just to sit down and say the situation was merde.

First to quit mid-decade was my great dining room manger, Tony Angotti, who had held the service staff together with an iron fist before heading off to Las Vegas. After he left, the remaining team members started vying for each other's reputations and salaries, given that it was plain that we could not go on paying flush-times salaries in the downturn days of the Civic Center. After Tony, Noreen left, and then Steven. Finally, a year later, Mark came in from Napa to the boardroom when we were all actually discussing the problems in Napa and quietly told me, as a gentleman, that he was through at Stars.

That was the second time I should have gone down into the basement, turned on the gas, and lit a match. My beneficiaries were the core team members, and they would finally have owned Stars, or whatever was left of it.

After the team broke up I changed my will to benefit a home for the retired donkeys of Calcutta—showing what I thought of the endless stream of new managers who came in. They were impressed with the reputation, the honors on the walls, and the superlatives lavished on me and Stars, but they had never lived them. Now Stars had no one apart from me who knew fact from legend. Dressing these new people up as consorts was a challenge as big as showing any interest in the process myself. To find a way out, and to recover from the exhausting holiday season, I took off for my spiritual homes—Paris and a large, luxury hotel room.

Chef of the Year

In January 1996, after my obligatory walk in the Tuileries Gardens outside the hotel, I went to find solace at Rudolf Nureyev's grave, where I laid an enormous bouquet of white lilies for this friend who had died of AIDS. As I stood there in the rain, the television cameramen, who had showed up because it was the anniversary of his death, asked me to pick up the flowers and put them down again (and again). I politely refused. Something in me snapped when they became angry. I now look back at that moment as the birth of my growing realization that I was as little interested in the sacrifices of being a star as Rudi was, just before he died, in the porno tapes he insisted I buy for him. After weeping into a couple of dozen Bélons at La Coupole with a Brazilian picked off the Avenue Foch, and realizing the beautiful flesh at the table with me held no emotional support for me anymore, I canceled my visit to Guy Savoy's new concept which everyone was talking about (that all famous restaurants should have a café), and called Air France. Given my history with Guy and with this café concept, even back to the days of Panisse, I realized all the ironies at play. But it was time to gird my defenses and set off for New York, where I was to get up onstage and accept an award without noticeably looking around to see who was still throwing stones.

At any other time I would have turned down anything as patently self-serving as an organization like Chefs in America. But they had managed somehow to get Carnegie Hall, an Oscar look-alike statuette, and Lee Iacocca to present it. No one outside of the community of chefs would know that it meant nothing, and it was good for at least temporary emperor's clothes, hiding the fact that the year looked like it would be very naked indeed. Full dressing occurred, however, when a few months later I received my real Oscar, this time for the Outstanding Chef in America from the James Beard Foundation. It was a very much bigger deal, and invitations to donate money and services flowed in, as did customers.

We did the usual benefits and dinners to much acclaim (Cystic Fibrosis in Florida, International Association of Culinary Professionals for Julia Child, at Stars for Pavarotti, Placido Domingo, and Martha Stewart). But the Citymeals-on-Wheels at Rockefeller Center that summer was a grim wake-up call. I did not want to spend the usual ten thousand dollars on the trip, so decided to do a tomato stand and have the growers pay for it. The tomatoes showed up an hour before the event, were unripe and ordinary, and for the first time ever, the event was rained out. If I had trouble grasping large-scale disasters, I certainly knew a small one when I was standing in the middle of it. But when I suggested to the new team members that we cut our losses and split, they were confused. The old team would have had us packed up and out of there before even I realized we should go. Standing there in a new and ineffective location (instead of our usual in the center of the rink) with bad supermarket tomatoes, I just wasn't interested in summoning up the old bravado: It was a mess so call it a mess, and get out. The new staff expected miracles from me, and I was running out of them.

Right after the tomatoes and Mark Franz's dinner for Jacques Pépin, I answered the phone on one of the rare nights I was working as maître d' at Stars. It was the Pacific Grove, California, police: My brother had just been killed. This several times wounded Green Beret, Special Forces, and 101st Airborne soldier with three tours in Vietnam at the height of the war was killed getting on his ten-speed bike on the grass verge of a park in the center of town. He was on his way to celebrate his birthday with his family when some kid ran him over.

I walked over to the bar, had a glass of champagne, and considered my options. I picked up the phone and found the people I wanted to talk to just arriving at their offices in Tokyo.

"Right," I said to Sapporo and Sony in separate calls, "if you are still interested in Stars, let's talk."

The next morning, feeling the false resolve of unrealistic decisions, I made the list of potential buyers. Japan was at the top, then my friend in Thailand (even with rumors of a palace coup confirmed when I called and the Queen, in hiding, was sitting next to him), followed by Golden Harvest Films in Hong Kong (the Stars Singapore group) and the developers in Palo Alto.

I was ready to sell.

Stars Around the World

The first franchise with its promise of big returns was Palo Alto. In 1994 the down payments paid the new management team and, as business in the Civic Center started to drop off a few million here and there, some of Stars's expenses as well. It seemed a good interim plan to keep Stars afloat until the Civic Center reopened.

Then things started to get strange in Palo Alto. Jim Baer, the attorney representing the owners, was also the project's construction manager. With his claim to us of his perfect decision making, perhaps there was perfection to his overseeing a construction project that had different versions of working drawings. Perhaps.

The project took on an unreal glow.

Stars Palo Alto finally opened in 1995 to three-star reviews. But when the inevitable cost overruns became known, Jim put all the blame on me. The investors, just as inevitably, took his word. To try to get a grip on the difference between the project's fact and its fiction, I took an afternoon off with the perfect margaritas of the Zuni restaurant and waited for a call from Jim to tell me not to come back. Over the third cocktail I wondered what it was about me and the kinds of people with whom I was involved.

First there were the Jesuits in Australia, then the sexual predators of English schools: I'd more or less outrun them all. So far so good. My friend of the "Champagne Palace" in Boston was purely psychotic, but I never held it against him unless he was dangerous, which he was quite often toward the end. Then he would be hauled off to the bin. Alice could be actually quite adorable, but often hostile when threatened (which was quite often), so I decided that if she believed so strongly it was her restaurant, why not let her have it? Doyle Moon was very charming and had an outsider's healthy respect for the possibility of being damaged by insiders, and I could relate to that. And he was a lot of fun when in the mood for a few lines of coke and some wonderful drinks. But he was hostile too when someone threatened to come between him and his getting what he wanted. I found his killer instinct a bit fascinating (as long as I was not on the list of his victims), and I envied his single-minded strength in destroying his friends, once his fondness, loyalty, and often endless tolerance for them were replaced with paranoia and greed.

But I found nothing to admire in Jim Baer.

And, he believed in the perfect rightness of his descisions—no matter how objectionable or flawed.

When the entire franchise fee from Palo Alto went to the Stars management team, I answered with interest a potentially lucrative call for a consultation from the owners of the Hotel Vancouver. They wanted to redo its dining room. After my first visit, I was hooked. Not only did I like the regional general manager and his wife, the migrating whales, and the otters on Vancouver Island competing with bald eagles for salmon, I fell in love with the region and its ingredients. When I attended a festival of British Columbia foods and for the first time tasted cloudberries and the wines from the Okanagan Valley, I knew the region was in the same phase California had been when I started at Chez Panisse. I loved the enthusiasm of the chefs and the farmers who were supplying them, and the very unjaded way in which they appreciated what they were trying to do.

So when a new development opportunity became available in Seattle in 1997, in a building that was to finish off the revival of the new downtown, I jumped at the chance. Since 1980 I had been telling the press that Florida and the Northwest were the only two culinary regions of America that were left to develop and received only raised eyebrows in response. But by the mid-nineties it was obvious to all what we had known in California for years—that the best berries, mushrooms, pinot noir, and fish were now from Alaska and the Northwest, not California.

Following my culinary nose, I decided to open a Stars five blocks up from Seattle's waterfront market—a Stars that would help make America's newest regional food. I told the architects that I wanted the same kind of huge bar overlooking the dining room as in Stars San Francisco but that we'd hide most of the kitchen with a big oyster and seafood bar for casual and single diners. It would be a celebration of local seafood, a visual statement of where we were and what kind of food we would be emphasizing. I wanted a big fireplace separating the bar and the dining room to give the feel of the Northwest's lodges; I knew that anyone coming up the escalators out of the Seattle rain and seeing a hearth with a roaring fire would not be able to resist coming in.

But that was two years before the opening, and at the same time an old friend from Hong Kong called and said we should meet: he was developing a team to open entertainment restaurants in Asia and then in the United States. They wanted the Stars concept. Always one to travel at the drop of a hat, I flew to Singapore to meet his group, where I would be dealing with three very civilized and ethical principals: the owner of Golden Harvest Films, the chairman of the board of the city's biggest investment house, and the Board of Tourism and its minister, who very usefully, was in charge of Singapore's work visas. To the extent that I could feel secure with any human beings at this time, I warmed up to the appearance of successful, rich businessmen, well liked in their community, and a government that ran a state as well as any ever had. I accepted the project.

My slightly criminally minded publicist took one look at the franchised Stars Singapore team leader and warned me not to trust him in or out of my sight, saying that there was more snake in him than man.

I didn't see it.

I could see that he hadn't much experience with money unless it was someone else's: his spending was like that of a kid who had been given the keys to a billionaire's cash vault. He made me nervous when he talked about budgets, blithely skipping through a three-year projected budget awash in red ink. He signed a lease the restaurant could never afford, and talked about losses as inevitable, even part of the plan. I had never *planned* to lose money in my life, but nothing I said fell on open ears, so I kept quiet. The owners of Stars Singapore were very big guys in finance; I figured they knew something I did not.

All doubts flew momentarily from my brain when I climbed up the ladder and put my head through the hole hacked in the floor of the hundred-year-old building across from Raffles in the heart of Singapore.

I gasped in joy.

It was a room I had waited a lifetime for: a hundred-foot-long Palladian rectangle with a row of Doric columns five feet away from each of the long walls, a big shuttered window centered between each column. Here was classical, grand colonial, tropical architecture at its best. When I learned it had been the dormitory for the boys of the Sacred Heart orphanage, I could almost see the same lineup as my school in England, with its long rows of bed-chair-bed-chair.

The other locations—an old Chinese spice shop, a government building on a hill—were beautiful, but this city-block convent with its little cathedral that would be our banquet hall was unique in the world. And after seeing the outdoor fast-food restaurants and the exotic markets filled with eight kinds of mangoes, huge baskets of rambutans and mangosteens, of headily fragrant pineapples and sugary finger bananas stacked in small mountains next to bamboo baskets filled with thirty-pound red snappers, octopus, garoupas, and exotic striped moray eels that were the most beautiful fish I had ever seen, I knew all my fantasies from my upbringing—of tropical fruits and verandas filled with elegant white suits and cool gin and tonics—could come true here. It was a world to which I was happy to escape. Over drinks at Raffles I signed the contract, holding back a desperate eagerness to say, Why not buy Stars instead of merely franchising it?

The finished Stars—with its pizza oven and rotisserie oven at one end of the dining room and huge bar at the other, a spiral staircase in between joining the Café below with the main Stars—was magnificent. Drew Nieporent, a man of many famous restaurants on both American coasts, said Stars Singapore was the most beautiful restaurant in the world.

I thought about buying an old chophouse and setting up shop in Singapore, letting a management company operate all the restaurants. But when, after a few months, the local team failed to get even to first base in how to operate a Stars, when they seemed more loyal to each other than to the owners, and more interested in glamorous special events than in everyday operations, I knew that they were marching to a different drummer, that their music was more Pied Piper than victory march. After helping them open the restaurant I returned to San Francisco, until my next contracted visit.

When I returned to Stars San Francisco, in the depth of the Civic Center's demolition, I was determined to get a grip on the operations and to build the restaurant back up. But as construction of the new courthouse across from Stars's entrance began, huge barricades went up that isolated the area even further.

Since there is never a better time to strike successfully then when someone is down, the bottom feeders appeared; first with little bites, then in a wholesale frenzy.

Blood in the Water

First was the telephone call from the FBI: How well did I know Andrew Cunanan? Gianni Versace had been murdered a few days before, and Cunanan was the suspect, along with anyone who "knew" him. But because the real contacts had been (and still were) customers of Stars, I told them my lips were sealed.

They didn't like that.

The next day it was around town that I was mixed up in Versace's murder.

I got on a plane to Singapore and returned a week later.

I saw it on the evening television news the night I got back. An attorney in a wheelchair had invited a news camera crew into the men's bathroom at Stars and had filmed him bashing backward and forward, "trying" to get into the toilet stall, which, no surprise to anyone, he could not. Soon there was a lawsuit on my desk. The press howled in righteous outrage, and more inspectors, TV, and activists showed up across the street at Stars Café: they objected to the marble bathrooms—which had been installed at vast expense a few years before, inspected, and passed as conforming to the Americans with Disabilities Act.

It turned out that the perfectly accessible stall openings were one-quarter of an inch short of what was required by the newest regulations. Out they all had to be ripped.

I had to give interviews in the bathrooms when they were finished. So this is what it has come to, I thought to myself: I really am in the toilet. I thought of Singapore, the strictest city in the world, where this would have been done via a letter in a dignified way instead of with barbarians at my gates.

The only people embarrassed by all this (other than me) were the fifty representatives of the Japanese Hotel and Restaurant Association, who had been my hosts in Japan and were now visiting Stars. They had come to California to see Napa and buy wine for the five hundred hotels and restaurants they represented. But our visit to some of Napa's most prestigious wineries ran aground on the new grandeur spreading through the valley. The Japanese were snubbed. Having their day in San Francisco and at Stars declared their "Day," and having the presentation to them by Mayor Frank Jordan helped to smooth their feathers, but they suggested between the (very polite Japanese) lines that I move to Kyoto, which they knew to be my favorite Japanese city. More and more I looked forward to trips to Singapore, Hong Kong, and Australia, where I seemed to be able to do little wrong, in contrast to San Francisco, where I seemed to do little right.

My efforts to sell Stars to Sapporo and Sony came to a civilized nothing after the Japanese experience in Napa and their tour of the Civic Center area, now falling into the fetid laps of the homeless.

Moving on, I turned the old Café space in Stars into JT's and a cigar room to show what I thought was the next trend: comforting, sensible, unadorned, single ingredient–driven food. That approach was a few years premature, and also by now I was spread too thin emotionally. I could not deal with a new generation of staff who had no idea what I was talking about when I said that a great chef knows when not to get in the way of perfect ingredients: a piece of impeccably fresh turbot, for example, needs no more than a made-to-order lobster coral butter sauce, into which a sprig of tarragon has been infused for ten seconds.

I was not up to starting all over again. And there was no extra money or time now to take the new managers and staff to the Crillon in Paris (to see how breakfast was done), to Lameloise in Burgundy or The Four Seasons in New York (to see how service was done), or to Maguy Le Coze's perfect Le Bernardin (to show how perfect unadorned fish was done). At a lecture at the CIA in the fall of 1995, I begged the first graduating class of the bachelor's program to have a little humility; I said that spending all that money to become chefs was really only the beginning of the journey. The stunned silence that followed told me I should never have left Hong Kong, where the staff knew I knew more than they did, and would listen as long as I made them money—and as long as they could call me names in Chinese under their breath that would have stripped the paint off the culinary walls of fame in America.

Back in San Francisco, things became worse with the new mayor: The deal to buy out Stars and put it in its new location was revived, but it never seemed to be either in or out of favor. The cupboard was empty.

The Cupboard Is Bare

Denise Hale and I drank the last of the Cristal in Stars's cellar on New Year's Eve 1995.

Her husband (with Al Wilsey one of the last great San Franciscan tycoons with any style) had just died, and she and I had spent a lot of time together while he was in the hospital. Every night during that time we would sit at midnight in Stars, drinking and feeling nothing, not even the alcohol. We made a vow to be out of San Francisco for the next New Year's Eve. I told her that it should be in Hong Kong, and that I would show her the wonderland of Singapore, where nothing bad ever seemed to happen. Or Manila, from where I was hoping something good in the way of money would arrive.

Benjamin Bitanga, that cheery Manila pirate who had helped wrest Stars from Doyle, had always thought of it as "our" restaurant. Now he was back to the rescue, agreeing that I should sell part or all of Stars to keep it afloat until the opera and ballet came back in 1997. I had already been to Manila and met the group, who adored Stars; a year later, with rumors that Stars was broke, they were scared off.

At the end of 1996 I was easily persuaded to spend New Year's in Singapore, though it was a toss-up what needed my attention more that evening: Singapore Stars for its first December 31, or San Francisco Stars for its twelfth. But I knew I had cut most of my emotional ties with San Francisco when I decided to be away for New Year's Eve. I took Denise Hale and my other two favorite San Franciscans, Bruno and Urania von Ristow, on a Christmas cruise on a chartered yacht around Hong Kong and gave them a champagne lunch. In Hong Kong I felt truly at home. At the Peak Café the staff, who had not seen me for six years, cried when I walked in. The at-home feeling was intensified in Singapore, when at three on New Year's Day morning, we walked a mile back to the Ritz-Carlton, Denise bedecked in Bulgari, feeling completely safe: not a homeless person in sight, let alone a thief. Neither one of us wanted to return to San Francisco and face the music—she of lawsuits piling up from her stepchildren (other than Liza Minnelli), I of what was going to happen if the cash from a Manila, Hong Kong, or Bangkok deal did not come through, or cash from the franchises didn't start to flow. The Thai connection was proving elusive, potential deals with Hong Kong–MCA and/or Disney seemed far off, Manila was in weekly contact but agonizingly evasive, and Stars Singapore, with its impossible rent, was hemorrhaging money and my percentage fees.

But at least Andrew Yap, the new owner of Stars Singapore, would arrive in San Francisco in a few days, supposedly in a buying mood. The word was he needed something to go with his Italian "cigarette" boat collection.

Andrew was due at the Stars management offices at 3:30 one day in early 1997 to sign the letter of intent to buy Stars. By 4:45 he had not shown up or called. At 5:00 he did show, explaining that the airport weather had held him up and that he now had only a few minutes to talk before his plane to Singapore. Of course I knew all the airlines' schedules to Asia by heart, and could see for fifty miles out the office window. I excused myself and called the San Francisco airport: there had been no fog or delays in two days. I walked back and listened as Andrew explained that the original offer of several million dollars (which had brought us to the table that day) could now be no more than one. I rose, told him I was grateful for all the work he had done, and said I did not want to be responsible for him missing his plane. His mouth sagged slowly open, then quickly shut. He stood up, buttoned his coat, and instantly dropped the fatherly tone with which he had broken the news of our ruin. I escorted him to the door with just the polite but very firm faceless timing I had learned in Hong Kong.

The next day I flew to New York to present the Beard award to 1997's "Best American Chef." My publicist insisted I take my Yorkshire terrier Harry up to the podium with me: As yesterday's news, how else could I draw the cameras? My beautiful copresenter, the New York socialite Nina Griscom, said, "Harry, get a life," but everyone knew she meant me.

Back in San Francisco there was no end to the mounting bills. Only the scheduled return of the opera and ballet to the Civic Center and the holiday season private parties—each of which I was forced to guarantee to cook myself—saved our cash flow, if nearly destroying me.

Back in the Philippines I met the investment group again, now excited (having seen the recent San Francisco cash flow) about opening a Stars in Manila. I phoned my comptroller with the great news of more franchise fees, but his news was less good. On my desk was another employee complaint which, because of the impending sale, we took to confidential mediation.

The mediation judge was a Stars customer, but since I had never talked to her, she did not have to disqualify herself from the case. She took me aside and said the whole thing was "pure extortion." But did I want to settle or face another lawsuit?

I didn't. I knew I hadn't the money to fight but was horrified when I realized I didn't have the desire to, either. Twelve years before, a settlement would have been $3,500. The waiter trial had cost hundreds of thousands. Now a down payment on a discrimination case would be $125,000. At a break in the hearing negotiations, the two employees had dragged me into the ladies' room, their ever-tear-filled eyes suddenly quite dry, to assure me that this was not personal, nothing to do with me.

I tried to remember that it was nothing personal when a few hours later I walked out of the chambers with the last of our money gone.

When I drove off, I laughed; here I was in a new Mercedes, and now I wouldn't have a dime to my name.

Cloud Cover

In early January 1998, when I scheduled a meeting for the Stars managers and the board, no one showed up except the Stars attorney, the COO, and me. No words were necessary. We knew that we alone could not keep the endless line of vendors at bay. No one could blame them. They had been living on the same promises of Asian funds for the last three months that we had.

Then a check for the Stars Manila franchise came through from Bitanga's group. The money dented the vendor bills but didn't hold out for long. But on my first morning in Manila in March, to see the site and to shake hands, a call came through to my room in the Shangri-La hotel. It was Andrew Yap.

We met in the enormous foyer lounge next to a garden of royal palms. I told him that I still had plans to refurbish Stars in time for the reopening of the performing arts halls in the Civic Center, but that I would need financing. Andrew looked at me with barely concealed cunning and told me that if he were to refinance Stars he would have to own it. I paused delicately, for as long as I could.

"Fine."

We shook hands after mine had stopped shaking.

As I wandered out to my car, I wondered if the shaking of my hands was from sadness or relief. But now, assuming the deal went through, everyone would get paid.

After a stop in Singapore to check on Stars, and a promotional tour on Crystal Cruises, I returned to San Francisco and cooked again for the Meals-on-Wheels, for the fifteenth anniversary of the AIWF held at Michael's in Santa Monica, and with gritted teeth, for the AIDS Emergency Fund. But my mind was on the sale and what would happen if it fell through. Then Andrew and his team finally believed me when I advised them to hustle to be ready with their organization (and Stars's new appearance) by the opening of the performing arts season in September. The due diligence ended on June 3, 1998; the money was due on the twelfth. On the fourth I cooked a big dinner for Shafer Vineyards, on the seventh I flew to New York for Citymeals-on-Wheels at Rockefeller Center. I made two appointments on the twelfth: one for an overhaul at my favorite salon, and the other (tempting the gods) for the movers to come and get all my papers and personal goods from Stars.

The money was due by noon, so I made a spa appointment for eleven-thirty. Whatever the outcome, I was going to have needed a massage. When my cell phone rang, I felt my heart miss several beats: It was the office at Stars saying they had given the cell phone number to the bank but had no news. Of course I had already given the number to the banker, so the second time the phone rang I was calm, thinking the bank would not bother to call saying it *wasn't* there. It was. All delicious several seven figures of it.

The next day I held a meeting to hand over Stars to its new owners and formalize the occasion with the staff. Then I headed to the airport for the closest tropical beach that was at the height of its mango season.

At Rosewood's Las Ventanas al Paraiso I had an ice chest full of ripe mangoes put next to the hammock on my roof garden and stocked up on champagne and fresh pineapple juice.

Paradise indeed this was.

At last it was over.

I put on the earphones and listened to Gregg Allman's "I'll Be Holding On."

I did.

Third Interlude

Dinners for Stars

WHEN CECIL BEATON gave a party in the 1920s, the food was seriously considered, as it was whenever Lord Peter Wimsey sat down with friends. Jumping forward four decades, at my Harvard College table with friends I followed their classicist example and served a consommé marmite or even a garlic broth after a rich first course. I did not go so far as to think there had to be a fish course before the main, let alone a roast after a braise, and poultry as well as meat, but we did our best.

By the time Stars was well under way with private parties, it could be said of the San Francisco's gilded set's pet, Jo Schuman, that "the best thing she makes for dinner is a reservation at Stars." And that the food had to be good, but most particularly small, chic, not too odd (no feet, eyes, scales, or feathers), and sit easily on the stomach. After all, one's guests might have just arrived by plane from eight time zones away, just had a four-hour lunch with the same people they were about to eat dinner with, and did not want to bulge out, even in the tiniest way, of the unique, made-for-the-evening Ferre, de la Renta, or Dior.

Jo gave a dinner for Michael Gross when he was on the road for his book, *Model: The Ugly Business of Beautiful Women*, a tricky business with Anne, Carmella, Elaine, and Jeanette at her table, so the wine with the main course ("Will everyone know how expensive it is?") was d'Yquem, distracting them all from the scattered standing ovations given to Joan Collins fresh from *Private Lives* across the street and the opera star Samuel Ramey, as they arrived ten minutes apart.

No food could be riveting enough to stop heads snapping up when Nureyev walked in on the arm of the magnificently fabulous Kenneth Jay Lane–covered Dodie for the party given him after the opening night of *The King and I* by Carole Shorenstein Hays. One did excuse oneself for staring at the couture babushka on Natalia Makarova or the Cossack sable on Danielle Steel, especially after Rudi pulled at the baggy pants of his Kenzo and told Dodie they made "his bum look big." One had to look somewhere.

Sometimes the conversation was so fast nothing else could keep up. Nan Kempner opened one lunch, when asked about her travels, with "Well, one cannot live by blood alone." She was referring to an impoverished member of royalty she had met at Valentino's party in Rome—or maybe she had met him at Malcolm Forbes's birthday party in Tangier. Both events were all anyone could talk about—as well as about who from San Francisco had been invited. Denise had, and everyone knew it.

With moments like that I knew the food had to be serviceably delicious but uncompetitive for attention. Rose Marie Bravo's (then at Saks) lunch for the impeccably groomed Georgette Mosbacher dropped the bombshell that her new perfume cost fifteen hundred dollars an ounce. That brought silence to the table and, for an endless minute, the food was the center of attention. After all, Vicky Tiel's perfume, launched at a Stars dinner the night before with the same guests, was only three hundred dollars, even if she did call it Nudes All Around. And Denise Hale's Jungle Gardenia from Walgreens cost only twenty dollars! No one knew which one it was, or how much it cost, that Jimmy Galanos was wearing, but the sweet smells of success were definitely in the air, and overpowering the aromas of food and wine. If it wasn't perfume it could be smoke. So for George Hamilton, fresh from introducing me to Imelda in Manila, and now introducing his line of cigars, we served lobster in champagne and finished with peaches and cherries soused in ten-year-old Old Weller bourbon.

So social food by the eighties and nineties had to service jaded if always appreciating palates but never distract from the real business at hand: chat and people summing up (only the other diners in the room "watched"). The young people, as Ann Getty called them, paid a bit more attention. Viscountess Serena, in a very un-English comment about the food, adored her chicken at Denise's dinner for her and her husband, David, Viscount Linley, in town to show off his new book, *Classical Furniture*. With guests being introduced with names like Prince Alexandre de Borbon–Dos Sicilias y de Hasbourgo-Lorena, one could not eat with one's mouth full of complex food. And with the "young people" I could be more in charge if I had to be. Billy and Gavin always knew what they wanted. And since Stars donated the food at the fund-raising dinner for 180 guests of the United States Holocaust Memorial Museum organized by Auschwitz survivors and by Gay and Lesbian Campaign leaders Tyne Daly and Mark Leno, I chose chicken. "Banquet chicken was raised to new heights," raising $150,000 that night alone. Even though I cooked the chicken myself, I knew it was really Michael Tilson Thomas sitting at Stars's grand piano and playing "Fascinatin' Rhythm" that covered up the fact that it was only chicken, after all. Then there was

A Dinner for Sophia Loren

March 31, 1995

Mushroom Timbale
fava beans and purple asparagus

Smoked Pheasant
oven-roasted vegetables and lamb's lettuce salad

Ginger Mousse
warm ginger cookies

By this time I had told my chefs the menu rules for special dinners at Stars many times: By all means remember that there might be persons at the table too polite to disrupt the evening by saying they had the flu, that their jet lag was worse than an overdose of antihistamines, that they were on a diet, that they were really vegetarian, that they were allergic to shellfish, that they had just arrived from an inescapably late lunch, that this would be their eighth social meal in a row, that they hated lamb, or couldn't look rabbit in the face. And that raw garlic or onions were never served.

The idea of the timbale was its small size (apart from the ease of mass-producing it while still keeping the same quality as if it had been cooked to order for four people), so that guests could pick at it and make it look as if it were mostly eaten—just in case they hated mushrooms, or cream. Then they could eat the fava beans and push the color-coordinated asparagus around if they were nervous about it, as some people are. The pheasant was breast only, delicious but innocuous in its way, and once again, one could pick at it and eat the vegetables or salad instead. As for the ginger mousse: small again (everyone is allowed to pick at dessert), and no one can resist cookies four minutes out of the oven.

The Italian consul general and his wife said this dinner was the highlight of Sophia's and Carlo Ponti's visit to the Bay Area, even when Herb Caen had announced in advance the menu and the fact that the dessert sounded like the name of a Tenderloin stripper. In this case, everyone ate everything. I was nervous because I had been told that Sophia ate only pasta for lunch (I was not going to cook pasta for an Italian) and sandwiches for dinner. And what food could compete with those lips (signature "coral nude"), those eyes, that hair, cheekbones "so defined you could hang laundry on them," and "those, hum . . . that poitrine." More worried than I was were some of San Francisco's beauties who were, as Cynthia Robins of the *Examiner* said, "in a swivet" and grabbing their cleavages every time Sophia swept by. All except Daru, whose own famous poitrine held up perfectly. Bob Colacello was worried only about his Neopolitan Brooklyn family Italian or, in his own case, Bensonhurst. Everyone agreed with San Francisco's greatest beauty (here unnamed) that Sophia at sixty was "the most glamorous woman in the world."

Dinners for Couture

Dinners for couture were the most difficult because one had to assume each of the guests was as figure conscious as anyone could be. And that having to wear (because he was the guest of honor) a Calvin Klein (in town for a fashion show at I. Magnin and Denise's dinner for him at Stars), for example, that had not been worn since the beginning of the season and now many dinners later might not fit, could leave a bad taste in the mouth no matter how good the food.

For Vicky Tiel it was beluga and potatoes washed down with magnums of 1983 Roederer Cristal; for Jil Sander ("She's fantastic. The female Armani," I had said to the press) it was grilled Nantucket scallops with tomato-basil sauce; for Bill Blass, grilled wild Pacific salmon with sweet corn and heirloom various-colored tomato salad with peach cobbler to follow; and for Oscar de la Renta with Danielle Steel in a Ralph Lauren military tunic (she had checked her Oscar coat) and Nan Kempner ("I just love Stars") and New York's Rose Marie Bravo ("You outdid yourself. I can't tell you how much I miss Stars") it was Japanese eggplant timbale with chilied crab ("now Oscar's favorite dish").

When Gianfranco Ferre came to town and Denise gave a dinner or lunch at Stars, I could rev the food up a bit. After a few weekends at the Hale Ranch with Gianfranco, I knew him well enough to know he would have been disappointed if I hadn't. It was a dinner for "star-gazing and grazing":

Dinner for Gianfranco Ferre

Celery Root Gratin
scallop hash & lobster vinaigrette

Grilled Lamb Medallions
arthichoke bottoms filled with chickpea puree

Wild Strawberry Soufflé

Gianfranco dined on plain rice. "I'm not well," he said, "it must have been the caviar on the Concorde."

It was a typical Saturday night. The time quoted to walk-ins was one hour and forty-five minutes, with everyone waiting for the opera crowd to leave at 7:45; Paul Pelosi had just incapacitated the dining room manager into a fit of giggles by telling the valet parker Solomon, "Park my car in her trunk," as Jo Schuman pulled up in a stretch limo; the giggles left five reservation lines blinking with a promise of more scenes if those diners ever showed up; a gossip columnist was on the phone wondering what I would serve for the *Harper's Bazaar* editor Liz Tilberis's dinner (curried crabmeat soufflés) to promote her new book *No Time to Die*; Mayor Willie Brown had a reservation for 8:00 and didn't show; Danielle did show up with her matched Graff "D" flawless diamond twins, and I had not alerted the security or insurance companies; Francis Ford Coppola was there for drinks only (had to get back to work) but after a drink decided "to stay for starters," making a scramble for the staff to set another place at Denise's already tight table; but then the great Escada-tiger and rhinestone-covered Charlotte "Tex" Swig kissed her husband, George Shultz, good-bye, so he wasn't staying; Bob Colacello lost his pen—then it was found with Francis signing autographs; Peter Coyote lost his diamond ear stud, so Dodie's otherwise *very* conservative husband borrowed Frances Bowes's gold bead ones, first trying them on himself and thereby reducing the rather fey maître d' to yet another fit of incapacitating giggles; and there was a birthday party in the Grill Room and a bat mitzvah in the other private room that needed his attentions. Matthew Broderick was competing with that year's gold medalist downhill skier from the Bay Area for the ogling of women, and leaving not a few of my guys serving the oyster bar slack-jawed and weak-kneed. The Fat Boys across the dining room were showing ogling diners their necks and arms, heavy with more Los Angeles gold and New York diamond-district bracelets than all the socialites put together. A cockroach had found its way up from the basement, despite the weekly bombing, and was doing a Rockettes routine along the wainscoting next to a particularly fastidious and now hysterical prima donna; the Stars doctor was dining on the edge of the Ferre party and drinking a twenty-five-year-old Petrus, which I was hoping no one in the party would see and then ask for; and Jim and Jo O'Dea were at their usual table and alcoholically itching for a fight.

"It's pure San Francisco," the O'Deas told Pat Steger of "the Social Scene."

"I couldn't care less who's here," said another patient customer. "I just want a table."

Dinners for What Glitters

Particularly close to the metaphor in my heart was the dinner we did to help launch *Faking It*, Kenny Jay Lane's book about what was not real but still glittered. I repeated the menu we had just done for the hostess, Denise (for gold-plated David Rockefeller), though without the 1983 Dom Pérignon en magnum.

Black Truffle Custard
prawn vinaigrette

Capon Breast with Lobster Sauce
fava beans, wild asparagus, garden peas

Passion Fruit Soufflé

Warm Ginger Cookies

Kenny was dressed in a double-breasted glen plaid suit and yellow tie, long before they became powerful, and had a warm cookie in each hand as he regaled the table with stories of Sophia Loren, Judith Leiber's objets (he did the first ones using dime-store plastic bracelets), the Duchess of Windsor, and Jackie Onassis (he told her he couldn't find any faux cabochon jewels of poor enough quality to copy the $250,000 piece of junk that Ari had given her).

Not junk, glittering, and definitely not fake was Dede Wilsey's diamond the size of an iceberg, and almost the same color, though not below the waterline. It was so large that when Nancy Pelosi saw it, she literally stopped talking in midsentence, not an easy feat for a politician (someone wagged). Denise's diamond-and-sapphire David Webb necklace shone like a stand of Christmas lights, and Sally Jordan's watermelon slice Judith Leiber minaudière looked more delicious than the soufflé (someone else wagged). Others raved about the soufflé with gossip columnist Pat Steger, saying that if most of the jewels were not real, at least the real J.T. was there, but wondered about the two matching open rose-size diamond-looking brooches on Ann Getty's left shoulder.

Definitely real were Connie Wald and Princess Genie di San Faustino, as were the gorgeous pink ranch roses from Denise's country garden: "I talked to my roses for a week and told them not to let me down." Some of them did, so Ray Reddell had to step in with a few hundred of his own old-fashioned ones, and so started a real revolution in which roses—old or new—were considered chic.

David Pleydell-Bouverie, who owned the Sonoma ranch on which M. F. K. Fisher lived, said the decorated dining room looked "quite chic." Five hundred candles in pink-lined (more flattering to anyone over forty, as most were) shades were set amongst every white lily available strewn across the green-moiré tablecloths sprinkled with little gold stars. H.R.H. Prince Alexander of Yugoslavia wondered all night if the stars were real, until Constance Towers (married to John Gavin) plastered a few stars across her décolletage before getting up to sing "My Romance," really meaning "yours" (the Hales'), so that wasn't real. But Mitzi Gaynor's response to Carol Channing calling out that she couldn't hear her singing was real enough: "Tough."

The night went on longer than the premiere of *War and Peace,* playing that same night at the Opera House, and definitely real were the thousands of dollars lost to Stars (we had closed Stars that Saturday night for Denise) by not having the hundred or so people coming over for champagne at the end of the performance. For the lesser thousands in tips lost to the staff, I reminded them of Dodie's remark when looking at the crowded dance floor: "Don't dance with anyone you don't like."

Musical Chairs

Some people, no matter what we did, were never happy where we sat them. But all was forgiven if they liked to eat, and the kitchen could show off. A trim (in grand opera terms) "superstar" Luciano Pavarotti in 1994 could not find a place that made him happy, or at least we could not. No drafts were allowed (understandably, given what a cold could do to his performance), and no one was permitted to walk behind him. But he wanted to sit in the center of the room, where everyone could see and greet him.

I put him near the kitchen and was the only person allowed to walk behind him. The drafts (I was proud of the constant 100 percent outside air change at Stars) we solved by putting first a napkin ("don't be stupid") then a paper cocktail napkin on the hair-thinned back of his head. He rather liked that. As he did the dinner ("un grande complimento—una cucina grande")—or just loved Stars because we used to sneak him ice cream onto the café table onstage during *Bohème* when he was supposed to be on a diet.

Un Grande Complimento

Golden Oyster Mushroom Timbale
mussels, nasturtiums, sage flowers

Wild Turkey and Rabbit-Filled Pasta "Pillows"
truffled celery root

Braised Beef Cheeks
ramps, carrots, red mustard gremolata

Warm Apricot, Hazelnut, and Pear Tartlet

"The beef cheeks were a hit at the dinner," Pat Steger reported in "The Social Scene," "but before getting down to the beef, Luciano got around to hugging and kissing a few cheeks." Of course the O'Deas were there, getting ready to try to top Patty Rouas, who, clad in the latest Hervé Leger, looked disapprovingly at Pavarotti and said in a stage whisper, "The waif look is out. Full figures are in."

Lunch for a Pet

Not all celebrities were two-legged. Some four- were Stars's regulars. Like Bentley, a famous seventeen-year-old basset hound.

The San Francisco journalist Rob Morse reported that "on Tuesday Warren Hinckle (journalist extraordinaire himself) threw a touching wake at Stars for his beloved Bentley, who had to be put to sleep. Actually, it was a pre-wake, because Bentley attended. Chef Jeremiah Tower served Bentley magnificently. We'll miss him, but maybe not his fleas." The meal was attended by San Francisco's district attorney and sheriff in case anyone became stroppy about dogs at the bar. Jack Davis, the man who made mayors in that town, had arranged the postprandial transportation to Pets Unlimited, a wide-load and superlong-bedded open truck, onto which a kennel had been strapped in place of the usual bulldozer.

Bentley's Lunch

Grilled Ground Chuck
with bacon

Evian in a silver dish

"His ashes," said Hinckle, "will be delivered to Art Agnos, who, when he was mayor, once kidnapped Bentley and threatened to do away with him." Not everyone likes dogs lapping up spilled Bushmills at the bar.

Dinners for Media

"With your fingers. Just tear them apart," said Martha Stewart. And she should know, as "the elegant expert on entertaining." She was talking not about the fawning reporters but the quail.

White Oregon Truffle Salt Cod Puree
lobster and oyster vinaigrettes

Quail in a Brioche Nest
filled with foie gras, black truffle sauce

A Mere Trifle
wild blackberry sauce

Actually, for this, another Jo Schuman dinner at Stars (1994), the quail were boneless, so a single swipe with a knife would have done quite well.

Denise Hale ("San Francisco's most gracious and successful party giver") had helped Jo plan the party, and it was a perfect time for Martha and Denise to compare notes on what makes for perfect entertaining. The men at the dinner (even Denise's husband and another who kept his private jet on hand for their trips to Hong Kong) had to listen to "There are so few interesting men," but they were too busy to listen: Martha was signing their copies of *Menus for Entertaining* even though Denise had predicted no men would be interested ("even empresses can be wrong").

But if you do have a very attractive man, like the Comte de Chandon de Briales at Stars, as guest of honor, then surround him with ladies. Martha agreed. So did all the men with Denise: "Always have on hand some very attractive girls who are amusing, very beautiful," because the most important ingredient for a successful party is the choice of people.

Especially the unattached: "You have to have single people. You can have couples and it's a quiet dinner, but it's not a party." Denise knew this well—she asked the advice of the greatest party expert before Martha, Elsa Maxwell.

"My child," replied the diminutive and rotund trouser-roll Elsa, "be ruthless whom you invite."

Both Denise and Martha agreed with Dodie's dance advice: Invite only the people you like, and never bores.

"A bore is a bore is a bore."

Choose from the many walks of life, and choose people as different as possible as long as they are interesting: "Whatever they do they have to be the best at it."

CHAPTER 8

Long Live the Revolution

Victory Farms

THE JANUARY 2002 day started with the light of a pink sunrise promising to radiate in desert red onto Camelback Mountain behind us. It was one of those perfect Arizona winter desert mornings, the temperature already picking up to around seventy degrees, the air clear, smelling like clean dust and doused campfires. I was at the Roaring Fork in Scottsdale, Arizona, with its owner, Robert McGrath, filming my new television show, *America's Best Chefs*, on chefs recognized by the James Beard Foundation. We met Gina Collins at her Victory Farms truck in the parking lot while she pulled out a small mountain of vegetables and greens picked in the cool of the early desert morning. Robert, Gina, and I decided on what mix of greens we would use on the show and for that day's Roaring Fork menus. The next supplier's truck had every kind of fresh and lightly dried chili I had ever seen or heard about, and a stack of fresh cream and its butter that made my mouth water.

For years, starting at Panisse, I had tried to convince Vella Cheese company and others in Sonoma to give me some unpasteurized cream so that I could make sauces like the French, and for years they all stubbornly refused. Then I tried to get this cream from the Reading Terminal Market in Philadelphia, knowing full well that the Amish and Mennonites would not fool around ruining cream and butter by boiling the milk. But no dice. They would not ship unpasteurized cream across state lines.

So thirty years later, in a parking lot in Scottsdale, Arizona, dipping the fingers of one hand into a gallon of real cream and holding in the other canary yellow butter that had come from a large family of Mennonites neighboring this farmer's property, I was moved almost to tears at what had finally come to pass.

While waiting to film the legendary happy hour at the Roaring Fork, we chilled some Gosset champagne. I took my first sip of this fabulous hand-made wine, spread some hand-churned butter on my hand-forged tortillas warmed over the fire, and sat back to watch the sun go down. Looking up at Camelback turning magenta in the moments before night fell, and knowing that we would soon be facing a 4:00 A.M. call for the filming of a perfect sunrise over the Arizona desert, I poured another glass of rosy champagne, remembering that, in the immortal words from the Pink Panther, champagne has the minimum of alcohol and the maximum of companionship. I remembered also the day before in Los Angeles, when the Farmers' Market in the middle of winter brought home to me in this wonderful victory of the revolution in the way America dines. No better example existed than a winter farmers' market in Southern California.

Any winning restaurateur these days realizes that outstanding cooking starts with superb ingredients, and that a menu should be conceived from the marketplace rather than abstractly thought up. The cornucopia of January in Santa Monica was as plentiful as that of New York in August or September: "sweet tooth" wild mushrooms that looked like giant hedgehog mushrooms; the cabbage family in all its glory—cauliflower, cavallo nero, and several broccolis; purple, pink, and fire engine red mustard leaves; radicchio that was not magenta with white stripes but the other way around and with lime green stripes running though the leaves as well; the onion family in all its glory—still-sweet cipollini (because picked that morning), fresh green garlic, every variety of chives with some of them flowering; Thogmorton Farm's vast array of fruits dried in the sun—white peaches, nectarines ugly when dried but with a perfume that made me swoon, six varieties of pears, hideous-looking but delicious persimmons, and an encyclopedic selection of dates, fresh and dried; ripe pomegranates and fresh-crop walnuts; and best of all, if I could possibly choose, all the citrus of Southern California at the peak of its season—Meyer lemons, kumquats, clementines, tangerines, "sweet lemons," five different kinds of grapefruit, crosses of grapefruit and oranges like pomelos, and a few others of mysterious parentage, like "manellos."

At the end of my walk in the market I ate a little box of wild strawberries from Lore Caulfield, who usually sells miniature and diminutive roses but that day had just a few handfuls of these precious fraises de bois.

The New Chef

Less wild than the strawberries were America's new breed of chefs (or even the aging ones), despite the *Wine Spectator* in 2001 calling them "restless, reckless, and relentless." What was going on with America's top and aspiring chefs as the century passed into a new one, I wondered, as I was about to tour America.

I found it odd that the Chez Panisse Web site was the only one of a restaurant on *Gourmet*'s list of the nation's top fifty restaurants that did not feature, let alone mention, the name of the chef. Just the service charge. Which brought up also the question of what made a famous chef as the new millennium began. Perhaps there was a clue in *Gourmet*'s saying that Alice Waters "is not so much a chef as an impresario." A concert master. Certainly by 2000 the best American chefs did seem to be marching to their individual music.

According to *Gourmet*, Thomas Keller of Napa's The French Laundry aspired not so much to cook good food as to pursue fundamental truths revealed through food; Wolfgang at Spago Beverly Hills served up passion and seriously glamorous dining; Alan Wong in Honolulu was a true fusion of an organic, street-level blend of Chinese, Poylnesian, and mainland American, lightly seasoned with imports from Japan, Mexico, and Korea—proving that Trader Vic's was the original fusion food forty years earlier; Charlie Trotter was likened to "The Aleph" (per my favorite poet, Jorge Luis Borges), or that point from which every single thing in the world can be seen and from which Charlie cooks; the sublime food of Ken Oringer in Boston was all about intensity of flavors, drawing on those of Maine, Japan, and Spain; Nobu Matsuhisa was "the Escoffier of all things great and raw"; Clark Frasier and Mark Gaier (they learned the salad aesthetic at Stars) grew the greens in their kitchen garden so that the leaves' "immediacy is breathtaking"; Tom Douglas, in the wonderfully fun Palace Kitchen in Seattle, created "campfire cooking fit for kings" (and more); even my old undergraduate-vacation stomping ground Galatoire's, where I consumed more fried oysters and shrimp rémoulade than any human should, was still a restaurant that made one "giddy with pleasure"; Marcus Samuelsson at Aquavit made herring (and more) first acceptable and then chic; the always superb Le Bernardin of the always impeccable Maguy Le Coze and Eric Ripert was as if the Romans had built a temple to fish and shellfish cooking; the genius over the years of Jean-Georges Vongerichten, who gave us the absolutely brilliant early Vong (with a recently departed Stars chef), was now giving a lot more; and the "piercing intelligence" of Daniel Boulud's approach to classical French cooking got more flavor out of a single bell pepper than *Gourmet* thought most restaurants did out of a whole truckload of foie gras.

I found these chefs now to be anything but reckless: perhaps restless, since most chefs in this culture must be, and often relentless in their passionate pursuit of perfection and reward. They had good models: in Southern California, Michael McCarty and Jonathan Waxman starting in 1979, and a few years later, Wolfgang Puck's publicized California style; in the north with Panisse, the Santa Fe Bar & Grill, and Stars; with the example of women cooks standing right up there at the finishing line with the men: Mary Sue Milliken and Susan Feniger of Los Angeles's Border Grill, Cindy Pawlcyn of Napa's Mustard's, Lydia Shire of Biba in Boston, Susan Spicer in New Orleans, and Odessa Piper of L'Etoile in Wisconsin.

The next wave of chefs brought on now established and influential greats like Robert Del Grande in Texas at Café Annie, Mark Miller of Coyote Café in Santa Fe, Stephan Pyles of Routh Street in Dallas, and Robert McGrath of Roaring Fork in Arizona; in the South with Frank Stitt of Highlands Bar & Grill in Alabama, Paul Prudhomme, who taught America gumbo and to eat blackened fish, and Norman Van Aken, who brought America new Florida cooking.

In the late eighties Americans dined off the superstar chef hype and thought Thai–Pacific Rim food or Tuscany were the perfect antidote when they could not get a table at Le Cirque. A grilled steak Fiorentina with nothing else on the plate, or some grilled perfect fish with nothing but olive oil and lemon, cost the same as Dover sole in lobster sauce, so was now comfortably chic. Drew Nieporent brought the chic but accessible restaurant downtown, and Charlie Trotter brought it uptown and won the Beard Award as America's best chef. Mario Batali left Stars and went on, with his partner Joseph Bastianich, to conquer America with its best Italian food at Lupa and Babbo, not to mention fish at Esca, showing that settling down into a personal style and refining it was what the turn of the century in America promised for the decade to come. The new chefs had found their own voices and vision, landing on their feet with courage and confidence: at a temple of perfect food like Daniel Boulud's, the menu is broken out by ingredients: asparagus, lobster, and salmon (to name a few). Adornment in America was left to the David Rockwell dining rooms.

Gone are the days (for now) when a chef would be featured in German *Penthouse*, as I was in 1988, next to the naked centerfold and as a "Jet-set-Guru." Now it is much more an article in *The New York Times* about "How a celebrity chef of the '80s got his stove back," as Jonathan Waxman opened the Washington Park in April 2002 and had the confidence to put on a dish that is seen as his signature from Michael's and Jams: the roast chicken with French fries and watercress from 1979. After years of being a media darling, Jonathan, who coalesced his style around Alice Waters and me (according to Michael Batterberry of *Food Arts*), is no longer flying off to Paris's Taillevent for lunch (my old style) but is back in the restaurant. So far he has not been seen naked in front of a blender, or with his name on a pot.

Trying not to call the kettle black was my last act as a restaurant chef. In 2000 the journalist Adam Nagourney called me for *The New York Times* to talk about an interview I never gave. The article had been done for the *San Francisco Chronicle* under the aegis of my old nemesis Michael Bauer, and he called it "The Rise and Fall of a Star, or How the King of California Cuisine Lost an Empire." I was in Stars Manila when it appeared, producing a panic in my press-loving and worshiping Filipino friends, who were mystified when, reading my own press for once, I laughed out loud and long. It was a good article, the photographs showing me in the arms of the beautiful Urania von Ristow, on my red BMW, cooking langoustines, as a young chef in a Valentino suit talking to Richard Lawrence Balzer, and with bejeweled Denise Hale, who is captioned as having "stuck with Tower through all the ups and downs." A lot of the article is about what Stars was like sixteen months after I sold it and never set foot in it again, and what it was like when it closed a year after that for remodeling, a night that its once chef Mark Franz was quoted as saying was like being at your ex-wife's funeral. Both he and the wonderful Stars Café chef Loretta Keller, who had gone on to open her own café, Bizou, laughed at Ruth Reichl's evaluation that the prevailing Berkeley attitude, "'Oh, it's OK, it's good enough,' was never good enough for Jeremiah. He brought this amazing style into the community and everybody—men and women—were in love with him. He was like a character in a movie. We were all walking around in Birkenstocks," said Ruth, "and here he comes this English gentleman."

When Adam printed that I said Alice didn't know a little vegetable from a rotten one, I did for once regret not having handled that interview in sound bites. What I had told him was that the true story of her enormous contribution has not been told, and that he should interview her to get it. I said that her real contribution did not have a lot to do with the early revolution, that in the beginning she did not know commercial vegetables from truly great ones, but that she had learned. Much of her story came later, especially after Sibella Kraus came onto the scene in the early eighties and planted those little lettuces in Alice's garden. That was the beginning of her actually great contributions, things like her advocacy for farmers' markets, for sound and sustainable agriculture, for Slow Food, and for the Chez Panisse Foundation, which underwrites the Edible Schoolyard as well as the Garden Project at the San Francisco county jail. Ask her about all that, I said. Not about a perfect peach.

America Rediscovered—Again

The irony about new American cooking in 1988, as pointed out in a San Francisco newspaper, was that hardly any chef in the country claimed to be cooking American food. Even if discovering America was what it was all about, each chef took the clue from California and looked to his or her own backyard. How many cuisines were there in the United States anyway, and was this new emphasis on regional cooking "a profound reawakening or another exhausting trend"? The always intelligent writer Jay Jacobs said it was a game of culinary Star Wars, with every chef grabbing his or her Warholian fifteen minutes of fame. The chefs who had been there at the beginning disagreed. Jimmy Schmidt defended the superior flavors of any vegetables picked closest to you that went straight into the pot; he said that the celebration of regional food is merely recognizing food for "its true worth, rather than a marketing-created worth," and that some regional foods were so highly charged from childhood they would never be trendy and disappear. That was an optimistic view of American childhood, but every chef agreed that when a vegetable or fruit is ripe, ready, in season, and in your own backyard, it's the best.

Larry Forgione of An American Place agreed, but added a caution not to forget new techniques and combinations like, for example, Emeril Lagasse's food at Commander's Palace. Most of the chefs voiced a vision that the pull of working with locally superior ingredients was so strong that regionalism was here to stay, that great cooking would always be ingredient driven. John Makin from his restaurant in Napa Valley said that the next great leap in regional cuisine "will be chefs moving out of urban areas and setting up restaurants in the country side where farmers knock on their back doors with ripe products at the height of freshness." As the chef who had opened his kitchen back door to wandering amateur foragers sixteen years earlier, I loved the historically innocent freshness of that comment when it was wryly told to me. Stephan Pyles and I were the lone voices of dissent in this vision, seeing an end to regionalism but not to the force of perfect ingredients, wherever they came from. We saw a sort of "culinary harmonic convergence," and I predicted that regional cuisines would exist for some time but would result in a codification of an American cuisine.

And that is what happened, building on the tradition started at The Four Seasons in New York in 1959, fueled by its own foragers, and creating what Jeffrey Steingarten at *Vogue* forty years later called "a completely contemporary American haute cuisine." In 1979 Michael McCarty had to rely a lot on his contacts in France to get the ingredients he wanted, but by the late eighties and early nineties every chef around America was encouraged by the spiritual, public relational, and financial rewards of encouraging local producers. The revolution became evolution in full flower.

This process was relatively quick and complete because it had been going on throughout the United States in pockets known only locally and regionally except for a few famous ones, such as Wisconsin cheeses, New England cider, or Southern hams. Not many were aware nationally that Makin's 1988 prediction that restaurateurs would flourish in the country-side, where farmers would knock on their back doors, had been going on, for example, in Wisconsin for sixteen years, or that Odessa Piper had been doing just that from the center of Madison for almost as long. "We did sort of lose our way after World War II, and only slowly have we been coming back to our senses," said Odessa. It was an American victory after the war to feed the whole country abundantly, "fast," and cheaply, but at what now seems to have been enormous cost to our health and well-being. So for her it was time to bring out the "baby pictures": working with her suppliers from the moment of the development and growing of an ingredient and following the ingredient though all its stages to find its optimum moment, flavor, and use.

In 2002 Adrian Hoffman at San Francisco's One Market restaurant voiced the current concerns about American cuisine—as well as an answer to them—quite succinctly in a *Gastronomica* magazine interview. He was uncomfortable with the catchall phrase "American Food," since it seemed to say more about a lack of culture, a lack of soul, and even more important, a lack of focus. Having grown up in a world after the age when Americans gave picnics fit for a Russian prince or filled cantaloupe melons straight from the field with hundred-year-old Madeira and stuck them down a cool well for the next day's lunch, he had no American romantic memories of a lost time. Making the lack of background and clear culinary tradition even more difficult to deal with, he said, were the copious resources and the "maze of food cultures" in California and the United States. The idea that the "awful, generic term *continental* be revived and applied to California Cuisine" terrified him. The only clear way out of the morass of temptations, he said, is to focus on the culture and traditions of a specific cuisine, and to give new color and expression to them by paying homage to the local farmers and artisanal purveyors who provide superb ingredients.

The circle has been completed: it's Joe Baum's "new-old food in a new-new setting" all over again, driven, as always, by ingredients.

The Fourth Ingredient Revolution

Ever since 1973, when I introduced the Panisse version of the famous Lyonnaise salad with warm, bread-crumb-crusted fresh goat cheese with walnuts and nut oil dressing, or the cassoulet made from our own geese, it was clear once again that the simplicity of the food was symbiotically married to the purity and allure of its raw materials.

A 1986 interview with me about California cuisine was titled "It's Time to Rediscover Marketplace Cuisine," and went on to list my principles of cooking: knowledge and respect for the region or locale in which one is cooking; flexibility in mixing traditional recipes with the fresh products at hand in the marketplace; simplification of presentation and service; seasonality; and rationality in the number and balance of dishes on a restaurant's menu. In late 2001, John Mariani in *Esquire* magazine summed up the new chefs' cooking: "simplifying, removing extraneous ingredients from their plates, and focusing more on the essential flavors of the main ingredients."

The first revolution in American fresh ingredients occurred in what we did at Chez Panisse with freshness and local California ingredients; the second started to occur in the last two years of the seventies, when *local* started to mean international because of the revolution in air-shipping of fresh ingredients, like the ones I introduced to the California dining public at the California Culinary Academy; the third was when American chefs picked up the mantra from the first revolution and helped spread farmers' markets and new supplies of organic, local, sustainable ingredients across the land; and the fourth is the current extension of the second, or the instant international Internet marketplace. *Local* and *fresh* and *seasonal* now mean wherever there is a field of superb ingredients, refrigeration, and an airfield nearby: South African wild mushrooms in New York in June; haricots verts from West Africa in California markets; fish from ten thousand miles away fresher than local East or West Coast United States locked in by storms.

An event around 1990 called "Tasting of Summer Produce" in Berkeley brought the public into the same space as the restaurateurs and the farmers who supported them, and made everyone realize what a powerful union the three main players made: Supplier, chef, and restaurant customer could change completely the culinary scene of a locality in just twenty years. More events like "What's Cooking in the Park," which paired Central Texas growers with local restaurant chefs, occurred throughout the nineties, so that by 1996 the public no longer saw this union as a Berkeley phenomenon. In a seemingly unlikely place like Austin there sprang up a store called The Gardens, a Whole Foods Market, and farms for restaurants like Boggy Creek. Jeffrey Steingarten's (*Vogue*) end-of-the-millennium prediction that there was a restaurant crash in the air, or that the next trend would be a gay cuisine, did not come true. Certainly his horror of famous chefs expanding their empires and leaving the new restaurants in the hands of inexperienced, lower-paid staff was often true. But the choice of where to go in America to find the ingredients heretofore the realm of famous chefs was no longer a mystery. The culinary magazines like *Bon Appétit* celebrated these sources and started publishing the addresses and Web sites or where to find them. The choice of "local" and "fresh" expanded beyond mine of the seventies, when I could not find a green bean that I liked.

A supplier like Portland's Nicky USA, for example, published its quality guidelines, which were no longer fresh versus frozen. Their rules go right to the heart of it all, to the kind of farming that is sustainable over a long period of time. By the end of the decade, these standards became the norm rather than the exception for small producers supplying restaurants of conscience. Nicky supplies rabbit, quail, geese, poussin, squab, wild turkey, chukar, guinea fowl, Muscovy duck, fallow venison and bison, to name a few, and all the suppliers must follow Nicky's rules: raise the animals humanely, on feeds without medication, animal by-products, or hormones; and they must be all "free range," like the lamb from Oregon's Andersen Ranch, which enjoy a pasture grass diet on the hills of the Willamette Valley. I have long thought that the healthiest food in America is the food cooked in its best restaurants. That is a claim I could not have made thirty years ago, and I can make it now because the chefs get the healthiest ingredients and pay attention to doing as little as possible to them in their cooking.

Chez Panisse in 2002 used Western Grasslands Beef; in May of that year, ranchers showed up at San Francisco's "Open Market Day" to talk about how their "healthful, sustainably-reared local beef" was raised. That moment was a long way from merely thirty-four years earlier when Western ranchers would have shot at anyone with long hair from the radical streets of Berkeley preaching organic farming.

The newsletter from GreenLeaf in San Francisco was a manifesto of the revolution. In May 2002 a chef could have bought organic fresh green almonds, a product Richard Olney introduced me to in France in 1974; I begged local suppliers for them for years to no avail. He ate them with cherries, over which I pined because they were so superior to the two varieties that I could buy back in the United States. But now from a 2003 newsletter, I could have bought Brooks, Burlat, and King Bing cherries, as well as unirrigated fruit from the foothills of the Sierras. My dishwashers used to have to spend hours carving the rosemary skewers, now I could have bought them; rose and rose geranium flowers I had to steal on my way to work—now here they were in a list that included also rue, fresh hearts of palm, popcorn shoots, cardoon, rocolla or wild arugula (the best), lovage, nepitella mint, berggarten sage, peppercress, and lemon balm. Stars lettuce mix (which once took eight hours a day to make) was now just a phone call away: the tender lettuces mix was sucrine, majestic red, black jack, red perella, brunia, little gem, spreckles, freckles, roger, dark lolla rosa, four seasons, and green tango. It was enough to make one break into dance.

On rereading James Lipton's *An Exaltation of Larks,* which celebrates bounty and calls a collection of songbirds in the high months of summer an "exaltation," I wondered what the collective name for all this bounty should be. Strolling though Manhattan's Union Square farmers' market in 2002, seeing what New York, Long Island, and New Jersey alone can produce in August, I thought that the word had to be *revolution.*

The first stand had bambino eggplant as well as white ones, purple ones, and purple-and-white-striped ones looking like a Karl Lagerfeld coat; there was Texas tarragon; Caribbean oregano; basil green, purple, and Thai; rosemary, thyme (lemon and flowering), black peppermint, lemon verbena, and seven kinds of mint, including apple. At stand number two I saw an entire regatta of radishes—watermelon, black, French breakfast with their white tips and white icicle (all white), as well as a whole section of tiny and giant red round ones; parsley root; tatsoi; long squash runners and their blossoms; mounds of tomatillos; small round carrots as well as long ones; bushels of limas; baby turnips; five kinds of beets; red, yellow, orange, gold-and-green-striped cherry tomatoes; cranberry beans; microgreens; and pinterelle dandelions. At New York's Fox Hill Farm potato stand there were Yukon gold, whites, reds, russets, small red, carola, Norland red, brintje, Desiree, Augusta, Russian banana, agria, and French fingerling. But it was the onion stand that trapped me, as it always does.

It was next to a stand selling old-fashioned roses, so the heady perfumes of the Duchesse de Brabantse mingling with the smell of the glisteningly fresh onions made my mouth water. I saw a bread stand nearby, as well as some Vermont "European style" butter, and was tempted to make an onion–rose petal sandwich on the spot. After all, in Sydney as kids we used to make nasturtium ones. All I needed was some sea salt and Lampong pepper. There they were, those onions, in all their glory: salad whites, cooking yellows, rocambole, shallots on the stem, garlic tops about to flower, scallions large and small and white and red, purple and snow baby pearls, gold coin, luscious leeks, red cipolle, small red Italian, Kelshe (sweet and mild), and the Walla Walla sweets. I took home the Walla Walla, sliced them thinly, marinated them in fleur de sel and freshly squeezed blackberry juice for twenty minutes, and served them with a sauce of the rose petals ground up in a mortar with egg yolks and lemon juice, adding light French yellow extra-virgin olive oil to perfume and color the mayonnaise.

In February 2002 in Chicago with Charlie Trotter I saw Farmer Jones's (truly) Ohio microgreens, lettuces and herbs that had grown in hoop houses when it was freezing outside, the temperatures actually concentrating the sugars (their "natural antifreeze"). In Wisconsin I was taken through the revolutionary Janie Crawford's lamb farm before cooking this superb meat with Odessa Piper at the farm. A week later I was cooking at Clio with Ken Oringer, the James Beard Foundation Outstanding Chef of the Northeast and chef of one of the top fifty of *Gourmet*'s best restaurants in America. His food, it said, has an "intense clarity of flavors with subtly (and brilliantly) Asian-inflected dishes." I'm not sure what "inflected" food is, but I do know that the black bass and lemon tempura with Korean smoked salt and a little "hit" of intensely dressed microgreens on the side was one of the best dishes ever put in front of me. The next dish I had was a "London broil" of "giant squid," if you call a fifty-pound squid a giant (which I did after seeing the size of its head). Even more astonishing than the head were the slices across its midsection, each slice eight inches long and an inch deep. In my mind I knew *giant* had to mean tough, so I was bowled over when, on biting down on a slice of this favorite food of the sperm whale, I immediately knew why it is: tender as milk-fed veal and as full of juices as capon breast poached gently in olive oil.

But the squid, caught one mile off the Chilean coast and ten miles into the depths of the ocean, didn't surprise me as much as the elvers (very juvenile eels) that had been caught on their way from the Sargasso Sea to the Scituate River in Massachusetts, and brought into the kitchen of his restaurant by Ken's fish supplier Joe Norton. Ken called the dish of elvers his "linguine with clams." The elvers looked more like capellini, and the other ingredients were garlic, hokkigai and surf clams, red chili flakes, and the best olive oil I have tasted in years. For a first course we pulled some live deep-sea scallops out of the tanks at Joe Mullaney's Harborside Fish

Market and cut them for sashimi. The scallops quivered under my fingers as I sliced them, and twitched as we applied the sauce of white soy sauce, aji Amarillo, ginger, garlic, and yuzu juice. On top of the scallops Ken put some fresh Maine sea urchin roe. Sublime.

On the way to Scituate it occurred to me that my Massachusetts heritage and half Irish background made me misty-eyed that the seafood available in Boston, a culinary wasteland except for oysters and scrod when I lived there in the early sixties, should now be as bountiful (again) as the oceans of Galicia and as passionately well cooked as in any French three-star seafood restaurant in Antibes.

In January 2003 I received a letter explaining what ingredients I could expect to find in Minneapolis in February for my cooking demonstration promoting my new book, *Jeremiah Tower Cooks*.

We have a great game supplier with Pekin duck, pheasant, and rabbit; any meat, including whey-fed lamb; fish and seafood no problem either. Of course, the White Earth Land Recovery Project's wild rice comes from here. Also fresh hothouse herbs, and a large Asian community with great markets. We have a Farmers' Market on full alert for whatever fresh ingredients you need: you can have the best, freshest organic eggs, farmstead butter, purest cream, goat cheese, and an extraordinary aged sheepsmilk cheese—all from pasture-pampered animals.

Obviously the ingredient revolution has worked. What about the ingredient-driven food?

The New Food

American restaurant food has come a long way since the "sentimental" menu that Marion Burros reported was created recently by Alice for Marion Cunningham at Chez Panisse. The diners' comments included:

"Marion would never put truffles in her chicken."

"Marion would want iceberg lettuce."

"Marion doesn't eat oysters."

Marion's mind was more on cookies.

Consider the confidence of England's most popular chef, Jamie Oliver, in his simple and straightforward from-the-heart cooking. In a recent article on new English food, he said he is willing "to give it a go" with whatever he has seen that intrigues him, like Peruvian food: "It has a really good social vibe, like tapas with lots of little bowls of this and that, a really refreshing way to eat." Or at the Fat Duck in Berkshire, England, the chef takes whatever he fancies from the past fifty years of techniques and fresh ingredients to make his own kind of food, like sweetbreads cooked in hay and salt crust, crusted with pollen, and served with cockles à la plancha and parsnip puree, or red mullet served with a velouté of cocos beans with licorice and vanilla. A reporter thought the mullet dish might be at odds with traditional tastes.

Which traditions, I wondered.

How old does a dish have to be before it becomes a tradition? Is El Bulli in Spain too new, even when everyone in the world is whipping up foam?

The new American food has the same lineup as Jeffrey Steingarten used in *Vogue* to describe the newness of the "nouvelle cuisine" movement in France and its impact on America: "hand-raised ingredients [nothing new in France], bought that morning [as it always had been], cooked at the last minute [new], and eaten only in season [as always], the return to cooking's regional roots [had been going on for decades in France and Panisse], and the banishing of formulaic sauces [very new]."

I had read this article just before I toured the country by car as we passed the millennium. I wanted to see what was going on culinarily in the towns of America rather than just what had been reported was happening for years: now that the home cook could find ingredients in supermarkets that once were available only to top restaurants. I found two major things happening: within the culture of towns along the interstates, the quality of available ingredients had overtaken that of the restaurant food using those same ingredients, and that the planning of menus in the best of America's chef-owned restaurants had moved toward synthesis and away from shock.

The new supermarkets all seemed to have the word *fresh* somewhere in their names. All over America, even in unlikely places like Marathon Cay in Florida, I saw radicchio Treviso, mascarpone, American goat cheese, and perfect little green beans. And given this new shopping, all that good American home cooks needed was a television show to push them again to the stove. Why wouldn't anyone try Mario Batali's latest easy raviolo (when you can use the fresh wonton wrappers from your superfresh super-market); or Lydia Shire's fresh tomato sauce; or make a sauce for steaks out of salted anchovies (imported foods shelf), fresh basil, spring garlic, and new crop (not rancid) organic hazelnuts from Oregon; be entertained enough by Emeril to feel at ease cooking whatever he shows; give Martin Yan's Peking duck a try once having seen it on his new *Chinatown*; or use

the barbecued pork or roast duck in America's Chinatowns as the ultimate fast food at home, just chopped up with fresh herbs and cilantro on
top of pasta or a cabbage salad; or cook some white corn posole from Los
Chileros de Neuvo Mexico, who specialize in "gourmet New Mexico
foods"?

A fast look at restaurant menus in nineties America shows that the earlier, wilder throwing of ingredients into the air like cards to see how they
fell has settled down into more personal visions. Ingredients are chosen for
their harmony on the plate rather than for pure novelty, as in "look what
I've found." The Square in London showed a perfect example of the new
surefooted cooking, its menu listing dishes like pea soup with morel chantilly, or steamed zucchini flowers with scallops and buttered crab, and a
soup of peaches and strawberries with champagne.

Some visions remained true to the original: In August 1996 I went to
the Chez Panisse twenty-fifth anniversary party and for fifty-five dollars
and 15 percent service charge we had:

Hors d'oeuvre

La bouillabaisse de Lulu

Salade du jardin

Compote anniversaire

Sorbet de cassis

The menu took me back to twenty-three years earlier, when I had to spend
many hours trying to find fresh ingredients for my bouillabaisse at Panisse,
shopping in Oakland, Berkeley, both Chinatowns, and from any foragers
who had been out fishing and gathering. At this anniversary dinner, I wondered where all the famous ingredients had gone.

The next day at Stars Singapore I was back cooking foie gras sandwiches, boning rabbit saddles, baking oysters and spiny lobster, making
roast chicken broth (served with ginger, foie gras, and Chinese black bean
custard), and stuffing alternately red and white Belgian endive leaves with
quail egg and lobster rémoulade. Or inventing desserts with fresh lychee,
rambutan and mangosteen or ginger and jasmine flower sorbets.

But if you want to know why Chez Panisse was voted the single best
restaurant in the United States in 2001 by Gourmet, it was because of the
green beans: "Sharply vinegared" and served as a first course with "an art-
fully rumpled heap of beyond-organic herbs," a drop of jelly, and "a swath

of mayonnaise," the beans "vibrated" on the plate. Along with half a soft-boiled egg, this dish was reviewed as "the loveliest conceivable expression of a great cultural region." Really? Jean-Georges Vongerichten at Jean-Georges in Manhattan is from the opposite school of American cuisine according to the award list: Chez Panisse is devoted to displaying nature at its best, Jean-Georges determined to bend nature to his will.

If those are the extremes, the September 2001 Share Our Strength dinner at Gramercy Tavern was not, even though one of the hors d'oeuvre was a ragout of sea urchins. In fact, this entire menu reads like my list from the first days at Panisse of the things I could get only by bringing them myself illegally: foie gras, brandade, prosciutto, cured hamachi, osetra caviar, and goat cheese. The menu could not be more indicative of what is going on now: what is being cooked, its use of various languages and culinary terms, and its drawing on ingredients from all over the world.

Sydney's Rockpool:
salad of squid ink noodles, smokehouse bacon, garlic, chili, and coriander

New York's Cello:
breaded Maine sea scallops, caramelized endive, and Sauternes nage

Seattle's Rover's:
Alaskan halibut, rabbit hearts, and turnips with a Walla Walla onion and pinot noir sauce

New York's Union Pacific:
ragout of veal with a green paprika foam

New York's Gramercy Tavern:
roast capon with foie gras, artichokes, and sherry vinaigrette

Paris's Petrossian:
Coca-Cola Cajou of Coca-Cola emulsion, fruit and spice cookie, coconut sorbet and cashew sables

If any dish stood out from the others, it was Neil Perry's squid ink noodle salad, showing the sure hand with new-old food he's had since the Blue Water Grill opened in 1986. His flights of fancy are kept under control, and the dish was as memorable for its harmonious tastes as for the proper cooking techniques, which ensured kindness to the diner's body.

But harmony and inspired self-control of perfect ingredients achieved a height that we could never have found or done at Panisse or Stars, or Los Angeles (or anywhere in America) twenty years earlier, at a dinner at the

James Beard House in May 2001, organized by Charlie Trotter, David Bouley, and Australia's great Tetsuya Wakuda.

Wakuda
Scallop with foie gras, citrus & soy jelly

Bouley
Striped bass, fennel-braised with saffron rose olive sauce

Wakuda
Confit of Tasmanian soft-smoked ocean trout with kombu

Trotter
Organic veal shank with soy beans & hijiki seaweed sauce

Bouley
Braised beef cheeks with Catskill Mountian ramp spaetzle

Trotter
Three custards: green tea panna cotta, chamomile crème caramel,
Assam tea brûlée with melon sauce

Bouley
Chocolate tart with pistachio ice cream

The dinner was a paean to flavor. And textures. Tet's dish was a two-inch round of perfectly fresh sea scallop sliced an eighth of an inch thick. On top of it was a round of foie gras cut in exactly the same proportions. Nothing else was on the plate except for a little citrus juice, soy jelly, and olive oil. Absolute heaven. As the *Chicago Tribune*'s Bill Rice said at the end of the meal, when we were all almost speechless: "Sometimes simplicity is just downright that simple," reminding me how far we had come in twenty years. A year after Spago opened in the early eighties in Los Angeles, Wolfgang Puck, Jerry DiVecchio of *Sunset* magazine, and I were interviewed at the western regional conference of the Newspaper Food Editors and Writers Association. The reporter noted that we all insisted on the importance of quality ingredients, as if that was indeed news. I wanted to talk about simplicity which, I said, was in those days going to the outer limits often like a runaway horse, and that since we were at the beginning of an eclectic, we-can-do-anything cycle, the quality of ingredients was the only thing to provide stability. In 2001 Ruth Reichl was quoted in *The New York Times* saying that I was "the one that started pushing the envelope and demanding better ingredients." This Beard House dinner organized by Charlie Trotter in the same year proved that the envelope was bulging with new talent. And when that talent embraces the best of the past, the present, and looks to the future—as does Jean-Marie Lacroix at the Rittenhouse Hotel in Philadelphia, or as Rick Moonan cooks at his RM in New York, or as Vincent does at his Vincent in Minneapolis—the power of simple, masterly food reigns.

Flavor Rules

I would sum it all up as a sensual love for the flavor and texture of beautiful ingredients. And knowing how to marry them.

Robert Finigan wrote me in late 2001 about Boy (Michael) Bauer's latest off-the-tracks voluptuous excitement over the food at the redone Clift and its Asia de Cuba dining room. Bob could hardly get over the bananas with fried calamari, but he was floored by Chinese-style fried rice with guacamole. Bauer's take, by contrast, was "marvelous" food. Bob wondered if "marvelous" meant the sheer marvel of being able to think it up, cook and plate it, or whether the food was wonderful to eat.

"When you conceived Stars," he said, "you brilliantly had the idea of an upscale bistro just right for its place and time, perfectly prepared dishes of historical and regional significance with excitements around the edges perhaps not previously experienced by most Stars' patrons." I would say to Finigan that I am well out of the sphere of Boy Bauer's power to make kings out of burgeoning princes and princes out of reigning kings; and that what turns me on now are clean, pure, rich, and totally inspiring simple and complex flavors. They may be Tet's scallops with foie gras, or a mixture of cuisines like the fused cooking style that was born when the Sichuan Chinese in upper Manhattan, cohabiting with the 1960 Cuban immigrants, married two cultures of chili-flavored food. It was the movie *Woman on Top*, déjà vu all over again.

As guidelines in this culinary wooing of different cultures, ingredients, and flavors, I told my chefs to remember always their first paint box. You discover the primary colors, and since they are so wonderful, you feel they must be even more wonderful mixed together. But all you get is brown. Mud. It's the same with ingredients and flavors. A muddy result means that all the flavors stay on the same note, or slightly different ones all at once, without any structure—just noise. A clear flavor has incredible clarity and purity. The clarity of a kilo tin of beluga caviar is in its "Here I am."

As Bill Rice said, sometimes simplicity is just that simple.

Appreciations

MY THANKS to the team at Free Press/Simon & Schuster for accepting the book and to Martha Levin and Liz Stein for rescuing it. Thank you to Rachel Klayman and David Edelstein for their enthusiasm and hard work in the earliest stages. To my English professor sister, Mary Tower, for her constant support and editing. Thanks also, as always, to Lisa Queen, my agent at I.M.G., for believing in and working so hard with the book. And to Richard Collier, my friend and my attorney in San Francisco, who spent years making sure this story would end well.

Special thanks to all the players in this history, and to George Lang for supplying me with original archives relating to the real beginning of new American food at the early Restaurant Associates and The Four Seasons.

January 2003

Bibliography

Every book listed is in my library (except for one), and I have read them all. Any omissions tell a story, though not always.

A.W. *A Book of Cookrye*. London: Edward, 1591.

This book is as early as you need to go back in English. It is small, easy to read, and apart from how to cook a crane, a curlew, a bustard, and a bittern, it shows the first faint stirrings of a modern organization table service for later centuries.

Acton, Eliza. *Modern Cookery for Private Families*. London, 1845 and 1855.

Because she has "truffles potted in butter" prepared "for the breakfast table," and that will always get my vote, and because she was a favorite of Elizabeth David (who gave me the book in 1974). My standby carrot soup of Chez Panisse early days was from Acton, using water instead of stock for pure vegetable flavors, as did Richard Olney and Marcel Boulestin before him. This is a book that comes from "instinct and sheer intelligence rather than experience," and it is more interesting than that of the later Mrs. Beeton, who copied her.

Adams, Charlotte. *The Four Seasons Cookbook*. New York: Crescent Books, 1971.

Read the foreword by James Beard for an introduction to perhaps America's most influential restaurant of the twentieth century. And notice the fiddlehead ferns, fried parsley, wild asparagus, and a large American wine list as early as 1959.

Alexander, Victoria, and Genevieve Harris. *A Taste of Australia: The Bathers' Pavilion Cookbook*. Berkeley: Ten Speed Press, 1995.

Because the Bathers' Pavilion restaurant on the beach at Balmoral (near Sydney) was the West Beach Café, Trumps, and Michael's (Los Angeles) of Australia all rolled into one. What was New California decor and cooking became the New Australian here—along with Tony and Gay Bilson's Berowra Waters Inn, Neil Perry's Blue Water Grill at Bondi, Phillip Searle, Damien Pignolet, Tetsuya Wakuda, and a few others.

Alford, Jeffrey, and Naomi Duguid. *Hot Sour Salty Sweet.* **New York: Artisan, 2000.**

"A culinary journey though Southeast Asia," and no journey in the area of the Mekong Delta (southern China, Laos, Thailand, Cambodia, and Vietnam) has ever been more mouthwateringly photographed or written about—ever.

Ali-Bab. *Gastronomie Pratique.* **Paris: Flammarion, 1928.**

A book that includes a regime for how to eat very well without getting fat, showing that we did not invent concerns over eating healthfully. A very fashionable book for chefs to have read in the eighties. It grasps all your senses and elates the historian in you without a hint of cobwebs; rather it blows them away. It certainly did for me in 1974, when I used it at Chez Panisse, and then later at Stars.

Allen, Ida C. Bailey. *Mrs. Allen's Cook Book.* **Boston: Small, Maynard & Company, 1917.**

Quite before her time with health concerns, her answer being to banish all bad cooking, even though she overcooks the vegetables by ten minutes.

America's Cook Book. **Compiled by the Home Institute of the New York Herald Tribune. New York: Charles Scribner's Sons, 1937, 1940; rev. ed., 1942.**

Included because my mother bought it the year I was born, and cooked with it for forty years. My copy is covered in food, stained, and dog-eared. And because it is very Rector's (restaurant) and a prequel to Beard. He must have known this book, or Josie Wilson did, when writing his monumental *American Cookery.*

Anger, Kenneth. *Hollywood Babylon II* **(American ed.). New York: E. P. Dutton, 1984.**

I lived with Kenneth while he wrote the first *Hollywood Babylon,* almost ten years before this book was published. And because it shows Nick Ray and others in the film industry who, because of Alice Waters's boyfriend at the Pacific Film Archive at the time, were very much part of the scene of Chez Panisse. And because the cover shows what too many hamburgers, if they are not truffled, can do for you. Poor Liz.

Arenos, Pau. *Los Genios del Fuego.* **Barcelona: Peninsula, 1999.**

If you want to know what is going on in the most recent frontier of cooking, this is the book. It is visually in the style of *White Heat* and then Charlie Trotter's books, complete with the drawings done by the chefs to show how to present the dishes. All about ten geniuses of Spain in the vanguard: Ferran Adria, Jean Luc Figueras, Santi Santa Maria, and so on.

Aresty, Esther B. *The Delectable Past.* **New York: Simon & Schuster, 1964.**

The best contemporary of the fast passes at two thousand years of cooking, and still one of the easiest, most amusing, and educational to read. See also Jean-Louis Flandrin.

Aron, Jean-Paul. *The Art of Eating in France: Manners and Menus in Nineteenth Century France.* **New York: Harper & Row, 1975.**

An absolutely fascinating book! Its accounts of the magnificent Very's restaurant in Paris inspired me in 1976 to start thinking of the Stars concept: Could I have the likes of my hero Grimod de la Reynière eat there or in a café next door every week as he did at Very's?

Arzak, Juan Mari, and Ferran Adria. *Arzak & Adria 2000– 2001.* **Spain, 1999.**

This book was written to show the food that turned one century into another. These men should know. And the photograph of one of the world's great foods, el jamón ibérico (that most perfect of hams) makes my mouth water.

Audot, Louis Eustache. *La Cuisinière de la Campagne et de la Ville.* **Paris: Audot, 1818.**

This is the only book on this list that I do not have and have not read, but I mention it because I have been told it was the French home cookbook for a century after its publication and because again, that early on, it is about women's cooking.

Baldick, Robert. *Dinner at Magny's.* **New York: Coward, McCann & Geoghegan, 1971.**

One of the three books that really made me want to come up with the Stars concept and success. Just a brilliant book, and not only because the author is a fan of Huysmans! Magny's was the watering hole "of the leading novelists, critics, historians, and scientists of nineteenth century France."

Barry, Naomi. "Escoffier." *Gourmet,* **October 1989.**

Because Naomi is a wonderful writer, and she really gets her man in this article.

Batterberry, Michael and Ariane Batterberry. *On the Town in New York: From 1776 to the Present.* **New York: Charles Scribner's Sons, 1973.**

Because these authors were in love with New York when it was not fashionable to be, and visionaries to see that the town would become the world's best culinary scene again, especially if anyone knew about its very colorful and creative past. Think truck farms run by a single restaurant (Delmonico's) on Long Island in the late nineteenth century.

Beard, James. *American Cookery.* **Boston: Little, Brown, 1972.**

This book shows that Jim knew how to take his place in history. Still, it ain't no Ali-Bab.

———. *Delights and Prejudices.* **New York: Atheneum, 1964.**

The best of his books, and maybe the only one he actually wrote. The true James Beard—or at least one of them.

———. *Fish Cookery.* **Boston: Little, Brown, 1954; new ed., 1976.**

Not the greatest book, even though it does have recipes for fresh sardines. But in 1976 James was already pointing out the severe marine "ecological changes" since the first edition. And because the inscription to me in 1976 says: "For Jeremiah—who knows so much! Love, James Beard."

———. *The James Beard Cookbook*. With Isabel E. Calvert. New York: E. P. Dutton, 1961; rev. ed., 1970.

Note that the copyright is 1959 to know how he was thinking that early on. In 1970 the publishers hail this as a classic, "as essential to the modern American kitchen as the stove itself." James calls it "a basic cookbook." Not as good as the Rector's 1928 book, and it is already diluted by the home economics virus of the period after the world wars. But a Beard classic nonetheless.

Beaton, Cecil. "The Art of Table Decoration." *Gourmet*, December 1969.

Beaton is impeccable, and this advice is still amusing for the twenty-first century. In 1969 I read and recorded in my culinary notebooks: "A treat need not be a luxury; a banquet need not include caviar. Imagination is the most important ingredient."

Beck, Simone, with Louisette Bertholle and Julia Child. *Mastering the Art of French Cooking*, Volume I (only). New York: Alfred A. Knopf, 1961.

The book (especially the first volume) that launched a thousand young cooks into vats of butter, cream, and wonderful cooking.

Beebe, Lucius. *The Stork Club Bar Book*. New York: Rinehart & Company, 1946.

One cannot visit the twentieth century without saying hello to Lucius Beebe. And this book, from one of New York's "various plush and chromium cocktail zoos," is all about the last time the city was at its height.

La Belle France: A Gourmet's Guide to the French Provinces. Preface by André Maurois. New York: Golden Press; London: Paul Hamly, 1964.

A stunning book that was countless years of inspiration for Chez Panisse and, early on, for my regional festivals. Perhaps no book more than this one inspired Alice Waters. See the newer and equally magnificent version of Robert Freson, *A Taste of France*.

Bemelmans, Ludwig. *La Bonne Table*. New York: Simon & Schuster, 1964.

A true New York boulevardier in the old style; incredibly civilized stories of his "lifetime love affair with the art of dining" in the now mythic places like L'Ousteau de Beaumanière in Provence, Le Pavillon in New York, and la Tour d'Argent in Paris. Everything from sausages and beer to caviar and champagne. Material originally from *Playboy* in 1960 ("Caviar"), *Holiday*, *Town & Country*, *Vogue*, and *The New Yorker*.

Bey, Pilaf [Norman Douglas]. *Venus in the Kitchen or Love's Cookery Book*. New York: Viking Press, 1952.

Did the great Harry Cipriani know of this book when he wrote *Heloise and Bellinis*? This book is even more wonderful.

Bianchini, F., and F. Corbetta. *The Complete Book of Fruits and Vegetables.* Illustrations by Marilena Pistoia. New York: Crown Publishers, 1975.

The colored illustrations tell more than a photo ever could. When this book came out, I bought it immediately and showed it to my partners at Chez Panisse with glee: Here were the things that I wanted to grow, the wild radish, the purslane, Treviso, New Zealand spinach, and the sea rocket and borage I had cooked with in Maine. I was given a copy by Linda Guenzel, who wrote *The Chez Panisse Menu Cookbook;* she inscribed it by quoting Larousse on what is a vegetable, and then said: "You, the high priest of all culinary, have given us vegetables as Larousse may never have known."

Bittman, Mark. *How to Cook Everything.* New York: John Wiley, 1998.

The new *Joy of Cooking.*

Blanc, Georges. *The French Vineyard Table.* New York: Clarkson Potter, 1997.

The most visually evocative and beautifully done of the French chef books of the nineties, by my favorite French country chef, who carried on the cooking of the amazing women of Vonnas and Lyons.

Bober, Phyllis Pray. *Art, Culture and Cuisine.* Chicago: University of Chicago Press, 1999.

A very impressive and illustrated culinary history that "examines cooking through the dual lens of archaeology and art history." Finally someone who can explain what that classic period of reclining while dining was all about.

Boeckmann, Susie, and Natalie Rebeiz-Nielsen. *Caviar.* London: Mitchell Beazley, 1999.

Called the definitive book, it probably is, if you read it with the Inga Saffron book. The book inspires one to go out and eat caviar—while one still can.

Borrel, Anne, with Alain Senderens and Jean-Bernard Naudin. *Dining with Proust.* New York: Random House, 1992.

This could have been a very silly book. But the food is real, thanks to the great Parisian chef Alain Senderens, who understands the grand presentations of the era. The food in the very good photographs is historically correct and delicious looking. What a way to learn history, with Nesselrode pudding, Spiced Beef in Jelly, and the "Lunch at Reveillon: scrambled eggs with bacon, lobster American style, hare à l'allemande, rose and macaroon preserve." Divine.

Boulestin, X. Marcel. *Ease and Endurance.* London: Home & Van Thal, 1948.

Elizabeth David gave me this book on "the first day of summer, 1978," after a seven-hour lunch. It shows how Boulestin covered the twenties, thirties, and forties, mixing artists, socialites, and food. See page 90 for the description of his new restaurant in Covent Garden. He used the artists of the day, creating a decor that should make decorators today gasp in admiration. And because thirty-five years later I tried to buy the place.

———. "Finer Cooking." *Vogue*, London, 1923–.

Read anything by Marcel, and this is a very good introduction.

———. *What Shall We Have Today?* London: William Heinemann, 1931.

If you want to see Elizabeth David before Elizabeth herself, this is her hero and mentor with his relentlessly modern mind. As a young man he was secretary to the Colette-Willy ménage, then escaped the drama of that household and, already an Anglophile (taking Colette to tea at the English Dairy in Paris), fled to England, taking with him a few Modiglianis that he had bought for twelve pounds. *Simple French Cooking for English Homes* came out in 1923, written for single people and working women who have to cook without much money or time. Sound familiar? Think Richard Olney, only fifty years earlier: "All these soups . . . must be made with plain water. When made with the addition of stock they lose all character and cease to be what they were intended to be." No statement could be more "modern" in every way, or more cutting edge. Also because he says that on charcoal is the only way to grill.

Boulud, Daniel, and Peter Kaminsky. *Chef Daniel Boulud.* New York: Assouline, 2002.

A day in the life of Daniel, and a wonderful book if you can get past the crazy graphics. I can.

Bradley, Richard. *The Country Housewife and Lady's Director.* London, 1727, 1732, 1736; repr. 1736 ed., London: Prospect Books, 1980.

A vastly entertaining and intelligent book with recipes inspiring for now—look at the Sorrel Tart and the Small Suckers of Artichokes. Not at all esoteric, until we get to the Viper Soup.

Brillat-Savarin. *Physiologie du Goût.* Paris: Michel Levy Frères, 1873.

Is any comment necessary? Well, perhaps: see Lucien Tendret.

Brown, Eleanor, and Bob Brown. *Culinary Americana.* New York: Roving Eye Press, 1961.

One hundred years of cookbooks, published in the United States from 1860 to 1960—so an invaluable bibliographical resource.

Brown, Helen. *Helen Brown's West Coast Cook Book.* New York: Little, Brown, 1952.

Helen was an absolute favorite of James Beard. This was stuff for the public, *McCall's, House & Garden,* and so on, and is so very American. It gave me the nerve in 1976 to start putting the origins of ingredients on the menu.

The Browns. *America Cooks.* New York: Garden City Publishing, 1940.

"Favorite Recipes from Forty-eight States," including Scuppernong Pie and a traditional breakfast from the Shenandoah Valley. Packed with Americana before the canned and frozen foods.

Bullock, Mrs. Helen. *The Williamsburg Art of Cookery.* Williamsburg, Va.: Colonial Williamsburg, 1939.

Very entertaining, but what rivets me is the account of the books consulted for this work: Hannah Glasse, Miss Leslie, John Farley, Mrs. Mary Randolph's *The Virginia Housewife*. Perfect taste!

Capon, Robert Farrar. *The Supper of the Lamb.* New York: Doubleday, 1967.

An inspiring book. Included here for the preface; for the dedication, which is to his wife, whom he calls "the lightning behind all this thunder," because he believes that an onion can save you from hell, and because he says, "The world exists, not for what it means but for what it is. The purpose of mushrooms is to be mushrooms; wine is in order to be wine: things are precious before they are contributory." That is the cook's true guide.

Carson, Rachel. *The Silent Spring.* Boston: Houghton Mifflin, 1962.

A huge influence on me in the early sixties, which later, in the early seventies, made me want to start growing our own produce and recycling for the restaurants.

Chamberlain, Samuel, and Narcissa Chamberlain. *Bouquet de France.* New York: Gourmet Books, 1952.

Defining the art of a culinary tour, in the days when you could just drop by almost anywhere in France and get a good meal. A sensibility we should recover.

Cherikoff, Vic, and Jennifer Isaacs. *The Bush Food Handbook: How to Gather, Grow, Process and Cook Australian Wild Foods.* Balmain, Australia: Ti Tree Press, from the 1990s (year not listed).

This is serious book. Not a Birkenstock in sight. It shows how seriously the Australians took over from California in reworking regional aesthetics to make a new culture and cuisine. Fascinating book and beautifully presented.

Child, Mrs. *The American Frugal Housewife.* Boston: Carter, Hendee, and Co., 1832.

One can tire of the thousands of "household management" books, but this one is small and powerful. And this woman, at a time when a woman could not go into the supper room at a party unless escorted by a man, was a newspaperwoman, magazine editor, gardener, novelist, poet, reformer, and a friend of Whitman, Lowell, and Bryant. She also hid runaway slaves, and her first important antislavery writing in America nearly ruined her.

Cipriani, Harry. *The Harry's Bar Cookbook.* New York: Bantam Books, 1991.
My hero.

———. *Heloise and Bellinis.* New York: Little, Brown, 1986.

When I read this book I knew that Harry and Tom Margittai were having as much fun as restaurateurs as I was!

Cocteau, Jean. *Past Tense (Diaries)*. New York: Harcourt Brace, 1987.

Because the highly intelligent Ezra Pound thought Cocteau was the most intelligent Frenchman he had met, along with Francis Picabia. For "Eggs Picabia" see Alice B. Toklas's cookbook.

Colette. *Prisons et Paradis*. Paris: Librairie Arthème Fayard, 1986.

For the truffles and her sensibility about everything, including food.

———. *The Pure and the Impure*. New York: Farrar, Straus, and Giroux, 1967.

"To receive from someone happiness—is it not to choose the sauce in which we want to be served up?"

Conrad, Barnaby. *Absinthe*. San Francisco: Chronicle Books, 1988.

Now that absinthe is legal again in Europe, and being manufactured in Thailand as well as in Spain and France, one should read about this most subtle green elixir to be sipped at "the green hour" because, as someone said, "Absinthe makes the heart grow fonder."

***Cooking*. Edited by Barbara Kafka. Stamford, CT: Cuisinart Publications, 1978–.**

Great little magazine edited by the phenomenally brilliant Barbara Kafka. Writers are Naomi Barry, James Beard, Gault and Millau, Abby Mandel, Elizabeth David, and so on. Read also all the books by Barbara, including the wonderful book *Roasting*.

Core, Philip. *Camp: The Lie That Tells the Truth*. Foreword by George Melly. London: Plexus, 1984.

Not just because the book is dedicated to me, "champagne en campagne," but because it covers a lot of my early imprints and aesthetic lessons: Aubrey Beardsley, Cecil Beaton, Prince Yusupov, the Sitwells, the sixties, Robert de Montesquiou and Boni de Castellane (the Belle Epoque's most elegant men), Jean Cocteau, Edward James, Ronald Firbank, Diaghilev, D'Annunzio (the perfect peaches, in the perfect bowl, all wrapped in the perfect silk scarf—all made at his villa), Noël Coward, Colette, Carême (who made the campiest remark of all of them about the Fine Arts being five in number, including pastry making, of which architecture is a branch), Capri, Jean-Michel Frank, Christian Bérard, and Lou Reed. These are all the people who made the most of their faults, because after all, "Camp is a disguise that fails."

Courtine, Robert. *The Hundred Glories of French Cooking*. New York: Farrar, Straus & Giroux, 1973.

A book wonderful for its unparalleled illustrations—the beautiful chefs in boots, the photo of Curnonsky at lunch, the fish market section at Les Halles. Treat yourself.

Cox, Mrs. Samuel R. *The Parker Cook Book.* Abilene, TX, 1932.

Not the Parker House hotel cookbook, but in this one, for the Presbyterian church, they still ate caviar, and the nonalcoholic drinks are state of the art.

Craddock, Harry. *The Savoy Cocktail Book.* London: Constable & Company, 1930.

If you haven't seen the design of this perfect Art Deco book, you are really missing out. The ultimate recipes, and then there is the foreword to the wine section, by Colette.

Crowninshield, Frank. *The Unofficial Palace of New York: A Tribute to the Waldorf-Astoria.* New York: Waldorf-Astoria, 1939.

For the Sert murals, the chapter by Elsa Maxwell, and the American menus with Diamond Back Terrapin, Chicken California Style, Roast Mountain Sheep, and Basket of Lobster, all at one dinner in 1899. See the 1937 menu for an "Idaho Dinner," which then called out the origins of the ingredients: Snake River, Twin Falls, Sawtooth Range, Jerome County, Boise Valley, and Lone Pine, Idaho.

Culinaria. Cologne: Konemann, 1998.

Huge, glossy books that entice you to pick them up and then make you think nothing this obvious-looking could be good. They are, and full of gripping information and illustrations. The United States, France, and Italy are the ones I have.

Curnonsky. *Traditional Recipes of the Provinces of France.* Translated by Edwin Lavin. London: W. H. Allen, 1961.

The book from which I did the famous Curnonsky festival at Chez Panisse, and the book I used to give as Christmas presents. A beautiful book—if a bit recherché.

David, Elizabeth. "Edouard de Pomiane." *Gourmet,* March 1970.

Because it opens with "Art demands an impeccable technique; science a little understanding."

———. *French Provincial Cooking.* New York: Harper & Row, 1960.

I was handed this book on my first day of work as executive chef at Chez Panisse by Gene Opton, the woman running it at the time, and was told it was the bible to cook from. Very great book, and Elizabeth's main work as far as most people are concerned.

———. "Marcel Boulestin." *Gourmet,* August 1969.

The article that turned me on to Boulestin, and again on to Elizabeth.

———. "Norman Douglas." *Gourmet,* February 1969.

Because on the back page of Elizabeth's copy of *Old Calabria,* Norman wrote: "Always do as you please, send everybody to Hell, and take the consequences. Damned good rule of life."

Davidson, Alan. *The Oxford Companion to Food.* **Oxford: Oxford University Press, 1999.**

In the tradition of the great dictionaries of food (see Dumas), this is Alan at his best—erudite, and not afraid of his always-riveting opinions. A must for food reference today.

Davis, Irving. *A Catalan Cookery Book: A Collection of Impossible Recipes.* **Edited by Patience Gray. Paris: Lucien Scheler, 1969.**

Inasmuch as some knowledgeable people say that right now the best and most daring food in the West is in Spain, and because I have loved this book and the food in it since it was published. Rabbit with snails indeed! Pretty good with monkfish too—the snails, I mean. In the early seventies people thought I was mad for pushing this food and this book. See Arzak and Adria, and Pau Arenos.

De Croze, Austin. *What to Eat and Drink in France.* **London: Frederick Warne, 1931.**

Written "for tourists so they can choose from any province [of France] the typical local dishes." Important early Chez Panisse source.

De Gouy, Jean. *La Cuisine et La Pâtisserie Bourgeoises.* **Paris: Lebegue et Cie, 1896.**

Because this book is understandable to all, "à la portée de tous," and because you will need this one to explain all the other ones—French cookbooks, that is.

De Groot, Roy Andries. *The Auberge of the Flowering Hearth.* **New York: Bobbs-Merrill, 1973.**

This book blew me away, made me fall in love with France again, love De Groot again, and after I made everyone read it, and saw they loved it, set me off on a cooking frenzy of renewed enthusiasm at Chez Panisse in 1973. One of the books you would take in an overnight bag—your only luggage—when banished to a desert island. Also a huge favorite of Alice Waters.

Douglas, Norman. *South Wind.* **1917. (Reprinted many times since first publication.)**

"'You are quite right,' the count was saying. 'The ideal cuisine should display an individual character, it should offer a menu judiciously chosen from the kitchen workshops of the most diverse lands and people—a menu reflecting the master's alert and fastidious taste.' *Southwind,* XXXVI." Quoted in my journals, July 26, 1970.

Dubois, Urbain, and Emile Bernard. *La Cuisine Classique.* **Paris: Chez les Auteurs, 1856.**

Not just for the illustrations of those divine garnishes stuck on skewers (like whole truffles pierced with cockscombs and crayfish), or for the uniquely understandable descriptions of pièces montées, but because this book tells exactly what the difference is between the two services, French and Russian. From what I still hear of these terms bandied around in culinary academies, this book should be reread. Also the style of the recipes is beautifully direct, straightforward, and definitive, and just before the similarly inspired Escoffier.

Ducasse, Alain. *Flavors of France*. New York: Artisan, 1998.

Finally a book by a chef (one of the most famous in the world) that is the food you can cook from, and the photographs show you can. Alain knows that more than four main ingredients on a plate is too many.

Ducasse, Alain, and Jean-François Piege. *Grand Livre de Cuisine d'Alain Ducasse*. Paris: ADP, 2001.

Not since Prosper Montagné did the *Larousse Gastronomique* (1938), Escoffier his *Le Guide Culinaire*, and Henri-Paul Pellaprat his *L'Art Culinaire Moderne* (1935) has a chef accomplished a work that codifies the cooking of a nation and the time. This one does. An enormous achievement.

Dumaine, Alexandre. *Ma Cuisine*. Paris: Pensée Moderne, 1972.

Richard Olney, in our correspondence in 1973, told me to read this. Dumaine became my model—I wanted a restaurant like his, that people would think "worth the journey."

Dumas, Alexandre. *Dictionary of Cuisine*. Translated by Louis Colman. New York: Simon & Schuster, 1958.

My bedside reading in college, and I could not wait to buy the unedited version. I never tire of this book. See Alan Davidson and Waverley Root. This edition was severely cut; the new, less edited one is Alexandre Dumas, *Le Grand Dictionnaire de Cuisine* (Turin: Henry Veyrier, 1978).

Dupleix, Jill. *New Food: From the New Basics to the New Classics*. Port Melbourne, Australia: William Heinemann, 1994.

Tells the story of why the nineties were not going to be the eighties. This woman loves to think, eat, write, and tell you all about it. Very clever indeed.

Durack, Terry. *Yum*. Port Melbourne, Australia: William Heinemann, 1996.

Yum indeed. By the husband of Jill Dupleix, this book is very nineties, or the new Australian intelligence, the worldwide view. There is a list of who he thinks are the best chefs and restaurateurs in the world at the time of his writing, including my favorites Bruno Loubet of London's L'Odéon, Georges Blanc, of course, Arrigo Cipriani, and Pierre Koffman.

Durrell, Lawrence. *The Black Book*. Paris: Obelisk Press, 1938; New York and Paris: Olympia Press, 1959.

Because the book opens with "Today there is a gale blowing up from the Levant," the wind withering the soft gold shavings of hair along the thighs. "The very nipples turn hard and black on the breasts of women, while the figs roast." Who needs a cooking lesson? And if it isn't about food it is all the senses that cooking conjures up. The hero tastefully identifies the scent on the air: "It's the girls' bogs again!" Such an amateur of odeurs must be admired. How did he know it was girls? This is the book to read if dining alone.

Ebert-Schifferer, Sybille. *Still Life.* **New York: Harry N. Abrams, 1999.**

A thousand words to describe what food was on artists' and other people's minds—and then there are the paintings.

Escoffier, Auguste. *Le Guide Culinaire.* **Paris: Flammarion, 1903; 3d ed., Paris: E. Grevin, 1912.**

There was an edition in 1907 as well, but the 1912 has the introductions of both the second and the first, and these are the beginning of modern cooking. Do not overlook the mention of his "maître" Urban Dubois. And the pieces on stocks and "fonds" are the bible to this day. Also the book I used for the Escoffier festival at Chez Panisse in 1974, which put the restaurant on the local and national map.

————. *Ma Cuisine.* **Translated by Vyvyan Holland. London: Paul Hamlyn, 1965.**

My first cookbook, or the first that I read constantly from cover to cover, and the mainstay reference for my recreational graduate-school cooking binges and early lessons.

Escoffier, Auguste, ed. *Le Carnet d'Epicure.* **Paris, 1908–1912 at least.**

A lesson in culinary history that cannot be missed. Check out the Salad Folle— with haricots verts, foie gras, lobster, hazelnut oil, and so on—in 1908, sixty years before everyone thought they had invented it.

Evelyn, John. *Acetaria, A Discourse of Sallets.* **London: B. Tooke, 1699.**

Because three hundred years later everyone agrees this is one of the truly delightful early cookbooks: the dedication is totally mad, the preface about the "universal plantation" deranged, 90 percent of this "cookbook" is about gardening and life, only 10 percent recipes (a delicious one for artichokes). Not a cookbook at all, but read it and see how serious and how much fun the seventeenth century was for cooks.

Farley, John. *The London Art of Cookery,* **7th ed. London, 1792.**

Farley was the "principle cook at the London Tavern." If you do nothing else with this democratically approached and concisely worded book, look at the plates showing the arrangement on the table of the various dishes per course—many books talk about this "French" service, but few show how it was done. This is "Simple Food," and the recipes are beautifully written.

Farmer, Fannie Merritt. *The Boston Cooking-School Cook Book.* **Boston: Little, Brown, 1937.**

A bit overrated but historically interesting, and do not bother with any editions after this one. Read "a few rules for successful dining": as in use foods only at the height of the season, use generous-size plates so the food is not crowded, think always of the wine and how the food will affect it, and so on. All this in 1937!

Fashions in Foods in Beverly Hills. Beverly Hills: Beverly Hills Woman's Club, 1931.

If there was any doubt what America ate after the fall of American food (post–World War I) and before the Revolution, here it is. Carrot Ring, Tamale Pie, Goulash, Cottage Cheese Salad, Wakimoli Salad, and Divinity. Most of it pretty good, which is why most of the country is still eating it!

Fielding, Daphne. *The Duchess of Jermyn Street: The Life and Good Times of Rosa Lewis of the Cavendish Hotel.* Boston: Little, Brown, 1964.

Because if you did not see the show from the BBC more than three times you are deprived. The way I always wanted to treat my customers, and did. An absolute inspiration for any truly inspired restaurateur! From kitchen maid to culinary genius, mistress of the king, and prankster extraordinaire, one of the great individualistic women of the century. And discreet to boot.

Firbank, Ronald. *Concerning the Eccentricities of Cardinal Pirelli.* London: Duckworth, 1926.

Thank God there is one mention of food, "white menthe" (and then only because the dog was covered in it); otherwise I could not include this inspiration of my college years.

Flandrin, Jean-Louis, and Massimo Montanari. *Food: A Culinary History from Antiquity to the Present.* New York: Columbia University Press, 1999.

Jacques Pépin said this book is "essential reading for the historian and the lover of social studies as well as the modern cook and gourmet." The title says it all: If you are interested in food, this is the book for you.

Foods of the World. Edited by Time-Life Books, James Beard and Michael Field, consultants. New York: Time-Life, 1970.

I have to mention Michael Field. Cathy Simon, Michael Palmer, and I cooked a lot from his *Michael Field's Cooking School* when we were in college. I could never get a straight answer out of anyone, let alone Beard, about what he was like. When asked, Beard would get quiet, as when he knew someone was talented, admired the talent, but for some private reason didn't want to praise it. Anyway, these books were of enormous excitement and inspiration to me and my friends. I could not wait for the mail to bring the new issue. *Vienna* was good, *Classic French* wonderful, and *American Cooking: Southern Style* was the one most of my friends cooked from and the one that got us all on to Thomas Jefferson and hams. Still a great read.

La France à Table. rue de Castellane, Paris, early 1930s.

A magazine with writers like Colette, Gaston Derys, Austin de Croze, Curnonsky talking about cooking. When they talk about cooking in the ashes of the fire, for example, it is the true flavor of the regions and countryside of France.

Franz, Mark. *Farallon.* San Francisco: Chronicle Books, 2001.

Definitely a chef's book. For those who love to cook fish and want to know all about it, Mark tells you how.

Freson, Robert. *The Taste of France.* New York: Stewart, Tabori & Chang, 1983.

One of the most stunningly beautiful photography cookbooks ever, and one that created a style. The writers include Richard Olney, Ann Willan (La Varenne), Jill Norman (Elizabeth David's literary executor), Alan Davidson, and Caroline Conran.

Fussell, Betty. *I Hear America Cooking.* New York: Viking Press, 1986.

Because she educates us away from the traps of slavishly believing in "authentic" and "regional" without knowing where the worth of the concepts lie.

Gattey, Charles Neilson. *Foie Gras and Trumpets.* London: Constable, 1984.

For those who love to give grand and expensive parties, or who love to read about them. You have not lived until you have read about Kessler's "gondola party" for the English king, or "the Awful Seeley Dinner" when Little Egypt was served naked from a pie and the police had to raid Sherry's (again). The Savoy, Boulestin's, the Waldorf, Delmonico's, Rector's—all these great restaurants and the dish about them is all here.

Gibbons, Euell. *Stalking the Wild Asparagus.* Philadelphia: McKay, 1962.

The father of foraging, and the book that inspired me in the sixties, on the beaches of Maine and at my Massachusetts farm, before I got into the restaurant business, to grow my own and to forage.

Ginor, Michael. *Foie Gras: A Passion.* New York: John Wiley & Sons, 1999.

A book about this delicious fat that really works. The best I know in English on the subject.

Glasse, Hannah. *The Art of Cookery, Made Plain and Easy,* Alexandria, Va.: Printed for the author, 1805.

Because, according to John and Karen Hess, it was "the most popular cookbook in the colonies." And for the section on American cooking.

Gopnik, Adam. "Is There a Crisis in French Cooking?" *The New Yorker,* April 28 and May 5, 1997.

A piece of extraordinary intelligence. The fickle muse of French cooking, and where does she sit?

Gordon, Peter. *The Sugar Club Cookbook.* London: Hodder and Stoughton, 1997.

The jacket says that Gordon is the Alastair Little (eighties) of the nineties. He's cool. A book of the "de rigueur" (though I hope not "rigor mortis") Marco Pierre White design school. He's really searching the world for great flavors, but see the Australians ten years earlier.

Goloub, Hélène. *100 Recettes de Cuisine Russe.* Paris: Self-Published, 1924.

Perfect recipes for a cuisine that, for a dinner party, is still the most impactful.

The Good Cook. Richard Olney, consultant, Editors of Time-Life. London and Alexandria, Va.: Time-Life Books, 1979–?

The best how-to teaching books there are, especially the English edition, and a series that I worked on with Richard, as well as doing a few of my own in Virginia. This series changed "how to" food photography for good.

Griffini, Orso Cesare, and Frances E. Vieta. *I Tartuffi.* Rome: Trevi Editore, 1973.

The book that, when I bought it in 1974, made me want to be the first to bring fresh truffles to California—and I was.

Grigson, Jane. *The Art of Charcuterie.* New York: Alfred A. Knopf, 1968.

It is not generally known how influential this book has been, but every time you taste a succulent double pork chop in America, it is because the chef read this book. All the brining done now in American restaurants is because of Jane. Cook pork or poultry without this book? Not well.

———. *British Cookery.* New York: Atheneum, 1985.

A celebration of regionality by this most wonderful of women. Superb.

Guenzel, Linda P. *Beyond Tears: The First Eight Years.* Illustrations by David Lance Goines and Wesley B. Tanner. Berkeley: Chez Panisse, 1979.

The collection of menus from August 28, 1971, to December 30, 1978, the day before my last day at the restaurant. The first chef was Victoria Kroyer, who later opened Pig by the Tail charcuterie across the street. I was the second. Linda knew this was the important period, as did Darrell Corti when he sent a funeral wreath in 1974: "Chez Panisse can never be this great again."

———. *The Chez Panisse Menu Cookbook.* New York: Random House, 1982.

The inscription in the copy given to me by Linda is "To Jeremiah—The inspiration, the raison d'etre, the *creator* of so much on these pages—without you, there would be no Chez Panisse, no cookbook. Truth shall triumph."

Guérard, Michel. *La Cuisine Gourmande.* Paris: Robert Laffont, 1978.

This and the Troisgros book, with its revolutionary food and plate presentations, changed it all for young chefs in the United States. Nora Ephron said that this food did not have any impact on the way Americans eat at home, but to the extent that food magazines or TV shows have any effect on that eating, she's wrong. But she's right inasmuch as, in the hands of untalented cooks, the food became "non-nouvelle cuisine," prompting Paul Bocuse (the self-proclaimed leader of the Young Turks) to say that "so-called" nouvelle cuisine "usually means not enough on your plate and too much on your bill."

Guillot, André. *La Grande Cuisine Bourgeoise.* **Paris: Flammarion, 1976.**

This is the "cuisine bourgeoise," as opposed to the "cuisine de la noblesse" that existed before the French Revolution. The three principles of this cooking are the best products (not the rarest), diversity of the dishes that can make up menus, and the rule of economy (nothing wasted). This book explains also how the change in politics and constitutions set the culture of how we eat today. Read the brief historical analysis of the rise of bourgeois cooking.

Hartley, Dorothy. *Food in England.* **London: MacDonald and Jane's, 1954–1975.**

I can't remember if Elizabeth David admired Hartley's scholarship or not (God help anyone whose work she didn't), but I find the book great reading. Look at the unique and amazing sketches of ranges and roasting equipment. The food, she says, is "old fashioned, the way we [English] like it." And when it's "open apple tart after the pig," with clotted cream, so do we all.

Hay, Donna. *The New Cook.* **Sydney: Murdoch Books, 1997.**

There are several books in this series of material from Australian *Marie Claire*, and I find them all visually inspiring. The photographs and the contents never fail to make me want to cook, and to conjure up new dishes. The price of the books is very right.

Hazan, Marcella. *Essentials of Classic Italian Cooking.* **New York: Alfred A. Knopf, 2001.**

The way to get the best of the genius of Marcella in one book, this one comprising both *Classic Italian Cookbook* and *More Classic Italian Cooking.*

———. *Marcella's Italian Kitchen.* **New York: Alfred A. Knopf, 1986.**

Because, as I said on the back cover: "A perfect book : . ."

Herbst, Sharon Tyler. *Never Eat More Than You Can Lift.* **New York: Broadway Books, 1997.**

If you like books with "sayings" on food and wine, this is it. My favorite has always been what Lily Bollinger said about champagne, and she would have known: "I drink it when I'm happy and when I'm sad. Sometimes I drink it when I'm alone. When I have company I consider it obligatory. I trifle with it if I'm not hungry and drink it when I am. Otherwise I never touch it—unless I'm thirsty." On my tombstone I hope.

Hess, John L., and Karen Hess. *The Taste of America.* **New York: Grossman, 1977.**

Read this if for no other reason than it made most of the famous names in the United States purple with rage, spluttering with outraged pride. I adored it. Seemed to me to hit what was going on with the commercial food industry in America at the time fairly squarely on the mark.

Hess, Karen. *Martha Washington's Booke of Cookery.* New York: Columbia University Press, 1981.

When I recommend centuries-old cookbooks here, I do cringe slightly with fear at how difficult the print and the language may be to decipher. Let alone some of the terminology. This book is completely noted and annotated ("*layes* is an old word for layers; *porringers* are individual bowls") and therefore makes easy and fascinating reading of this family manuscript and treasure trove of "culinary secrets of some of our earliest colonists, part of our American heritage from England."

Hierneis, Theodor. *The Monarch Dines.* London: Werner Laurie, 1954.

Memories of a cook at the court of Ludwig of Bavaria. I am still trying to figure out why I was given this book on my twenty-first birthday! I do know that I took one look at the photo of the kitchen at Neuschwanstein, and at the one of the dining room at Schloss Linderhof, and knew I had to live in that kitchen or make a house like it. Pure Minoan arches and vaulted ceilings. Every anniversary of Ludwig's last meal (before strolling out of the embrace of his valet into that of the lake) was celebrated in my restaurants.

Hirtzler, Victor. *The Hotel St. Francis Cook Book.* Chicago: Hotel Monthly Press, 1919.

Quite a modern book still. The "art of cooking developed in the hotel business, which, in America, now leads the world." The book is organized with a breakfast, lunch, and dinner menu for each calendar day of the year with some recipes selected from each. The food is caught halfway between Europe and the United States, and is very schizophrenic about the choice of English or European languages to name the dishes. But nothing American is left out. There is no grip on the book's own region of California yet, except for the oysters.

Holyfield, Dana. *Swamp Cookin' with the River People.* Berkeley: Ten Speed Press, 1999.

Like *White Trash Cooking,* this little book has a ring of truth, is hilarious, and I love the photographs of Louisiana swamp critters and how they are cooked outdoors.

Hom, Ken, and Pierre-Jean Pebeyre. *Truffles.* Paris: Hachette, 2001.

If anyone knows more about black truffles than the Pebeyre family of Périgord, I don't know who it could be. And until you have cooked Ken's tastou (truffle sandwiches) or the oeufs à la cocque, sauce truffe (soft-boiled eggs with black truffle sauce), you have not lived to the fullest. The photograph of Pierre-Jean's grandfather Alain sniffing truffles through his long, white beard has been constantly on my kitchen (or restaurant) wall since my first days at Chez Panisse.

Hopkinson, Simon. *Roast Chicken and Other Stories: Second Helpings.* London: Macmillan, 2001.

Wonderful unpretentious essays by this chef who started Bibendum restaurant in London.

Huysmans, J. K. À *Rebours*. Paris: Fasquelle Editeur, 1955.

An important book to understand the sensibility of the nineteenth-century fin de siècle and the world of Ritz and Escoffier. It is the book that, along with Rechy's *City of Night*, ruined my twenties, as Gide's *Faux-Monnayeurs* did my teens.

Jackson, Stanley. *The Savoy*. New York: E. P. Dutton, 1964.

You don't have to have stayed in one of the Thames suites to appreciate the wonderfully English understated outrageousness of this book, and its social history of several eras.

Janson, Charles William. *The Stranger in America*. London: Albion Press, 1807.

All about the "genius, manners, and customs of the people of the United States," written by a European. You get an idea of the view from the following excerpt (about an American woman in an English household) that "is truly characteristic of American politeness." When asked to drink tea she replied: "Tea, indeed! No— I have drank [*sic*] none of that cursed stuff since the affair at Boston. I swallow a beef steak or a piece of fat pork for breakfast and supper, and wash it down with a quart of cider—that's my way!" No Thomas Jefferson in that woman's family!

***The Joy of Truffles*. Cologne: Evergreen Benedikt Taschen, 1998.**

One of the most beautiful food books ever published. The photographs of food set the standard. The photo of the braised black truffle with sherry butter makes me want to dive into it.

Kaytor, Marilyn. *21: The Life and Times of New York's Favorite Club*. New York: Viking Press, 1975.

The other book that made me think of creating the Stars concept. This is the book if you want to know the history of the first fifty years of the twentieth century in New York, and was there ever a more debonair restaurateur than Pete Kriendler?

Keenan, Brigid. *Dior in Vogue*. Foreword by Margot Fonteyn. New York: Harmony Books, 1981.

Look at Le Coudret, Christian Dior's Mill House near Fontainebleau. The dining room and the photo of Dior, chicest of men, making raspberry liqueur in the kitchen of the same old mill house with his very un-chic dog Bobby. As for the mill: "There were white walls and dark beams, stone-flagged floors, simple furniture gleaming with the patina of age and care, big country cupboards smelling of lavender." The unpretentious style of a gentle genius.

Keller, Thomas. *The French Laundry Cookbook*. New York: Artisan, 1999.

The book that raised the bar for chefs' cookbooks to infinity. Stunningly beautiful, inspirational, and challenging for most.

Kennedy, Diana. *The Cuisines of Mexico*. New York: Harper & Row, 1972.

I bought this in 1974, and it still inspires me. The front flap says Kennedy is in the "tradition of Elizabeth David and Jane Grigson." Personal, opinionated, and true. As a cookbook should be. See also the new books, including *My Mexico*.

Kettner's. *Book of the Table.* **London: Dulan and Co., 1877.**

Because it is an inspirational book that believes that "If the nature of the ingredients be well known, much fewer will do."

Knapik, Harold. *Haute Cuisine Without Help.* **New York: Liveright, 1971.**

A charming book by a friend of Alice B. Toklas, for whom he cooked. He wrote it to show that you don't have to be French to cook superb food. Even in 1971 he wanted to tell the public about the horrors of canned anchovy filets, and the glories of salted whole ones. This is all about the origin and the quality of the ingredients. Read the bit about poached eggs.

Kuh, Patric. *The Last Days of Haute Cuisine: America's Culinary Revolution.* **New York: Viking Press, 2001.**

Another look (and a very intelligent one) at the story of *California Dish.*

Lang, George. *Nobody Knows the Truffles I Have Seen.* **New York: Alfred A. Knopf, 1999.**

And I wonder how many know the huge achievements of George Lang and the contributions (see The Four Seasons, Restaurant Associates, and how we view catering in America today) of the amazing George. Read about it all here. As well as in other books.

Lanta, Anna Tasca. *The Heart of Sicily.* **New York: Clarkson Potter, 1993.**

Because surely in any cook's heart there is a little or a lot of Sicily? I adore this book (see the photos of tomatoes drying in the sun and how it is *really* done), this family, and their wines grown in the heart of Sicily.

La Varenne, Sieur de. *Le Vray Cuisinier François.* **Amsterdam: Chez Pierre Mortier, 1651 (Larousse).**

This father of French cuisine started his career as chef by pimping for Henri IV, the king who wanted a chicken in every subject's pot. My bible when I was a lad, *Larousse Gastronomique,* told me that La Varenne's "recipes can be used today," so I did. I used the raspberry vinegar recipe and later, at Stars, the squab cooked in it. (See *Jeremiah Tower's New American Classics*).

Lawrence, R. de Treville, Sr. *Jefferson and Wine.* **The Plains, Va.: Vinifera Wine Growers Association, 1976.**

Not just for Jefferson's letter in 1787 to Château d'Yquem asking to buy some wine, or his wine-loving correspondence with my ancestor John Rutledge, but the one of two books that in 1976 made me think of American food, and of calling it "California," in particular.

Lawson, Nigella. *How to Eat.* **London: Chatto & Windus, 1998.**

How could anyone resist a title like that? And Nigella tells us so charmingly. See her other books and television show as well.

LeDuc. *Crustacés, Poissons et Coquillages.* **Paris: Jean-Claude Lattes, 1977.**

The book from the restaurant in Paris that changed the way we all looked at cooking fish. A big influence on me in 1977.

Leslie, Miss. *Directions for Cookery in Its Various Branches.* **Philadelphia: Henry Carey Baird, 1853.**

What this woman, writing with huge success (in sales) for other women who have to cook for their husbands, hates: "washy soup, poultry half raw, gravy unskimmed, and vegetables undrained; to say nothing of ponderous puddings, curdled custards tasting of nothing, and tough pastry." Many of the professional cooks on line in the United States today don't know about skimming sauces. And she knew then that bad food makes bad moods, and that only food cooked according to proper procedures is good for one's health.

Lewis, Edna. *The Taste of Country Cooking.* **New York: Alfred A. Knopf, 1976.**

My copy is marked "From James Beard, August 1976." After I read it, and after my California Dinner at Chez Panisse, I knew we were onto something emphasizing American food, as Jim had told me all along.

Machen, Arthur. *Dog and Duck.* **New York: Alfred A. Knopf, 1924.**

Because: "If a man talks to me of the sacred cause of Humanity, I lock up my few silver spoons." And "But he who speaks well of port is, as the Greeks said of their best men, beautiful and good."

McClure, Michael. *Meat Science Essays.* **San Francisco: City Lights Books, 1963.**

This was a bible for me as a college freshman, thanks to my roommate, the poet Michael Palmer. A book "that may turn out to be a significant one for his generation. Its themes are suicide, death, revolt, sexuality & drugs; Artaud, Camus, and liberty"—all the things that obsessed me in the sixties, other than Escoffier's *Ma Cuisine* and John Rechy's *City of Night.* And for the essay on cocaine (so that the night it was introduced to Berkeley, on top of the low freezer in the kitchen of Chez Panisse, I was ready). And for the culinary chapter: "The Mushroom."

Margittai, Tom, and Paul Kovi. *The Four Seasons.* **New York: Simon & Schuster, 1980.**

"The ultimate book of food, wine, and elegant dining" is what the cover says, and certainly the restaurant is "one of the world's great restaurants." Read also the foreword by James Beard, who calls the restaurant "a gastronomic legend." How true.

Marinetti, Filippo Tommaso. *The Futurist Cookbook.* **Italy, 1932; London: Trefoil Publications, 1989. Translation: Bedford Arts, San Francisco, 1989.**

Because the New York chef David Burke proved Marinetti correct, probably without even knowing it: Tyrrhenian Seaweed Foam with Coral Garnish, for example. And Excitant Gastrique. And because the book is hilarious and vastly intelligent.

Marron, Fred J. *Jean-Louis: Cooking with the Seasons.* Charlottesville, Va.: Thomasson-Grant, 1989.

The ultimate chef's photograph cookbook of its time, and one of the best and most influential of the last part of the American twentieth century. Having nothing to do with the seasons, but all about presentation, and style-setting presentation it is, a style that capped the eighties and sent the young nineties into a swoon. Thousands of up-and-coming chefs aspired to this cooking, with mixed results.

Marshall, A. B. *The Book of Ice.* London: Simpkin, Marshall, Hamilton, Kent & Co., n.d. Another publication of his, *The Table,* was published in 1886.

Given to me by Elizabeth David, "a reminder of your summer with me in London 1978. With Love." Because we both wondered whether the first household ice cream makers were in the United States or England. Read about cucumber ice cream, white coffee ice cream, Spanish nut and cookies ice cream. All a hundred years before Ben & Jerry's went public.

Médecin, Jacques. *La Cuisine du Comte de Nice.* Paris: Juillard, 1972.

Given to me by Alice in early 1974, this, Elizabeth David, and (for me) Richard Olney were the books that formed Chez Panisse until I decided to take it truly regional in 1976. A book that influenced a lot of people, many of whom went "Mediterranean."

Menon. *La Cuisinière Bourgeoise.* Paris: Guillyn, 1746.

One of the great cookbooks of all time, as both Richard Olney and Elizabeth David told me over and over again until I read it: "Simple dishes, good ones, and new ones, for which I have given easily understandable instructions." And a book that was one of the first to write about women's cooking in the home.

Montagné, Prosper. *Larousse Gastronomique: The Encyclopedia of Food, Wine, and Cookery.* Introduction by Auguste Escoffier and Philéas Gilbert. Edited by Charlotte Turgeon and Nina Froud. New York: Crown Publishers, 1961.

Get started on this translation, then buy the earlier French editions for all the edited-out details in the English-language editions. The book other than Escoffier's *Ma Cuisine* that I read ceaselessly in college.

Montagné, Prosper, and Prosper Salles. *Le Grand Livre de la Cuisine.* Paris: Flammarion, 1929.

A beautiful monster of a book, with Philéas Gilbert (partner with Escoffier in *Le Guide Culinaire*) doing a preface, and Henri Béraud's look at the future that would suggest the pot-au-feu had hyperbolic magic mushrooms in it. Read it for the lunch menu of February 2, 1926, the centenary of Brillat-Savarin. It is the menu that Béraud regretted "all his life that he had not assisted at its preparation." I now regret not having been there. And what an extraordinary modern menu it is, considering how mad they could have gone, being that close to the previous century: "rissoles of foie gras and sausages cooked in Chablis for hors d'oeuvre, Beaujolais for aperitif; an 'omelet du Cure' with La Mission Haut-Brion; stewed eels in a coulis of crayfish, Cheval Blanc; a truffled turkey, Côte de Nuits of

Bouchard; Salade de l'émigré; Cheeses, another Bouchard Reserve; pyramids of meringue with vanilla ice cream flavoured with rose petals, Heidsieck and Pol Roger; Fruit, coffee, cognac, liqueurs." Now that's a lunch!

Morris, Helen. *Portrait of a Chef: The Life of Alexis Soyer.* **Cambridge, England: University Press, 1938.**

As a model chef "Soyer was vain, a poseur, a fop, an eccentric, a brilliant inventor, and a magnificent organizer." He was the "lie that tells the truth." And he designed the vast kitchens of the Reform Club. And he once fed 22,000 poor people Christmas dinner for free. Anyone who thinks he or she is a grand chef should read this book first.

Nignon, Edouard. *Eloges de la Cuisine Française.* **Paris: Edition d'Art H. Piazza, 1933.**

A true Scorpio, and slightly mad. And a brilliant foreword by Sacha Guitry that I have quoted often. Read also Nignon's *Les Plaisirs de la Table* (Paris: Jacoub & Aulard, 1930), which is truly a pleasure. No one has more fun than Nignon. Also because if you look under the bed of any of the most famous chefs since 1960 (at least literate ones), you will find one of Nignon's books. Nignon was chef at Paillard in Paris, then at Claridge's in London.

O'Donnell, Mietta, and Tony Knox. *Great Australian Chefs.* **Sydney: Bookman Press, 1999.**

If you had any doubt that the culinary revolution moved to Australia after California, before moving on to England, this book will convince you.

Olney, Richard. *The French Menu Cookbook.* **New York: Simon & Schuster, 1970.**

Because it was dedicated to Georges Garin, the inspiration, if an irascible one, for the Young Turks of the seventies in France. As in vegetable purees. And because when I read this book when it came out in 1970, I began a correspondence with Richard, and it was my personal (not the official) bible when I started at Chez Panisse.

————. *Simple French Food.* **New York: Atheneum, 1975.**

Not just because my book is inscribed "For adorable Jeremiah," but because when Richard told me he was going to write it, I said we would have to do a two-week festival of the dishes at Chez Panisse to introduce him and his food to California.

————. *Yquem.* **Paris: Flammarion, 1985.**

Because it is fascinating to see the menus from 1867 to 1985 that have served this famous wine, including the one I did at Chez Panisse in 1975, "An American Menu," with only Sauternes served with the food. The pairing of rich roast beef with d'Yquem came from Prince Yusupov (the one who assassinated Rasputin) as told to me by the mentors of my teens, Count Cheremetev and my Russian uncle.

Orwell, George. *Down and Out in London and Paris.* **New York: Harper and Bros., 1933.**

For anyone interested in working in the restaurant business, this book is a must, before reading its pupil, *Kitchen Confidential* by Anthony Bourdain.

Pellaprat, Jean-Henri. *L'Art Culinaire Moderne.* **Castagnola, Switzerland: Jacques Kramer, 1956; or see the English translation as *The Great Book of French Cuisine*, New York: Thomas Y. Crowell Co., 1966.**

That is exactly it: a great book. What it was like to eat at Maxim's, if you don't have their book.

Pépin, Jacques. *Complete Techniques.* **New York: Black Dog & Levanthal, 2001.**

A compilation of the brilliant how-to photographs of *La Technique* (1976) and *La Méthode* (1979) that helped me through so much in the kitchen, since I was never taught professionally, and when I started at Chez Panisse, there wasn't anyone else who was either. Thank you, Jacques.

Peterson, James. *Sauces.* **New York: Van Nostrand Reinhold, 1991.**

The first person after Escoffier's introduction to stocks and sauces to get it right—perfectly. A book that I wish I had written.

Petits Propos Culinaires. **Edited by the Davidsons. London: Prospect Books, 1979–.**

A wonderfully mad and fascinating little collection of books, and in this first edition Nathan d'Aulnay (Richard Olney) and I printed recipes for use in the Time-Life *Good Cook* series. Elizabeth David was intrigued and did "Hunt the Ice Cream," the wonderful Elizabeth Lambert Ortiz did "Coriander," and in later editions, like No. 26 in 1987, the booklets were already looking at Australia, with the visionary "Symposium of Australian Gastronomy."

Picture Cook Book. **New York: Time Inc., 1958.**

Full on 1950s. Look at page 119: The shoes are more beautiful than the food, not to happen again until the nineties and Manolo Blahnik! And page 154, the clothes at the barbecue! Then look at the restaurant section and see the food of Fernand Point (see below), the photograph and food of the great Alexandre Dumaine at the Hôtel de la Côte-d'Or in Saulieu (see above), and Ernie's in San Francisco, just to see the very spooky photo of the chef Ermete Lavino, who is the identical twin to the Ernie's chef of thirty years later, Jackie Robert. Yes, this book is a treasure of the mouth-hanging-open-in-wonderment variety.

Point, Fernand. *Ma Gastronomie.* **Wilton, CT: Lyceum Books, 1974.**

You have to love a man who drank a magnum of champagne while being shaved, and who was the culinary father to Paul Bocuse and a host of other Young Turks, like Thomas Keller in Napa, and Tony Bilson in Sydney.

Pollan, Michael. *The Botany of Desire*. New York: Random House, 2001.

A book on apples, potatoes, marijuana, and tulips that reads like a thriller. A perfect book.

Pomiane, Edouard de. *Cooking with Pomiane*. Oxford: Bruno Cassirer, 1976.

One of Elizabeth David's favorites, and one she told me to read for writing the Chez Panisse menus. And because he had a radio show on food in the 1930s, as well as tried to teach the French to eat the way we do now: with health in mind, but without sacrificing great flavors and meals.

Practical Housekeeping: A Careful Compilation of Tried and Approved Recipes. Wilton, Ohio, 1876.

This is the mother of all housewives' companions, dedicated to the "Plucky Housewives of 1876, who master their work instead of allowing it to master them." The material later (1883) became *Buckeye Cookery*, which was reprinted by Dover.

Ramsay, Gordon. *Passion for Flavor*. London: Conran Octopus, 1996.

The foreword is by Guy Savoy, the French chef that we Americans trounced in 1983 in Newport in front of one hundred U.S. food journalists. Another book after the school of Marco Pierre White, a very nice book to cook from, and a new "cuisine légère" all over again. Richard Olney liked Gordon's restaurant Aubergine, though perhaps not for the cappuccino soup presentation.

Ranhofer, Charles. *The Epicurean*. New York: Dover, 1971.

By the chef at the great Delmonico's in New York (this material is from 1862 to 1894). A book I bought in February 1974, but the bell did not go off in my head until two years later; when reading it again, I saw that all the menus used English words and terms, and I saw the dishes inspired by California (the corn soup from Mendocino) and immediately wrote the California Regional Dinner, which started a revolution.

Rann, Evelyn. *After the Theatre Lunch*. Buzza Company, from the1930s.

This little pamphlet book has a beautiful and charming late Deco design that could easily be the inspiration for David Lance Goines, of Chez Panisse poster fame. The written material is straightforward with a lot of class: very American.

Rawlings, Majorie Kinnan. *Cross Creek Cookery*. New York: Charles Scribner's Sons, 1942.

One of the ultimately American cookbooks, and it inspired me to do a Florida Regional Dinner at the Santa Fe Bar & Grill in 1982. When I was asked, "Is this Floridian cuisine?" I answered, "It should be." Rawlings gives the recipe for the divine Black Bottom Pie.

Rector, George. *The Rector Cookbook*. Chicago: Rector Publishing, 1928.

The only nonliving restaurant other than Delmonico's that was a model for Stars of San Francisco: "Rector's was the supreme court of triviality, where who's who went to learn what's what." The customers were "champions, challengers, opera stars, explorers, captains of industry, and lieutenants of sloth; gamblers, authors, and adventurers, [and] all celebrated their temporary successes with a night at Rector's." The book has very American food at its best. The European heritage was there, but it was worked over into a new image and taste. My grandmother's favorite book—for her cook.

Reynière, Grimod de la. *Almanach des Gourmands.* **Paris: Chez Maradan, 8 vols., 1803–1812.**

The first book that Richard Olney told me in 1973 to buy and, with my first spare money from Chez Panisse, I did. Four of them. Wonderful, brilliant, and an inspiration to many great chefs and writers (see Lucien Tendret).

Ripert, Eric, and Michael Ruhlman. *A Return to Cooking.* **New York: Artisan, 2002.**

The first chef's cookbook that measures up visually after Thomas Keller's book, *The French Laundry Cookbook,* and surpasses it in usability by the home cook. One is swept along by the personal passion of Eric and his rediscoveries.

Ritz, Marie Louise. *César Ritz.* **Philadelphia: J. B. Lippincott, 1938.**

Because whatever ideas you have about perfectionism will forever change after you have read about this genius's work habits. Mine did.

Rodriguez-Hunter, Suzane. *Found Meals of the Lost Generation: Recipes and Anecdotes from 1920's Paris.* **Winchester, Mass.: Faber & Faber, 1994.**

Hilarious, and a must for anyone who wonders how to put on a party without a lot of money.

Rombauer, Irma S., and Marion Rombauer Becker. *Joy of Cooking.* **Indianapolis and New York: Bobbs-Merrill, 1975.**

One of the greatest cookbooks ever. Originally published in 1931, it now makes later editions of Fannie Farmer look like Mobil guides. If you had to have one cookbook, this could be it. See Bittman.

Root, Waverley. *Food: An Authoritative and Visual History and Dictionary of the Foods of the World.* **New York: Simon & Schuster, 1980.**

My favorite dictionary of food, along with Alexandre Dumas's and Alan Davidson's two hundred years later. See also *The Food of France* and *The Food of Italy.*

Sackville-West, Vita. *V. Sackville-West's Garden Book.* **London: Michael Joseph, 1968.**

Because Alice Waters gave it to me on May 7, 1974, thinking that this was what I was talking about as I was pushing starting a farm of our own. Obviously she had never seen Sissinghurst, where my mother used to take me on tours, or known about the inherited fortune that maintained it. In California we ended up with lettuce and a few geese.

Saffron, Inga. *Caviar*. New York: Broadway Books, 2002.

Subtitled "The Strange History and Uncertain Future of the World's Most Coveted Delicacy." So read it and eat it while you can.

Saint-Ange. *La Bonne Cuisine*. Paris: Larousse, 1927.

Because she is a cult. Decide for yourself if it is by 1927 "the most practical cookery book in the French language" (Elizabeth David) or not. It is certainly more practical for the home cook than Escoffier's *Guide Culinaire*, and it is one of the first cookbooks truly in love with precision. It is interesting that Elizabeth adored this book, since her books are anything but precise from the point of view of anyone but a natural cook.

Sanger, Marjory Bartlett. *Escoffier*. New York: Farrar, Straus & Giroux, 1976.

One of the best books about the Man.

Sarris, Stan, and Rodney Adler. *Banc*. Sydney: New Holland, 1999.

An Australian version of the "day in the life" of a restaurant, beautifully photographed, and with good recipes of food and drink.

Schlosser, Eric. *Fast Food Nation*. Boston and New York: Houghton Mifflin, 2001.

"The dark side of the American meal," a view of what is wrong with modern America through what it eats. Brillat-Savarin's "you are what you eat," come horrifyingly true.

Schofield, Leo. "California Cuisine," Australian *Gourmet*, April 1986.

Sometimes it takes an outsider to see.

Schuman, Charles. *American Bar*. New York: Abbeville Press, 1995.

After the *Savoy Cocktail Book*, and on a par. The best book on bartending and drinks now.

Serventi, Silvano. *La Grande Histoire du Foie Gras*. Paris: Flammarion, 1993.

An exceptionally beautiful book, superbly done, and with it and Michael Ginor's book, you have the whole foie, as it were.

Simon, Andre. *A Concise Encyclopaedia of Gastronomy*. London: The Wine and Food Society, 1940–1948.

Brilliantly told and organized by category, like "Fish" and "Meat." On buying fish: "Look at the fish, it tells its own tale." The section on "Ham" is the best on the subject I have ever seen.

Sitwell, Edith. *English Eccentrics*. London: Penguin Books, 1971.

How could you have an informed sense of humor about the twentieth century if you have not read this? Or feel so well about how much you drink? Not as much, one would hope, or as colorfully, as Squire Mad Jack Mytton, who drank eight bottles of port a day, and his horse, Baronet, not much less. He spent half a million (tens of millions today) doing it, and set fire to his nightshirt to cure the hiccups. A barrel of fun, as it were.

Slater, Nigel. *Appetite.* **New York: Clarkson Potter, 2000.**
Subtitled "So What Do You Want to Eat Today." This book will always answer that question that never ends. Nigel is a genius.

Smith, Delia. *Delia's How to Cook.* **London: BBC, 1998.**
A friend of mine in London said of Delia that all her recipes always work. If you are interested in basics, Delia's television shows and books are the ones to watch and cook from. She is the doyenne of British cooking at the moment.

Solomon, Charmaine. *Encyclopaedia of Asian Food.* **Boston: Periplus Editions, 1998.**
Exhaustive and fascinating. Charmaine has always known the most from a Western perspective, and she was one of the first to know.

Spoeri, Daniel. *The Mythological Travels.* **New York: Something Else Press, 1970.**
Magic mushroom surrealism unsurpassed.

Steingarten, Jeffrey. "Meals of the Millennium." *Vogue,* **November 1999.**
Because this, and anything Jeffrey writes, is worth reading.

Stout, Rex. *Too Many Cooks.* **1938. (Reprinted New York: Bantam, 1983.)**
Because in 1970 I read it again and listed the wonderful food in praise of America: Creole Tripe from New Orleans; Missouri Boone County Ham—cooked with vinegar, molasses, Worcestershire sauce, cider, and herbs; Chicken in Curdled Egg Sauce—almonds, sherry, Mexican sausage; Tennessee Opossum; and Philadelphia Snapper Soup. See next entry, *The Nero Wolfe Cookbook.*

————. *The Nero Wolfe Cookbook.* **New York: Viking Press, 1973.**
The Nero Wolfe mysteries were some of the first books I read that made me want to cook, and here are the recipes.

Szathmary, Louis, advisory ed. *Cookery Americana.* **New York: Arno Press, 1973.**
A series of twenty-seven cookbooks, including *Fifty Years of Prairie Cooking,* that "chronicles a fascinating aspect of American social life over the past 150 years." Truly an insight into what we have lost in the menu since the First and Second World Wars. Most of the household management and church societies material that fills these books is not "cottage cheese omelet" and "rinkum tiddy."

Talleyrand, Charles-Maurice.
Anything on the lifestyle of this great diner is worth reading. A man who continued, because of a complete lack of scruples, to eat famously well throughout the people's revolution against excess, and lived through all the next royalist,

imperial, and populist regimes. After all, his chef was Antonin Carême, one of the greatest chefs of all time, and mentor to Escoffier as well as Dubois and so on. And because Talleyrand was the first to figure out that entertaining should be tax deductible.

Tendret, Lucien. *La Table au Pays de Brillat-Savarin*. Mâcon: Protat Frères, 1892.

"A small masterpiece" Richard Olney calls it. This book inspired many, like the legendary Alexandre Dumaine, the greatest chef in France in the mid–twentieth century. The famous Poularde au Vapeur is from Tendret, going from Dumaine on to Fernand Point and his pupil Bocuse. The Aga Khan would go to France just to dine on this sublime chicken at Dumaine's.

Tirel, Guillaume (Taillevent). *Le Viandier*. Paris, 1373–1380, Paris: Techener, 1892. Pichon and Vicaire.

Tirel was the head cook to French dukes and to Charles VI. Read this if for no other reason than that this collection of manuscripts is the first French cookbook, and to learn to cook with almonds, and for the miracles of verjus in cold soups thickened with almonds. Oeufs de Truite (trout eggs) not bad either.

Toklas, Alice B. *The Alice B. Toklas Cook Book*. 1954; New York: Doubleday, Anchor Books, 1960.

A book "of character, fine food, and tasty human observation," according to Janet Flanner (American journalist in Paris), the book that I cooked from endlessly in college, and then afterward cooked from for the Gertrude Stein dinner at Chez Panisse. Try the Eggs Francis Picabia, but the most food-splashed page is for "A Tender Tart," everyone's favorite kind.

Toulouse-Lautrec. *Chez Maxim's*. New York: McGraw Hill, 1962.

Alice Waters's favorite book, and looking at the photo of the countess in her fifties mink entering Maxim's to greet the owner, Louis Vaudable, you will know why. For the lovers of chicken "in half mourning," this is it. And because, with the Baron de Ladoucette, I had one of the best meals ever at Maxim's.

Tower, Jeremiah. "Crowned with Roses—A Four Second Perfume." Unpublished, 1972.

"Memoirs of a Harvard Graduate, 1961 to 1972." In the introduction I wrote, "I will speak, like Arthur Machen, of certain tastes. But unlike he, who dared retribution by admitting a Germanic liking for apple sauce with his roast goose when nationalism made such an admission risky, I will dwell on a revival, and so avoid the ire of all but the most dull."

———. *Jeremiah Tower's New American Classics*. New York: Harper & Row, 1986.

My first cookbook.

Troisgros, Jean, and Pierre Troisgros. *Cuisiniers à Roane.* Paris: Robert Laffont, 1977.

The other book that changed American chefs' views of cooking and presentation of their food. See Michel Guérard.

Trotter, Charlie. *Meat and Game.* Berkeley: Ten Speed Press, 2001.

I mention this one to remind you to look at the whole series of Charlie's restaurant cookbooks.

Tsuji, Shizuo. *Japanese Cooking: A Simple Art.* New York: Kodansha International, 1980.

The first book that we saw in America to set down the art of this cooking and, arguably, still the most influential.

Villas, James. *American Taste: A Celebration of Gastronomy Coast to Coast.* Foreword by James Beard. New York: Arbor House, 1982.

Because when I was planning the Celebration of American Chefs for 1983 as the first big function of the AIWF, this book was the inspiration to make me insist, against the pressure of New York and Los Angeles chefs, that we find chefs from all over the land. And because James Villas is the writer who champions simple American food, and knows more about it than anyone. See below.

———. "From Our Abundant Land: At Last, A Table of Our Own." *Town & Country,* June 1976. Read also *Villas at Table: A Passion for Food and Drink.* New York: Harper & Row, 1988. And *Between Bites.* New York: John Wiley & Sons, 2002.

All Villas's books are fascinating and historically important.

Visser, Margaret. *The Rituals of Dinner.* New York: Grove Weidenfeld, 1991.

A book on the "origins, evolution, eccentricities, and meaning of table manners." Fascinating. How and why we eat together.

Warne, Frederick, & Co. *Every-Day Cookery: For Families of Moderate Income.* Covent Garden, London, c. 1900.

This extraordinary little book, of only 150 pages, by a publisher who did "useful books," "model manuals," and so on, sold this for one shilling and actually thought that roast partridge on a platter with its garnish of vegetables, or a whole turbot, was for moderate income (in those days, chicken was the luxury poultry). Read this delightful book and see why Elizabeth David adored it so, how it formed her style, and why she gave it to me.

Warner, Richard. *Antiquitates Culinaire; Or Curious Tracts Relating to the Culinary Affairs of the Old English.* London: R. Blamire, 1791; repr., London: Prospect Books.

Because it includes *The Forme of Cury,* thought by most to be the finest of the old English cookbooks: "a roll of ancient English cookery, compiled about 1390, by the master cooks of Richard II." Read it now, eat the latest and best food in London now in places like St. John's, and remember the fourteenth century.

Wechsberg, Joseph. "Brillat-Savarin." *Gourmet,* March 1970.

Thank God someone has some objectivity about this god of gourmets. And because anything by Wechsberg is worth reading. See also his charming *Blue Trout and Black Truffles,* New York: Alfred A. Knopf, 1966.

White, Marco Pierre. *White Heat.* London: Pyramid Books, 1990.

A visionary book (as you can tell by the countless imitations after it was published) that set the style for a "day in the life of" a restaurant and the handheld camera that is part of the action of the restaurant.

Wolfe, Linda. *The Literary Gourmet.* New York: Random House, 1962.

Because this book is beautiful and really fun to read. Because The Four Seasons restaurant tested the recipes, appropriately, since its "imaginative modern cuisine is based on the best achievements of the past" and "brings these historic recipes once again to life." Tripe from Shakespeare, crayfish soufflé from Gogol, crème au chocolate ice cream from Dumas, suckling pig and kasha from Chekhov, velvet cakes—naturally—from Wilde, and for the dinner at the château of the Marquis de Vaubyessard, to which Emma Bovary goes, "one of the most seductive dinner parties in literature," the perfumes of "the flowers and of the fine linen, the fumes of the viands, and the odor of truffles" all enveloping Emma as she enters the dining room.

Woolf, Virginia. *Orlando.* London: Hogarth Press, 1928.

The dinner Orlando did at the embassy in Constantinople at the end of the great fast of Ramadan: "gold plate . . . candelabras . . . negroes in plush breeches . . . pyramids of ice . . . fountains of negus . . . jellies made to represent His Majesty's ships . . . birds in golden cages . . . gentlemen in slashed crimson velvet . . . oceans to drink," and so on. The 1978 Orlando dinner was the last that I ever cooked at Chez Panisse.

Index

About the Author

JEREMIAH TOWER began his career as chef and co-owner of Chez Panisse in Berkeley, California, and later ran several other successful restaurants, including Stars in San Francisco. He is the author of *Jeremiah Tower's New American Classics* and *Jeremiah Tower Cooks*, as well as the host of PBS's *America's Best Chefs*, and is currently working on the companion book, *America's Best Chefs with Jeremiah Tower*. In 1996 the James Beard Foundation named him the Outstanding Chef in America. Tower lives in New York City.